THE

JANITOR

A Novel
By

J. M. (Mike) McEniry

To KAREN,
— an ouple of mercy!
Thanks for the TLC!
Mike McEniry

This first novel is dedicated to the men and women of the United States intelligence community who have always believed that what they were doing would make this world a better place to live.

My heartfelt appreciation to my wife and soul-mate, Peggy Lou, for her encouragement, support, and editorial assistance.

In Memory of:

Wallace Clemens Bentley, II
January 27, 1937 - to - November 30, 1993

Fly on, Marine...Semper Fi!

ACKNOWLEDGMENTS

The author wishes to gratefully acknowledge his thanks for the assistance given to him by a former CIA 'contractor' (who still must remain nameless), and for the encouragement offered by friends both in and out of the military establishment.

A special thanks to Colonel Dick Francisco, USMCR (Retired), and the late Colonel Merle Kime, USMCR (Retired), with whom the author had the distinct pleasure to serve and fly in the U.S. Marine Corps Reserve, for their background information of the Korean conflict.

Deserving acknowledgments also go out to fellow writers. Herbert A. Crowder for his wonderful editing, suggestions to fix the shortcomings in the initial draft and his encouragement, to Kregg P.J. Jorgensen for his editing and supportive help, to fellow Marine aviator and author Joe Weber. Kudos and thanks to C. Norman Noble for his early lessons in diction, grammar and dialogue and to János L. Wimpffen, Ph.D. and Lauren Perry and Barbara Sterk for their assistance in the proof-reading and organization of the manuscript, and to Robbie Shinn for her final re-write editing.

A special word of appreciation for the early encouragement from Jeffrey Beales, who acted as my first agent, incited a lot of early interest in the project and kept me at the task of finishing it when I thought it wouldn't be of interest to anyone.

CHAPTER ONE
EXPEDITING AN APPOINTMENT
San Salvador, El Salvador - 1969

The two men sitting in the car were not speaking. They were intently watching the courtyard gate of the American Embassy from a block away. They were dressed casually and both were wearing aviator-type sunglasses. The slanting rays of the late afternoon sun highlighted the dust motes in the air. There was little or no traffic, vehicle or foot. It was hot. The windows of the car had to be down and the flies were everywhere. They were noisy and aggressive. The men had to constantly bat them away.

The driver spoke without turning to look at his companion, "Where is he? He should be coming out this entrance, mi Coronel. It's nearly four o'clock."

The driver was Dominique Paredes. He was addressing his boss, Colonel Emilio Raphael Cordero. They were both from Venezuela and had been together since the abortive Cuban 'Bay Of Pigs' disaster.

Cordero had been a favorite of his Central Intelligence Agency Training Advisors and quickly rose in rank. He had handpicked Paredes, while training, to be his right hand man. During the Cuban invasion they both narrowly missed being taken prisoner. Since that time

1

Cordero had switched his activities from the CIA to the U.S. State Department, doing operations for 'State' in Guatemala, Panama and Columbia. He had recently taken up temporary residence in Costa Rica, awaiting further assignment. Cordero had been told by State that he would be the next head of Security in El Salvador.

The Catorce Familias, the fourteen families that ran, or influenced the running of El Salvador, had requested help from the United States Government. The Cuban Communists were usurping the police authority, stirring up the populace and spreading terrorism in El Salvador as well as in the other Caribbean and Gulf of Mexico rim countries.

The U.S. State Department appointment had been promised to Cordero but so far nothing had happened. It was taking too long. Something had to be done. What Cordero and Paredes were doing this day was designed to expedite State's decision process.

Colonel Cordero had bestowed the rank of Lieutenant on his companion. It was one of his many ways of keeping his second-in-command in line while not letting him get too close, either in a personal relationship or rank. He enjoyed having someone to ridicule, believing in the leadership-by-intimidation school. He had always been a bully. He carefully picked his people for those types who wouldn't stand up to him. He had chosen well with Paredes.

Cordero turned to his driver, answering his last question. "You heard the same report from Carlos that I heard. And Carlos is *your* man." Colonel Cordero continued insolently, "Do you not have faith in his powers of observation? We know where our quarry is going to go for his dinner. We know what table he usually occupies and his favorite waiter. We know that he leaves the embassy at the same time each day for his evening meal, even if he is going back to the embassy later."

"Si, my Coronel, I'm impatient. Forgive me." He turned to Cordero, "Carlos is my man, as you say, and he did

2

a beautiful job. There are close to twenty-five pounds of Semtex in the briefcase, the Semtex you ordered to have it appear as Cuban terrorist activity. I was not aware of the fact that Semtex would leave an identifying trace, one known to be from the Eastern Bloc countries." Paredes raised both hands in a quick upward gesture, "There will be no mishaps. He will not escape that much explosive."

"And the arming device?" Cordero asked.

"Another work of art; it is fool-proof. Carlos reversed the switch. Opening one of the briefcase clasps will start the timer and...But look! There he is, that's him!" Lieutenant Dominique Paredes sat up straight behind the wheel. He started to reach for the ignition.

"Wait," Colonel Cordero said quietly.

Both men watched as their mark turned and walked in a direction that would take him away from them. The man was young, maybe thirty-two. He was over six feet, slight of build and had red hair. His tan linen suit looked out of place. His skin was nearly as red as his hair where it showed above his shirt collar. He would stand out above the crowd, both physically and in coloration, anywhere in this Central American country.

Cordero spoke reflectively as if merely thinking out loud, "He looks too young to be the intelligence representative. He looks more like the Agricultural Attaché he is posing as." Turning to Lieutenant Paredes he added, "All right, drive on, I want to get to the restaurant before he does."

Paredes started the car, slipped it into gear and drove at a leisurely pace. They didn't look over as they passed the young American. It was five blocks to the restaurant. They would have plenty of time to get there and order a quick snack before their quarry arrived.

There was a convenient parking place across the street from the restaurant. Paredes parked. They both got out of the car, reaching into the back seat for two identical black briefcases. Crossing the street they entered the restaurant, removed their glasses and made their way toward the back. The head waiter came scurrying up to them. Cordero gestured toward an empty booth near the back wall. It was early and most of the patrons were seated toward the front of the restaurant.

"This will be fine. Please direct an efficient waiter to our table; we only have time for a light repast." Cordero spoke in a soft, gracious manner. He had selected a booth next to the one the American usually used.

"Si Senor." The head waiter snapped his fingers toward a waiter nearby and quietly gave him instructions as he came up to him.

Colonel Cordero and Lieutenant Paredes slipped into the booth, putting their briefcases under the table. In a matter of moments the waiter placed menus in front of them, nodded and stepped back. The two men glanced at the menus and then ordered.

Carlos had done his surveillance well. He had eaten at the restaurant enough times to know the fastest item to order. That factor had been added as part of the overall planning.

When they were served, Cordero asked that their check be brought to them now since they were pressed for time and wouldn't be wanting anything else. The waiter returned shortly with the check in a leather folder, placing it discretely on a corner of the table.

They had started eating when the mark came in. He waited for the head waiter to come and show him to his table. The way the head waiter treated this customer was indicative of his special status as an important patron. Carlos had reported that the American received very special attention.

The mark was served a drink in moments after he was seated. He looked the menu over for a while. By the time he had placed his order Cordero and Paredes were finished. Cordero had already placed currency in the check holder, making sure that enough corners of the money were visible. Paredes reached under the table, quietly opened the arming clasp, glanced at his watch and retrieved the other briefcase. This was the crucial moment. They had to get out of there without someone noticing that they had left another briefcase under the table. Their planning was timed so that the flurry of activity around the mark would mask their departure.

As they were leaving, the head waiter started toward them. Cordero motioned toward their vacated booth, in a manner indicating payment had been left at the table.

They made good their exit.

Once outside Cordero looked at his watch. As they started across the street to their car he asked Paredes, "How long?"

"Ten minutes, as we discussed, mi Coronel."

They got in the car and leisurely drove away.

The sound of the fierce explosion could be heard over the traffic noises even six blocks away. Neither occupant of the car took notice. Their thoughts were on other matters; Paredes on his plans for their exit from the city and country. Cordero's mind, on the other hand, was on matters that would hasten his appointment to the promised security position in this small country.

As head of security, Cordero knew that he would not only have untold opportunity for great wealth but would also be able to satisfy his inner needs. There were some new methods of interrogation he was anxious to try.

CHAPTER TWO
HEADQUARTERS, CENTRAL INTELLIGENCE AGENCY
Langley, Virginia - 1969

Clyde Hayner had his feet up on the corner of his desk. He didn't notice the scuffed, brown wing-tip shoes. He couldn't see the run down heels, just the outside edges. They say that a man's shoes are a picture of the man. In this case, it was true. Clyde Hayner was that sort of man, *scuffed, with run-down edges.*

He was of slight build, had thinning, mouse-gray hair and wore glasses with steel, almost-round frames. He looked more like a small town high school teacher than an employee of the Central Intelligence Agency. Approaching his mid-forties now, time had not been kind to Clyde Hayner. The excitement of being a member of the agency had long since passed into the reality of boredom not exclusive to government work, but more to the middle age reality that life was slipping rapidly by.

He was looking out the window at the light snowfall drifting down. It was the first week in November, a little early for snow he was thinking. He loved this time of year; the crispness in the air, the trees bare, even the soft lighting of the fall sunshine, all of it. It just felt good. The holidays would be coming soon and that was one thing that Clyde could still get a little excited about. If only he didn't have to deal with the dispatch still in his hand.

Clyde ran the El Salvador desk in the Central American Department of the agency. He had given up going field-operational a long time ago. He was quite content to have events stay nice and quiet. His desk was supposed to be one of the quieter jobs in the department. At least it had been until Castro decided that he wanted to control the countries around the Gulf. Castro was making pretty good progress, until the agency had been forced to counter his activities. Castro was focusing his attention on countries with areas of unrest, injustice to the little people and great disparity in the distribution of wealth. His ploys didn't work in Venezuela, where the country was rich in oil and the people were treated rather fairly. But El Salvador qualified. Castro's people had managed to stir things up in El Salvador pretty well. The Department of State folks had responded rapidly to the cries for help from the Salvadorians. Once State determined what Fidel Castro was up to, the Central Intelligence Agency had been brought in.

  The agency's primary operations-type on-site, the Case Officer, had elected to eat in the wrong restaurant, at the wrong time, and had perished in a bomb explosion that had killed twelve people and seriously wounded several others. It was strongly suspected that he had been fingered, or it could have been someone else who was the target, or it was just bad luck. Whatever the case, the agency had to replace the operator with another agent, at least on a temporary basis. They had chosen Whitey McFrank, since it was known that he had a personal relationship with Alfredo Cellini. Cellini was head of the fourteen families that literally ran El Salvador.

  Hayner looked at the dispatch again. It was from Whitey.

  McFrank wasn't even full time on the agency payroll. He was part-time, one of the old re-treads from the big war. He was a former operative in the Office of Strategic Services, known as the OSS. Some time had passed between the disbanding of the OSS at the end of the war and the creation of the new intelligence agency some two years later.

The Cold War had created a need for an international intelligence agency. President Truman had no intention of giving Hoover and the FBI any more areas of operation and power than they already had. He confined their activity to internal national operations. The new agency was to be responsible for *outside* of the country; areas of possible conflict or those that posed a hazard to the United States. The Cold War was in full swing.

Helping to create the nucleus of the new agency, General William "Wild Bill" Donovan, who had headed up the Office of Strategic Services, called together many of his former OSS members for a thinly disguised reunion. It was actually a recruiting effort for the new agency.

Whitey McFrank was one of the few who had declined a regular commission in the new agency but had accepted part-time contract work. That had been twenty years ago and he was still doing odd jobs. His specialty was "janitorial services"; cleaning up other people's messes.

Clyde hadn't run, or controlled Whitey before, or anybody like him, but he had heard some of the stories.

Whitey's full name was Ernest Herman McFrank. Nobody called him by his first or middle name. In his early years he had been prematurely gray. Now his hair was pure white. He had been saddled with, and used the moniker "Whitey", for as long as anyone could remember.

Whitey had spent much of the big war behind German lines. His parentage was German and he spoke the language fluently. It had been said that during the war, one of his primary targets was the famous German Commando, Otto Skorzeny, who was responsible for getting Mussolini off of the Italian mountain top and flown to Berlin. Whitey got close enough to get one shot at Skorzeny. Otto's canteen had deflected the shot and he had escaped. They met after the war in a prisoner-of-war camp where Skorzeny was being interrogated. Skorzeny looked up when he saw Whitey approaching; he had recognized him and, while rubbing his hip, said, "It's still sore!"

But such is the stuff of legends.

The agency had initially called Whitey in to temporarily replace the operator who had been killed. But, more importantly, he was to determine the type of support the Salvadorians needed and to interface with the appropriate Intel people in the El Salvadorian government. His secondary mission was to determine if the bombing of the restaurant was directed at Americans specifically an American Embassy official--and to clean up any messes he came across from either the communists or created by our own agency people. That was Whitey's specialty; janitorial services.

Castro's influence manifested itself by communist-inspired guerrilla and terrorist activity. It had been easy for him to insert teams into these Central American countries and to provide them with assets provided by his new ally, the USSR. The teams would recruit from the locals and start out with minor hit-and-run events that would be successful. The success attracted more recruits. Then, with their group expanded, activity could escalate. Recently, the escalation was caused by the El Salvador State Police themselves, who were roaming the countryside, suspecting everybody, over-reacting and not using a whole lot of good sense. They had been overly corrupt and out of practice for any real police work. Their interrogation attitude and methods only served to anger the populace. This further stirred up the natives in an escalating fashion. Communism would start to look good compared to the activities of their current government. Things had gotten out of hand.

Now, with his all-white hair and carrying more weight than he should, Whitey looked just like an old man. Clyde couldn't understand why the company still used him. Whitey had been sent down to El Salvador in response to the need for an operational operator to sort things out. The Department of State had received a request for an intermediary from the "Catorce Familias"; the fourteen families who ran that country. The Familias had screamed for help. State realized the severity and nature of the growing problems and brought in the agency, who in turn, had sent Whitey down there as a temporary replacement for the murdered intelligence officer. Now Clyde had to run him. He looked at Whitey's dispatch again and the last paragraph held his attention. *'The head of the Catorce Familias, one Alfredo Cellini, says that the State Department was going to make a certain Colonel Cordero available to work with the El Salvadorian State Police--and where was this man?'*

There had been some talk about a Colonel Cordero but Clyde didn't know the details or status. He'd have to check. He took his legs off his desk, got to his feet, walked out into the hall and down to his Section Chief's corner office. He knocked quickly a couple of times and then, without waiting, walked in.

Peter Jorgensen looked up as Hayner came in. "What's up, Clyde? You look harried," he asked in a conciliatory manner.

"I just got this from McFrank in El Sal," Clyde replied as he handed the dispatch from El Salvador to his Section Chief. "Take a look."

Jorgensen took the dispatch and read it carefully. As he was reading, he motioned for Clyde to sit. After a couple of minutes the Section Chief looked up.

"This doesn't appear to be out of the ordinary, Clyde. I don't know if you've been briefed on Cordero. We inherited him from State. His full name is Emilio Rafael Cordero. He is originally from Venezuela. He was involved with us in the Cuban Invasion attempt. He is very anti-Castro. It is my understanding that he has done a couple of things for State since then. Cordero is in Costa Rica right now, supposedly on vacation. We are aware of the fact that

State recommended him to the families through the embassy people down there. I think he's just what we both want; that is, the families and the agency. We can count on him taking direction pretty well and he supposedly runs a tight ship. I don't think it'll take Cordero too long to straighten things out, and it keeps the agency in a position of plausible denial. I'll get him up here. Send a dispatch to Whitey and tell him to get back to Cellini with the confirmation that Cordero will be on his way. Don't commit to any time-table."

"I'll get right on it, Chief," Hayner rose and left the office.

Peter Jorgensen just looked at the closed door Hayner had walked through. He remembered some of the things that he had been briefed about Cordero. The Colonel was one ruthless son of a bitch! And, he was certainly ambitious. That could be a problem. However, with fourteen families watching over things, there should be ample warning of anything getting out of hand.

Clyde got back to his office, wrote out the dispatch to McFrank and, on his way to the message center, stopped at the section's secretary long enough to tell her he would be gone for the rest of the day. He had a twenty-mile drive home, no chains and his tires were damn near bald. He just hadn't planned on snow this early. Well, it may have been the least of his worries, but *his* worries were here, in front of him; and the Catorce Familias, with *their* problems, were a long way away.

SAN SALVADOR, EL SALVADOR

Two days later Whitey McFrank stopped by the embassy and picked up his mail. They still called it mail. The only people who were supposed to know where he was, when on assignment, was the company. The only mail he ever got was a dispatch, or two, or three, with instructions from someone sitting behind a desk and hundreds of miles away. God! He hated office pinkies; folks who were not ever in the field, never in harm's way, never got shot at. Their biggest risk was driving to and from their office.

After reading the dispatch from his Control; it turned out this one wasn't as bad as some. It looked like the company was actually going to do something in response to a field man's request. It was almost too good to be true. No time table, of course; that would make his job too easy. He must be getting old, he thought. Everything was pissing him off; the heat, the assignment, the Familias, his mail, warm beer, no women--had he left anything out? Shit! He headed back to his hotel. He would have to arrange a meeting with Cellini and change into a clean shirt before going over there; that is, if Cellini wanted to see him today.

When he called he was told, "Si. Senor Cellini would like to meet with you as soon as possible. A car will be sent." This only served to make him surlier than he had been before.

He took his time changing into his last clean shirt, being careful to renew his antiperspirant. He wondered how long he was going to be down here on assignment. Still standing in front of the mirror, Whitey looked at his body carefully. Getting fairly heavy around the middle. The mirrored face looking back at him had been described as cherubic; the face of a kind, well-meaning grandfather type. He had often wondered about that description. However it helped him blend in, which was good for his line of work. Clear pale-blue eyes, still striking at his advancing age. His hard body wasn't what it used to be, though.

His favorite past time was martial arts and working out with other martial arts advocates. He was entitled to *all* of the belts; white, brown, black and some that hadn't been named as yet. When his schedule allowed, he taught deserving and carefully selected students; passing on advanced martial arts moves as a form of entertainment.

12

Entertaining himself, that is. His appearance certainly hid the man underneath. *Enough musing,* he thought; *on to the business at hand.*

He was running out of clothes. Whitey would have to remember to ask his control how long he would be staying. He hadn't been able to turn up anything on the bombing that would indicate any of the other twelve dead people being a deliberate target. He had determined that the agency operator ate there on a regular basis. Aren't they training these people? That is not a very good habit. What surprised him was that someone knew the young man was the "Intel". His Agricultural Attaché cover had been a good one, and his stupid habits were certainly not what an Intel-type would have displayed. There was no question in his mind that the young intelligence agent had been the target. It was made to appear as somewhat typical of terrorist activity. Almost a bit too pat. He had sent the report with the facts of the matter, along with his personal analysis, some time back. His job here was essentially finished. They would be replacing him soon.

When he got to the lobby, Whitey saw the car waiting outside at the curb. The Latinos could be prompt when it suited them.

The doorman saluted and hurried across the sidewalk to open the rear door of the limousine. He was barely seated and the door closed when the driver launched into the stream of traffic without even bothering to clear himself. *These people are nuts*, he thought. *It would be just his luck to survive all the years of agency work only to die in an automobile accident!*

The drive didn't take long. They arrived at the gate of the fenced estate. Even though he was expected, he was carefully looked over by one of the two guards posted there. The second guard stood well back and alert. Whitey was asked to show identification before the car was cleared to proceed. The drive into the estate grounds to the main house was S-curved and the foliage arranged to make speed nearly impossible. Whitey had always been impressed with the care that had been taken to insure proper security on this estate. The car pulled up to the main entrance of the house. Here the guards carried only side arms, whereas the gate guards had carried Uzi sub machine guns.

The car door was opened and Whitey was escorted into the mansion. The cool interior was a marked contrast to the outside heat of the day. The coolness was due to the thick walls and general construction techniques used in this part of the world. Heavy air conditioning was not in wide use in El Salvador yet, other than in modern offices.

Once inside the hacienda, the guard accompanying him was replaced by a servant. As he followed the house servant down a hall, Whitey noticed a bulge under his jacket that was obviously a side arm. Security was tighter than it had been when Whitey was last in to see Cellini. He had been thinking about how long it had been when they came to the door of the library. The servant knocked and, when answered, opened the door and stepped back to let Whitey enter. Cellini rose and came out from behind his desk with his hand outstretched to greet his guest. He was about six feet, elegant, and casually dressed; a good looking man in his mid-fifties.

"Senor White, I'm so glad you could come right over. It has been too long since you have been in my home. I had heard that you were back in my country," Senor Cellini mentioned nonchalantly. "You should have called."

"Senor Cellini, it is good to see you as well. My arrival was to have been kept under wraps. It was the matter of the restaurant bombing. But then, nothing escapes you, Alfredo. Yes, I should have called. My apologies." Cellini gestured acceptance. Whitey continued, "It does seem to have been quite a while. Are you still doing a lot of flying?"

"Not as much as I would like to. The time seems to be so short, what with all the trouble we have around here.

It has, as you know, become quite deadly in my country. The last time you were here was over the unfortunate occurrence with Reggie? They kidnapped his son, kept him tied up for three months. Then, when the ransom was negotiated, they dropped him off at the gate in front of Reggie's house. He had been shot through the head. We asked you to come down at the time, and only gave you the name of the killers, not the complete story."

"Yes, I remember. I was puzzled at the time as to why you didn't give me more information. I thought then that you may have wanted to get the go-ahead from the rest of the families."

"What you thought was true, only it was more than just that. I wish now we had accepted your price at the time. Since then we have spent many times what you would have charged and with no results. The grief was a cause for blindness and indecision. The family couldn't make a decision about anything--funeral details, or revenge. Nothing! I felt bad about your long trip."

"Well Alfredo, it is good that we can speak of this now. I would still be glad to help you out on that one. It would be difficult, but not impossible. The people involved will all have gone to ground and be harder than hell to find. But that much ransom money is hard to keep secret. It leaves a long trail."

"I agree, it would be most difficult. Perhaps we'll look into it again," Alfredo sighed, then changed the subject. "The family and I are going over to La Progresso for a few days. We would be honored to have you join us at the beach house. Can you spare the time from your present assignment?"

"Alfredo, thank you, but I am going to have to decline. Perhaps another time."

"I'm sorry you can't make it. Yes, another time then." Cellini turned back toward his desk and found a chair, gesturing for Whitey to sit down in another one close to his.

"Well, to the reason for your coming to see me today. You are aware, of course, that there have been two other abductions recently of prominent citizens. One of them is a distant cousin. There have been no requests of ransom yet. Our family does not expect to see the cousin alive again in any case."

Now was time for business. The informal atmosphere had changed significantly to one of formal business. McFrank had spent enough time in this part of the world to recognize the somewhat abrupt change and to not be offended.

"Senor Cellini, I'm sorry. Yes, I knew about the kidnappings. I didn't know that one was a relation." He thought, *"It doesn't surprise me, most of the prominent people in this country are related to one or more of the fourteen families."*

"Thank you for your sympathies, Senor White, these are difficult times, but we will prevail." Cellini paused for a moment, lost in thought, then continued. "Do you have some good news from our friends in Washington?"

"Yes Senor Cellini, I do. They have agreed with your request and suggestion that a Colonel Cordero be made available for your State Police assignment. They did not make me aware of the timetable. However I was led to believe that it would not be long before he would be here."

"Aah, that is good news. You will keep me informed, of course."

"Of course, Senor Cellini."

"Will you be able to join us for dinner, or shall I call the car?"

Whitey politely declined the dinner invitation. Senor Cellini stood up, reached over and pressed a buzzer on his desk. He gestured and walked Whitey across the large room. They made their farewells at the door to Cellini's office.

16

Whitey was quickly escorted to the entrance door. The car was in the same place where he had left it. During the ride back to the hotel, Whitey reflected on his visit with Alfredo. The invitations to the beach house and to dinner had seemed forced. There must have been a lot on his mind. It wasn't like the Cellini that Whitey had known in years past.

The following day, Whitey's mail indicated that he was released to return to his domicile in Seattle, pending further orders. It suited him just fine. No details about Cordero, nothing, just that he was released to return to domicile, pending further orders.

Normal operating procedures dictated that unless a specific action was spelled out, it wasn't to be done. Okay. Fine. It wouldn't take long to get airline reservations out of El Salvador. However, due to their relationship, Whitey called Alfredo and advised him that he was leaving but would be in touch.

His next call was to Sandy, his soul-mate, lover and who also happened to be his wife of a few years. She was something else, that one. She only asked to be told when he would be coming home if possible.

Two days later he was watching the cold rain bouncing on the taxiways as the Boeing 727 rolled out on landing at Sea-Tac International Airport, located between Seattle and Tacoma. He would be home in a little over an hour.

While waiting down in the baggage claim area for his luggage to make its way to the carousel, Whitey went over to the phones nearby and called Sandy. That way she knew she had an hour to prepare herself for his arrival.

And maybe the second thing Whitey would do when he got to the apartment would be to put his suitcase down.

CHAPTER THREE
THROWN TO THE DOGS

Colonel Emilio Rafael Cordero was annoyed. He and Lieutenant Paredes had finally made it back to his Costa Rican base of operations. They had come out of El Salvador through Honduras. Leaving San Salvador, they had traveled north through Santa Ana and then Metapan, crossing into Honduras late at night. The area is quite mountainous, the roads a joke; and the officials of Honduras are bored and difficult to deal with, even with the usual bribes. Both Cordero and Paredes were traveling on Costa Rican passports, using different names. They did not want to leave any trails of movement in or near El Salvador.

Scheduled air service was supposedly available in Gracias. But when they arrived they found that it was no longer available and the closest air service was Erandique.

Paredes had been tasked with the overall planning; the hit in San Salvador, and transportation, which included the air service at Gracias. Cordero had become quite put out with his lieutenant for this oversight.

A straight line distance between Gracias and Erandique was only about thirty miles. The mountains and poor roads about tripled the mileage. And to make matters worse, the car had developed over-heating problems. Paredes had purchased the car in Nicaragua and it was to be sold or abandoned after their need for it in El Salvador. Paredes had obtained illegal El Salvadorian license plates, and then changed back to the Nicaraguan plates for the border crossing into Honduras. This was one of the reasons

18

for their problems with the border police. There were currently bad feelings between Honduras and Nicaragua, and the Nicaraguan license plates initiated the hostility from the border guards. But then, Honduras always had bad feelings for someone!

Paredes was able to sell the car in Erandique, for pennies compared to the purchase price. They booked tickets aboard a local flight out of Erandique to the Honduran capital, Tegucigalpa and from there to Managua, in Nicaragua. Then, using their own passports, on to San Jose, Costa Rica.

With the exception of the last leg, the travel had been brutal and the accommodations primitive. Cordero had been riding Paredes hard about his overall planning; the poor choice of car, the re-sale price, and the lack of air travel.

But that wasn't what was really annoying Colonel Cordero at the moment.

They had no sooner arrived at the hacienda Cordero had leased, when his current concubine, Carmeletta, came running up to him crying and carrying on. Cordero wasn't in any mood to deal with this hysterical woman. In fact, women were very low on the Colonel's priority list. He didn't really care about this woman's problems. But something she said had caught his attention. He finally couldn't ignore the words coming from this woman's mouth.

"I've been raped! Pablos, the beast, took me and forced me to do all kinds of vile things, my Patrón. He beat me..." Her voice trailed off and her sobs increased in volume, "And he said that you had the penis of a little boy and that he had one of a man!"

It was this last comment that had caught Cordero's attention and enraged him.

Pablos had been recently recruited and brought into his force and probably didn't understand the rules. He was young, cocky and very good looking, almost pretty. Cordero doubted very much that he raped the young girl; had sex with

19

her, yes. There was no doubt in his mind that this much of Carmeletta's ravings were true.

The Colonel was tired, dirty from his long trip and didn't wish to deal with this now. *But such is the burden of command,* he thought.

"Enough woman!" Cordero pushed her away. Turning to Paredes, "Have Pablos brought to me in the study, now!"

"Si, mi Coronel!" Paredes hurriedly left to do as he was told. Inwardly he was delighted that his Colonel had something else to think about other than the stupid things that had occurred getting back to Costa Rica.

The Colonel started off down the hall, motioning for the girl to follow. Once inside his study, Cordero turned to the woman, "And you are certain? This Pablos raped and beat you? I don't see any bruises. Where are they? Show them to me."

"Uh, they are not where you can see them, the insults and threats were more hurting than his blows...." Carmeletta was afraid to go on. She knew that Cordero would want to examine her very closely. She had bruised herself in a few discreet places in preparation.

He slapped her hard. "I said show them to me. Be quick about it." Cordero was determined to get to the bottom of this.

Carmeletta was glad that she had the presence of mind to bruise herself. She had done it the first night, and again later. The self-inflicted bruises weren't bad enough to show for long. She didn't know when Cordero would return, only that he would. Pablos hadn't noticed the bruises. She made sure that they only made love with the lights off.

She removed her blouse. She wasn't wearing a brassiere and her breasts were her best asset. She moved in such a way as to make them sway provocatively. They were not over large, but pert, the nipples standing up. One of the bruises on her rib cage was just below her left breast.

Cordero wasn't interested in her breasts or the small bruise. He made a gesture indicating his impatience. She lifted her skirt. The remaining self-inflicted bruises were on her inside thighs. She pointed down.

"Get up on the desk. Spread your legs!" Cordero snarled.

She did as she was told. Cordero stuck his hand into her crotch and tore her underpants off. He then grabbed her roughly and squeezed. She screamed and started to cry.

They were interrupted by a rap on the door to the study.

"Cover yourself, woman!" Cordero said, removing his hand and wiping it on her skirt. When the blouse went over her head, he pulled her abruptly off the desk, then walked over and opened the door.

Paredes stood there. Behind him were two men holding Pablos between them.

Colonel Cordero addressed the men, "Tie him and then leave us. Wait outside. Paredes, you stay! The girl started to say something. Cordero whipped back around and shook his finger in her face. "*You!* Be quiet!" Cordero's mood was darkening.

Pablos was now obviously quite frightened. He was afraid to speak. His eyes kept darting back and forth between Carmeletta and Colonel Cordero.

Paredes pushed Pablos down into a straight-backed chair that he had pulled out from the wall. He stood back.

Cordero stepped forward and looked down at this pretty one. Carmeletta told him that Pablos had forced her to use her mouth; suck him, and then he had sodomized her. The thought crossed Cordero's mind that it would be interesting to do the things to Pablos that he had done to her.

Normal sex, in almost any form, was not exciting to Cordero. Inflicting pain and using power during a sexual act was more to his liking; sadistic actions in either homosexual or heterosexual acts--it didn't matter. Doing those things to this pretty one before him was tempting. It was just a passing thought, however, he had other ideas for this one. A plan was beginning to form.

Faster than the eye could follow Cordero reached out and back-handed Pablos just as he started to look up. A large ring that Cordero wore on his right hand tore open the cheek of his victim. Blood splattered the front of Pablos' shirt. He let out a surprised scream.

"Carmeletta tells me that you forced yourself on her. Is this true?" The Colonel spoke quietly, almost kindly.

"No, my Coronel, no. I didn't know that she was your woman....it was only after I had made love to her that the other men told me she was your woman...I didn't know...I didn't know." His head fell forward as he sobbed and then fell quiet.

"Did you strike her?"

It took a little longer for Pablos to answer this time. "Yes, yes I struck her. But that was before I knew. The men didn't tell me for some time....I didn't know, my Coronel, that she was yours."

"Did you say things to her about your manhood?"

Pablos looked up, surprised at this question. "I don't understand. I said many things to her about what I could do. About my member, about my manhood. She told you this?"

"Yes, she told me this." Cordero turned and walked slowly back across toward his desk. The thought that had been forming in the back of his mind became clear. It was time for a lesson to the men. It was a shame to waste this one, but the man had been stupid to let his cock rule his brain. Cordero didn't have much respect for men like this.

He turned back to the man in the chair. "Pablos, I'm going to have to punish you. I'm sure you understand."

Pablos nodded his head, looking down. The blood from his torn cheek was still dripping onto his shirt front. A fear was starting to build within him. He didn't know what was in store for him, but it couldn't be too bad. He knew that

Cordero was organizing a military force, and he had always done what was asked without question. His only wrong had been this stupid woman. She was as much to blame, and the other men had thought it a big joke. How bad could his punishment be?

"Paredes, take him out to the dog's yard. Strip him and stake him to the ground. I want all of the men there as well."

"What's this? Why strip me? What is going to happen? The dogs . . . why the dogs? What? Pablos thought.

Paredes opened the door for the two men who were waiting just outside. They came in and lifted Pablos to his feet and took him away. He was starting to whimper. The men looked at him with disgust.

Colonel Cordero was left alone with Carmeletta.

"Now as for you, my *Little Puta,* since you have allowed yourself to be used by one of my men, you might as well have all of them." He raised his hand as she started to say something, "Don't try to be something you're not. This can be a good thing for you if you don't act like a 'puta', but act with class. We will not speak of this again."

Carmeletta broke into tears but thought better about trying to change Cordero's mind. She had been with him for over a year and knew this man well. Their infrequent love making had been awful. He was a sadist. Normal sex didn't happen. Everything had some form or another of cruelty or vile perversion. Once he had almost killed her. But, the other benefits of being the concubine of the leader were many.

She had longed for normal lovemaking. To just be held would be wonderful. This was why she had approached Pablos. It had been so long since she had been with someone who seemed to care about her. He had been a wonderful lover--gentle, sensitive and caring. They had even spoken about leaving together.

23

And then the men found out about them.

Pablos, the fool, couldn't keep his mouth shut. He had to brag. Why was it that men had to let everybody know about their conquests? She had tried to warn him but the fool wouldn't listen! So now the price must be paid. Only this time she feared for her life.

But the Colonel wasn't directing his anger toward her. He seemed almost calm. In fact, if she didn't know better, she thought he appeared relieved. Maybe she didn't know him as well as she thought she did.

Carmeletta knew he was right. If she acted the lady with the men, she would be able to control them. If she was careful. Maybe it wouldn't be too bad.

When the Colonel's instructions had been followed completely, Paredes came for Cordero.

"Mi Coronel, all of the men are in the yard. We are ready." Paredes knew what was coming and was looking forward to the spectacle, especially the part he was to play.

Colonel Cordero kept four Dobermans that he had personally trained. They were obedient to him in some special ways. He used them as guard dogs in the hacienda's compound, letting them roam free in the fenced estate after securing for the night. They only barked when an intruder was found, and then, only to attract their master's permission to go beyond whatever it took to neutralize the victim. They had been trained to hold their victims.

Colonel Cordero walked out into the compound and over to the dog run. He took his time. It was important for the men to observe his power. He had changed into a clean uniform shirt and trousers. The ever-present aviator sun glasses hid any emotion that he may have felt.

Pablos had been stripped naked and was staked, spread-eagled, on the ground. The men were wondering what was going to take place. Cordero walked over to the fence and barely nodded to his lieutenant. Words weren't

24

necessary. What the men were about to see had taken place at other times. Paredes knew what he was to do.

Now. It was now. The special treats that his Colonel sometimes bestowed on him. Lieutenant Paredes smiled and slowly pulled out a switchblade knife. As he pressed the button to release the blade it flashed in the sunlight. He bent slowly over the helpless man staked out on the ground. Reaching out he slashed across Pablos' stomach, just deep enough to draw blood. Pablos screamed in pain and terror. Moving down to his feet, Paredes cut the inside of Pablos' thighs from his groin to his feet on both legs. He carefully avoided his genitals.

Pablos screams didn't slow down the merciless actions. The cutting continued on both arms in the same manner; cuts just deep enough to draw blood. In his growing terror, Pablos started to urinate. This brought nervous laughter from the men. The urine ran into the cuts on his stomach causing more pain.

Cordero spoke quietly to his lieutenant, but his voice carried to the men, "Now, release my little pets so that they can enjoy the fun as well."

Pablos now realized the full extent of his fate. "No-ooo, please...have mercy. I didn't know...I didn't know!" His sobs grew in intensity. "Mother of God. Please not this. ..No-ooo..."

Paredes moved over to the kennels and opened the gate. The dogs moved quickly to where Pablos was held down. They waited--waiting for their master's release.

"Comer!" Cordero said, which was Spanish for "eat".

The dogs immediately attacked the helpless man. Part of their training had been an introduction of blood with their food. Pablos started screaming and kept screaming. The watching men were taken by surprise. Some laughed, a couple of them started retching. The others appeared to be too stunned to do anything.

Paredes took special note of those men who were retching or who appeared to be disapproving of the action taking place in front of them. They would bear watching. He wanted a special type of man under his Colonel's command. Paredes knew what his master wanted.

It took Pablos a long time to die.

Colonel Cordero thought it had been a good lesson for the men. It was not a waste of a man after all.

CHAPTER FOUR
THE APPOINTED POSITION

The same morning Whitey was released to return to Seattle, Colonel Cordero was being shown into Peter Jorgensen's office. Jorgensen rose and met him half way across the room. There was quite a difference between the two men; Jorgensen, right at six feet, fair hair and complexion, dressed in a double breasted blazer with school tie and tan slacks, the Colonel about five feet eight, typically dark complexion, black hair and eyes, and wearing an expensively-tailored European silk suit. One of them looked like a successful stockbroker and the other like a well-heeled gangster.

"Did you have a pleasant flight, Colonel?" Peter asked as he directed Colonel Cordero to a couch. Peter took a chair close by.

"Si. It was a long one, but it gave me enough time to make up a list of some things I'm going to need when I get to El Salvador."

"Did someone tell you about that?" Peter appeared to be a bit surprised. His thoughts went much further. *"It was unlike a Latin to get right down to business in this direct a manner. Then there was the matter of 'El Salvador'. Who had let this so-called Colonel know about that?"*

The answer to his thoughts came quickly enough.

"No, Senor your people are very quiet about those things. I have not just been enjoying my rest in Costa Rica. The words, they travel fast in that part of the world. It is no secret that El Salvador is having some problems. Some of your government people and a member of the Catorce Familia, have discussed my helping the Salvadorian government. It appears to be time." He stated this slowly and with conviction.

"Well, your surmise was accurate, Colonel. The families are anxious for you to take a special assignment with the State Police. They do not want their Army involved at this time. There is apparent need for the ferreting out of some guerrilla groups operating in El Salvador, inspired by our Cuban friends."

"Si that confirms the things I have heard. It is felt by some in Costa Rica that they could be next."

"Well, all things are possible, Colonel. We can certainly discuss it at the appropriate time." Jorgensen paused for a moment before continuing. "I believe you said that you had a list of required items. Can these be supplied from our bases in Panama? Do you have the list with you?"

Colonel Cordero opened his briefcase and took out a large sheaf of papers. They were hand-written. He handed them to Peter.

After glancing over the first two pages, Jorgensen looked up, "These are not standard items in our inventory; they're all Eastern Bloc manufacture. I assume you have your reasons for the specific items listed." He continued to look at the Colonel, waiting. Cordero nodded in the affirmative and Jorgensen went on. "Right! I'll get someone on this immediately."

Jorgensen got up and walked over to his desk. He picked up the phone and spoke briefly. A few moments later there was a soft knock and the door opened. It was Peter's secretary. He handed her the sheaf of papers and she left without a word.

Turning back to Colonel Cordero, Jorgensen said, "We'll go on down to the briefing room. Clyde Hayner has the current situation and details you'll need to know."

Without saying anything, Cordero rose and gestured for Jorgensen to lead the way.

The briefing took close to two hours. They returned to Jorgensen's office.

"Unless you have other wishes, Colonel, I think we should eat here in the cafeteria. It isn't fancy, but the food is good." Jorgensen said.

"As you wish, Senor," the Colonel replied.

Peter Jorgensen thought for a few moments and then decided this was as good a time as any to discuss the agency's position on the assignment of the Colonel to El Salvador.

"Colonel Cordero, perhaps we should talk for a moment about the job you're going to be undertaking." Peter waited for any objection that might be forthcoming. When there wasn't one, he continued, "Your financial arrangements with the familias is your business. For your ongoing cooperation with the agency, my government's contribution will be two hundred and fifty thousand dollars, deposited in your account as agreed upon some time ago. Is that agreement still valid?"

It was very quiet. The silence became awkward. Finally Cordero cleared his throat and spoke slowly and quite distinctly.

"Senor Jorgensen, You will find as we work together that I am a man of my word. I fully realize 'The Company', as you and your people like to call it, did not select me to work with the Catorce Familias. The fact that your State Department made all of the arrangements, including the amount to be paid into my bank account, does not in any way change our working relationship. I understand completely the major difference between strategy and tactics. State sets the strategy and The Company, the tactics; or operations if you prefer. Perhaps you would feel more comfortable if I put it another way. I fully understand the Golden Rule. He who has the gold makes the rules! And, you have the gold!"

Jorgensen was surprised at the candidness and understanding displayed by this man standing before him. It put things in a slightly different light. He had been prepared to encounter some difficulty in dealing with someone of this type, including having to negotiate the funding. Thinking, *he was surprised, and maybe....no, just leave it at surprised.*

"Colonel, I meant no offense. Sometimes it is best to get things said directly and out in the open. That way there will be no misunderstandings."

"No offense has been taken, Mr. Jorgensen," Cordero paused and thought for a moment. "But I do have another request."

"Other than the list of special equipment? What would that be?"

"My contact from your agency in El Salvador," the Colonel replied.

"We had planned on using Hayner, whom you met today, and dispatch from here for any specific instructions. Do you have other thoughts on this?"

"Yes. I like to work face to face with my...how you people put it....my control. That way there will be no misunderstandings." The emphasis on the word misunderstandings hung for a moment, and then Cordero continued, "I wish that person to be your Mr. McFrank. He is known by my people and I have been told that he is in El Salvador now".

Jorgensen took a moment to think, then replied, "Why don't we go to lunch and then we can talk about this some more."

"Of course, Senor."

SEATTLE, WASHINGTON

McFrank had been home for three days when he got the call to check into the local agency office. It usually meant that there would be another offer of a contract, or a question on his report that couldn't be discussed on the phone.

The drive into downtown Seattle was a short one from Capitol Hill, where Whitey and Sandy lived. It was after the morning rush hour. Traffic was light. Whitey pulled into the parking garage under the Federal Building. He parked, locked the car and went over to the elevator. The local Central Intelligence Agency offices were on the eighth floor. Operations were on the seventh floor. This always puzzled him, this attempt at security. The agency address was in the telephone book, and the offices were listed on the building directory in the lobby of the building.

He punched the button for the seventh floor. When the elevator stopped and the doors opened, he went out, turned left down the hall around a corner and went into an unmarked door.

Inside was a small anteroom without any furniture. He walked over to the inside door and pressed a buzzer set into the wall. A voice came over a speaker that wasn't in sight, "Identification please."

"McFrank," Whitey said into the air.

There was an audible click and Whitey turned the doorknob and went in. The door opened smoothly, despite the fact that it was specially constructed steel, painted to appear to be a standard wooden office door. He closed the door behind him. The heavy click confirmed the locking mechanism was in place.

The inner office was three or four times larger than the anteroom. Along one wall were file cabinets; and on the other wall were TWX machines, facsimile 'sends and receive' machines and even an old Western Union telegraph machine.

Just inside the door was a desk for the Duty Officer. Seated behind the desk was a young man Whitey had met and seen a few times but didn't know very well. He did remember his name; it was Anthony Walker. He liked to be called Tony.

"How were the southern climes, Mr. McFrank?" the Duty Officer asked.

"Just fine. Hot, a lot of flies and bad food. You said you had some important mail for me."

"Yes Sir," Tony handed Whitey a large envelope. "You had better open it here in case you need to reply, or. . ." His voice trailed off when Whitey looked at him. There wasn't much else he needed to say. He had no doubt said too much as it was.

Whitey went over to one of the chairs in front of a TWX machine, sat down and opened the envelope. The first page was from Clyde Hayner, El Sal desk at the company headquarters. The rest of the pages contained what was obviously a long shopping list for some very particular items, Eastern Bloc automatic weapons, shoulder-fired rocket launchers, ammunition, explosives, caps, fuses--the list went on for several pages. It looked like somebody wanted to start a war. He turned back to the first page.

It was a set of orders, ordering him to Active Duty again. Not a request, but an order. This was a bit unusual especially since he had just come off orders. One sentence jumped out at him, --*Colonel Cordero has requested you, by name, to be the on-site control. You will interface between local Case Officer and Colonel Cordero...*

Shit! And then another word jumped out ...indefinite.

Shit! And Double Damn! *Well okay.* He thought. *One thing about being part time, he was able to negotiate the fees, within reason, of course. This time it wasn't going to be within reason. His turf was Europe, not Central America. South America was okay in some places but Central America was a mystery. Nobody could tell what was going to happen next. 'Unstable' was just the beginning word, followed by 'volatile', and 'violent', all mixed in with that special brand of Hispanic machismo permeating everything in both Central and South America. His relationship with Alfredo Cellini was what tied him to the area. The only good thing about it was that now it had a clear-cut purpose. The bad guys were Castro-Communists. They were very well defined. Even if this area was not his turf, he could get into the purpose and feel good about what had to be done.* He turned back to Anthony Walker.

"Give me a message blank, Tony."

"Here you go, Mr. McFrank. I'll be happy to encode it for you."

"What do you mean encode it? Aren't your lines secure?"

"Yes Sir, but look at the front of that envelope that I just handed to you.

Whitey looked for the envelope, found it and saw the security classification stamp. "Yeah, I see. Okay, I'll have this for you in a couple of minutes. Is there a typewriter in here with all this equipment?"

"Yes Sir, the one here at my desk. If you want to use it, I'll go get some coffee. Would you like a cup?"

McFrank got up and walked over to the desk, waiting for Tony to vacate his chair. "That would be fine, Tony. Make it black please."

Anthony Walker got up quickly and seemed happy to get out of the way and even out of the room, for that matter, by the way he hurried out.

Whitey sat down at the typewriter and soon finished the message. It was order acceptance, negotiated front load price, with the monthly rate; and he added a cut-off date of three months, which would make the orders re-negotiable at that time.

That should stir things up at the El Sal desk.

He glanced up as Tony came back into the room with the coffee. Whitey got up and moved over to another chair. Passing Tony, he took one of the cups from him.

Tony sat down and looked around. He was about to ask where the message was. Whitey saved him the trouble.

"It's still in the typewriter, Tony."

Walker took it out of the typewriter and read it over. His eyes got big when he came to the money parts. He had the good sense not to say anything.

"I'll get this out right away. You don't have to sign it or anything. Do you want a copy?"

Whitey thought for a minute, and then replied, "No, now that it is all special classification, I don't have any suitable secure file area at home. Just use my file here at the office. Put a copy in there when you're finished. And here, put this top copy of the orders in the file also. The rest of these papers are operational and I'll keep them with me." Whitey rose to go, grimaced and commented, "This coffee is terrible. I'll leave the cup here. See you around, Walker."

"Right, Mr. McFrank, have a good, uh . . . we'll see you when you get back. Into the office, I mean."

On the drive back to the apartment, Whitey thought about how he would tell Sandy. Ernest Herman "Whitey" McFrank was a very private person. Not one to talk much about what he was thinking. It was probably due to the line of work he was in. But this time things were different. As much as he hated Central America, he believed in the mission. And, he had just returned from a contract. And now another one right on top of it. He knew she would be disappointed. He wanted to explain how he felt about it to her, and the money thing and how it was getting close to retirement for him. It would be his choice, not the company's. If this mission went well he could almost make enough in the first three months. The second three months--

and there would *be* a second three months, would make it icing on the cake, so to speak.

What the Hell, all he had to do was stay alive, keep Cordero alive and put a smile on Cellini's face. Cellini was really the only one who mattered, beside himself, that is.

He was a little surprised at Cordero's request. Whitey didn't know the man. And he didn't know how Cordero could know anything about him. It was something to think about. He just did not believe in coincidences. There were a lot of things he didn't believe in and that kind of thinking had kept him alive for a long time.

CHAPTER FIVE
A NEW CONTRACT

The next morning, promptly at eight o' clock, the special telephone rang. Whitey answered it on the second ring. He had been in his den, studying some sailboat designs that Sandy wanted him to look over. He had been expecting the call.

"McFrank." He listened for a moment then replied, "About a half hour."

He turned to find Sandy, who had come to the open door of the den. Before he could say anything, she came over to him and placed a finger on his lips.

"I know, you'll be back soon."

They had talked long into the night. He had told Sandy things about his various agency contracts that hadn't ever been discussed before. She was surprisingly calm about it. Sandy also understood that this could very well be his last contract. He had explained that, though it was operational, it wasn't very dangerous. He would be controlling on-site. He would not be directly involved operationally. There was always some degree of danger, of course, but other than being apart for probably six months, this could be a fairly decent twilight cruise. And a cruise it would be. They would have enough money for the sailboat they wanted and enough left over to do some serious blue-water cruising--for a good many years, in fact.

She understood. Her understanding was enough for him.

He turned away, opened the top right-hand drawer, took out his Detonics and slipped it into the custom holster that fit the small of his back. Sandy was still standing there.

"Just the office, and I'll be back."

Without waiting for a reply he brushed by her and out to the closet for his jacket. He stopped at the front door and looked back at Sandy. She had come out of the den and was standing in the hall. They looked at each other for a long moment without saying anything. He turned and left.

When Whitey got to the company office he was told to see the Seattle Chief of Station, Harold Roberts. Whitey went to the Chief's office, knocked once, went in and closed the door behind him.

Roberts was standing in the middle of his office holding a sheaf of papers as Whitey walked in. He turned, facing Whitey and spoke in a direct manner. "I've been briefed on your orders and, by the way, since you accepted the assignment, you're back on Active Duty effective today. The pay rates that you requested and a three-month contract have been approved. I've also been briefed on your list of special items." The Chief was getting right down to business. He went on. "From what I've been told, the best local variety store is in Vancouver, B.C. Is that what you had in mind?"

Whitey walked over to a chair near the desk and sat. "I was going to give it a shot, yes."

Chief Roberts sat down behind his desk. "It might interest you to know that Otto Schwartz is in Vancouver at the moment. We've been working a gambit with a couple of amateurs, nothing serious; and Otto won't come into this country for anything, anyway."

This bit of information got Whitey's attention. He knew Schwartz. Schwartz was probably the largest arms dealer in West Germany. It was a well-known fact, in the intelligence community, that he had personally provided all of the hardware for the Algerian uprising against their French landlords. It was also fairly well known that Otto's mother had the misfortune that day to elect to use her son's Mercedes to do a little shopping. She didn't get any farther than trying to start the engine. Any number of people would have gladly wired up the car to go boom, but most folks in the Intel community bet that it had been the French. The French get very aggressive when messed with. In any case, Otto Schwartz was not a very nice person. But, he could supply just about anything a person wanted in the way of arms and ordnance. With Schwartz in Vancouver, Whitey could deal directly with him, not through a daisy chain. He liked that.

"I would appreciate getting word to Schwartz, through your gambit or whatever, that I have some business for him."

Roberts nodded. "The thought occurred to me when I saw your mail and the list of items being requested. How had you planned on moving the package?"

Whitey thought for a moment before replying. "I hadn't worked through that one yet, but considering the sensitivity of Cordero's arrival and his mission, I don't think commercial channels would be appropriate. The material should be flown into an out-lying field where there are either no customs folks or those that are there can be bought, and would stay bought. I'll have to work it out from the El Salvador end."

"I thought as much. I've taken the liberty of asking the two amateurs who have been working the Schwartz Gambit to come down today. They're in the other office." Roberts motioned to Whitey to hold still and then continued, "As luck would have it, they're both Marine pilots and actively flying in the Reserve out at Sand Point. We could have them detailed to the agency on a limited contract."

Whitey chuckled. "Not that it's any of my business, but how in the hell did you get mixed up with amateurs? And Marines to boot?"

"McFrank, I'm surprised at you. What do you have against Marines?" Roberts was openly amused at McFrank's attitude.

"Nothing really, it's just that my experience has been that they don't really follow outside orders well. They have a tendency to improvise on the spot. Usually the improvisation works well. It's just the unpredictable factor I question." Whitey paused for a moment and chuckled again. "Perhaps that's a bit harsh. Follow orders? Of course, just in the manner maybe. Actually I guess I was making a bad joke. But that's beside the point. Seriously, how did you get involved with these two?"

"It's kind of interesting. They have an aircraft brokerage company, buying and selling large aircraft. Many of the major airlines are getting rid of their early jets and preparing for the jumbos. The smaller airlines around the world are looking to upgrade their piston fleet with these well-maintained domestic jets. It's my understanding these two have a program worked out with Pan Am for the DC-8's that have the spare fifth engine pod under their wing." Roberts paused for a minute to gather his thoughts, then continued. "Whatever. They have been working with several foreign folk and when they started conversations with some Germans, the subject regarding 'tactical goods' came up. Not too surprising with Krauts. When the lads figured out that it is against the law for an American citizen to deal in any kind of arms without a specific arms license, they gave us a call. One thing lead to another and they ended up carrying a wire for us in a couple of meetings with Otto Schwartz in Vancouver, B.C. And they've been able to keep Schwartz there for going on ten days now. Frankly, I think you'll like them, Whitey. They're kind of ballsy."

Whitey waved his hand as if it didn't matter much. "Okay, that answers my question. Let's go meet these two aspiring spooks."

"No, I think we'd be better off bringing them in here." He reached for his intercom, "Chris, would you ask Barnes and McGarrity to step in here?"

There was a muted reply and then Roberts depressed the intercom key again, "Thanks Chris."

A moment later the door to Robert's outer office opened and two men who appeared to be in about their mid to late thirties entered. The first one was about five feet ten and of medium build. He had receding dark hair that at first glance made him appear to look the older. There was a no-nonsense look about him, comfortably confident. The second one was a little taller--probably six feet, with dark hair and appeared to be a bit amused by all of this.

Roberts stood, as did Whitey, and made the introductions, "McFrank, I'd like you to meet Doc McGarrity and Harry Barnes. Gentlemen, this is Ernest McFrank his associates call him Whitey."

Handshakes and brief pleasantries were exchanged; and then the Section Chief gestured for them to sit, and he went back behind his desk. No one spoke for a minute. Roberts gestured to Whitey, who took his cue.

"What got you two into the spook business?"

McGarrity and Barnes both looked at Section Chief Roberts, who nodded his okay. McGarrity, the no-nonsense one, took the lead without hesitation.

"Smoke and I....or rather Harry here and I, have been brokering a few airplanes internationally. We started dealing with a German buyer and the next thing we knew he was asking about tactical goods." McGarrity paused for a moment and then continued, "He started out asking about Mustangs, P-51's, and then on into some pretty heavy ordnance."

"Like what?" Whitey asked.

"It started with hard-point racks, then gradually evolved into what goes on them. Finally he wanted the wing-mounted fifty caliber machine guns for the Mustangs and then other specific items--drop tanks, rockets and the like," McGarrity replied. He tilted his head and raised his eyebrows as if to ask did Whitey want more.

Whitey bored on. "Then what?"

"Well, we knew where there were some Mustang parts and thought we could find some of the racks and drop tanks. Didn't really know about the other items this German was asking about. Then it occurred to us that this might not be too kosher. I asked around a bit and found out that it was against the law for an American citizen to mess around with arms without a license. We decided to call the CIA."

Whitey didn't quit. "Why the CIA?"

"After looking in the telephone book under Government Listings it was thought that the only folks who would be interested in some Kraut wanting to buy machine guns was either the CIA or the FBI. The CIA was international to our way of thinking. What's your point? We're here aren't we? And we've been cooperating with Mr. Roberts here, trying to get this German to come into the United States." McGarrity was getting a bit tense and it showed.

"Easy, Doc. I'm just trying to understand how you lads got involved. I'm also wondering if you want to get further involved. And how much time you would have free to spend in the process." Whitey had eased off considerably. "You called Barnes 'Smoke' earlier? What's that all about?"

Barnes spoke up for the first time. "It's my moniker from fighter-pilot days in Korea; a nickname. Like yours. Looking at your hair, I think I can see why they call you 'Whitey'."

Whitey ignored Smoke's last comment about his own nickname but continued. "Chief Roberts tells me you both were Marine pilots. Do you still fly?"

Barnes took the question. "We're both in a Reserve Squadron out at Sand Point, flying AD's. Weekend Warriors."

41

"Either of you have any multi-engine time?"

"Sure, the R5D, R4D-8's and bug smashers. Why do you ask?"

Whitey had a puzzled look on his face. "I'm not familiar with those designations. They're Navy aren't they?"

"Yeah, the R5D is a C-54 or civilian DC-4, which is an unpressurized four engine Douglas transport. The R4D-8 is the C-47, DC-3, or Gooney Bird. Actually the R4D-8 is really a Super DC-3; a modified version of the old DC-3. A bug smasher is a twin-tailed Beechcraft, a small transport; the Navy designation is SNB, the Air Force calls it a C-45. It's a small twin-engine military trainer. Beech also builds and sells them for civilian executive travel." Barnes looked like he was lecturing before a class. "Answer your question?"

"Yeah, okay, I think I get the picture. Would you be available to do some charter work that could take you away for a month or so?"

"I don't know." He turned to McGarrity. "Doc, what do you think?" Barnes asked.

McGarrity directed his answer to McFrank. "What Harry's driving at, Whitey, is that we don't like to miss our week-end Reserve drills. We even work out our international business trips around the drill schedule. The Reserve is important to both of us. Whatever we do for you would have to be approved by the Marine Corps."

Now it was Whitey's turn to look for assent. He looked at Roberts and waited for the Chief's response.

Roberts said. "Gentlemen, it would still be government work. I think we could satisfy the Marine Corps that you would be getting your flight hours in another fashion. Is there anything else that could prevent you from taking on the charter work Whitey mentioned? Any family considerations?"

Barnes and McGarrity looked at each other as if this was a new concept. They both started to say something at the same time. Barnes gestured for McGarrity to go ahead.

"The consideration is not family. The consideration is how long the charter would take. How much danger was involved? How much money was involved . . . and what, or how this would be presented to the Marine Corps. Those are the considerations, gentlemen." McGarrity turned to Barnes, "That about it, Smoke, did I leave anything out?"

"You did good, Doc, especially since this is the birthday day and all."

"Birthday? I don't understand." Roberts was confused.

Smoke spoke up, "This is November tenth, and it is the Marine Corps Birthday. It is a date revered by Marines."

Roberts appeared a bit taken aback but recovered, "Oh, I see. Well, you've spelled things out rather clearly. We will address the points you have raised at another time. If Mr. McFrank doesn't have any further questions..." His voice trailed off. When he didn't get any indication from Whitey he continued, "You are free to go. We certainly appreciate your coming down to the office and giving of your time. I'll be in touch shortly." Then he added as an after-thought, "Oh, and...Uh, happy birthday."

With that he rose and held out his hand to both. They shook. Roberts led them to his door, and they were gone. He returned to his desk, sat and looked at Whitey with a raised eyebrow.

Whitey was quick to respond. "Well, my first inclination is to tell you that you're out of your fucking mind. However, expressing my opinion to my superior in that manner would not look too good on my fitness report." As intended, this brought a ready smile to Harold Roberts. "And I think you are on to a very good solution to the task at hand.

However, and this is a big however, what in hell do you intend to say to the Marine Corps? I thought we didn't do that sort of thing. But before you answer, I have a second reservation that I'll state for the record. And that is, these two are very typical. How did you put it? I believe 'ballsy' was the term; and I think they carry a very high unpredictability rating."

"That may be, Whitey. I'll submit you've had a great deal more experience in reading field people. But I feel they will do what they are told and will improvise only if they are put in a position where they feel they have to. They have been very anxious to do things our way in the work they did in Vancouver. I have every confidence that would be the case at this end of the operation. The problems, if there are any, and there probably will be, will be at the El Salvador end of the operation. That will be up to you. It's your planning, your control and your network. In that part of the world things have a tendency to not remain predictable and it certainly wouldn't hurt to have a couple of people who are capable of working their way out of a deteriorating situation."

"Okay, you make a very valid point. Let's have them do the Schwartz contact with the shopping list without committing them to the whole operation." Whitey thought for a moment then added, "And you haven't said how you intended to handle the Marine Corps."

"I agree, one step at a time. I'll go ahead with your shopping list; pricing and delivery considerations. Why not let Peter Jorgensen ponder our selection of these two, their fees and any other items that would have to cross his desk anyway, just that you're considering them. That way it will include the Marine Corps, since they are members of the Active Reserve. Believe it, Whitey, you know that we do detail people to the agency from other branches of the service. Granted, they are usually full active duty personnel.

But the enlistment or use-permission procedures are the same, and strictly voluntary, of course."

Whitey stood up. "Okay. Turn the shopping list over to the lads so they can get it to Schwartz. I'm going to need delivery and cost data as soon as possible anyway. I think it's a good idea to go ahead and check with Jorgensen on the other details about these two jar-heads--can we use them, budget and, you know, the usual stuff." Roberts nodded in agreement. "I'll wait to hear from you then." With that, Whitey turned to leave.

Roberts got up also, "Well I'm sure this will work itself out. I have a lot of confidence in these two. But the final decision will be up to you; it's your operation, Whitey. I should have some answers for you in about three or four days. Why don't you and that lovely wife of yours take a little time off?"

"Good idea, Chief. I'll do it." Whitey took his leave.

Roberts waited for a couple of minutes and then pressed his intercom. "Chris, will you step in here please?"

Chris Mavis was a young thirty-five, slight build, with a nice body. She was married and the mother of a little girl. She had been Robert's most private secretary for eight years. He felt that she could probably run the section better than he could. She had a very good mind; and, more importantly, knew when to keep opinions and things overheard to herself. She came into the office and softly closed the door behind her.

"Yes Sir?" she asked.

"Chris, I'd like you to call McGarrity and have him come in tomorrow morning. If he asks, you can tell him we have another errand in Vancouver for him, and for Barnes, of course. I'll brief them, but have the McFrank-List copied and ready for them to take. Will you have time to copy the list before you go home tonight? I would just as soon not give it to one of the clerks."

"It won't be any problem, Sir. Are there any restrictions about calling Barnes if McGarrity isn't available?"

"That will be all right," Roberts noted the time and then went on to say, "Would you try to get Peter Jorgensen for me?"

"Yes Sir." Chris went back out. A few moments later Robert's intercom came alive. "Director Jorgensen is on line one, Sir."

Roberts picked up the phone. "Peter, Harold Roberts here. If you have a few minutes, I have a rather unusual situation to put before you. . ."

Three days later Roberts called Whitey.

"McFrank," Whitey answered in his usual manner.

"Roberts here. Our two amateurs have the list in-work up north. I've discussed their further involvement with Langley. No problem, however no formal moves will be made in that direction until you make a decision one way or the other to use them. It's your call."

"I will have to think about it. Let me know when they get back to you with price and delivery details. I'll let you know my decision then. And I do appreciate it being *my call.*"

"Right then," Roberts replied and hung up. Conversations were held to a minimum on these lines, or any other non-secure line, for that matter.

Whitey hung up. He sat staring at the phone, thinking. *Roberts was beginning to sound more and more like a Brit. In fact, it seemed to Whitey that he had worked more for the Brits in the past few years than for the agency. This recent caper in El Salvador being the exception. And now Marines. What next, he thought, Mom, apple pie and the Fourth of July? It wasn't that he had anything against Marines. The truth of the matter was that he hadn't ever worked with them. His experience had been with the Army and special units of the Army. He had always heard that Marines were like Army Rangers, or Airborne; special troops for special jobs. Elite troops of any kind were always unpredictable. Maybe it was their independent attitude, or superior attitude. And they all thought themselves bullet-proof. Or maybe it was just his own attitude. He was a loner and preferred to work that way. But things had to get done and he couldn't do it all by himself.*

CHAPTER SIX
THE MARINES HAVE LANDED

A week later Harold Roberts called Whitey into the Seattle office. Chris took him right into Roberts' private office upon his arrival. Whitey was a little surprised to see the two amateurs in Roberts' office.

"Ah, Whitey, the gentlemen here have all of the data you have been waiting for." Roberts rose to shake McFrank's hand. He gestured him to a chair and continued, "McGarrity, you want to do the honors?"

"Yes Sir," McGarrity stood and handed a thick sheaf of papers to Whitey. "We were able to get Schwartz to work pretty fast on the package, Whitey. It's all here; pricing and delivery to Vancouver."

The last comment caught Whitey's attention. "Vancouver, did you say?"

"Yeah, we thought that you would want to examine the shipment, or whatever. Wasn't that okay?" McGarrity replied.

"Yes, that's fine. I'm just a little surprised Schwartz would go along with it. He usually likes to deliver in London. He has a secure network there. Did he resist or question Vancouver at all?" Whitey asked.

Doc McGarrity thought about it for a moment, then turned to Harry Barnes. "What do you think, Smoke?" Doc turned back to Whitey, "I just handed Schwartz the paperwork and asked for price and delivery to Vancouver. Do you recall anything else, Smoke?"

"No, that's the way I remember it going down. It was just a done deal. I got the impression this was the sort of thing he had been waiting for. We have been kind of stringing him out a bit, you know, in keeping him around here." Smoke addressed this last comment to Whitey.

McFrank busied himself looking through the papers. He turned to the last page, looking for the total amount of money. He found what he had been looking for, glanced up and directed a question to Doc McGarrity. "All of the prices, including the total amount, are in dollars. Did Otto give you any idea of the currency he wanted? Did he mention anything?"

"Yes, as a matter of fact, he mentioned that the listings are all US dollars but he didn't care if the monies were in dollars or German Marks. In fact, I asked him if a check would be all right and he looked at me real funny. No sense of humor. He didn't answer me." McGarrity said with a chuckle.

Whitey seemed to ignore this attempt at levity. He had been looking at the delivery information. "Did he point out that the delivery would be six weeks from the date of order and the point of delivery would be Vancouver?"

McGarrity returned to a more business-like attitude. "Yes, he made a special point of this. He wanted to know if the monies could be raised in that period of time, or if there would be any problem. I told him I didn't believe there would be any problems but delivery would have to be made to a place where the shipment could be examined without attracting any attention."

"Hm-mm," was Whitey's only reply. He appeared to be in deep thought. The room got quiet. Finally, Whitey looked over at Harold Roberts for a moment then stood up, in order to face both McGarrity and Barnes directly. "At our last meeting you gentlemen were candid in answering the question of your interest in further involvement. I will be just as candid and to the point. Do you want to further involve yourselves?" He held up his hand. "Wait, before you answer. Hear me out." Whitey hesitated for a moment to be sure he had their attention, "Washington has cleared using you to fly the shipment to the operational area. They did not go to the Marine Corps with any request, and won't, until it is certain that you will be involved. The company frequently uses people from other branches of the service, so this is not an unusual request. Normally the personnel are 'active duty', but the policies and procedures are the same. To continue with your stated concerns, the element of danger is low; there isn't any war or hostility going on in the operational area. However, there is always possibility of risk and this operation is no exception. Finally, there will be a substantial sum paid at the completion of your contract." He paused for a moment to allow the information to sink in. "I'm sure you have some questions."

Doc looked over at Barnes then back to Whitey. "Can we have a few minutes alone before we answer?" He asked.

Roberts rose and said, "Whitey, why don't you and I get a cup of coffee and leave these two to discuss your offer." He walked over to the door without waiting for a reply. One wasn't necessary. Whitey followed him out and closed the door.

It was quiet for a moment then Barnes looked over at Doc, "Wa-ll, a fine mess you got us into this time, Ollie."

Both of them started laughing. It was getting out of hand until McGarrity motioned Barnes to quit. "Wa-wa-well, it looks like we had....we had better....uh, just help these folks out," Doc responded, in his best Jimmy Stewart impression.

Barnes replied, "I think we decided a long time ago we couldn't live forever, and things have been pretty tame around here of late. I'm in."

"Are you sure? Do you want to check on getting your liberty card from Shelly?"

Shelly was Smoke's live-in girlfriend of about a year. She was a stewardess for Braniff, about five feet four, from the south, still retaining a charming accent. She had dark hair that she kept in a page boy, and large pale blue eyes that would even make Paul Newman jealous.

"Doc, I don't have those kinda problems. Shit, we've been leaving notes to each other as it is. Shelly isn't senior enough to bid a decent schedule. She doesn't question what or where I'm going. It isn't a problem. How about you, any problems yourself?"

Smoke knew Doc was between wives, and not seeing anyone on a regular basis, but the question was asked anyway, out of politeness.

"No, I'm okay. Let's go get those two spooks and find out where it is that we're going to be when we get shot at, and how much it's going to be worth."

"But Doc, didn't you hear what Whitey said? There aren't any hostilities in our operational area."

"Right! We're going to be flying in enough guns and powder to start a small war, so what the Hell, we'll be welcomed with a band and dancing girls. We'll step out of our polished aircraft, onto the red carpet that has been rolled out and the girls will ignore our crooked smile but straight teeth, and throw our Adonis-like bodies onto the turf and have their way with us!"

"And that's the way, uh-huh, uh-huh, I like it, uh-huh." Smoke sang, mimicking a current rock and roll tune.

"Smoke, I can't believe you. You have the morals of an alley cat." With that, Doc went over and opened the office door, stepped out and told Chris that they were ready to continue. He came back in, stopped for a minute and looked at Barnes who was casually smoking a cigarette. He couldn't help but think of how he had gotten mixed up with this totally insane, but lovable idiot.

They had met in Korea in 1952. Doc remembered he had been sitting at the Acey-Deucy table when this newish-looking Second Lieutenant came into the squadron ready room. It was the back end of a Quonset hut.

"Is this VMF-Two Twelve?"

"Sure is. The home of the Devil Cats. You came in the back door. What can we do you out of?"

"--Uh, I'm Lieutenant Barnes. I just came over here to check in. I've been at MAG-Twelve Headquarters and they told me to report over here."

"Well Barnes, I'm not the Duty Officer. Go right through that door and they'll take care of you. When you're through, come on back here and I'll relieve you of some of your Acey-Deucy money. By the way, I'm Doc McGarrity."

"A pleasure, Doc, but Smoke is my game. Do you get much chance to play anything around here?"

"Sure, if the weather gets bad or the Air Force forgets the Marines have landed and are here to help them. They control the OPS over here."

All fighter pilots have a moniker, or nick name. Usually there is a story behind how the handles get applied. For example, "Doc" got his when someone accused him of being "an operator". He had worked some kind of miracle procuring some supplies from the Air Force. And, more importantly, he got away with it.

The weather stayed bad for about a week. There was time enough for Harry Barnes to earn his nickname, "Smoke". It sure as hell was his game. At one time or another, every pilot in the squadron was ready to kill him. Smoke is that kind of a card game.

They flew together a lot and became close friends.

And that's the way Doc McGarrity had met Harry Barnes.

The door opening behind him brought Doc back to the present. He moved over to where he had been sitting before and waited until Harold Roberts and Whitey McFrank came in and took their places.

Whitey got right down to business. "You've made a decision?"

"Yes we have. We're in; that is, unless you only pay minimum wages. We would like to know the operational area, the substantial funds mentioned and the equipment we would be flying."

"Fair enough," Whitey said. "The area is Central America, the monies will probably be in the twenty-five to fifty thousand each range, depending on the length of time spent, success of the mission and my recommendations. The equipment will be up to you, being either a DC-3 or C-45. I personally would prefer as small an aircraft as possible, to allow more latitude in the selection of a landing site."

Barnes and McGarrity looked at each other, shrugged; and this time Barnes took the lead. "Where will the airplane come from, how much time will we have to refresh ourselves in the aircraft type and what is your general timing?"

Harold Roberts took the floor, "The airplane can be here anytime appropriate to the schedule. We will need a nod from Langley Virginia, however, and the ultimate schedule will be set by Mr. McFrank."

"How does the money thing work?" McGarrity asked.

"What are you asking, Doc? We can give you an advance, monthly check, or whatever you need," Roberts replied.

McGarrity nodded his understanding, "The question is, I mean...it sounds like we will be gone for more than a couple of weeks. I wouldn't want things to just pile up."

"This office can be of assistance in that area. You can leave your payables with Chris Mavis and she can handle them in a subtle manner. We won't use CIA stationery or checks, Doc." Roberts thought it was his turn for a bit of levity.

This even got a chuckle out of Whitey.

Roberts continued, "We have six weeks to wait for the material to get shipped in to Vancouver. The approval from the agency is only a matter of a day or two, including the coordination with the Marine Corps. I'll put in the request for the airplane when you let me know what you want to use. As soon as Langley gets back to us, you'll both be on the payroll. We'll advance you whatever you want against the twenty-five thousand each and/or set up a payment schedule. In the unlikely event you don't survive the mission, the agency has a double indemnity policy. Your next of kin would receive a lump sum payment, tax-free, of one hundred thousand; the doubled amount based upon the fifty thousand dollar maximum contract fee..."

Doc interrupted, "Well yes, that is certainly reassuring. I can't stand the decision as to which one of my ex-wives would get that amount. Actually, the best plan would be to leave it to all of them and let them fight over it. A great idea if only I could watch." Doc was not impressed.

Smoke, on the other hand, thought it was very liberal of the agency and said so. "This has got to be a real first for a government agency. You guys certainly take care of your own. I'm impressed. Can I name anybody as my beneficiary?"

"Certainly, but don't you want your wife to get it?"

"She isn't my wife yet. We just live together."

"Oh, I see. Well, it is rather unusual, but we can manage that one."

Doc dismissed all of the money talk with a wave of his hand. "Let's get back to the guts and feathers of this project." He turned to McFrank. "Whitey, can you give us some idea of the weight and cube of the shipment so we can figure out which airplane will do the job? Some of the items are obvious, but how things are packaged are a mystery to me, and that will determine the configuration of the shipment."

"I can do that, Doc. Give me a day or so and I'll get back to you. I can pass the information direct in such a way, weight and cube, so it won't be sensitive information. I don't know if Mr. Roberts has explained the level of secrecy this project carries. That should be explained and you should be made aware of the procedures which must be adhered to accordingly."

Roberts responded, "That will be done before they leave here today, Whitey."

Doc broke in, "Another thing, Whitey. Once the type of airplane equipment has been determined we need to sit down and work out the flight plan...primarily fuel considerations. I don't imagine the air field that you will be selecting will be a full-service, fixed base operation, with red carpet treatment. We'll probably have to carry enough fuel to get in, land and back out to where we could refuel."

"Why don't we just plan on coming back here in three days?" Whitey sounded a bit exasperated, "That way we'll have the agency and Marine Corps approval factors out of the way. I'll work out the weight and cube data you need and I'll bring some maps of the area that I have in mind. You will be able to do some hard planning." Whitey was no-nonsense this time.

Everyone agreed this was a plan. Whitey took his leave.

Roberts asked the two Marines to wait for a moment and went out of his office. He was back shortly with some forms. He handed one to each of them.

"I don't know if you've ever seen one of these; it is a disclaimer. By law I have to tell you that you are not to divulge your association with, activities for, or intelligence information received from the agency, without approval."

Doc started to say something, Roberts held up his hand. "Wait, Doc, there's more."

Roberts cleared his throat and continued in an official-sounding voice. "Do you understand that your employment with this agency is in the national interest of the United States of America and that you cannot communicate the matters, material or anything else related with your specific contract, other than to those designated as essential, and cleared for this project on a need-to-know basis only?"

Both Doc and Smoke nodded assent. Roberts went on.

"Do you understand that if questioned about your activities, you will use the cover story that will be provided? That if questioned by superiors, you will use the cover story provided? That you will not now or ever communicate your association with, or specifically use the name or nickname, or refer to this organization by which you are employed, to anyone without express written approval of the employer, and should you violate the contract, you could be prosecuted to the maximum extent possible?"

Doc and Smoke looked at each other for a moment, then nodded.

"Say it. Say that you understand, Gentlemen."

"Uh....I understand," Doc said.

"Yeah, I understand, too," Smoke said. "I assume that I can't say anything to Shelly."

"Right. You couldn't even if she were your wife. Now sign the disclaimer that you're holding in your hand. You are officially employed by the Central Intelligence Agency of the United States of America, subject to final approval by Langley and the Marine Corps, and you will abide by the rules thereof."

It was obvious that Chief of Station Harold Roberts had given this speech many times. He certainly knew it by heart. He took the signed forms and placed them in a file on his desk.

"That's it then, Gentlemen. If you don't have any questions you're dismissed." He held out his hand. Both Marines stood, shook his hand and left.

CHAPTER SEVEN
THE BRIDGES AT SINANJU

They were standing, waiting for the elevator when Smoke started to say something. Doc motioned him to stay quiet. The elevator arrived and they stepped in. There were two other people in the elevator so they continued their silence. Once outside Smoke turned to Doc.

"Let's go have a drink. We've got to talk about this! I feel like I've just been read my rights!"

"Dammit, Smoke, you had all the chance to say '*NO*' to it upstairs. What the hell were you doing up there, playing hero?" Doc said this with more than a trace of sarcasm.

"Fuck no, that's not it at all. What am I going to tell Shelly? She's not cleared. You heard what Roberts said. What can I tell her? She's due home tomorrow. *THAT* is what I want to talk about!" His voice was getting louder.

"Okay, okay....relax. Where do you want to go? I'd like to get away from the downtown area. Doing spook things makes me think I see spooks behind every fern, in the elevators, down the hall and everywhere we go. I don't even feel comfortable standing here in the street talking about it!" Doc wasn't smiling. It didn't go unnoticed.

"Well, you're driving, Doc, but how about either the Sky Room or if you don't mind driving me home, how about the Red Baron?"

"What do you mean, I'm driving, how the hell did you get downtown?"

"I took a cab, Doc. Shelly has her car out at the airport and my Porsche is in the shop. I had to get a goddamned service appointment from a Kraut asshole, and if you miss an appointment, or if you're late, you play hell getting in! They demand and expect promptness!" Smoke was speaking in a deliberate German accent. "I love my Porsche, but dealing with the service people is a major pain in the ass. I feel like reminding them that we won the fuckin' war! I was rather hoping that I could talk you into a ride home. I'll buy the drinks at the Baron...how's that?"

"Yeah, yeah, yeah, no problemo, but yass, you will buy the drinks, Ol' Buddy. It has been more than awhile since you loosened your purse strings. Which reminds me, your last couple of expense accounts, for our little company ventures, were a tad on the high side, or should I say, somewhat excessive. Are we not dividing up the spoils enough that you have to pad your expense account?" This time Doc was smiling.

"Hey, Sport! You were the one that taught me all about how to do expense accounts when we worked for Pacific Airmotive. You were my boss then, you're my associate now. Is this going to be your new policy? You check my expense accounts and then I get to check yours? How about fuck you! Strong letter to follow! I spend expense money as if it was my own. Which in fact, it is, since it comes out of the profit. You do your thing and I'll do mine and, in the meantime, don't you have anything better to do than to rummage around in my files?" Smoke was starting to work some anger up.

Doc motioned for Smoke to start walking toward the lot where his car was parked.

"My car's down in the lower lot." Doc gestured across the street, "No, Smoke, I was not rummaging around in your files checking your expense account. I was looking for the Viscount package from Aer Lingus that we're working. When I came across your expense account I was just surprised how you could find any way to spend money in Ireland. I think they close the country at eight o'clock in the evening. For my part, I think the whole country is as bad, if not worse, than Cedar Rapids or Omaha!"

"Well, you're right. But on the last couple of trips over, I fell in with some bad guys from the Aer Lingus Flight Operations Department. It gave me a whole new perspective on the Irish. They could have been Marines. They can be bad." Smoke gestured wildly. "What the hell are we talking about all of this for? I've got a problem!"

"Is this the start of a snivel, or are you working up to a major whimper?"

"Doc, I'm serious. Shelly was getting a little bent about our screwing around up in Vancouver. I did a very stupid thing. I mentioned we were doing a thing for the government. She's brighter than the average bear and quickly had it figured out which part of the government we were doing favors for. She was just getting started bellyaching before leaving on the flight she's on now. She doesn't forget; it will pick up right where she left off when she gets back."

"What the hell prompted you to say anything about this? You're not married to her yet."

"Boy, do you have a lot to learn! When was the last time you had a live-in?"

They got to the car. Doc unlocked the passenger door and went on around to the driver's side. Smoke got in and unlocked the driver's door from the inside. Once Doc was inside, Barnes went on to explain.

"Well, if you remember, when we were talking about this caper at the onset, we were speaking in a very guarded manner on the phone to each other. It sounded suspicious to her. Shelly thought that I was getting involved with some chick up in Vancouver. She nailed me with it and I told her she was mistaken. You and I were just doing some work for the government and couldn't talk openly, or much about it, since you could never tell who might be listening! That was probably not the thing to say. But, it was what I said. I had to cover my ass somehow. I didn't want her to think I was having an affair." Smoke threw up his hands in disgust. "Anyway, there you have it. I have a problem and I need your help."

"Well, Mr. Barnes, if it is too much of a problem, you can stay here and keep our company going. I can always find a co-pilot who's looking for adventure."

"Doc, you're starting to piss me off. I'm not staying here and letting you run off to have all of the fun! I just need some help in telling Shelly so she won't worry and will be here when we get back. If we don't come back, it won't matter. She'll have enough money to find some pleasure in life without me. It'll be difficult, granted, but I'm sure she'll find a way."

"Hey! I'm not going to help you tell Shelly anything!" Doc continued, taking his eyes off the road and glancing over at Smoke, "I'll help you sort out the best way to present this sudden urge to serve, but you're telling her on your very own, my dear friend." Doc said this with some finality.

Smoke understood Doc's position. "Of course, I didn't expect you to stand in front of Shelly and plead my case. What do you take me for?" He glanced away for a moment, then continued. "Better yet, don't answer that! Let's get going."

The evening traffic hadn't started to build as yet. They got out of the downtown area in a reasonable fashion. During the drive out to West Seattle not much was said. They arrived at the Red Baron, parked, and went in.

As they walked into the darkness of the Red Baron's reception area, a voice came from out of sight. "Well, well, well! If it isn't the Bobsie Twins on Land, Sea and in the Air. Heavy emphasis on the in the air!"

Smoke turned and looked over his shoulder, "Howdy Beveree, as you can see I even brought the good doctor with me. Line up the abortion cases!"

He had recognized Bev Handy, the chief hostess whom he had gotten to know over some period of time during his frequent stops. Bev was an attractive lady in her early forties. She was into jogging and it showed. The Red Baron restaurant was only about six blocks from Smoke's house. He was fairly well known in the establishment.

Barnes went on, "If you're doing the bar at this early hour, how about a couple of Dewar's 'n rocks."

"On their way, Bird Man. Go sit and I'll bring them to your table. I don't think Heidi is in there yet."

Heidi was one of Smoke's favorite bar maids. She looked like something out of a Wagnerian Opera; braided blonde hair, rather muscular, very German. All that was missing was a helmet with horns or a black uniform with a swastika arm band and a whip. Black leather boots would complete the picture. She was enough to make a masochist salivate! Smoke loved her.

"Jezzus, Smoke, is Heidi the one with the muscles?"

"Yeah Doc, Heidi is right out of Mein Kampf. If it weren't for Shelly, I'd be hopelessly in lust!"

"Smoke, you're sick! Shelly is the best thing that ever happened to you. You should probably marry the girl. Are you playing around on her already?"

"No fuckin' way, Doctor. But I do have my little kinks. And if I were going to play on Shelly, I think I would start with Heidi. I mean she has outrageous tits, and an ass you could crack an egg on; truly a gorgeous hunk of woman flesh! No, I'm not even thinking about playing on Shelly. We don't have an agreement or anything like that. It hasn't even been discussed. Shelly is in no frame of mind to make the total commitment, as she puts it. We haven't even agreed to not date anybody. It just isn't talked about. Damnedest thing. But this is why I need your help with how to tell Shelly about this urge to serve, as you so aptly put it."

"I don't get the connection," Doc was puzzled.

They had made their way into the dimly-lit bar part of the Baron, went to what had become their table and sat down. They were alone. It was early afternoon. The late lunch folk had left and the afternoon early drinkers hadn't started arriving yet. Heidi wasn't behind the bar. But, good to her word, Bev had finished fixing their drinks and was on her way over to their table with them.

"It's good seeing you again, Doc. Things have been way too quiet around here," Bev said as she placed their drinks on the table.

"Thanks, Bev. It's good seeing you too. You're looking great. Hasn't Smoke kept you folks entertained enough?" He motioned toward Smoke. "Oh, and by the way, this will be his tab."

"Well, he does come and go. But since he got his steady live-in, we only see him here when his lady is on a flight. Ain't love grand?" Bev replied.

"It sure is. And any time that *your* man starts giving you a hard time, just remember the doctor is in for you any time." McGarrity said with a grin.

"I will keep that in mind, Doctor Mac," came the fast retort. "I'll be in the lobby. Give a yell if you need a refill and Heidi isn't here yet."

"Roger that," Doc then turned to Smoke, raised his glass and said, "Well, Ol' Buddy, here's to your plea bargain tomorrow night. Is that when Shelly gets back?"

"Yeah, that's her schedule. I've got to think about this a bit."

"Why don't you call Roberts and ask for the so-called cover story he mentioned? When do you suppose we'll get that?"

"That's a good idea. I got the impression he was reciting from memory some written text. That's what it sounded like. But you're right. He did say cover story, didn't he?"

Two drinks later, Heidi showed up. She checked their table and two other people who had come in and were sitting across the room. Smoke's eyes followed her every movement.

"Damn, she moves good!" he observed.

"That she does, that she does. How about just one more for the road, I still have to drive back through town to Queen Anne Hill. I'm starting to feel these. Bev pours a good drink."

Smoke got Heidi's attention and raised his glass indicating a refill for both of them. There wasn't much more to talk about. They drank their last drinks quietly. Well, it was quiet except for the clicking of Smoke's eyeballs as Heidi walked back and forth from behind her bar and the growing customers in the room. She did move well.

Finally, with a sigh, Smoke got up, reached for his wallet and laid enough money out to cover the tab, including a generous tip.

Doc rose and they made their way out, pausing long enough for Smoke to say good-bye to Heidi. Doc went on ahead and chatted with Bev. Smoke caught up and they left.

The Red Baron was about six or seven blocks from Smoke's house. It didn't take long to make the drive. They both saw Shelly's car from about a half block away.

"I thought you said Shelly wasn't due back until tomorrow night, Smoke."

"She isn't supposed to be here tonight. But it looks like she is. Do you want to come in for another drink?" Barnes asked.

"Nah, as I said, you're on your own, Ol' Buddy. No way am I getting involved with your lame-ass plea for mercy!" Doc said with a chuckle.

"Fine pal you are. Who covered your six at the bridges on the Sinanju? Who called for the Navy when you had to ditch? Who is the best fuckin' friend that you ever had? I ask these questions while pleading for support, and you're going to ignore me!"

"You got it! I'll repay all of those things when it doesn't involve a woman. I admit it, I'm truly a coward! Now you know the real truth, Smoke. Women scare the shit out of me!"

"Okay, okay, I'm off...into harm's way! And without a wingman. Nobody to cover my six. God! What a way to go!" Smoke raised the back of his hand to his forehead in a forlorn gesture from silent movie scripts.

Doc pulled up to the front of the house, stopped the car and reached across to open the passenger door.

Smoke looked down at the arm in front of him that was opening the door, then up at Doc with a look of dismay, "That's it, huh? I'm on my own? This is it?" Smoke was starting to really bitch.

"That's it. There it is. You got it. Call me tomorrow when you can talk. If you can talk." Doc waited patiently for Smoke to get out of the car.

Smoke did get out, then leaned back in for a last comment, "Right, I'll do that!" And with his last remark, closed the door somewhat firmly.

Doc drove away, chuckling. Smoke had gotten to him though. Korea and those goddamned Sinanju bridges. What a cluster fuck. It was a wonder any of them were still alive. Korea was getting close to twenty years behind them, but Doc remembered as if it were yesterday. It was the type of thing he would rather forget, but Smoke's words put him right back there. The bastard! It all came flooding back. . .

KOREA, 1952

The Sinanju Bridges! Hollywood didn't make a movie out of those bridges, but they sure as hell should have! The Air Force B-29's had been hammering a bunch of bridges on the Sinanju River, up North of P'yongyang, for months. The bridges were still standing. The Marines were called in to try it their way after the Air Force somehow couldn't get the job done with their high altitude saturation bombing.

All of this bombing activity made the gooks think that we thought the bridges were important so they had moved more anti-aircraft equipment around there than the Krauts had around the Polesti oil fields in World War II.

The brass decided to try another tack. Turn it over to the Marine close air support squadrons. The Marine Air Group command decided to do this assigned mission in one shot. It was to be a "group grope". Two squadrons of Corsairs and a squadron of Douglas Skyraiders; the fighting arm of Marine Air Group 12.

VMF-212, the Devil Cats, got five, four-plane divisions into the air the day of the "group grope". One of the divisions consisted of Salty Wells, Division Leader, Tex Randolph, his wingman. McGarrity had the Section, with Smoke on his wing.

The mission was pretty straight forward.

For the ordnance load, Salty and Tex carried seven five-hundred pound bombs and Smoke and McGarrity had three one-thousand pound and eight two-hundred-fifty pounders on each of their planes. Plus, of course, a full load of 20mm cannon ammo for the wing guns. (The squadron aircraft consisted of F4U-4's which were equipped with four 20mm cannon, unlike the earlier models of the Corsair from W.W.II that had eight 50 cal. machine guns.) No wonder they called the Corsair squadrons the "Heavy Haulers". The airfield at K-6 was all Marsden Matting, the steel stuff with holes in it left over from the big war. When you taxied out with a full load of ordnance on that matting, the wings shook like they were going to break off. None did. Getting airborne was some kind of drill, though.

Smoke and Doc had closed the squadron bar at midnight and then gone over to the sniveler's bar. This was over in a Quonset Hut that was also sleeping quarters. It was run by one of the pilots called Blackjack Joe Duncan. Blackjack Joe was from Boston. The drinks cost a little more, and you ran a tab. A funny thing, Blackjack Joe usually wanted folks to settle up their bar bill if a hairy bunch of missions was coming up.

Blackjack Joe was at one end of the bar doing his books when Barnes and McGarrity came in.

"Hey guys, how about bringing your tab up to date?"

"What the hell do you know that we don't, Blackjack?"

He went back to his books "Just settle up before you leave tonight."

Doc turned to Smoke and said under his breath, "The son-of-a-bitch has better G-2 than our own Intelligence Department G-2. I wonder how the hell he does it. Tomorrow must be a doozy!"

"Jee-zus, Doc, maybe we'd better wrap this up. I hate pulling G's with a hangover."

"Shit, Smoke, how the hell would you know, you haven't pulled G's without a hangover since you left flight training."

Barnes thought for a moment before he replied, "Yeah, you're probably right, but I'm far from sober now anyway."

"Okay, Smoke", Doc turned back to Blackjack Joe. "Right, Duncan, but if we're going to pay up, how about digging into the safe for some of that good Red Label, instead of this swill you've been passing off as Scotch?"

"Well you fuckin' guys can stop your sniveling 'cause I'm switching the Scotch over to Red Label anyway. And here's your tabs, you can start a new one tonight."

Smoke and Doc drank up, settled their bar bill and headed for their hut to hit the sack. It was a very short night. Piss call was at 0400.

The briefing was attended by the three squadron's pilots, crowding into VMF-212's small ready room. The MAG G-2 Officer, a full bird Colonel, strolled in.

"Attention on deck!" someone yelled out.

As the pilots started to rise the colonel spoke out, "Be seated, Gentlemen. I'll try to be brief. As you have heard, the Air Force 29's haven't taken out the three bridges on the Sinanju. And now the task has been handed down to us. Each of your three squadrons are assigned to a specific bridge. You will 'do it, until you get it right', to coin a phrase. And by that I mean if your bridge isn't taken out, you'll have to go back again. Gentlemen, this is not a milk run. The gooks have moved a lot of AA (anti-aircraft) into the area. I would strongly urge you to get it done the first time. We're going to stagger target times to reduce air traffic in the fire zone. Two-Twelve, you'll have the first and the third wave, Three-Twenty-Three, you'll be number two and four. One-Twenty-One, you'll have the first and fifth. You can go in with Two-Twelve since your bridge assignment is the farthest east. Any questions gentlemen?"

"Colonel, just how bad is the AA?" one of the pilots asked.

"Well, there's a hellava lot of it. But the good news is that due to the Air Force high altitude work, it is essentially oriented to high altitude. This is one of the reasons we got the mission. The Lords above feel that going in low, like they perceive is the Marine Corps way, will give us a chance to succeed. And that is another very important reason to get your bridge on this first attack. They'll be ready for low work next time, if there has to be a next time."

This last remark got a groan from the troops.

"Any more questions?" He paused, looking the room over. "Okay. If not, your squadron commanders each have their briefing folders and will go over specific target info with you."

He gathered up his paperwork and turned to go.

"Attention on deck!" was called out. As the pilots started to get to their feet the Colonel turned back.

"As you were, Gentlemen, carry on and good luck!"

He didn't say he'd like to be with the troops, or any of that bullshit, but Doc got the distinct impression he certainly wouldn't have ducked it either. For a G-2 Officer, this was a pretty ballsy guy. Word has it that he flew a lot of the photo recon missions himself.

The overall impression was the squadrons had been given a job to do that the Air Force had screwed up. The MAG Commander had every confidence that his Marines could do the job.

The briefing covered ordnance assignments, run-in angles and suspected and known gun emplacements. The G-2 intelligence data was pretty thorough. Including the bomb tonnage the 29's had dropped. It was a hellava lot! The many pictures showed it. The area around the bridges looked like a moon-scape, pock-marked with craters everywhere.

When the squadron briefing was over, Salty took a few moments to outline their procedures. He said the runs would be in pairs. He and Tex and then Smoke and Doc, in order to concentrate their ordnance. Pickle everything on the one run. The division call sign would be "BAKER".

The take-off was typical, black as pitch once they got beyond the runway lights. They were heavy, naturally, and it was always a jolt to have to "go on the gauges" and still look for the exhaust and the dim formation lights of the airplane in front of you. There were big rocks out there in the dark. Making contact with them could ruin one's whole day.

The join-up went well. Salty kept them pretty tight. They had to orbit the field twice for the other divisions in their outfit to get together. The other squadrons were also going to be taking off and joining up.

The flight north to the Sinanju went pretty smooth. The sky was starting to get light. It was going to be a fairly clear day.

Salty decided that since they were would be the second division to roll-in, using ten thousand feet for their initial, or roll-in point, wouldn't give them much time to get on- target, as they would pickle their bomb loads at about four thousand. But it wouldn't give the gooks much time to zero-in on them either. At least that was Salty's plan. The fact still remained, they had to take those bridges out. Either that or make a career out of this very undesirable target area.

The flight seemed to take forever. Doc kept checking and re-checking his position in relation to Salty, then checking Smoke over on his right wing. Smoke was in tight, for a combat hop anyway. Not tight like the Blue Angels, of course. Although any of the pilots in the squadron were capable of flying that tight, it just wasn't done in combat. He motioned for Smoke to move out a bit.

The division continued to climb. Doc could feel the tightness starting in his gut. He knew this to be the first sign of the fear that builds as one is going into harm's way. He was almost beginning to get used to it. One never does, however.

Doc thought that fear can also be tasted. It is rather metallic. As fear builds you feel a flushness and you can feel and hear each heart beat--a pounding that increases. At this point one starts looking forward to the actual mission. Anything to get busy and forget about all of the things that could happen. It's almost a rush, too. Whatever it is, one thing for sure, it isn't fun! Those that say it is should really be locked up somewhere where they can't hurt anybody. God! The things you think about! You can bunk with a guy for months, fly his wing or have him on your wing, but fear isn't something one talked about. Oh, occasionally someone will mention that they had the shit scared out of them, or other words to that effect, but no in-depth discussions. And it isn't a macho thing either. You don't really know what it is. Doc just knew that each pilot must feel this way, or at least he hoped so. Doc would hate to fly with a guy who was indeed fearless. That sort would probably get them all killed!

They reached ten thousand feet and Salty leveled them out. He motioned for Doc to move out. Doc realized that he had closed up pretty tight also. Doc, in turn, motioned Barnes to move it out again.

Sinanju was pretty far north, almost to the Yalu and China. It had given Doc too long to think.

But now, flying looser, he was in a better position to notice their surroundings. The growing dawn light was expanding down into the valleys below. He could see a haze layer in between and connecting the hills with an occasional cloud puff on top of the inversion layer that was causing the haze layer. They were about six thousand feet above the haze and broken cloud layer. It gave a feeling of some security even though Doc knew the radar guided guns of the gooks couldn't see haze or clouds; they saw through the stuff. It was a false feeling of security.

Doc heard the lead division radio chatter with arming procedures. They were approaching the first bridge. This was the Devil Cat's target. They had to take it out now, or keep coming back.

Suddenly the air started to fill with black puffs. The gooks had found them and were laying up a barrage.

"My God!" Doc said aloud. He couldn't believe the intensity of the AA fire! How the hell were they going to get through all of that? Most of it was above them, but it wouldn't stay that way for long.

"DOC, WAKE UP!" It was Salty transmitting to him. McGarrity hadn't been paying attention. Salty had apparently been giving Doc hand signals to "arm".

Doc looked over his right shoulder and passed the signal to Smoke to arm his ordnance. Doc looked back just in time to see Salty and Tex roll-in on the target.

Jee-zus Kee-rist, everything's happening too fast! Doc thought. He quickly looked around for the first division of four aircraft that had been ahead of them. He couldn't see any of them. He didn't want to lose Salty in the haze. He rocked his wings to signal to Smoke that they were rolling in.

"SHIT! Here we go!" Doc yelled out loud, followed by a rebel yell that only he could hear.

He spotted Tex just pulling out and could see hits from Salty's run. Doc concentrated on the mid-span of the bridge and pickled the two one-thousand pounders from the outer wing hard points. The pull out was low. "Pull gees, pull gees," he was thinking, and finally back up he went into a climb. Something made him glance over to his right and there was Smoke practically even with him. Doc could see a big shit-eating grin on his face.

"WE GOT HITS, DOC," Smoke transmitted, "HOW COME YOU DIDN'T PICKLE ALL OF YOUR ORDNANCE?"

Shit and double shit!! Doc looked down quickly at the stores selection arming switches. Sure enough, it was exactly like he had selected. The two one-thousand pounders from the wing hard points had been selected, not "Salvo". He still had a lot of ordnance on board, another one-thousand pounder on his center line hard point and all of the two-hundred-fifty pounders on each wing. He was going to have to go in again!

"BAKER ONE, THIS IS THREE, I HAVE TO GO BACK IN. I'LL JOIN YOU OUT OVER THE WATER." (Their briefed rendezvous point, in the event they got separated, was to the west out over Korea Bay.)

"ROGER DOC, BE CAREFUL."

Doc looked over and motioned to Smoke that he was breaking away. Smoke shook his head as if to say "No".

Doc couldn't believe it. Again, he passed the lead to Smoke and this time, before Barnes could acknowledge, broke over the top of him and started down again. Doc made sure his ordnance switch was on "Salvo". He spotted the third division in its run and slid in behind the number four man. Doc could see everybody was getting hits on the bridge and it looked like the Devil Cats were going to do it in this one mission. He sure as hell hoped so. Doc could see the number four man in front of him getting clobbered by the ground fire. He had pickled his load, pulled up and then been hit. He was smoking. Doc didn't have much time to see more than that, he was at his release point. As he salvoed all of his ordnance he started taking hits from the gooks. Instead of pulling up, Doc broke left and dove for the river. The gooks had expected him to pull up like the aircraft that had been in front of him. In a moment Doc was on the deck, just above the river. Nobody else was hitting him, but he didn't know how badly his aircraft had been damaged. He was too busy to sort out his instruments for any clues. Doc had hunched down in the cockpit, trying to make himself smaller.

He started jinxing back and forth and threw in some up and down, hoping to throw off any gunners trying to track him. It seemed to be working because he wasn't taking any more hits.

Now he started to notice that the aircraft was shaking a little. Doc inched the throttle back. When he broke left after releasing his ordnance he had instinctively throttled up. In fact, everything was full forward, throttle, mixture and prop control. It took a few moments to set the power back to a proper fast-cruise setting. Doc scanned the engine instruments only to find most of them in the red or damn close. They were starting to come down now, though. Good 'ol Pratt & Whitney. The R-2800 could "take a licken and keep on ticken", as Timex used to say. The expression still stuck ten years later.

McGarrity was starting to settle down. He was alive. The airplane was still shaking some, but screaming along the river like a raped ape. Where the hell did that term come from? Doc was trying to picture what it would take to rape an ape. It wouldn't come together in his mind, but it set him laughing. He couldn't stop.

"DOC, I'M AT YOUR FOUR O'CLOCK . . . YOU'RE SMOKING A BIT. OVER."

The radio transmission brought him back to his senses. Doc quickly turned to check his four o'clock. There was Harry "The Smoke" Barnes.

"UH, ROGER THAT SMOKE. I TOOK SOME HITS BACK THERE. THE GUY IN FRONT OF ME TOOK A BUNCH, HE WAS SMOKING OFF THE TARGET. DID YOU SEE WHAT HAPPENED TO HIM? CAN YOU SEE ANY OF MY DAMAGE? I'LL PULL UP A BIT SO WE'RE NOT SO LOW." Doc was rambling on not knowing if he was making any sense.

He eased up to about five hundred feet. He had been skimming the surface of the river.

He felt another bump and then saw tracers going over his head. "Shit!" he said aloud. More ground fire.

"SMOKE! BACK ON THE DECK! WE'RE TAKING MORE FIRE!"

With that, he pushed back over and started to jinx a bit. Doc didn't know Barnes' position but knew that he could take care of himself.

Doc noticed they were coming to the mouth of the river. It dawned on him that the river's actual name is the "Ch'ongch'on". Nobody could pronounce it. At Sinanju, the river emptied into Korea Bay. They had always referred to the river as the "Sinanju". Doc couldn't believe the crap that went through his mind. He was getting shot at, his airplane had been hit and supposedly damaged. Lord knows how badly. He didn't know where his wingman was and he was *reviewing a geography lesson in his mind and rubbing his neck.*

He remembered the guys saying that when the shit really hits the fan the tight feeling that you feel in your neck is caused by your asshole coming up and choking you. It is said to leave brown rings around your neck. Or so the story went.

As quickly as it had started it was over. He seemed to be clear of enemy fire and out over Korea Bay. Doc started an easy turn to the south and began looking for Barnes. "SMOKE, WHERE ARE YOU?"

"I'M AT YOUR SIX, DOC. GIVE ME A COUPLE OF INCHES." Barnes was asking him to come back on the throttle a couple of inches of engine manifold pressure.

Doc throttled back on power a bit, eased his nose up to get off the deck and gave Smoke some more room to position. In a matter of moments he heard a couple of clicks in his headphones and looked over his right shoulder and saw that Smoke was in position on his wing. Doc nodded to him and signaled for a climb.

Doc ran through a plan in his mind to stay off shore. The southerly heading they were presently on would take them about direct to Chinnampo. If his bird decided to crap out, he was thinking that maybe ditching would be okay. He couldn't remember where all the enemy lines were, but by then he would know if his airplane was going to get him home or not. Anyway, from Chinnampo it was almost directly southeast to their airfield at K-6. It seemed like a plan.

"BAKER THREE, BAKER ONE, OVER." It was Salty calling him.

"BAKER ONE, BAKER THREE, GO AHEAD," Doc acknowledged.

"BAKER THREE, ONE . . . WHAT IS YOUR AIRCRAFT STATUS AND POSITION? OVER."

"BAKER ONE, THREE WITH BAKER FOUR. I HAVE POSSIBLE DAMAGE. I TOOK SEVERAL HITS ON MY SECOND RUN. 'FOUR' REPORTS EVIDENCE OF SMOKE. EXTENT OF DAMAGE NOT DETERMINED AT THIS TIME. ALL INSTRUMENTS IN THE GREEN, CLIMBING TO ANGELS TEN OVER THE BAY, SOUTHBOUND HEADING TO CHINNAMPO, OVER."

"ROGER THREE, WE'RE AT ANGELS SIX PROBABLY SOUTH OF YOUR POSIT . . . LEVEL AT SIX AND CONTINUE. WE'LL PICK YOU UP, OVER."

"WILCO ONE....YOU COPY FOUR?" Doc said as he looked over at Smoke. Barnes nodded and clicked his mike button twice.

At that moment the engine backfired. This got Doc's attention. A quick scan of his instruments showed him he was losing oil pressure and the oil temperature was rising. Now he knew what the engine smoke was about. He had been losing oil. The first hits must have found an oil line.

"BAKER THREE, THIS IS FOUR.....DOC, THE SMOKE IS GETTING PRETTY BAD AND IT LOOKS LIKE THERE IS SOME FIRE NOW. HOLD WHAT YOU'VE GOT AND I'LL MOVE IN CLOSER FOR A LOOK-SEE, OVER."

"ROGER FOUR."

After a minute or so, Barnes reported his findings, *"DOC, IT LOOKS LIKE YOU'RE ON FIRE FOR SURE. WHAT ARE YOUR INTENTIONS? OVER."* His tone had changed; he was obviously more concerned.

"STAY WITH ME HARRY, I'M GOING TO DIVE AND SEE IF THE FIRE GOES OUT. . .I'D RATHER DITCH THAN BAIL OUT, OVER."

"BAKER THREE, THIS IS BAKER LEAD," It was Salty. *"ROGER YOUR CONDITION, WE HAVE YOU IN SIGHT. WE'LL STAY AT ALTITUDE AND GET SOME NAVY ON THE WAY. BE OFF FREQUENCY FOR A BIT, OVER."* He had overheard their transmissions.

"ROGER   BAKER   LEAD,   WE'RE   GOING DOWN....LET'S GO, SMOKE."

"I'M WITH YOU, DOC."

McGarrity pushed over hard. They had almost reached six thousand feet when all hell broke loose. Maybe the dive would blow the fire out. He sure hoped so. He had really had enough excitement for the day.

Doc leveled out at about a thousand feet. The oil pressure was rapidly going away, but the dive had cooled things off so the oil temp was down, but the engine was running rougher. He looked over his shoulder and Barnes was still there. Barnes moved in for a look.

"DOC, THE SMOKE IS THICKER BUT IT LOOKS LIKE THE FIRE IS OUT. WHAT ARE YOUR INTENTIONS? OVER."

Before Doc had a chance to answer, the engine backfired and started shaking so bad he couldn't read the instruments. It looked like the decisions were being made for him. All the shaking probably meant the engine had finally run out of oil and was starting to either seize or break up, or both.

"SMOKE, IT'S ALL THROUGH....THE ENGINE HAS PACKED IT IN. I'M GOING TO HAVE TO DITCH, OVER"

"ROGER, I'M STANDING BY, GOOD LUCK."

He got to work. There was lots to do. Slow down; get some flaps out . . . open the canopy, line up with the troughs. Go with them, not across. Was that right? Shit! He hoped so. Okay, now tighten the shoulder harness. How cold was the water? It was getting late in this fall of 1952. Had they been briefed on water temperature? What difference will it make, he was going to find out in a few minutes.

"BAKER THREE, THIS IS BAKER ONE, NAVY HAS A SUBMARINE OUT HERE. THE CARRIER IS TOO FAR AWAY....ARE YOU DITCHING? OVER."

"SALTY, THIS IS SMOKE. DOC'S ENGINE HAS PACKED IT UP AND HE'S GOING IN, OVER."

"ROGER FOUR, I HAVE YOU BOTH IN SIGHT. WE'LL STAY AT ALTITUDE IN CASE WE NEED TO RELAY ANY MESSAGES. WHAT IS YOUR FUEL STATE? OVER."

"BAKER LEAD, BAKER FOUR, I'M FINE. GOT LOTS."

Doc was only half hearing all of this; the water was getting closer fast! He remembered what they had been told in flight training; there would be an initial impact, then a second hit. Then the airplane would nose over on its back. You had to wait for everything to stop, then you could get out. They had to do all that in the "Dilbert Dunker". It is an SNJ cockpit on rails that plunges into a swimming pool. It was sort of fun. Of course, the pool was fairly warm, there were divers in the water, standing by in case you turned the wrong way getting out of the cockpit. When the Dilbert Dunker hit the water it was hinged to go upside down just like what would probably happen. That was a drill. This was for real!

Almost there. Doc slowed some more and the Corsair settled into the water. Just like they said; it skipped once then nosed in and over on its back. A lot of confusion, bubbles everywhere. It was dark; cold. He got the seat belt undone and kicked down and out of the cockpit. His parachute hung up on the canopy and for a minute he thought he was going to go down with the airplane, then the chute broke free and he quit panicking. Doc thought hard for a moment, which way was UP. It was kind of important. Okay; there, up that way, it was lighter than dark and appeared to be in the direction the bubbles were going, so he did the same. Followed the bubbles. He was also aware that he was rapidly running out of breath. It was taking too long. After what seemed like forever, he broke the surface. Doc reached down and pulled the toggles on his Mae West life jacket. One of the cells blew up. The other cell had either a dud inflation cartridge or the cartridge was missing. The one cell was enough to hold him up while he found the manual blow-up tube for the third cell, and started puffing into it. The life vest came up full. Now to get the life raft free from his parachute seat pack. His hands were getting numb. Damn, the water was cold! He had to get into the raft fast or he wouldn't make it! After more stupid struggling he got the raft free from his parachute seat pack, found the toggle and gave it a hard yank. Thank God! That cylinder was full. If he ever got back he would check and re-check his survival gear carefully before every flight! Things were certainly like they had told him in flight training. There weren't any surprises; except maybe the cold and how quickly it takes your strength away.

Now to get into the raft. He didn't remember ever practicing this little maneuver. The first two attempts were pretty dumb. Third time was the charm, though. He was in, on his face, but in. He carefully turned over and looked around. The airplane was still afloat, nose straight down, tail out of the water. Doc looked up and saw Smoke circling. Barnes had his canopy open and was looking intently at him. Doc waved. Barnes rocked his wings to acknowledge. Doc heard a bubbling, looked back around and his Corsair was gone.

The sea was relatively flat. There were rolling waves running about two to three feet. It was just enough to limit his visibility. It wasn't too uncomfortable. If he wasn't so cold, it wouldn't have been bad. He was starting to worry about exposure.

That was about it for what seemed forever. Doc was trying to move enough to generate some warmth but without tipping the raft over. Mr. Barnes was circling overhead. Occasionally Doc could see Salty and Tex, but they were much higher. Then he remembered hearing Salty tell Smoke that they would stay at altitude to relay radio messages. Salty had said something else about the Navy, but he couldn't remember what it was.

Smoke made his next pass lower and rocked his wings a lot harder. Then Doc saw another Corsair. It wasn't from their squadron, he noticed the letters on the tail, and it was from VMA-312. They were the squadron from MAG-12 that was based aboard the carrier. Apparently he was here to relieve Barnes.

His guys had to be getting low on fuel. That was it. That's why Smoke had made his last pass so low to get his attention to let him know what was happening, Doc thought, as he waved back at Smoke. Then Smoke was gone.

Doc saw another Corsair higher. He was probably doing the high radio relay.

The combination of the light rocking of the wave action and the disappearing adrenaline was enough to put him away. He didn't know how long he had been nodding off when he heard a rumbling. The next thing he knew he saw a submarine bearing down. It was very close. Doc turned the raft to see it better. He saw a crewman with a heaving line. The crewman threw it. It was too far for Doc to get to. The crewman threw it again. Doc kept trying to get to it, but he didn't have any strength; his arms wouldn't work. He saw another crewman run along the deck and dive in toward him. The sub had stopped about fifty yards away. In a few moments the crewman was swimming alongside with the heaving line.

"How ya doin' fly-guy?" he asked.

Doc tried to talk but his teeth were chattering too much. He managed to grunt something in return. God! It was good to see him. Doc noticed they were being pulled toward the sub.

He didn't remember getting out of the raft and down below but when things had settled down, he was wrapped in wool blankets and sipping a cup of hot, very hot coffee. The sub skipper came by and stuck his head into the Officer's Wardroom where he had been taken.

"How do you feel?"

"Pretty good, Sir, at least I'm thawing out. I'd like to meet the crewman who dove in to help me, though."

"Sure enough, I'll send him in. Can we get you anything else?" he asked.

"Maybe some dry clothes in a bit."

"Not a problem, in fact I think that's being handled," he turned as if to go, then swung back, "We've alerted your squadron that you're in the good hands of the Submarine Service."

Doc nodded his thanks as the skipper left the wardroom.

A bit later a round-faced, smiling crewman stuck his head in, "You wanted to see me?"

"If you're the lad who jumped into that cold water to help me, I do. My name's Doc McGarrity, what's yours?"

"Rosillini, Thomas Haines....uh, Sir," he responded, "You looked like you could use a hand."

"Well, I sure needed one. And I hold mine out to you now! Where are you from?"

"Seattle." The sailor replied as he took the offered hand.

"No shit! So am I. Where did you go to school?"

"O'Dea High School, the Catholic school." He replied with a grin, "How about yourself?"

"I went to Broadway. We lived on Capitol Hill. My folks are still there."

"You've got to be shitting me! Me too. We live on Boylston," He was really surprised, "...In the two hundred block."

"I'll be damned!" Now it was Doc's turn to be surprised, "We live on the five hundred block on Boylston, down near the Cornish School of Art. I mean my folks do. We moved there when I was a freshman at Broadway."

Neither of them could believe it. They just looked at each other for what seemed forever. Finally Rosillini said he had to get back to his duty station. Doc told him they'd get together when this crap was over. Rosillini laughed and went on his way.

Doc called after him, "Tom, what's your home phone number?"

"I'll get it to you before you leave, Lieutenant," He called back over his shoulder.

After a bit one of the crew members brought him some dry clothes to put on. Later, the ship's doctor, a Chief Hospital Corpsman, directed him to one of the officer's staterooms and suggested that he lie down for a while. No sooner had his head hit the pillow, than Doc was sound asleep. It had been a long day. A very long day.

Yeah. He had remembered all right. In the thinking about every detail he had damn near run off the road. *Well shit! Maybe that's why Smoke was his best friend. He not only laid his ass on the line, he had covered mine. What more love can one man have for another? Or something like that. Wasn't there a line from some classic story about one man taking another's place in France during the revolution to ride the cart to meet Madame Guillotine?*

But Smoke has to deal with his own woman problems. I can't even deal with my own! Doc thought about it from almost every angle, and it still came out the same.

CHAPTER EIGHT
THE PLEA BARGAIN

Smoke watched Doc drive off and then turned and made his way up the bank, cutting across the front yard. He lost his footing a couple of times on the slippery grass. It occurred to him that maybe, just maybe, he might be a bit in his cups. Wonderful! And his lovely lady was home a day early. He was going to have to tell her he would be gone for a bit. Damn! Just wonderful! He got to the door and fumbling with his key, finally got it unlocked. He went in.

"Hi honey, I'm home," he managed to call out without slurring.

Shelly stuck her head around the corner from the kitchen, looking into the living room. She spotted Smoke, "Surprise, surprise! I made it home a day early. And you're just in time. I'm fixing some dinner. It's a chicken casserole dish that I found out about from your secretary, Hunter. What a neat recipe. It's called 'Opulent Chicken'. I hope you haven't eaten yet. It's really something. Artichoke hearts, mushrooms, white wine, boned chicken breasts and you serve it over wild rice. Sounds good, huh!"

Harry Barnes just stood there grinning. Shelly looked at him closer.

"Harold, have you been drinking? Dammit you weren't going to do that. You were probably out with that partner of yours, playing Marine! Well, were you?" Shelly was not pleased. Her usual southern charming manner of speaking was noticeably absent. She had her hands on her hips and was advancing in a menacing manner. Her face was inches from his own, though she had to strain looking up, she was so close.

Barnes was backing away. "My car's in the shop, Honey. We had a meeting downtown and Doc gave me a ride home. We stopped at the Red Baron for just a couple. I didn't know you were home. I didn't expect you until tomorrow night, Honey-Babe."

"Don't 'Honey-Babe' me. Just a couple of drinks, my ass! You're drunk! And what was this big meeting all about? Is this more of that government stuff?" She was getting worked up.

Smoke was trying to think how to talk about this. "Yes, well it is, sort of....more government stuff, that is. We have picked up a contract to fly a special charter. There is a lot of money involved and it is perfectly legal. Nothing to land anyone in jail. The money's good. It will make our year, so to speak, in this one trip."

"Smoky Barnes, if it is government, and legal, and you're going to make a lot of money....it has to be dangerous. Don't string me along, dammit! What's going on?" Her anger was beginning to turn to concern.

"Honey, don't worry. It's just a trip down south. Both Doc and I have been assigned to another government agency by the Marine Corps. It's sort of like two weeks active duty; you know like we do in the summer with the Reserves, only a little longer. The pay is good and there isn't any danger to speak of." He paused for a moment, then added, "And even if there is, they have provided good insurance coverage for us in the unlikely event that something happens. You'd be well taken care of."

"Smoky, I don't want to be *well taken care of.* I want you. I just happen to love you, you big jerk! Can't you get that through your thick head? Besides, how can there be insurance if we aren't married." She was starting to soften.

"Shelly, I'm crazy in love with you too. I made arrangements to make you my legal beneficiary. As for the

84

job, it's just that I got to do what I got to do. This job is important and I'm flattered that I was picked as one who could get the job done. If the Marine Corps thinks the same way, it could lead to a faster promotion. I don't want to stay a Captain forever."

"I thought you told me you didn't want to get promoted, and that's why you get in trouble from time to time. If you got promoted you would get promoted right out of the squadron. You said there weren't that many billets for majors." She turned back to the counter where the chicken dish was being prepared. "You're going to have to get your stories straight. Which is it?" The softness had gone away again.

"Uh, well, it could put me in line for a squadron command.   This will bring me to the attention of Headquarters, Marine Corps. If I get this job done in a timely manner there's no telling where it could lead to." Smoke thought that he might be reaching.

"Bullshit!"

He was right. He had been reaching. He wasn't ready for this. The year with this woman had taught him that he needed a clear head to deal with her.   Her straight forwardness, although part of her charm, was very disarming. He tried another tack.

"Sweetheart, I really can't talk about this job. It comes under some special classification. But trust me, the pay is good, the danger is not a factor, and it could get me some nice recognition with the Marines." He paused for a moment thinking. "And, I've agreed to do it. What else can I say? You have given me more reasons to stay alive than I've ever thought possible. I wouldn't do anything to hurt you, Honey. I'll only be gone about three or four weeks and you're going to be working most of the time anyway."

She had turned back to him. She shrugged and looked up. "If you've agreed to it, I guess there isn't anything more to talk about. I just get nervous when you and Doc start getting restless. I listen to you two talk about just one more little teeny, tiny, friendly little war. And I know you keep looking around for some kind of a rush. I sometimes think you're both adrenaline junkies. Isn't flying around one weekend a month in those Skyraiders, or Spads as you call them, enough? And you're both making lots of money selling those big airplanes. So I know you are not doing the thing for the money. And, *DAMMIT* Smoky! You can't keep on getting in harm's way forever without getting hurt! It has to catch up with you. You both have cheated fate too many times. Doc is Doc. You are you, but I'm worried about you!"

"Look Honey, you know I'm a good pilot. Just because I'm not interested in working for the airlines doesn't mean anything! We've talked about all of this before. I just don't cotton to the idea of seniority commanding all of everything in the cockpit. While I'm trying to get senior enough to command a left seat, one of those 'senior citizens' can kill us all! How many times have you told me about some of the idiots you've flown with? The airline scenario is just not my cup of tea. I fly with a lot of those guys in the Reserve. They are not happy campers. They love the money--except for the junior guys, but the flying is a real bore and the politics are brutal. It's not for me."

"Okay, you'll just have to do what you have to do. You are the one that keeps hinting around about our getting married. This is just an example of why I'm not anxious to run down the aisle with you. But okay, I'll try not to worry too much. But you better not get yourself dead, you jerk, or by God I'll kill you!"

After she realized what she had said--after it had a few moments to sink in, she started to laugh. Smoke joined her; starting with a giggle that soon grew to uncontrollable laughter. Their laughing increased until they both fell to the floor, unable to get their breath.

When they finally ran down, Smoke took her into his arms and kissed her. Still in an embrace, he spoke in her ear, "Welcome home, Shelly girl. I would have stopped at one or two drinks if I had known you'd be here. In fact, if I had known you'd be home I wouldn't even have stopped for one drink! It was my idea, not Doc's. I really just needed a ride home. The Porsche is in the shop again. Do you have to check that chicken stuff or anything?"

"Uh-uh, it's simmering on low and will be okay. It can wait," Shelly said into his ear huskily.

They were still in an embrace, on the floor. Further conversation wasn't necessary.

CHAPTER NINE
PLANNING

As Doc was unlocking the door to his apartment, he could hear the phone ringing. He ran to grab it. Catching his breath, he answered, "McGarrity."

"Doc, this is Whitey. I'm glad I caught you." He paused for a moment, and Doc could hear the rustling of papers. Whitey continued. "I've looked over the material list and as near as I can guess, it will easily run ten thousand pounds. I haven't computed the cube yet. Do you need that?"

"No, actually the weight factor limits things rather dramatically. Uh, can you give me some idea of the shortest runway we'll be dealing with? Keeping in mind, obstructions at each end and that sort of thing."

Whitey took his time answering. He was obviously giving this some thought. "Well, it'd probably be safe to say that two thousand to twenty-five hundred feet would cover what I have in mind. Obstructions could be a problem. Trees grow fast in that part of the world." Whitey paused, deep in thought, then went on, "Are you saying the weight factor finalizes your aircraft equipment decision? Do I understand you correctly?"

"Yeah. Ten thousand pounds makes it a 'gooney bird', Whitey. There's no way in hell you can put that kinda weight in a C-45. The payload is easy for the C-47 and we can carry extra fuel in jerry cans or drums, if we have to. Two thousand feet, without an obstruction is okay. There was a time when I could get into eighteen hundred feet; but I had been flying one on a fairly regular basis and was pretty current in type. You know, in model. But, it has been awhile."

"Okay Doc, I agree with your decision. There are a lot of C-47's, or DC-3's, in that part of the world, and another wouldn't attract much attention. Maybe later this week we can get together at the office. I have some maps of the area and we can put our collective heads to it. Do you have any idea how long it will take you and Barnes to, uh. . .'get current'? Is that what you call it?"

"Yeah. We can talk about it at the office, Whitey." Doc replied. "I have someone in mind who might be able to spend time helping us get re-acquainted with the bird. I assume that check-out funds could be made available."

"No problem, Doc, it would be covered under 'expenses'. Okay, I guess the rest can wait until we get together. I'll call, or have someone let you know when would be a good time. Stay loose."

"Right. Take care, Whitey," Doc said as he hung up.

He thought about the training pilot that he had in mind. *Richard A. "Buck" Rowe. Here was a pilot's pilot. He had probably forgotten more about the DC-3 than Donald Douglas ever knew. Buck was raised in Alaska. He started flying about the time that he started wearing long pants. He used to say that his first real license was Commercial, Multi-Engine Instrument, with a DC-3/C-47 Type Rating! All at the minimum age, whatever that was. He didn't bother to slow down with a Private Pilot rating, like most folks do. For that matter, he used to say that he hadn't considered it a real rating anyway. Not for the kind of flying that his family did.*

Yeah, Buck knew a bit about the gooney bird. Doc was determined to get him for their refresher work. The kind of training and tips one could get from him weren't in any flight manual. Doc would start tracking him down in the morning.

He started thinking about what he could remember about the gooney bird. Actually there were some differences between the DC-3 and the C-47 besides the obvious difference in the passenger door. The C-47 had another section of the fuselage next to the standard passenger door that also opened. The two doors created a large freight-loading opening in the side of the airplane. The two models looked identical except for this visual difference.

Range and gross weight, which created the all-important payload, were different. The C-47 was created during World War II under a special contract to the Douglas Aircraft Company. Due to the larger opening in the door area, the fuselage had to be beefed up. This added weight. The interior would be bare, as befits a cargo aircraft, and this served to balance the added weight for the freight door, plus a little more. The engines, for the C-47, were specified to be an increased horsepower series of the original engine model. In fact, due to the large number of engines built during the big war, probably all of the DC-3/C-47's flying today carried this stronger engine. The bottom line was that the C-47 could fly farther and carry more than the DC-3. And the simple truth of the matter was that about anything you could squeeze into the airplane, it could take off and fly with. Of course, the catch came when you lost an engine or some other emergency problem, then the extra weight on-board played a major role in one's life expectancy.

Doc decided to look through his library for the aircraft specifications. He had aircraft/pilot handbooks on everything he had flown and some that he wanted to fly or thought that he might someday. After a bit he found what he was looking for. Yeah, there it was. He pulled the thick Pilot's Manual out of his book shelf, and started leafing through it. On paper, the C-47 could legally take-off weighing a total of 31,000 pounds, versus the DC-3 maximum take-off weight of 25,200 pounds. The range of the C-47 was a little over two thousand miles, while the DC-3 was right at fifteen hundred miles.

He knew it was something like that. Not bad, for old memory he thought.

Reading on, the C-47 was designed to carry full fuel, twenty-eight combat troops, with gear, and six thousand pounds of cargo for the two thousand mile range.

Hell, figuring a combat-equipped trooper at two hundred and eighty pounds, times twenty-eight is over seven thousand pounds plus the six thousand pounds allowed for cargo brings the total payload to nearly fourteen thousand pounds.

He remembered Whitey saying that we're looking at somewhere around ten thousand pounds for the toys he needed to get down to wherever he needed the stuff to go. Offhand that would leave thirty five hundred pounds, to be conservative, for fuel in drums or jerry cans. At six pounds per gallon that's five hundred and eighty gallons. Doc turned to the Fuel/Range charts. Cruise power at maximum gross weight would be ninety gallons per hour. The five hundred and eighty gallons would give them another six and a half hours of range. They would have to hand pump the fuel into the wing fuel tanks. But that calculates to a little over a thousand additional miles, bringing their total range capability to about three thousand miles.

He kicked the numbers around a bit more, putting the calculations on paper. Doc decided that fifty-five gallon drums would be the way to go. Six drums would be three hundred and thirty gallons at six pounds per gallon, netting out to just under two thousand pounds. That margin would more than compensate for the weight of the empty drums.

The whole thing was starting to look better and better all the time. Now the only thing left was to try to estimate how much shooting was going to take place. The money seemed all right but there *had* to be a reason for it.

And there was one more thing; he wondered what would come down the chain of command from Headquarters Marine Corps. He thought he should have a chat with his Commanding Officer, Colonel "Salty" Wells. He would have to check with Whitey or Roberts or both for permission to do that. He and Smoke had both flown with Salty in Korea and it wouldn't be a nice thing to leave him without his knowing what the hell was happening.

Doc made himself a scotch and water and sat down. He was thinking about Salty, Korea, the Marine Corps, how the hell it had all started. All that really came to mind was the fact that for as far back as he could remember, he had wanted to be a pilot.

Some things are never forgotten.

Sitting there, sipping on his drink, Doc remembered. *The early interest in aviation, the factors leading up to his selection as a Naval Aviation Cadet, then his first solo flight in an SNJ, first carrier landing and finally, graduation day. It was the day his mother pinned his wings on his breast. This last thought brought a misting to his eyes. It was suddenly a little hard to swallow. His mother was gone now, but the memory of that day, as she looked up into his eyes with the pride of a mother for her son, was etched into his mind and his heart forever.*

The following morning Doc placed a call to Buck and Meg's number in Canada. Meg answered, telling him that Buck was out of town but that she would have him call when she heard from him.

WASHINGTON, D.C.

Clyde Hayner pulled up to the half-opened wrought-iron gate at the Marine Corps Barracks at 'Eighth & I' streets. He turned in and brought his car to a stop for the gate guard, who had stepped smartly out of the small guard building. The open section of the gate was the lane closest to the guard house. Clyde rolled down the car window and produced his CIA identification card. The gate guard, a highly spit-and-polished Marine, took the card, checked the picture against the driver and executed a smart salute.

"Yes, Sir! How may I help you, Sir?" No rank was displayed on the identification card, but this Marine wasn't taking any chances. He knew the intelligence community often went about their business in "mufti".

"I'm looking for the Personnel Department, Headquarters Marine Corps."

"Yes, Sir! It is located down at the Navy Yard Annex." The Marine guard handed back the I.D. card and pointed back the way Hayner had driven.

"Oh really, how long ago did they move it, Marine?" Hayner asked as he put the card back into his wallet.

"About a hundred years ago, Sir."

Hayner looked puzzled for a moment, then said, "I've always thought of this as Marine Corps Headquarters."

"Yes, Sir. It's where the Commandant lives. I can understand your confusion." The guard was being very careful not to offend this visitor, "Do you know how to get to the Annex, Sir?"

"Yes I do. Thank you, Marine. Shall I back into the street, or would it be all right to pull in and turn around?"

"You can pull right in here and turn around over there, Sir," The Marine guard indicated the area to be used.

Hayner did as he was directed, coming back to the gate. The Marine saluted him smartly for the second time. Hayner nodded acknowledgment of the honor rendered. He drove the relatively short distance to the Navy Yard Annex, thinking *Moved a hundred years ago, indeed! Well, they sure kept it a secret!* He pulled into the parking area at the Annex and parked in a space marked "FLAG OFFICERS ONLY". What the hell, were they going to tow his car away or what? He didn't get much of a chance to take advantage of his CIA parking sticker. Let the Marine Security folks ponder on it. Besides, he didn't expect to be there very long.

He made his way into the reception area, showed his identification, and asked for the Chief of Personnel. He was told that would be Colonel Striker, and did he have an appointment. Hayner told the receptionist he thought that his office had made the proper arrangements for an appointment. After a few quick telephone calls, the receptionist confirmed that this was indeed the case, and told Hayner someone would be down shortly to escort him. Hayner busied himself by walking around the reception area looking at the various paintings on the wall depicting memorable events in Marine Corps history.

It didn't take long for an attractive female enlisted Marine to show up to escort him. Clyde wasn't sure just what her rank was. She was some kind of Sergeant, but Marine Corps uniform rank designations confused him. She was all business, despite her attractiveness, and quickly got him to Colonel Striker's office. She knocked at his door and when her knock was acknowledged, took him in and deposited him in front of the Colonel's desk.

The Colonel rose, holding our hand. "I'm Colonel Striker," The Colonel motioned Hayner to a chair, smiled and continued, "What can the Marine Corps do to help you, Mr. Hayner?"

Hayner shook the Colonel's hand with his right hand and handed the Colonel his CIA business card with his other. "Well, Sir, the agency would like to use a couple of your very fine pilots for a sensitive, short-term project," Hayner said as he took the offered chair.

"Do you have specific individuals in mind, or is this a general request?"

"We do have certain individuals in mind. I've brought their names and serial numbers. Just a moment." Hayner, searching in the thin attaché case that he had with him, found what he was looking for and handed a paper to the Colonel. "Here are the names and serial numbers, Colonel Striker."

The Colonel glanced at the paper and pressed the intercom on his desk.

"Sergeant Peale, would you step in, please?"

When the female Marine came in, Colonel Striker handed her the paper and asked her to get the two files. She was back almost immediately.

"Excuse me, Sir, but these are both Reserve Officers. They are not on active duty. Their files would be in Glenview."

The Colonel appeared shocked. He looked over at Clyde Hayner, "Were you aware of this, Mr. Hayner? Two Reservists? What in the world would the agency want with a couple of Reservists?"

"We were very much aware of the fact they were Reservists. They have been doing some work for us on a volunteer basis, and doing quite well, I might add. We're offering them a short-term contract to do some flying that will take them out of the country. Due to the time period called for, they are both very concerned about being gone during their week-end warrior bit. Is there some problem with this, Colonel? Is there some kind of difference between a Reservist and a *regular* Marine pilot? In some circles it is said that active duty is good training for the Reserves!"

This last remark did not please the Colonel. He got a bit red in the face and didn't answer for a few moments. Getting hold of himself, he finally did reply, "Well, the regular establishment doesn't quite share your views, Mr. Hayner! While we have a great deal of respect for the Reserve Program, we consider its purpose and function to be a standby force available to supplement the regulars during a time of need. Uh, with Congressional approval, of course. In the past, they have performed well, as a credit to the Marine Corps."

Hayner nodded his understanding at these remarks, but then pressed on, "That's all well and good, Colonel, but what about these two. We don't have time for Congressional action."

"Well, I didn't mean to indicate that Congressional approval would be required. I was referring to the entire reserve concept. As for these two, we can note their jackets with the information of our temporary release to your agency. However, the Fourth Marine Air Wing, Reserve Headquarters, Glenview, Illinois will have to grant their Leave of Absence from weekend drill attendance. That will be up to them to determine the status in relation to an *approved* Leave of Absence."

"I'm finding this hard to believe, Colonel. The task that we will be using these two Marines is for the 'good of the order' and you are saying that somebody in Illinois will be making a determination as to its validity before granting an *approved leave of absence*? Just how long is all of this going to take?" A degree of sarcasm was finding its way into Hayner's dialogue.

Colonel Striker noted the change in attitude. He spoke slowly, picking his words with care. "Mr. Hayner, I assume your people are operating under some degree of urgency. That being the case, I'll be happy to cut orders, indicating Headquarters Marine Corps approval, and forwarding them to Headquarters Fourth Marine Air Wing Glenview for their endorsement. We do have a chain of command just like you have, Sir! I'm sure Glenview will be equally prompt in addressing this matter."

"This is beginning to sound more like the cooperation I would expect to find here, Colonel. I haven't had that much to do with the Marine Corps in my career, but I've always had the utmost confidence and respect in your 'can-do' attitude and the Corps' ability to get a job done." With that, Clyde got up, extended his hand to Colonel Striker and then added, "Perhaps you can add a note to those orders to have someone from Glenview call my office. This card has my AUTOVON number on it."

The Colonel picked up the card from his desk where Hayner had put it and glanced at it to find the AUTOVON number. "Yes, I see it," He said as he rose to shake Hayner's hand. The Colonel then buzzed Sergeant Peale, who responded immediately. She waited while Hayner turned back to pick up his brief case and then escorted Hayner back to the lobby.

Hayner's car was where he had left it. It had not been towed or ticketed.

CHAPTER TEN
JUST A COUPLE OF HELL RAISERS

McGarrity was back in his company office. The meetings downtown had gone well. It appeared that the shortest field selected would be in the neighborhood of twenty-two hundred feet. Of the four airfields Whitey was thinking about, three were in the twenty-five to twenty-eight hundred foot category. Whitey would try to physically check them out for obstructions and general condition once he was back in El Salvador. There was another small item to consider, anti-government activity in the vicinity.

Rolling all of these factors together, the task was to find a suitable landing field. It would have to be one that could comfortably handle a C-47, was isolated enough for them to off-load a large amount of arms and ordnance, and all without attracting a lot of attention, yet was in friendly territory. There wouldn't be refueling available. The aircraft would have to be refueled from the fuel stores carried in the airplane, transferred from fifty-five gallon drums to the airplane fuel system. That would take time. Furthermore, the off-loading would have to be coordinated with Cordero and his people. One doesn't just leave a pile of guns in the middle of the jungle.

The airplane was on its way from Patrick Air Force Base in Florida. It would be flown in to the Tacoma Industrial Airport, scheduled to arrive in a couple of days. It was unmarked except for Venezuelan civilian registration markings; YV-WAWS.

The Seattle CIA Chief of Station, Roberts, had been advised that it looked like a dog but its engines and systems were in impeccable condition. Doc had picked Tacoma since it was a little out of the way, and there was a maintenance facility there operated by an old Alaska bush pilot, Ron Miller, who knew more about gooney birds than a lot of folks. In fact, between Miller and Buck Rowe, there would be no surprises!

Buck hadn't called. Doc had spoken with Meg, Buck's wife, and she was going to have Buck call when he checked in with her. It had been a week and Doc still hadn't heard anything. He decided he had better give it another try.

The Rowes' lived in Victoria, on Vancouver Island, British Columbia, Canada. They had a not-so-humble little cottage on Cadboro Bay. Buck was one of the few people who had done well in aviation. There was a saying that if one wanted to make a small fortune in aviation, one had to start with a large fortune. In most cases, the saying was accurate.

Doc had met Buck Rowe when Buck had been commissioned to set up a Beech Dealership at Tacoma Industrial Airport for, and financed by, a major timber company in the Northwest. It paid for itself by virtue of providing aircraft sales and parts to the timber company for its own fleet. Sales outside of that scenario were truly extra profit.

Doc had been a pilot-salesman in the Aviation Products Division of Pacific Airmotive Corporation's Seattle Branch. His job had been to fly around selling aviation products and parts in the greater Northwest and Alaska. Buck had become a customer and eventually a good friend. In fact, he had really put McGarrity in the aircraft brokerage business some years later.

Doc dialed the Cadboro Bay number, Meg answered.

"Meg, this is Doc McGarrity again. Have you heard from Buck?"

"Yes, Doc. In fact he called a few minutes ago. He just got in. This is the first time he's called in over a week. I told him you were trying to reach him. He's at the Flying Fireman hangar. You can probably still catch him there. Do you have the number?"

Flying Fireman was a Canadian company. It was a PBY operation that specialized in water-bombing forest fires. The amphibious PBY's were modified with a special scoop in the hull that would allow the airplane to skim the surface of a body of water and scoop water into an internal tank. This provided a fresh load of water to drop on a fire. The operation was based at the airport on Vancouver Island that served Victoria, B.C.

"Yeah, you told him that I'm trying to get hold of him?" Doc asked.

"I told him, but I think he said that he would return his calls when he got to the house. But try him now. I'm sure you'll catch him."

"I'll do that. Hope to see you again one of these days, Meg. Thanks and take care." Doc hung up and dialed the Flying Fireman hangar. When his call was answered, he asked for Buck.

In a few minutes, Buck answered the phone in his slow Alaskan drawl. "Hell-low, this is Buck Rowe."

"Buck, this is Doc McGarrity How the hell are you?"

"James Francis. It's good to hear your voice. What kinda trouble are you in now? Meg said that you'd called. I was goin' to get back to you when I got to the house."

"Well, I sorta want to rent you for a week to give Barnes and me a refresher in a gooney bird. Do you have any time at all?"

"I'm sure that we can work somethin' out. I don't know about a week, tho. I can't handle that much fear in my declining years. One of you, maybe; but both? In the same cockpit? Ha-ell, maybe I'll just talk to you from the ground. That'll work good and be a lot safer."

"There's five thousand bucks available to get the job done, Buck. We're going to have to operate into some short dirt strips and that sort of thing, refuel from drums...you know, a plush, first class airline operation."

"Doctor, what the ha-ell kind of a boondoggle operation have you got yourself into this time?" Buck sounded somewhat amused by all this conversation.

"It's not illegal, Buck. I'll tell you a little about it when we get together. Do you think you could squeeze Smoke and me into your schedule? Will five grand be enough? We're furnishing the airplane and fuel."

"Sure, given the time, I'd probably do it for the entertainment alone. But money is okay. I don't have anything against it. What's your schedule?"

"The airplane's estimated arrival is the day after tomorrow. I told the people who are bringing it in to use Tacoma Industrial. We can get started whenever you're available."

"Well, let me get home and see what's on the docket. I got your number someplace. Did you leave it with Meg?" Buck asked.

"Yeah, it's with the stuff I gave her when lookin' for you."

"Okay, we'll leave it at that, then. I'll let you know as soon as I can put a timetable together. Anything else?"

"No, that's it. I'll wait to hear from you."

They were finished and hung up. Doc thought about it. Buck was one special kind of friend. Not many like him around these days.

His next call was to his Marine Reserve Commanding Officer, Lt. Colonel "Salty" Wells. Roberts and McFrank had given him permission to tell him a little about the operation. Doc reached him at his Boeing

Company office. Salty was an instructor in the pilot training department.

Salty came on the line right away. "Wells here."

"Skipper, Doc McGarrity. Got a minute?"

"Sure, what's up?"

"You're going to be getting some funny messages from HQ 4th MAW. They'll be about Smoke and me. I have permission to tell you what we'll be doin' but it will involve our being gone for a bit and, as such, missing a couple of drills."

"Well, that doesn't sound too serious since, as you say, it'll be coming from Headquarters Glenview. But keep talking."

"Smoke and I are going to be doin' a little flying for a government agency down south. Way south. I've been told we'll get credit for the drills and the squadron can get credit for the flight time. But both of those two factors are up to you."

"Down south, you say. Is this an Air America thing? I thought they were only in Cambodia and Laos?"

"Skipper, I don't know about that. All I know is we're working direct on a contract. No mention has been made about Air America. The airplane is coming from Patrick Air Force Base, which is a major spook base. I don't know. Hell, I've probably told you more than I'm supposed to as it is. I had to get special permission to talk to you. I don't know any of the details of how the Marine Corps is going to handle this. All I know is that the agency folks went to Headquarters and told, or asked, them for our bodies for a period of time. I assume that Headquarters Marine Corps will issue something to our Reserve Headquarters in Glenview, who will issue something to the Detachment in Seattle and on to you. Other than that I don't have a clue, Sir."

"Well, I appreciate your calling me, Doc. You haven't said which agency of the government you'll be working for. I guess that I'll just have to wait and see what kind of paperwork they dream up. It should be interesting. While I've got you on the line, and you can keep this to yourself, we're losing our Spads. Reserve Headquarters' giving them to the Air Force for Nam. I was hoping for A4D Skyhawks, but they say we can't operate from Sand Point on a daily basis, due to the runway length. Anyway, I'm sorry to say it looks like we're getting R4Q's and having our squadron designation changed from attack to transport."

"Jezz-us Colonel, who'd you piss off?!!"

"Apparently everybody, Doc, but enough of that." The Colonel brought that part of the conversation to a halt, and then continued, "Both you and Barnes have prior transport time. I rather thought you could check out early and help transition the fighter jocks into the wonders and mystique of multi-engine operation. At least those who aren't flying for one of the airlines. I've even been authorized to offer 'Man-Days' to some of the former squadron chaps who are now flying with West Coast Airlines. And I understand that HQ 4th MAW are going to provide a couple of lads from the two Cherry Point R4Q squadrons to handle actual transition. Do you know how long you're going to be gone?"

"We've been told thirty to sixty days, Skipper, but you know how that can work. We're goin' to be flying a gooney bird. Both Smoke and I are getting a refresher in a couple of days. But shit, Skipper, Flying Boxcars? Damn! I've heard that they fly as fast sideways as straight ahead!"

"I have heard that also, but ours is not to question and it's the way things are going to be. There are other aspects in our favor. As a transport squadron, we'll have a heavier rank allocation. You know, both you and Barnes are coming into the zone for Major, either this year or next, so this could work in your favor, especially if the thing you two are embarking on finds favor with the top brass. And, if that is the case, it couldn't come at a better time, you two have managed to piss off a lot of folks in past years. I can't believe what it took to get you both promoted to Captain. I thought you were going to end up the oldest First Lieutenants in the Marine Corps. Still, to this day, I don't know what you did after Korea, and the trouble that you got yourself into. Thank God I wasn't there!" Salty said.

Doc didn't have much to say but he managed to mumble something like, "Well, we probably just had too much fun, Boss. That and running with the wrong crowd. Really, it was just a matter of associating with the wrong sort. We've been real good....up here....back home...."

Salty interrupted, "Which is why I was able to get you two promoted to Captain, like I said. But enough. Let me know when you hear anything more specific, and when I hear from Glenview, I'll let *you* know."

"Yes, Sir!" Doc replied, "We'll keep you posted."

"Good. I'll catch you later." Wells hung up.

As Doc hung up he realized that Salty Wells had indeed looked out for Smoke and him. What's more, Doc wouldn't ever want to do anything to embarrass him, or to make the squadron look bad. It was a shame about the Spads, but he could understand the need for this great airplane in Viet Nam. Damn thing carried the same ordnance load externally that the B-17 carried internally in the last big war. And like all propeller driven aircraft, it had the ability to stay on station for a long time. Yeah, he could see how they needed this remarkable airplane. It was the thought of Flying Boxcars that was a little disturbing. He couldn't think of anybody who had anything nice to say about them. Not much to look forward to coming home to. Well, like the Skipper said, 'It is what it is!'

HEADQUARTERS, 4th MARINE AIR WING,
NAS GLENVIEW, ILLINOIS

There was a knock on the door. Major Gilley, the 4th MAW Personnel Officer glanced up and called out, "Come."

Sergeant Alexander came into the office.

"What's the problem, Sergeant Major, you look upset?"

"Sir, this just came in from Headquarters Marine Corps. It's a bit strange. Or, at least, I've never seen anything like it." Sergeant Alexander handed him the message.

The Major took it, read it twice, to make sure he understood, then remarked, "I think the CG will get a kick out of this. If I understand it correctly, it appears that a government agency wants a couple of our Reservists for a period of time and we're to cut orders to excuse them from weekend drills. Do you read it that way Sergeant Major?"

"Yes Sir! But I think we're not supposed to cut orders, but endorse the orders from headquarters and pass them through. I've never seen anything like it before. Usually they cut orders for the *Regulars* and we cut orders for *Reservists*. It's nuts." He shrugged in wonderment, then added, "I've got Corporal Stacy pulling the files on the two Reservists. Shall I go check on what's taken him so long, Sir?"

"Good, I'm a bit curious about these two names. There's something familiar about them, Sergeant Major." He thought for a moment. "Go ahead."

Sergeant Alexander was back quickly with the two personnel jackets.

Major Gilley took the jackets and motioned for Sergeant Alexander to look over his shoulder.

"Here it is, Sergeant. I thought I remembered something about these names. See, they were both passed over twice for Captain. It took their CO writing a book about how they walked on water for them to get promoted. However, they have had good marks since. Probably just a couple of hell raisers."

"So it would appear, Sir. But look at their attendance record. It's one hundred per cent. The request to be excused from drills makes sense. It appears they like their Weekend Warrior life. I, for one, appreciate Reservists with that attitude, Major."

"Sergeant Major, you're absolutely right. I fully agree. I'll take this into the General. I'm sure that he'll be interested, if not amused. But now *I'm* curious. Why don't you call Headquarters Marine Corps on the AUTOVON and get any of their Active Duty disciplinary records. Who did these guys piss off? It had to be pretty good to be worth two 'pass-overs'."

Four days later, copies of the records came in. Sergeant Major Alexander looked them over, broke into laughter and took them to Major Gilley's office. He knocked.

"Come," the Major called out.

Sergeant Alexander entered the office, closing the door behind him.

"Major, these records just came in from Headquarters. You won't believe this. Our two aspiring CIA agents got into a world of trouble when they got back from Korea. It seems that while they were stationed at El Toro they got it into their head to 'moon' a Visiting Naval Officer's Wives Luncheon hosted by the El Toro Marine Officer's Wives! Read this, it's a real crack-up, if you'll pardon the expression," Alexander handed the files to the Major.

Major Gilley took the files and motioned for the Sergeant to sit. He started to read, a smile spread across his face, then a chuckle. Within a few moments he broke up completely. It took him some time to run down and to get control of himself. He caught his breath, paused, and then started to read out loud.

"In that First Lieutenant Barnes did, in the company of two other officers, exposed his bare derrière, in a bent-over bodily position, while on a stage at one end of the Officer's Mess Dining Room during a luncheon for Visiting Naval Officer's Wives, hosted by El Toro's Marine Officer's Wives for a period of time of approximately thirty seconds, controlled by the opening and closing of the curtain. In that First Lieutenant Barnes was positively identified by one of the visiting wives, he is charged with Indecent Exposure and Conduct Unbecoming an Officer...." Major Gilley stopped reading and looked up at Sergeant Alexander, addressing a comment to him, "Did you read this part? How *stupid* can it get? Some 'squid's' wife identifies a Marine pilot from his bent-over bare ass! I mean, even if she knew without a doubt who it was. Why would she want to admit the fact to the world? Serious stupid. Well, you see what he got? Thirty days in hack! Simple 'confined to quarters' when not on duty. That's pretty light for a court martial offense."

"I agree Major, but there's more to the story. If you read McGarrity's record, he came forward and admitted his involvement when Barnes got nailed. Wouldn't you have loved to be in the room when the Wing Commanding General was counseling these gentlemen in the errors of their ways? And only hack!" Sergeant Alexander said with a chuckle.

"Stop it Alex, I can't take much more. I'm too weak now. Whew! I haven't laughed this hard in a long time. Did you find anything else?"

"Yes, Sir. There was something in McGarrity's file about the potential damage to a naval vessel with an OE-2. I couldn't understand what the specifications meant. Maybe you can, being an aviator yourself. Here, Sir, I'll show you the charge sheet." With that, Sergeant Alexander turned to the page in McGarrity's file.

The Major took the file and read it through. Again, he chuckled a bit. But this time he was able to maintain control.

"I can understand your confusion, Alex. It appears that Lieutenant McGarrity was TAD (Temporary Attached Duty) to Camp Pendleton for purposes of training some helicopter pilots in the OE's. That's what you infantry types call a 'bird-dog'. It's a light airplane used for artillery spotting and forward air control missions. Anyway, it seems that our good lieutenant tried to land on a small jeep carrier anchored off-shore from Camp Pendleton. The Commanding Officer of the carrier wanted to press charges of a very high nature and it appears that the Commanding General at Camp Pendleton interceded on McGarrity's behalf. I can only assume that this was because of the excessive demands made by the Navy. Whatever the case, all he got was another thirty days in hack. I'll say this for these two, they seem to have led a charmed life. These offenses would have had me breaking up rocks in Leavenworth. Anything else on Barnes?

"He was banned from the Officer's Club a couple of times. It doesn't say what the charges were," Sergeant Alexander replied.

"Well, it's like I suspected before.... just a couple of hell-raisers."

CHAPTER ELEVEN
PLANNING OF ANOTHER KIND

"Whitey? Honey, come here. I want to show you something." Sandy called out.

McFrank came into the living room. He had been doing some work in the study, the small bedroom that had been converted into a study and library for his records and other non-sensitive papers relating to his special line of work.

"What is it, Love?"

"I want you to look at this boat design. It's a Perry Design." She looked up at Whitey from the drawings in front of her. "I think I told you that I found a Marine Architect right here in Seattle. He's starting to get some recognition, but still affordable. He takes a slightly different approach to some of his designs that really shows he gives a lot of thought to the needs of the blue water cruiser. I like his stuff."

"Yeah, Babes, I remember you talking about him. It's *Robert* Perry, isn't it?"

"Right. But look at this set of drawings. I just got them from him the other day. I'm going to have to return them soon."

"Nice lines. How big is it?"

"Honey, it says in the title block, it's a forty-eight. A Perry Forty-Eight is the design call-out. Forty-eight feet in length. I really like it."

"It seems big. I thought we were going to stay in the forty-one foot range. Can two people handle this boat?" Whitey asked as he sat down on the couch beside Sandy. He put his arm around her as he leaned forward to get a closer look at the drawings that were spread out on the coffee table.

"I talked to Perry about it. She's 'ketch rigged' and he has divided the fore sails up like a cutter rig; a jib and a club-footed stay sail. The stay sail is self-tending and the jib is roller- furled. It can be controlled from the mid cockpit.

"You've learned a lot, Babes. I'm impressed. All that nautical talk gets me excited." He gave her a squeeze. "Want to fool around?"

Sandy brushed his arm away in a good natured manner. "Come on Whitey, I'm serious. I want you to look closely at this design. I think I've found our boat."

"Okay, okay. Show me what you like about it. Being turned away from my husbandly prerogatives, however....well, I just don't know."

"Right. I deny you so much. You poor thing! Now, come on, quit kidding around." She pushed him lightly as if to turn him away. "We'll start at the aft cabin. It is just what you would like for 'fooling around'. The bed is queen-size. It isn't suitable for use under way but great in port. And Perry says that we would spend more time in a port than at sea and the accommodations should reflect that. This will be our home for a couple of years or more. Notice the good-sized head. It has an entrance at the forward end as well. I'd change that, close it off. Just forward of the head is the cruising cabin. Two bunks, both adjustable for heel. We would only need one. One of us would be on watch, at the helm. The other bunk could be converted to a work bench or something. This cabin is the main access to the big Perkins diesel engine."

"What's the horsepower?"

"Let me look. Here it is, it's eighty-five horsepower. Is that enough do you think?

"If that's what the architect called out I would think it would be enough."

"I guess. The other side of the engine compartment, the starboard side, is the companionway back into the Master Stateroom; and outboard of the companionway is a freezer underneath your navigation table. Radios, and all that stuff, are on top at eye-level. One of the things I like is the hanging locker right at the bottom of the ladder. It is large, and notice the grid in the deck for water dripping off of you. The hanging locker has a grid in the bottom of it for drainage, too. Mr. Perry says that one does get wet in the weather out there on the briny. I really like this boat, Whitey.

"What are we talking about, Honey? How much money?" Whitey looked directly at Sandy.

"A hundred-forty plus or there about. She would be Taiwan built. Perry says that we could take delivery of her there, saving a ton of money in taxes. Even considering getting there, extras that we would want and all, I think it would still be cheaper than buying something here. Even a used one. But building new will allow us to get what we want and how we want it." She caught her breath, "And, Honey, we can afford her!"

Whitey looked back at the drawings, now with renewed interest. "That's not bad. I would have thought a quarter of a mill. And yes, we've talked all about used versus new. As you've pointed out, this will be our home for some time. It will be small, in any size boat, compared to living ashore. I think new is what we want. You've done a great job, Sandy. I'm impressed. The closest we came before was the Hardin Forty-Five. And that was some time ago. She's Taiwan built, too. I liked that one, but there were still things that wouldn't be that easy to change. This is really a different boat. I like it and the price is right." He thought for a moment. "This contract I'm on right now will practically cover it. What do you mean *we can afford it?* What have you got stashed away?"

"Whitey, you can look at the accounts any time. I don't hide things from you. We've got more than enough right now to buy this boat, make any changes we might want and enough money to go away for a couple of years."

Whitey nodded without looking up. He was examining the drawings closely, going through each page now, and then back to the front of the drawing set. It was quiet. Sandy didn't say anything, letting her man learn about the Perry Forty-Eight. She had already done her look-through. She wanted this boat. She hoped that he would too.

It took about fifteen minutes and then Whitey looked up, "I agree. You've hit it, Kid. I can see some minor changes that we should talk about. I want you to find some real cruising people that have done it. Reading about all this in books is one thing but I want to personally talk to some who have been there, done that. We need to get smarter. But you've done a great job, Babes. I think this Perry Forty-Eight is our boat."

"Thank you, My Darling. I appreciate your confidence and recognition. It has been a lot of work. And now, My Pretty, I know just how to reward your naughty remarks. Come along." Sandy got up, pulling Whitey up with her. "Walk this way." She started out of the room, heading toward their bedroom, walking all hunched over. It was part of an on-going family joke.

Whitey followed meekly. All hunched over.

The next morning after their breakfast, while they were enjoying a last cup of coffee, Whitey spoke about the boat.

"When you return the drawings to Perry, why don't you ask him what it'll take to get the project started? Money? Planning? You know, what are the contracting details? Let's do it. Let's get the thing started."

"Honey, are you sure? You don't want to wait until your contract is over?"

"I'm sure. The contract will be a piece of cake, even with an extension. I'm ready to say that this will be it, my last contract. Go ahead and get started working out the details." Whitey shrugged a dismissal and changed the subject. "There's some talk about turning these apartments into condos. As much as I love this building we're going to have to make a decision soon, one way or another anyway."

"When did you hear that? About the apartments?"

"Yesterday, when I took the trash out I spoke with the 'super'. He's all worked up about keeping his job. I don't think he was supposed to say anything to any of the tenants. But he told me. For that matter, if the price is right we could buy it for investment purposes I suppose. Anyway, don't say anything to anybody for the moment. Let's see how it plays."

"These apartments are so unique. I guess that it doesn't surprise me. Shock is more like it. I mean the selling without telling anyone part of it. I'll keep my ear to the ground."

"Good girl. Let me know when you want me to meet with Bob Perry. I'm going into the office this morning. I'll be home for dinner."

Whitey got up from the table. Sandy got up with him and came into his arms.

"I love you, you wonderful man of mine. Thank you for your confidence about the boat. I'll get things moving. Hurry home."

Whitey kissed her and left for the office.

CHAPTER TWELVE
TYPE RATINGS

The C-47 had arrived on time. It proved to be in impeccable mechanical condition. The engines were near zero time; the engine logs listed a few break-in hours and then the flight time from Patrick Air force Base, in Florida, to Tacoma Industrial Airport, a matter of another twelve hours. The exterior looked like the bird had been ridden hard and put away wet! And *that* was the way it was supposed to look. It carried Venezuelan registration markings; YV-WAWS, and the paper work was complete. When McGarrity and Barnes would have to show papers, they were in order.

The delivery crew went over all of the logs, registration documents and conducted a walk-around inspection of the bird before Barnes drove them up to Sea-Tac International Airport for their commercial airline flight back south. McGarrity stayed behind to go over the maintenance logs with the mechanic friend of Buck Rowes'. There were no squawks; everything that was supposed to work, did work. There was an abundance of tie-down equipment for securing loads. The delivery crew had even pointed out some special reinforced tie-down rings that had been located strategically in the cargo area. They were identified with a red square as opposed to a red circle around them. In addition there were two fifty-five gallon drums up forward lashed to the deck, painted red and marked "100/130", indicating octane rating and that the containers were for the use of aviation gasoline. Each one was equipped with a hand crank pump with a hose attached, long

114

enough to reach out each fuselage side access over-wing hatch and to the farthest wing fuel tank filler cap on each side. The airplane had been prepared without any input other than the request for the fuel drums.

Now it was up to Doc and Smoke to get back in the saddle. Doc had arranged for Buck Rowe to fly down from Victoria the next day to start their refresher work. This gave the lads a whole day to review the handbooks and operating manuals.

Doc was sitting in the cockpit going over procedures and locating where all the clocks and knobs were when Barnes got back from Sea-Tac International. Barnes climbed aboard and made his way forward to the cockpit.

"Can anybody play?" he asked Doc.

"Sure, grab a chair and try to get smart again. I would like to remember how to start this thing and a few other pertinent doin's before Buck gets here in the morning. By the way, we're meeting here at 0630, 'Ol Buddy. Mr. Rowe likes to get an early start,"

Smoke slid over into the co-pilot's seat, "Find anything special, Doc? Or is this just another sterling example of Mr. Donald Douglas's finest hour?"

"No, it's pretty standard. It does have a Single Side-Band HF radio installed. I don't remember how to work 'em. Do you?" Doc asked.

"God no. Maybe Buck knows. They use 'em a lot in Alaska,"

"I'll ask him to check us out."

They reviewed various items, procedures and got most of the things out of the way that could be accomplished on the ground. They were both ready for the following morning.

It was 0620. Barnes and McGarrity were just finishing the walk-around pre-flight inspection when they heard an approaching airplane. Glancing up, they spotted the lights of an airplane in the dim early light of the day. It was on final approach. It had to be Mr. Rowe and he was on time. He must have cleared customs at either Boeing Field, or Sea-Tac, at five-thirty or so. What a way to live.

As he touched down they could see that it was Rowe's Beech Travelair. He turned off the runway in mid-field and taxied over to where they were waiting (there was only one DC-3/C-47 on the relatively small field), turned into a parking spot and shut down. Doc and Smoke walked over to the Travelair, grabbed some chocks and fastened a couple of tie-downs under the wings. Buck opened the door and slowly climbed out.

"Mornin', Gents. Looks like your airplane is carrying some strange registration markings. 'Yankee Victor'. What is it, Panamanian? "

"Morning, Buck. No, it's Venezuelan. Pretty trick, huh?" Doc said as he met Buck climbing down off the wing of the Travelair.

Barnes walked up and extended his hand. "Buck, I'm sure glad you could find some time for us. And you won't believe the condition of this bird. Its looks are very deceiving."

"Yes, it does look like it has been used a bit. Has Miller looked at it yet?"

Doc replied, "Ron Miller and I went over all of the logs as well as the bird yesterday. He gave it his full approval. I think you'll be impressed; new engines, fresh annual inspection and good radios. Which reminds me. It has an HF Single Side-Band radio. Can you check us out on the operation of it?"

"No problem. We'll do that last. All right, let's get to aviatin'. Who's first?"

Doc looked at Smoke, and reached into his pocket for a coin. "Call it." He tossed the coin into the air.

"Tails," Smoke said.

"It's heads. You get to be first."

They all got into the C-47. Buck climbed into the co-pilot's seat. Smoke into the pilot's seat and Doc pulled down a jump seat that fit between the two pilot seats and slightly to the rear. They started the engines, taxied out and down to the run up area. The tower wasn't manned until 0800, so they didn't have anybody to talk to. When the engine run-up was complete, Smoke called for the Take-Off check list, then did a crew briefing.

They were all set. As the instructor-pilot, Buck told Smoke to climb out to the west to five thousand feet. They would be doing some basic air work.

Take-off and climb out went smoothly. Once they reached altitude, Buck had Smoke do some stalls. Buck then shut-down one engine and had Smoke do some basic single-engine maneuvering. Then they headed back to the Tacoma Industrial Airport for practice landings.

The refresher training went on for the rest of the morning; alternating between McGarrity and Barnes. They stopped briefly for a quick sandwich. After lunch, Buck took the observer's seat, between the two pilot seats. He kept Smoke and Doc trading off as pilot and co-pilot, and by the end of the day had them making the mid-field turn-off, about 2200 feet, easily. It didn't matter if they had either engines or one. A few more hours of bug smashing and they wouldn't have any problems with short-field work.

Buck checked them out on the HF radio. It was simple the way he did it. They had to remember to extend the trailing antenna, and also to retract it before landing. The easy part was the use of Transmitting Tables for the most effective frequencies to use, versus time of day. The hard part was remembering the trailing antenna. Many pilots have forgotten to reel in the trailing antenna before landing. It has a lead weight about the size of a baseball on the end of a long wire antenna. It can be reeled out thirty or forty feet, but it has to be reeled back in or it goes away in a tree, around a fence rail or worse, when landing.

"Well, you two don't need me anymore." Buck gathered up his things. "Unless you want to give me a call after you spend a couple of days building some time. I can ride with you again to make sure you haven't picked up any bad habits. All in all, I think you're both okay.

"Buck, I really appreciate the time spent with us today. We'll get a check off to you. But I do think it would be a good idea for a wrap-up session," Doc asked.

"Give me a call on the day before you want to get together again. Hold off on the check, I'll send you a bill for the training hours. For now just go out and build some hours." Buck walked over to the Travelair and was soon on his way back to Victoria.

Doc and Smoke stood quietly on the ramp and watched the Travelair until it was out of sight. Finally Smoke broke the silence. "Damn! There goes one hellava pilot! I learn more about handling an airplane from just listening to that man speak, let alone being in a cockpit with him! What a day this has been--for me, at least. How about you, Doc?"

"It's true, it's true. He's one of the few who can make me feel like a Student Pilot all over again. Then, like you said, I learn a lot. What do you think? Do you want to hit it in the morning and get in five or six hours? We should probably do some instrument work, set up some procedures for shooting approaches. What Buck gave us for maneuvering power settings sure look like they'll work good. I'd like to try 'em some more, anyway."

"That's fine with me, Doc. Why don't we plan to meet here again around six tomorrow and just do it, okay?"

"Yeah, fine. You want to stop for a drink on the way back?"

"No, Shelly is home for a couple of days, so I'd better not."

"I don't blame you. Which reminds me, you haven't told me how your plea bargain worked out."

Smoke thought for a minute, then chuckled, "The chicken almost got overdone."

"What the hell does the chicken....*what* chicken...have to do with your plea bargain?" Doc asked.

"It's a long story, Doc. I'll tell you when we have more time and aren't tired or anxious to get home. At least, I'm anxious to get home."

"Okay, I'll see you in the morning. Go on. I'll have Miller fuel the bird so we'll be ready first thing. Give Shelly my best."

"I'll do that, Doc."

Smoke headed for his car and Doc went into the hangar to arrange the refueling.

Four days later, and with about twenty-five hours of C-47 flight time under their belts, McGarrity and Barnes felt ready for a check ride. Doc called Buck Rowe and set it up. When he was talking to Buck on the phone, the question came up about an official Type Rating. Both Smoke and Doc had military R4D (Navy-Marine designation for the DC-3) sign-offs in their log books, but neither of them held a civilian FAA DC-3/C-47 Type Rating on their Commercial Pilot's License. Buck said he could arrange for an FAA Check Pilot if they wanted. He went on to say he thought they were ready for it. The two Marines decided to have him do it. It would make them completely civilian legal.

They planned to train with Buck in the morning, land at Boeing Field for lunch and pick up the FAA Check Pilot. They could both complete their check rides and subsequent type ratings. Buck said he would meet them at 0630 the following morning at Tacoma Industrial Airport.

As always, he was on time.

Buck spelled out the work that was ahead of them. "Okay, Gents, here's the plan. The man in the left seat will be under the hood. You may or may not have both engines. We'll proceed direct to Olympia, do a VOR Approach and on to Sea-Tac International for a Precision or PAR-ILS approach, direct to the Boeing Field Outer Marker and a standard ILS approach into Boeing. This last approach will be to a full stop. All of the other approaches will be to the published approach minimums and you *will* execute the published 'missed approach' procedure. The FAA Check Pilot will grade you on crew coordination. The left seat, pilot-in-command, can call for anything he needs. However, be advised, if you touch the throttles they're yours. If you don't touch 'em, you can tell the co-pilot to set whatever you need--climb power, slow-cruise power--but you must be positive in asking for what you want. It's really best to only touch the throttles on advancing them for take-off, set your power, then tap them, which gives them to the co-pilot. Don't touch them again until final approach and landing. Do you understand?"

Doc and Smoke indicated that they understood.

Buck continued, "Call for your Check Lists, each of them. Climb Check, Cruise Check, Single-Engine. Remember, when the check pilot pulls an engine, call-out for *throttle* back, *prop* back, THEN call for 'Feather', identifying the bad engine, and then you ask for the Engine-Out Check List. This is the way the civilians play the game and this is the way that this check pilot will be grading you. Okay?" Buck didn't wait for an answer. "Let's get to work."

The training went well. Buck felt that they were both ready. They had time for a quick bite to eat before they had to meet the FAA Check Pilot. They parked on the ramp in front of Galvin's Flying Service and walked over to the Sky Room. Legend had it that Jim Galvin had serviced Bill Boeing's first airplane. Or so it was said. At any rate, he had been on Boeing Field a long time.

The Sky Room wasn't very crowded. Quite a few of the clientele knew Buck and some knew Doc and Smoke from the old Pacific Airmotive days when they flew out of

Boeing Field selling airplane parts around the Northwest. Even their favorite waitress, Darla, waited on them.

She was surprised to see this trio together at one time and had to comment, "This has to be some special occasion. Either you all lucked out and ended up with the same Parole Officer or you're out on some kinda work-release program!"

Such was the banter that was saved for the regulars, but it served to take the edge off of the check-flight tension. Buck assured them that they were both ready and to relax and just fly the airplane. The FAA folks were probably less demanding than a Marine Corps check pilot would be. And he was right.

They met the FAA Check Pilot on time and it turned out to be Hal Wilson, who knew Buck pretty well. He asked him, "You check these people out, Buck?"

"Oh, I had a little bit to do with it, but both of them have checked out in the Marine's R4D's. It was some time ago, but I've been working a refresher with them and thought they could use a civilian type rating. I think that they can keep from killing us, Hal."

This got a chuckle out of Hal Wilson and set a fairly comfortable ambiance for the flight check.

By five o'clock that day, both Harry "Smoke" Barnes and James Francis "Doc" McGarrity added a DC-3/C-47 FAA Type Rating to their Commercial Pilot's Certificate.

CHAPTER THIRTEEN
A BASE OF OPERATIONS

Colonel Cordero stepped out of the airplane and paused at the top of the passenger stairs that had been rolled up to the American Airlines Boeing 727. He looked around the Aeropuerto Internacional de San Salvador, surveying what was about to become his private playground. It was going to be a distinct pleasure to be the Head of Security in this rich little country. It would be a real money machine.

It was almost a shock coming from the cold of Washington, D.C. and stepping out of the air conditioned cabin of the jet transport into the heat and humidity of this Central American country. The climate appeared to be causing some ill effects on his fellow passengers. At least the Norte Americanos.

Cordero decided to check into the Pan American Hotel and rest for a day before calling Señor Cellini. He was traveling on his own Venezuelan passport and wondered if Customs would report his arrival. If they didn't, it would be one of the first instructions he would issue. Control. It was all a matter of control: the foreign travelers...their nationality; visa request, business interests or tourist; where they would be staying. All of this was very important. Colonel Emilio Rafael Cordero liked things nice and orderly.

Clearing Customs was a joke. His luggage wasn't checked, he was asked how long he intended to stay in El Salvador, and when he replied that he was planning on staying at least three months, he wasn't asked reasons, his business, where he would be staying or what he would be doing.

This was going to change. And quickly. That is, if he had anything to say about it.

Cordero caught a cab and told the driver to take him to the Pan American Hotel. The driver went directly, no excursions. Cordero tipped him accordingly. After checking into his room, he took a quick shower; and then placed a call to Costa Rica to his lieutenant, Dominique Paredes.

He was pleased that the call was answered immediately.

"Paredes here."

"Señor Paredes, this is Cordero. I'm at the Pan American Hotel in San Salvador. What is the status of our people?"

"They are well-rested and awaiting your instructions," Lieutenant Paredes answered.

"That is good. I will call you at this time in three days. In the meantime, if something comes up that I should know about, you can reach me here." Cordero spoke briefly.

"I will be awaiting your call," Paredes replied.

Cordero hung up. There wasn't any need for further conversation. Paredes had followed his instructions; no military titles were to be used on the telephone. Conversations were to be held to a minimum. Questions answered without unnecessary elaboration. Wiretapping was not illegal in this part of the world.

At nine the following morning Cordero placed a call to the head of the Catorce Familias; Alfredo Cellini. He was told Señor Cellini was not in. He asked that a message be relayed, telling Señor Cellini that Emilio Rafael Cordero was at the Pan American Hotel and was looking forward to seeing him at his convenience. The voice at the other end of the line assured him his message would reach Señor Cellini shortly.

Within the hour the telephone rang, it was a member of Cellini's staff. He asked Señor Cordero to hold, and in a moment Alfredo Cellini was on the line.

"Ah, Colonel Cordero, we have been anxiously awaiting your arrival. I have spoken with President Sanchez about your assignment and he is in full agreement. I am at my ranch. Would you be able to join me, Colonel? Perhaps we could talk about your plans in a more leisurely manner."

"I would enjoy that, Señor Cellini," Cordero said.

"Good. I'll send a car from our in town estate. How long do you need to get ready?"

"Thirty minutes is more than enough, Señor Cellini," Cordero replied.

"The car will be outside in thirty minutes, the driver will identify himself to you as 'Rosebud'," and without waiting for a reply, Cellini hung up.

Cordero elected to keep his suite at the Pan American for the time being. He intended to use it as a temporary base of operations until a more suitable place could be found. He was beginning to formulate a plan which he would discuss with Alfredo Cellini when the proper time availed itself. He made preparations to leave. The car would be on time.

Twenty five minutes later his phone rang. It was the desk advising him a car had arrived for him. Cordero asked that a boy be sent up to take his bags.

He followed the bellboy out to the curb in front of the hotel. There were three cars in front of the hotel, one was discharging two people, and the doorman signaled the driver of one of the other two cars. He came up to Cordero, politely nodded, and then looked up and said, "I'm Rosebud."

Cordero acknowledged and gestured toward the bags and got into the car. The fact that the doorman knew him by sight was disturbing. It would bear looking into upon his return.

Cellini's ranch was about twenty-five miles north of San Salvador. The trip took close to an hour due to the traffic in San Salvador and the narrow roads climbing to the higher elevations in the mountains surrounding the capital city. The ranch itself was at an elevation of about three thousand feet, which made the temperature and humidity comfortable. The driver left the main highway and drove slowly on an even narrower curving road that made high speed impossible. They soon approached a high, white-painted, stone wall. Driving beside the wall for some distance, they came to a closed gate. The driver honked twice and a man-door in the drive-in door opened and a man came up to the car. He carried what appeared to be an Uzi sub-machine gun over his shoulder. He had his hand near the trigger and, although relaxed, it was obviously within quick and easy reach.

The driver said "Rosebud" again and the gate guard nodded, went back through the man-door and then opened half of the double drive-in solid gate. The car drove into the compound and pulled to a stop in front of the main house. It was typical Spanish architecture; thick stone walls, no visible windows, just a large, double, main entrance door in the wall.

Two servants were instantly there; one, to open the car door and the other, to get any bags out of the trunk. A third stood at the open door to the hacienda as if he were directing traffic, which, in this case, he was. He stepped forward and greeted Cordero.

"Colonel Cordero, welcome. With your permission, I'll have your bags taken directly to your quarters. If you will come with me, I'll show you to where Señor Cellini awaits." He turned and led the way.

The inside of the house was comfortably cool. They walked down a long hall that was illuminated by sunlight coming from French windowed doors at the other end. Before reaching the end of the hall, the servant stopped before a large double door set into the wall. He knocked briefly and opened the door, stepping back to allow Cordero to enter.

Alfredo Cellini, head of the Catorce Familia, had been working at a large, ornately- carved desk across the study. He rose as Cordero came into the room and gestured toward a corner of the study where there were overstuffed chairs arranged in an informal setting.

"Colonel Cordero, I'm glad you could come out to the ranch. May I offer you some refreshments? Perhaps some limeade, or something stronger?" Alfredo Cellini said in English as he directed Colonel Cordero to one of the chairs. He took his seat in the other chair.

"I would prefer a whiskey, thank you. I am a little dry from the drive out. The roads were dusty," Cordero responded in English.

The servant who had brought Colonel Cordero to the study was still standing by the open double door. Cellini motioned to him and said in Spanish, "Juan, bring us some ice."

After the servant left, Cellini went over to a cabinet against the wall and took out a bottle of Johnny Walker Black label. He held it up to Cordero, seeking his approval. Colonel Cordero said, "It is my favorite."

Cellini nodded, poured a liberal amount in each of two glasses and continued in English, "I have a small gift. More a token of our appreciation, for your willingness to help us out."

He left the glasses on the cabinet and continued over to the desk where he had been working when Cordero arrived, opened a drawer and took out, an ornate silver belt buckle attached to a hand-tooled leather belt. He held it out in one hand and with the other, tripped a release on the top of it and the handle of a belt knife that had been disguised as part of the buckle's decoration popped out; the razor-sharp stiletto blade extended into the attached leather belt. Cellini deftly pulled it out. He waited a moment for the significance to sink in, then handed both the belt and the knife to his guest.

Cordero graciously accepted the impressive gift. "This is a beautiful piece of work. I will treasure it always, El Patrón. Gracias."

Cellini caught Cordero's use of the word *patrón*. It pleased him that the Colonel knew and respected his place in the scheme of things. He took his seat, leaned back, lit a small cigar, and then looked his guest squarely in the eyes. "Colonel Cordero, you come to us highly recommended. As you know, that bearded Son of a Pig in Cuba is behind most of the unrest in Central and South America. We have reason to believe he is directly responsible for the problems in Salvador. It is our wish to stop it quickly, before it becomes a major problem. The position being offered to you is a special position working with our State Police. They have suffered from a clear cut lack of direction. There is much evidence of pay-off for too many things. I want you to report directly to me. You will have your own organization. There has been talk in some quarters of having our army handle the situation. I, for one, do not think it would be the best approach. This is a very small country. It should not be that difficult to find the guerrillas and remove them. The people must be discouraged from assisting them. Let the communists concentrate on Nicaragua. I don't even want them staging in this country."

Cordero was surprised at the position being offered, but managed to hide his disappointment. "I understand, Patrón, it can be as you wish. I think that if the people can be shown that it is not to their advantage to support, in any way, activity against the state, it will serve to discourage guerrilla activity. If the guerrillas have to supply all of their own needs, it can severely limit their range of operation."

"Those are my thoughts exactly. We seem to be of one mind. Ah, here is our ice." Switching back to Spanish, Cellini continued, "That will be all for now, Juan."

He waited until the servant left the room before going on. "What are your immediate plans, Colonel?" He placed

127

some ice in each of the glasses, took one and handed the other to Cordero.

Cordero hesitated before answering, then decided to press ahead. "I was led to believe that I would be in charge of National Security and would be staying in the capitol." He took a sip of his drink to allow time for Cellini to say something. When nothing was forthcoming, he went on. "Now that you have made it clear what my assignment is to be I would like to have a base of operations, not too far from the Capital, but out of the city. I was even thinking of buying a ranch and staying here after my work is finished. Do you know of anything that would be suitable?" Cordero asked.

If Cellini was surprised about Cordero's mentioning National Security, he chose not to show his surprise or to respond to it. "Yes, I do know of a ranch. A family member has recently placed a piece of property on the market. He decided he wanted a ranch that had the room, and the terrain, suitable for a larger landing strip. He has found what he was looking for. The property he left is near San Julian, about forty-eight kilometers from San Salvador. It is in some fairly rugged country, about four hundred-fifty meters elevation, and not enough level ground to extend his landing field for the operation of a Lear Jet. As near as I can remember, the property consists of approximately one hundred acres. The manor house is large, old, but well-built and there are several other buildings on the property as well. It has been some time since I have personally been there, but I know that the former owner took good care of it," Cellini continued, "Is this the type of thing that you are interested in?"

"From your description, it sounds like what I had in mind. I do not have need for a landing strip long enough for a Lear Jet. How long is the existing strip?"

"As I recall, it is about seven hundred-fifty meters, or twenty-five hundred feet long, if you would prefer."

"That would be adequate for my needs," Colonel Cordero answered, taking a long drink. "Would it be possible to see it soon?"

"Of course. Would tomorrow be suitable?" Cordero gestured his assent. "Good. I'll have someone take you out there."

"Señor Cellini, I do have a question, a matter of curiosity. The identification by the driver, the term 'Rosebud', may I ask the significance?"

Cellini laughed, "One of my favorite American movies is 'CITIZEN KANE', where Orson Wells played the part of a man modeled after the famous newspaper publisher, William Randolph Hearst. And as he is dying, he whispers 'Rosebud'. It always fascinated me. Now, let's get on to the financial arrangements for your mission here."

The two discussed finances for some time. The special post, working with, but independent of the State Police, carried with it a favorable salary. In addition, the Catorce Familias would augment the salary with a monthly contribution. No mention was made of Colonel Cordero's funding from the United States Government. In addition, his position was defined; he would be operating somewhat independently, and not in connection with any elements of the Secret Police. He would not be able to track people coming into the country, among other things, as he had hoped. However, the pay from three sources was compensation for this lack of power.

The ranch property near San Julian turned out to be more than adequate for Colonel Cordero's plans. It was isolated and the surrounding country was ideal for security. The additional buildings on the property were suitable for housing the personnel he would be adding to his force.

Arrangements were made for the purchase and transfer of title. The Salvadorian Government had nationalized the country's Central Reserve Bank, formerly owned by the Catorce Familias, in October of 1960; some eight years previously. As head of the family, Alfredo Cellini was still able to exert considerable influence on the transactions, speeding them up.

Two weeks later Colonel Cordero moved into his new quarters. He had made arrangements for his Lieutenant, Dominique Paredes, to move the other men he had brought with him from Costa Rica. They were to form the nucleus of his planned flying squad. Their attitude was very much like his own. His people had been with him for some time; and not just for the money, they liked the way he did things. Colonel Cordero would recruit personnel as needed from the local population; carefully screened to fit his methods.

Colonel Cordero knew how to deal with guerrillas. When the guerrillas were in the field, they left their families behind in the village. It would be a simple enough matter to find the villagers in the mountains who were sympathetic and assisting the guerrillas. *Then* the Colonel would show the Catorce Familias how to discourage guerrilla activity.

CHAPTER FOURTEEN
THE REGULAR ESTABLISHMENT

McGarrity had slept in. It wasn't something he did very often. He just lay in bed, staring at the ceiling, thinking. He decided that he had been remiss in taking care of business lately. All of the spook stuff, the checking out and type-rating in the DC-3, was a lot of fun, but nobody had been watching the store lately. He and Barnes did have a company with all the attendant responsibilities, even if they didn't keep normal business hours.

Aries Enterprises had started life as a part time engineering firm. Doc had gotten involved in cryogenics about the time industry was coming up with the term. Cryogenics is the study of low temperature media. And by *low temperature,* a cryogenic engineer considers LOX, (liquid oxygen) lukewarm. Now liquid nitrogen and liquid hydrogen, are *cold*, and true cryogen's. Aries Engineering had been developing a frozen food air freight shipping container, designed into a 747 or DC-10 belly box. The project was a favorite design challenge for Doc. For three or four years it had been almost a hobby. Then he had made a chunk of money on an aircraft sale, actually for Buck Rowe; a purchase of three PBY's for Buck's Flying Firemen Company. Doc had decided to fund the cryogenic project with a portion of the proceeds.

The project was being worked on by a former Boeing engineer. There were a lot of Boeing engineers looking for things to do. Boeing had dumped 55,000 people out on the street. A group of engineers with a marked sense of humor had rented a large sign board with the message "Will the last person to leave Seattle please turn out the lights!" It made TIME magazine.

Doc had kept the project rolling from aircraft sales produced by him and Barnes.

Thanks to the company secretary, Hunter Herring, he and Barnes could afford to be gone a lot. But it was way past the time to go by the office and check on things and probably sign a few checks for Hunter.

Hunter was really something special. She was somewhere around her mid-thirties, happily married to a senior Boeing engineer, who had survived the purges, had three children, didn't look like she'd had three children and had a butt you could crack an egg on. She was stable and solid as a piece of granite. Hunter thought both McGarrity and Barnes were certifiably insane. She wouldn't sit still for nonsense of any kind. She had the uncanny ability to see through bull-shit, and was a direct person. At times, this latter attribute could be very intimidating. Hunter was an attractive lady. About five foot six, maybe a hundred and twenty-five pounds, penetrating eyes and trim figure. Her medium brown hair was currently lightly frosted. It was a good thing she was so happily married, she was the type of girl-next-door that Doc could really fall for. Something he didn't dare allow himself to think about.

He decided to get out of bed and call her.

She answered on the second ring. "Good morning, Aries Enterprises, how may I direct your call?"

Doc got a kick out of the way she handled the telephone. She made it sound like Aries Enterprises was some complex corporation in a three story building. The reality of it was that Aries consisted of Doc, the founder, Smokey Barnes, vice-president and Hunter, who really ran the company, Ross Bigelow, a cryo engineer, and a kid who came in after school to run errands, help Ross or sweep the floor.

The airplane deals had put the company on a paying basis and they could afford the luxury of a couple of full time employees. The airplane deals were far apart, but when they came through, the brokerage fees and commissions were substantial.

"Hunter, it's Doc here. What's going on that I should know about?"

"Boss, you've got several messages, three of them are overseas calls and several domestic. Are you going to be coming in?"

"Yeah. I'll be there in about an hour. Who are the overseas calls?"

"Two are from Aer Lingus in Dublin and the other is from Otto Schwartz in Germany."

"When did Otto Schwartz call?"

"He called twice, the first time was the day before yesterday and then again this morning. I told him you would be getting back to him before the end of the week."

"Good. Thanks Hunter, you do nice work. I'm coming in to the office. I'll see you in a bit." Doc hung up. He wondered what was happening with Schwartz. He called Barnes.

"Barnes residence," it was Shelly.

"Hi Shelly, Smoke up yet?" McGarrity asked.

"Yes he is, Doc. Let me get him for you. Oh, when are you going to come out? We haven't seen you in some time, well, that is, I haven't."

"Soon, Shelly, soon," Doc replied.

"Okay, I'll hold you to it. Here's Smokey." She handed the telephone to her honey.

"Hi, what's happening?"

"I just got off the phone with Hunter, you know, the one who's running our company, and she says Aer Lingus is after some words with us. That's your deal, Smoke. Can you break away long enough to handle it? I'm going into the office in about an hour, how about meeting me there?"

"Sure Doc, but it's not like I've been on vacation, we've been together, remember?" Harry Barnes sounded a bit annoyed.

"I know, I know. I'm just feeling guilty about all of the time we've spent doing other things. Schwartz has called a couple of times, too. I'll handle that, and you can deal with Aer Lingus."

"Sounds like a deal, Doc. Anything else?" Smoke asked.

"No, I'll see you in a bit then."

"Right. Take care." Smoke hung up.

Doc grabbed a bite to eat, showered, shaved and headed downtown. It was a quick ten minute drive off Queen Anne Hill...down to the Alaska Way Viaduct and over into Georgetown. They had selected an office and warehouse on Airport Way. It was about half way between downtown Seattle and Boeing Field. The location was chosen since it was equally convenient for all hands, except Hunter. She lived in Bellevue, on the other side of Lake Washington. But she had joined the firm after the vote and hadn't had a say. She never let them forget it either.

Doc pulled into his spot marked "President". He got out of his car, went into the building, and on into his office. In a moment, Hunter brought in a cup of black coffee and a hefty stack of mail.

"Here you go, Boss. Look this stuff over and then I'll bring you up to date on the payables."

"Thanks, Hunter."

It didn't take long to go through and sort the mail. Doc finished and asked Hunter to come into his office. She brought the check book and ledger. He signed several blank two-party checks, and looked over the payables. She had been doing a wonderful job.

"How much are we paying you, Hunter?" Doc asked.

"Fifteen hundred a month, Doc."

"Well, you're worth a hellava lot more than that, kid. Give yourself a raise to twenty four thousand a year. Make it retroactive to the beginning of this month." Hunter started to say something. Doc held up his hand and went on, "Don't worry, you're going to be earning it. Smoke and I are going to be gone for at least a month, maybe more. There's plenty of money in the bank. Keep Ross busy. He does like to diddle around. If he can get that prototype to hold temperature for forty-eight hours, we'll have a winner. I want it done with the liquid nitrogen. Don't let him use anything else. It's an inert gas, used in food processing, so it keeps both the FAA and the FDA happy. A couple of weeks ago, he was talking about trying the liquid hydrogen. I don't want him to do that. Okay?"

"Maybe it would be better if you spoke to him about it, Boss. He doesn't like to take direction from me," Hunter was almost apologetic about Ross's attitude.

"Okay, I'll speak to him. But I'm also going to make it very clear that in our absence, you're the leader around here. Maybe I should give you a new title. Would you like that?"

"It all depends. You and Harry have a pretty weird sense of humor. What did you have in mind?"

Doc thought about it for a minute. "No, this is serious. How about General Manager? You already have check signing authority. That title would give you all of the clout you'd need. And furthermore, if you need help or if Ross Bigelow needs a couple of bodies, go hire them. I'll be counting on you to run this damn company. What the hell, you've been running it for over six months anyway."

"That's very gracious of you, Mr. McGarrity. I would be proud to have the title." She took a deep breath, then as if none of this mattered, "I accept!"

"Good. Now try to get a hold of Otto Schwartz for me, if you would, Madam General Manager."

A few moments later she stuck her head back into his office. "Line two Boss, Herr Schwartz awaits."

Doc picked up the phone, "Guten abend, Herr Schwartz. McGarrity returning your call."

"Ya, ya. Guten abend. The shipment left Amsterdam two days ago, aboard the S.S. Dharma. She is scheduled to arrive Vancouver in seven days from now. Please have the agreed upon funds available after inspection. Verstandlich machen? You may contact me in eight days where we last met."

"How long will it take to unload and clear customs?" Doc asked.

"The shipment will be available for inspection within twenty-four hours after docking. Please be ready with the funds." Otto Schwartz replied.

"Good. I'll be there." Doc hung up the phone.

He thought for a moment, then picked up again and called Roberts at the agency. Chris Mavis put him right through. He was going over the details with Section Chief Roberts when Barnes came in and stuck his head into Doc's office. Doc motioned him to come in and finished going over the details with Roberts. He hung up and turned to Smoke.

"We're in business, 'Ol Buddy. The goods arrive in Vancouver a week from today. We'll be able to inspect the day after, according to our Kraut friend. I was just now talking to Roberts to arrange the funds. He says no problem."

"Looks like we got an adventure, Doc. I'd better wrap up the Aer Lingus thing and get my side of the business in order. Anything else?"

"Yeah. I'm promoting Hunter to General Manager. I gave her a raise to twenty-four thousand. Do you have any problems with that?"

"Hey. This is your company, remember? I just came on board doing the airplane things. You don't need my approval for anything. But it's about time you realized her worth."

"You're right. We haven't talked about it much but the partnership we established on aircraft brokerage I was going to change, making it all the way through. Since I incorporated this thing before you came on board, I guess I'll have to check with our attorney for how to do all that, unless you don't want the liability?" Doc said.

"You don't have to do that, Doc. I'm flattered, but I don't know anything about cryogenics or the other stuff that you're doing. But if it's what you want, fine. I'm happy to be your partner."

"Well, it's what I want. Airplane sales are not going to last forever. I'm going to need help with the sales and marketing of the container and you know how to sell. I'll call the attorney and get him on it. Go do your Aer Lingus thing and we can talk about it over lunch."

"Right then." Smoke spoke with a veddy British accent, straightening up and snapping a palm out British salute.

Doc called Hunter back in and they went over everything both of them thought that could, or would, come up in the next forty-five to sixty days. Doc mentioned that government checks would be coming in. She could just put them into the company account. Hunter suggested that he take a change of address card into the Post Office and have all of his mail sent to the office. This made a lot of sense to Doc. He explained that, in addition to the normal bills that would be coming in, he was paying child support for his son.

"I didn't know that you had a son or had ever been married, Doc. You've never talked about him."

"Yeah, but it didn't last too long. My flying got to her. I have a neat kid, though. I don't get to see him very often. They live in California. He's ten now. Maybe I'll get him in the summer now that he's older. Here. I'll show you his picture." Doc took a folder out of his desk. In the folder were typical school pictures. "His name is Barrett. Naturally, he goes by 'Barry'. I'll leave you the address and amount of the check. I usually send it on the twenty-fifth, so it'll get there by the first."

"He's a fine looking young man, Doc." Hunter handed the folder back.

Doc then asked Hunter if she had any objections to having his power of attorney. That took a little talking before she would accept the responsibility. She suspected the government charter he and Smoke were going to be flying might be a little dangerous from the way he was acting. Hunter was more than just a little bright.

"Now you're beginning to sound like you have some reservations, Hunter. Do you mind taking on this additional responsibility?" Doc asked.

"How do you think all of this sounds to me? I've only been here for six months, you promote me to General Manager, and then an hour later ask me to have your power of attorney. Then you tell me you're running off to fly some charter for some 'can't-talk-about-it-group' and you don't know how long you'll be gone. Oh, and you won't be calling in very often. Needless to say, I'm a bit overwhelmed. So what does this mean? Have a safe trip and if you don't come back I can spend all the money. Is that about it?"

It was quiet. Doc and Hunter just looked at each other. Finally Doc spoke up, "Well, you do have a rather quaint way of putting it. But, in a nutshell, that's about it. I would hope that you would divide things up. Or at least try to keep the company going. But, for God's sake, don't let Ross Bigelow do anything but engineering. Go hire a sales manager and do the container. I was going to call it Freeze Flight. Ask your husband for his advice. I don't care. Do whatever you want. If you hang it all up, try to save some money for Shelly and my kid. I don't have anybody else, Hunter. I'll be damned if I'll turn it over to my attorney. He's made enough money off of me as it is." Doc looked away, he had gotten to his feet and was now looking out the window of his office. He turned back, saying, "And don't forget to pay the taxes. Those folks will hunt you down. I'm not leaving yet. We'll talk some more about it."

"Okay, but you just better come back, you hear?" Hunter got up and went out the door.

Smoke came in, passing her as she left the office. He asked, "What's that all about? Hunter looked pissed."

"We'll talk about it over lunch." Doc returned to his desk and sat down. "What did Aer Lingus have to say?"

"The Viscount package is ours. Six standard birds in airline configuration, and one with an executive interior. I told you about the executive one. It would be a gas to keep it for a corporate airplane. It's really nice. This is the package that I want to off to Peru. It's not only the seven airplanes, but it includes a cockpit simulator and full rotable spares. Including engines. The good news is we're getting the entire package for six and a half million. There's lots of room for a considerable chunk of profit. I've been talking ten million to Peru."

"Sounds great. Let's go eat and you can bring me up to date on the details."

When they got back to the office, Hunter told Doc there was a call from Salty Wells. Doc motioned for Smoke to follow, went into his office and dialed the number on the message slip. It was at Boeing Flight Crew Training, where Salty worked, training crews for various models of the Boeing family of transports. After a short delay, Wells came on the line.

"Hi Skipper, what's up?" Doc asked.

"Orders came in last night from Glenview detailing you and Barnes to the CIA for '*an indefinite period of time involving flying*'. The squadron is to get credit for the flight hours logged. The Detachment called me this morning.

They haven't ever seen anything like this. I think the Executive Officer was a trifle disturbed."

"Well Colonel, can we pick up the orders this weekend? It's a drill weekend. We can do the weekend drill and then endorse the orders effective Monday. That way it won't screw up this drill." He was working around the system in the best possible manner.

"That'll work, Doc. But I would suggest that when the Detachment folks ask what's it all about, just tell them it is strictly on a 'need to know' basis. It'll drive 'em nuts." Salty was obviously somewhat amused about their reaction.

"Why Skipper, what are you suggesting? That we give our Regular Establishment a hard time?" He went on without waiting for an answer. "The fact of the matter is I was only authorized to tell *you* any of the details. And I had to get special permission to do that. So, your suggestion is a valid one. And you're right, it'll probably drive them nuts."

"Good. I'll see you both this weekend. We can have a couple of drinks and you can fill me in with whatever you're authorized to tell me." Colonel Wells hung up and went back to work.

Doc turned to Smoke. "You heard my side of the conversation. Our orders came in from Glenview, we're detailed to the spooks, like we requested. The squadron even gets credit for our flight hours. Isn't that some kinda deal."

"Damn right! Time's running out. We've got a lot to do, get this place sorted out, drill weekend, next week up to Vancouver to check the goods. Is that what Roberts said? You haven't talked to Whitey yet, have you?" Smoke asked.

"No, just Roberts, like I told you at lunch. He was going to let Whitey know. But, you're right, lots to do. Let's get at it." Doc replied.

SAND POINT, NAVAL AIR STATION SEATTLE

Saturday morning broke with a typical Seattle day; low overcast and occasional drizzle. *"It'll probably change to scattered showers later,"* Doc thought. He had been looking forward to this drill weekend. It looked like it would be the last time he would get to fly the AD-5 Skyraider. He had really developed an affection for the big lumbering Douglas dive bomber. Under the right conditions, it wasn't really all that lumbering.

By the time he got out of the shower and into his uniform, Doc noticed it had stopped raining. He grabbed a quick bite to eat and drove out to Sand Point; Naval Air Station Seattle. He got there in plenty of time before the morning squadron muster.

The air station itself carried with it a bit of history. It was built on a lump of land sticking out into Lake Washington, the twenty-six mile long lake bordering the east side of Seattle. The runway length was limited to the fact that it had the water of the lake on each end. The total runway length was just a little over five thousand feet.

The historical significance of NAS Seattle is the fact that the three U.S. Army Douglas bi-planes, which were the first aircraft to fly around the world in the late twenties, stopped there and refueled.

Doc checked his squadron mail slot, picked up the copy of the weekend drill Flight Schedule, was pleased to see he was scheduled to fly both Saturday and Sunday, grabbed a cup of coffee and had a seat in the Ready Room to await muster. He was barely seated when Smoke came in and made his way over to where Doc was sitting.

"Mornin', Captain McGarrity, Sir"

"And a good morning to you, Captain Barnes, Sir", Doc replied, and then continued, quietly and in a confidential manner, "By the way, I didn't tell you earlier this week but

Salty has asked me to not say anything about losing the Skyraiders, so don't you say anything, okay?"

"My lips are sealed," Smoke said.

"Good. From the looks of the schedule, it appears that I lucked out. I'm on the flight schedule both days. I notice that you only made it today." Doc pointed out to Smoke.

"Don't worry about me, Doctor, take a look at the schedule for the first launch tomorrow morning, the second page. One of those guys will cancel. Not to worry. I'll get his hop."

Doc looked at the second page of the schedule again and noticed that indeed the first launch had two of the squadron's heaviest boozers scheduled for the early morning launch. He laughed, "You're right. You won't have any problems getting on the first launch, just be suited up."

Whenever there was a pilot cancellation, the Ops Officer grabbed the first pilot handy that was in a flight suit and who looked halfway alert. It was important for the squadron records that all training hours scheduled were actually flown.

A few minutes before 0800 somebody spotted the Skipper coming into the Ready Room and called out, "Attention on deck!"

All hands rose to attention.

"As you were. Be seated gentlemen," Lieutenant Colonel Wells said.

Muster was taken, orders read, and the squadron got down to the business of the drill weekend. Those scheduled to fly, suited up. The other officers went off to their collateral duties. Colonel Wells asked McGarrity and Barnes to come into his office.

"Grab a chair, Gents," Wells motioned to two chairs in front of his desk, "Now tell me what you can about what the Hell's going on! The Detachment is all over my ass about you two. They wanted me to send you up to their office as soon as muster was over."

Doc took the lead, "Colonel, it's like I told you on the phone, I have special permission to give *you* some of the details, but for all the others, it's strictly on a 'need to know' basis. Barnes and I are to be detailed to the CIA for an 'indefinite period of time involving flying'. Our mission is to fly a cargo into a small Central American country. The cargo is classified. The purpose of the cargo is classified. The name of the small Central American country is classified, and the 'indefinite period of time involving flying' is so classified, *we* don't even know how long it will be. As far as we know, it is a down and back operation. Since you could easily have seen the aircraft flying around the area, I can also tell you that it is a C-47 with Venezuelan civilian registry markings. Smoke and I picked up a type-rating in it recently."

"Well, that's certainly interesting, Doc. What are you going to tell the Detachment?

"I thought I would tell them what they should already know. We're being detailed to the CIA for a special assignment involving flying....and the squadron is to receive credit for our flight hours, and that we are, in no way, to be penalized for any missed drills until released from the assignment. The rest is on a 'need to know' basis. I think that should do it, Sir."

The Colonel chuckled, "Yes, I think that should cover it. I wish I could be there. You two had better get a move on. Report back to me when they're through."

Both McGarrity and Barnes rose to attention, "Yes, Sir!" they said in unison, "With your permission, Sir!"

"Dismissed. Carry on, Gentlemen."

A short walk brought the two Marine Captains to the USMC Detachment Headquarters, located two hangars away. They reported in to the Sergeant Major. He took them immediately to the Commanding Officer's office, knocked quietly and went in. In a moment he was back out.

"The Colonel will see you now, Gentlemen," he said.

Barnes and McGarrity strode briskly into the office, up to about three feet from the Colonel's desk and came to attention. Doc spoke for both, "Captain McGarrity and Barnes reporting as ordered, Sir!"

Colonel Weston, a full bird colonel and a Regular officer, not a Reservist, looked up from his desk. "Stand at ease, Gentlemen. Do you know why I asked to see you?

"Yes Sir! Colonel Wells briefed us, Sir." McGarrity said.

"Good. Now tell me what this is all about. We have received some highly irregular orders regarding you two."

Doc looked over at Smoke, who nodded for him to do the talking.

"Captain Barnes and I are to be detailed over to the Central Intelligence Agency for a special assignment, for an indefinite period, involving flying. Our flying hours are to be credited to the squadron. Further, we are not to be penalized in any way for any drills missed during this assignment period. All other information regarding this assignment is on a 'need to know basis', Sir!"

"Captain McGarrity, I understand all of that. Those points are covered in the orders we received and are endorsing over to your Commanding Officer for endorsement over to you. I feel this Detachment has a 'need to know' just what the hell two Reserve officers of this command are doing with the CIA that *involves flying,* and how all of this came about!" The Colonel was not pleased.

"Colonel, with all due respect, Sir, I'm not at liberty to disclose that information to you, Sir. I respectfully suggest that the Colonel direct the question to the Commanding General, 4th Marine Air Wing, Sir."

"Do not get impertinent, Captain!" The Colonel said acidly.

Doc came back to attention. "No, Sir! That is not my intent, Sir. We have received explicit orders on what can and what cannot be said, Sir. We have not been cleared to discuss this matter with this command, Sir! Perhaps the Colonel has the rank to pursue the matter back through headquarters. I, for one, do not have any objections with the Colonel knowing the full details of our assignment. I'm just not at liberty to be the one to disclose the information, Sir!"

"I just might do that, Captain, I just might do that. These orders will be ready for you at 1600 hours today." The Colonel said haughtily.

"Sir, with all due respect, it is my understanding that Captain Barnes and I are to perform the drill weekend and then Sunday night sign the orders to be effective at midnight. Sir."

Colonel Weston didn't reply for a minute. Finally, he said, "That will be all. You're dismissed." He did not directly respond to Doc's comment.

"Yes, Sir!" both officers said in unison, stepped back one pace and executed an about face and left the office.

They didn't say anything until they were outside of the building. Smoke spoke first.

"Jeezus, what a jerk! I thought for a moment he was going to bring you up on charges, for Chrissakes!"

"I'll admit, I was a little taken aback, Smoke. Fuckin' Regulars. They do have to throw their weight around. He just couldn't *stand* for a Reservist to be involved in something he couldn't find out about. Maybe I'm being too harsh on him. He just isn't like the other Detachment CO's we've had. Maybe it's because he's a full bird Colonel and feels this assignment is beneath him. I don't know. But, you're right. He is a jerk!"

"Yeah, well things could be worse. We could be Regulars and have him for a CO!" Smoke said with disgust.

Doc laughed at Smoke's point. He checked his watch and then said to Smoke, "Will you brief Salty? I've got to suit up, I have a hop."

"No sweat, Doc. Enjoy."

They went back to the squadron hangar and separated, each to do what had to be done.

Later that evening, Doc and Smoke were at the bar in the Officer's Club when their Commanding Officer, Lieutenant Colonel Salty Wells found them. He walked up to them and said, in a jocular manner, "The least that you two trouble makers could do would be to buy your Skipper a drink!"

"Right you are, Colonel. What'll it be?" Doc asked.

"Johnny Walker over ice will do nicely, Doctor," came the reply. "By the way, although I'm sure that you are fully aware of the fact, you have really managed to twist the Detachment's tail. They are heartily pissed." Salty said with a degree of seriousness.

Smoke paid attention to his drink. Doc ordered the requested drink and continued the conversation with Salty. "Do you have any suggestions for Smoke and me, Skipper?"

"I would suggest that you just get the drill weekend behind you, maintaining a low profile and then disappear. When you return, your recent multi-engine experience will increase your value to the squadron and also to the detachment. These things have a way of sorting themselves out. Besides, I fill out your Fitness Report, not the Detachment! Thanks for the drink, Doc, you didn't really have to do that you know."

"I know that, Boss, but you take a lot of shit on our behalf, and this is one of the few ways that I can show our appreciation for your efforts," Doc said in a sincere manner.

Salty raised his glass and toasted, "A successful trip, and safe return, gents."

Both Doc and Smoke raised their glasses in return, responding with a "Here, here."

CHAPTER FIFTEEN
THE SHIPMENT ARRIVES

The drive from Seattle to Vancouver, B.C. is a comfortable two and a half to three hour trip. Whitey McFrank insisted on taking his own car. Barnes and McGarrity rode together in another car. To Doc, this seemed like nonsense. McFrank had just said to do it. It was for security reasons. They were going to stay in different hotels. Whitey said he would meet them where they would be meeting Otto Schwartz. Whitey didn't say how he would know where they would be. Doc hadn't asked.

Doc was driving and a lot was going through his mind. *It was rather relaxing just to get out of the office again. He and Barnes had not exactly been paying attention to business and there had been a lot of catching up to do. But he was pleased; Smoke had handled the Aer Lingus package well. It looked like it was over. The commissions on the deal were substantial. The company partnership for Smoke had been put through. Actually, it was just a matter of issuing a stock certificate. A lot easier than he had thought. However it brought something else to mind.*

He turned to Smoke. "Funny, I didn't know your first name was 'Harrison', I thought it was just Harry--and middle initial 'C'. What does the 'C' stand for? I guess I didn't ever know that you had a middle name; I didn't ever think about it."

"What the hell brought that up?" Barnes asked in an aggressive manner.

147

"It was the legal papers for the stock issue giving you a large percentage of the company, was what brought it up. What are you getting upset about?"

"Nothing. Well, I shouldn't say that. I always hated the name 'Harrison'. Don't know why exactly. I was named after an uncle. He had bad breath and always patted me on the ass." Smoke replied.

"What's so terrible about that? Shit, most relatives do those sort of things."

"When I was fifteen?"

"Oh." Doc couldn't think of anything appropriate to say.

It was quiet for a while. The long drive continued. It had started to rain. The swishing of the windshield wipers filled what had become an awkward silence.

"My middle name....the 'C', was for an aunt. I don't think you want to know about that."

"For Chrissakes Smoke, we're partners. We work together, we fly together. Shit, we'll probably die together, and now you're getting sensitive. I don't believe it."

"Okay, but promise you won't laugh." Smoke hesitated. He wasn't sure if he wanted to talk about it.

"Is it that bad?"

Yes, it's that bad. Just promise."

"OKAY!" Doc replied, raising his voice, "I promise, scout's honor." Doc turned to him and made the scout's three fingered sign.

It was quiet for a period, except for the windshield wipers. Smoke was thinking. He really didn't know if he wanted to talk about this. There didn't seem to be any way out of it now, so finally he cleared his throat and turned to Doc.

"It's 'Carvel'. The 'C' stands for 'Carvel'."

"Huh?" Doc said, surprised. He took his eyes off of the road long enough to look at Smoke.

148

"Carvel, the 'C' stands for 'Carvel'....and she wasn't really my aunt." He paused, then shrugged and continued, "She was my dad's secretary. He was fucking her. He'd bring her to the house, saying she was his sister. My mother never found out the truth, and even agreed to name me after her. I think my mother knew, or found out later, but she never let on. I never had a real aunt."

"So? What's so bad about that?" Doc asked.

"Hey. There's more. Uncle Harrison never married. He lived with another bachelor. He only brought his roommate to one family get-together, as I remember. My dad wasn't very nice to the roommate. My mom liked him, though. Every time she said anything to him, he would blush. My uncle just got mad. He never brought the roommate back."

Doc started to giggle, then broke down completely. He damn near lost control of the car. Barnes was getting more and more agitated the harder Doc laughed. He yelled at Doc.

"Goddammit! You promised you wouldn't laugh. You gave your word. What's so fuckin' funny anyway?"

"It just struck me that you were named after a gay uncle and your father's whore. That's what I was laughing about. I'm sorry, Smoke, really I am. But it is rather unusual, isn't it?"

"Sure, it's unusual. That's why nobody knows. And you better Goddamn keep it to yourself also!"

"Well Shit, Smoke, nobody has to know the details. Just the names 'Harrison' and 'Carvel' don't tell anybody anything. Get real, man. Relax. Take your pack off, Captain. Jeezus!"

"Well, don't you tell anybody?"

"Hey! Trust me. I won't breathe a word to anybody," McGarrity replied. He stifled a laugh that was trying to get out and cleared his throat to conceal it.

They drove the rest of the way in silence. Just the swishing of the windshield wipers.

The Bayshore Hotel is quite elegant. A beautiful view of Vancouver's harbor. Even with the difference in money--Canadian to US Dollar, the Bayshore is pricey.

McGarrity laughed as they were getting out of the car. "Do you suppose we're on Government per-diem for this, Smoke?"

"Abso-fuckin'-lutely, ma fellow 'merican."

Doc opened the trunk, pointed to the bags and handed the keys to the doorman who had just come over to them. The doorman motioned for a bellman to take the bags and handed the keys to an assistant to park the car. The bellman took the bags and led the two Americans into the hotel.

McGarrity asked the room clerk for adjoining rooms. He and Barnes were quickly checked in and shown to their rooms. Doc tipped the bellman, who left. Doc walked over to the door adjoining Smoke's and tapped lightly. The door opened.

"I'm going to go ahead and call Otto's hotel and leave a message that we're here. Why don't you get some ice? I had the presence of mind to bring some Dewar's." Doc said to Smoke.

"That's funny, so did I. But we didn't come up here to drink, Boss." Smoke went back into his room to get the ice bucket provided as a courtesy by the hotel.

Doc dialed the Internationale where Otto always stayed. The desk confirmed that they were holding reservations for Mr. Schwartz but he hadn't checked in as yet. Doc left a message for him to call upon arrival.

Smoke came back with some ice and Doc poured the Scotch. He stepped into the bathroom to add a shot of water into each glass. He came back in and handed one to Smoke. They raised their glasses and took a drink.

"How do you think Ross Bigelow took all of the particulars about Hunter's promotion, Doc.?"

"He wasn't all that pleased. I called him into my office while you were at the bank and advised him of Hunter's status. He tried to threaten me in a round-about manner. I just ignored him and went on to tell him that when he got the container to hold thirty degrees or colder for forty-eight hours there would be a bonus in it for him of five thousand dollars. He shut up real quick. I then told him when that occurred I wanted him to hire a couple more people to build up the other three belly boxes we got from Goodyear. Then he was to turn the package over to Pan American for their round-the-world flight that I've arranged. He left my office muttering. Smoke, he's a damn good engineer but suffers from tunnel vision. He wants the bonus bucks, so he'll be okay."

"That accounts for his attitude. I misread it. He must have just been real busy trying to figure out how to finish up. I didn't know you promised him a bonus. You've set my mind to rest. I was concerned," Smoke said.

"Hey, I'm pleased you're taking an interest in our company, Pal. Seriously, I think we have things pretty much under control for our great adventure. That is, if it doesn't last too long."

"You're right about that one, Doc. I just hope Shelly is as under control as the company."

"It's really none of my business and I'm not trying to make it my business but, as your friend, I really have to ask."

"Ask what?"

"Shelly. Are you going to make her an honest woman? You don't act like this is a passing thing. What's going on?"

Smoke wasn't quick to respond. He thought about it for a moment, then said, "Well, the truth of the matter is that I've asked her to marry me a couple of times but she hasn't accepted. This caper we're on now was mentioned as an example of why she's reluctant. I guess that I can't blame her. There hasn't been all that much conversation about it. It comes up. She says something like 'let's not rush into anything', or the like, and changes the subject. She professes to love me and I guess that I love her or it wouldn't have gone as far as it has. But we're not married and there are no plans in the immediate future for us to do that. Answer your question?"

Yeah. Sorry. I didn't mean to pry, Smoke. It's your business and I'm probably the last guy you want to talk to about marriage anyway. It's a wonderful institution. I just didn't enjoy living in an institution."

This last bit of shared wisdom brought a chuckle to both men. Doc and Smoke were just finishing their first drink when the phone rang.

Doc was sitting closest so he answered the telephone. "McGarrity."

"Schwartz here. Meet me in front of my hotel at nine tomorrow morning. I will take you to examine the shipment. Did you bring the funds?"

"The funds will be there, Herr Schwartz, and so will I. Barnes will be with me as well."

"Tomorrow then." Otto Schwartz hung up.

Doc hung up and turned to Smoke. "That arrogant Kraut bastard. I hope Whitey has the money." He paused for a moment to settle down, then continued, "We're to meet Otto at nine tomorrow morning in front of the Internationale. He will take us to examine the shipment. Whitey didn't tell me how to get hold of him or where he would be staying. Did he say anything to you?"

"Not a word other than just do as we always do. Check in, leave word for Otto and then to do as Otto says. Very spook-like, huh?"

"Yeah. Well, fine. Let's go and get a good dinner and hit the sack. Tomorrow should be a very interesting day.

At precisely nine o'clock the following morning, Doc pulled the car up to the portico of the Vancouver Internationale. Otto Schwartz came out of the entrance briskly and got in the back seat. Doc looked over his shoulder in an inquiring manner.

"Just head toward the harbor, and I'll direct you. You have the funds?" Schwartz asked.

"The funds will be there," Doc said as he started driving away from the hotel.

The drive didn't take long, Otto gave explicit directions. Doc kept glancing in the rear view mirror looking for Whitey. He couldn't detect anybody tailing them. Then again, he didn't really expect to be able to spot a tail.

They turned into a section of long warehouses. At Otto's signal, Doc pulled to a stop. Doc, Smoke and Otto Schwartz stepped out of the car and started toward a man-door within a pull-up door in the side of the building. Just as they reached the man-door, another car pulled up. Whitey got out of the car. He was alone. He had a briefcase.

"Guten morgen, Herr Schwartz," he said to Otto.

Otto Schwartz looked as if he had seen a ghost. He couldn't speak. McGarrity was surprised. He had never seen this German lose control, but he was seeing it now. Whitey came up to the three of them. He had the briefcase in his left hand. His right hand was behind his back. He watched Otto Schwartz very closely. Finally, Otto got hold of himself. He held out his right hand and spoke quickly in German. Whitey slowly took his handshake and answered in fluent German. They carried on a conversation neither Doc nor Smoke understood. Then, almost abruptly, Whitey gestured toward the man-door. Otto went over to the door and took out some keys. Finding the one he had been looking for, he inserted it in a new padlock on the door. It was obvious by his nervousness that he was still shook up over seeing Whitey McFrank there. McGarrity wondered just what had taken place between these two in years past. He was willing to bet that it was some kind of story.

They entered the darkened warehouse. Otto walked over to a switch on the wall and turned the overhead lights on. In front of them was a standard forty-foot ocean container. The double doors were open and the container was nearly empty. Spread out on the floor of the warehouse were several crates; some were stacked. They were all marked in German. Prevalent among the marks was the three-pointed star of Mercedes-Benz. It was obvious, even to someone who couldn't read German, that the crates were all identified as automobile or truck parts. Off to one side was a fork lift.

Otto Schwartz directed them over to a group of crates that were separate from the others. These were all spread out, none of them stacked on the other.

"Here is your shipment, gentlemen. Before we start opening crates, would you be so kind as to show me the funds?"

He directed this comment to all three, but more toward Whitey, since he was the only one with a briefcase. Whitey acknowledged the question and walked over to a crate that was waist high, laid the briefcase down, opened it and stepped back. The bills were still in bank-bound bundles, all U.S dollars.

"It's all there, Otto. But you can count it if you wish." Whitey said.

"If you say it is all here, I have no need to count it, Herr McFrank. But I do want you to examine the shipment. I'm rather proud of the condition. All the items on your list have been filled. No substitutions. The shipment is complete."

Whitey nodded, "I would be interested to see some of the more complex items."

Schwartz went over to the ocean container and came back with a crow-bar, hammer and a can of nails. He went to

154

the first crate and, using the crow-bar, opened it quickly. He stood up and gestured for Whitey to examine the contents.

Doc looked at Smoke and shrugged. All of this politeness seemed so incongruous after the security measures Whitey had insisted on. It was a puzzle to both him and to Smoke. They stood back and watched as Otto opened one crate after another. It appeared he was doing it in random order, but the items in each of the crates opened held Whitey's attention. Whitey and Otto were carrying on a conversation in German again. Whatever was going on appeared to please Whitey. The crates that held weapons were given special attention. The guns were new, still in a preservative, not unlike cosmoline. The other opened crates included fully automatic weapons, both hand held and larger sizes, rocket launchers, grenades, and some things that neither Doc nor Smoke recognized. At one point, Whitey gestured for Doc and Smoke to nail back up the crates that had been opened. They carefully resealed the crates. Whitey and Otto finished their examination. Doc and Smoke nailed up the last crate. This had taken the better part of the day. Now it was time to leave.

Whitey told Doc to drive Otto back to the Internationale. Whitey, would call them in two hours. Doc and Smoke were to be there and wait for his call. Whitey kept the briefcase with the money. This didn't seem to disturb Otto. They got in their respective vehicles and drove away.

Smoke and Doc went back to the Bayshore. They had dropped Otto off at the Internationale, on the way. Later, at a meeting in Doc's room, Doc said, "I could use a drink. How about you, Smoke?" Before Smoke could answer, Doc continued, "I'll get the ice this time. Why don't you get out your bottle?"

Doc didn't wait for an answer. He grabbed the ice bucket and headed down the hall to the ice machine on their floor. He was back in a couple of minutes, went over to the sideboard and mixed a couple of Scotches. Turning to Smoke, Doc asked, "What did you make of all that?"

"All of what? The thing between Whitey and the Kraut?"

"Yeah."

"They sure seemed like old, long-lost buddies," Smoke answered, thinking, and went on, "I wish that I understood German."

Smoke and Doc discussed the various weapons and ordnance they had seen. They agreed that for certain: it's one thing to see a list of items and another to see that list filled out and the hardware in front of them. Now they knew what ten thousand pounds of ordnance looked like. There were fewer crates than Doc had imagined. There would be plenty of room for the extra fuel drums that were going to be needed. That had been a concern. Whether or not they would have enough room. As for weight, they were still plenty okay.

The phone rang. Doc glanced at his watch. It would be Whitey. Things usually happened when he said they would. And he only 'said' when he was in control. Doc reached over and picked it up.

"McGarrity," he said into the telephone. It wasn't a long conversation. Doc listened a lot, only replying with short agreements. He hung up and turned to Smoke.

"That was Whitey, of course. He has rented another space a few bays down in the same warehouse where we were today. We're to meet him back there now and move our goods while we have the use of the fork lift. It's rented. Otto wants to load the container with the other items that aren't ours tomorrow and return the fork lift. If we do it now, the move that is, we can have the use of the fork lift. It sure seemed like a plan to me."

"Right. Sounds good to me, too. Let's get on with it." Smoke downed his drink and got up.

It didn't take a lot of time to move the crates. A fork lift makes short work of a ten thousand pound shipment. They were done in a couple of hours. Doc invited Whitey to have dinner with them. He agreed on the condition he could pick the restaurant. Little did Doc and Smoke know that Whitey's taste ran to very hot, spicy Chinese food. Vancouver, B.C. has a large Chinese contingent and Whitey knew just the place. It was quite an evening.

Over dinner, Doc asked Whitey, "I don't understand why Otto let you keep the money after showing us the goods."

"I kept the money because we hadn't taken possession of the goods. That German and I have done business before. He knows my style. He knew I would want to move our portion of the shipment and he trusted me to take only that to which I was entitled. I've arranged to meet him in the morning and will turn over the funds to him then."

"Thanks, I know it wasn't any of my business, it just seemed unusual. As you know, Smoke and I have been dealing with this guy for a while."

"That's okay, and you're right, it isn't any of your business. But I felt you were entitled to know due to the efforts you've both put into this caper. That's it for you two for now. You're free to return to Seattle. We'll get together in Richard's office in two days for final planning. You might want to consider wrapping up any personal loose ends and be ready to leave on short notice."

Whitey took care of the check. They said their goodnights.

Driving back to Seattle the following morning, Doc discussed the logistics of the situation. They would have to fly the C-47 to Vancouver, rent a truck and a fork lift, take everything out to the airport, load it on the airplane, return the truck and fork lift, file a flight plan for somewhere and take off.

157

It sounded simple to talk about. But things are not ever that simple. It had taken them a little over two hours to move everything a hundred feet or so. Maybe the thing to do would be to hire it done. Doc would have to check with Whitey on that one. But if the shipment couldn't pass that degree of exposure, what would the rest of their journey be like.

There were some things to think about, and some further questions that needed answering.

CHAPTER SIXTEEN
FINAL PLANNING

The meeting in Robert's office took place two days later at nine in the morning. Everybody was on time. Whitey was the last one to arrive. Chris Mavis, Robert's secretary, brought him in along with a pot of coffee and enough cups to go around. Harold Roberts, the Seattle CIA Chief of Station, seated everybody around a table in one corner of his expansive office. He turned the meeting over to Whitey.

"Do you lads have everything ready so you can leave at any moment?" Whitey asked of McGarrity and Barnes.

Doc took the initiative in answering, after glancing over at Barnes. "We're set. The only change I have to offer is disposition of funds. I've brought the particulars." With this, Doc handed Roberts a sheet of paper he had removed from his briefcase and continued, "You can see from this, I've given our company secretary my 'power of attorney' and she will not only be running the firm but will handle all of the financial factors we discussed a couple of meetings ago. Barnes is now a major stockholder in my firm, so the disbursement of funds coming to him will also be handled by my office. My secretary, Hunter Herring, does not know that your department of the government is the customer, but I assume the funds will be in the form of a standard government check. You can call her for any specific instructions or information, including our demise, God forbid, or anything else. I repeat, she doesn't know anything about what we're doing, who we're doing it for, or anything else. Just that we're doing a government contract charter and we'll be gone for some time."

Harold Roberts spoke up, "That makes a great deal of sense, Doc. I commend you on its simplicity. I'll see to it that funds are forwarded to your office promptly. The first payment on the day you leave, and subsequent payments thirty days apart, until your return. You owe my office an expense statement for the training costs you incurred."

"Mr. Roberts, I turned it in to Chris when we first arrived," Doc said.

"Good. I'll see to it that it is expedited through the system. I should have it in ten days or so," the CIA Chief of Station replied.

"I would appreciate it if you would identify that expense reimbursement check to Mrs. Herring. She is waiting for these funds to pay our charges at Miller Aviation and to Buck Rowe, who did the training."

"No problem," Roberts replied.

"If all of the financial matters are settled to everyone's satisfaction, can we get down to some final planning?" Whitey said with a noticeable degree of impatience.

"We're all yours, Mr. McFrank," Doc replied.

"I'll be leaving the day after tomorrow. Upon arrival in El Salvador I will determine the best location for the fly-in. You will be notified through this office. I will expect you to be able to give me an ETA by return notification," Whitey was speaking in a slow, very distinct, serious tone of voice, "Does anybody have any problems of any kind with this?"

Doc and Smoke looked briefly at each other, shrugged and nodded assent. Then Doc spoke up, "About customs. This gooney bird has Venezuelan markings, as we all know, and the cargo has paperwork, with the crates all carrying Mercedes-Benz stencils and so forth, but what's to prevent a customs agent from wanting to see a crate opened? The answer is nothing. I submit, gentlemen, the markings on

160

the aircraft will ring too many chimes. Can the company alert U.S. Customs to leave us alone?"

Roberts spoke up, "We don't do things that way, Doc. We can, and would do something after the fact. We would prefer you didn't get caught doing this."

"That's what I thought," Doc said, "As long as we have a few days, I think a plan would be to have Miller, down at Tacoma Industrial Airport, modify the plumbing so we can transfer fuel from the drums 'the company' folks provided for us, into a wing tank on either side, manually with the hand pumps while in flight. The C-47 has a thirteen hundred nautical mile maximum range, no reserve, as it is. It wouldn't take much more to be able to over-fly the States and land in Mexico. Mexican Customs people can be bribed to not look too closely at a cargo. I would hate to try to bribe an American Customs Official."

"How long would it take, Doc?" Whitey asked.

"I'll find out, but I don't think it would take more than a day or two. I'll let you know. But from what you have said, it looks like we have four days, at least."

"Right. Check it out. It just might be a great idea anyway. I can see how it could allow you to transfer enough fuel prior to landing, then be ready for an immediate departure . . . without having to do it....The fuel transfer, after you landed. I like it." Whitey said rather thoughtfully, thinking out loud.

Doc looked over at Whitey. He reached over and laid his hand on Whitey's arm. "I put a pencil to some of this, check it out. The direct distance from Vancouver, B.C. to El Centro California is seven hundred and sixty nautical miles. On down to Mazatlan is another seven hundred and thirty, nautical. We're looking at approximately ten hours of flight time and eleven hundred gallons of fuel. That's allowing for a decent reserve. That puts us pretty heavy out of Vancouver, but we would be dealing with nice heavy, cold air. The military flew the C-47 at a thirty-one thousand pound take-off weight." Doc picked up another sheet of paper out of his open briefcase, glanced at it and continued. "Departing Mazatlan, where it is hot and thinner air, we wouldn't need as much fuel for the leg into El Salvador. It looks like about seven hundred fifty plus, to maybe eight hundred gallons. Hell, that's the existing standard internal fuel capacity of the bird. Filling only four of the six fifty-five gallon drums I'm planning on using, would allow for plenty of reserve."

Whitey turned his head slightly and looked Doc straight in the eyes, "It's really your call, Doc. I understand fuel drums, but what are we talking about here? I thought there were only a couple of drums aboard."

"The company lads put two fifty-five gallon drums on board, tied down all nice and neat, with a hand pump in each one and enough hose to reach out through the over-wing window hatch to the wing tank filler necks on each side of the airplane. It sure wouldn't be too hard to add a couple more drums. There is a lot of room and the fuel weight is three hundred pounds per drum. I figure we'd need a total of six drums for an additional fuel weight of eighteen hundred pounds, out of Vancouver, B.C., like I said. I haven't figured the weight of the empty drums, but it isn't that much." Then, adding with a chuckle, "Sometimes it's just better to not know."

Whitey thought for a minute, then said, "Well, you and Smoke have to live with the situation. I would think twice about smoking in the airplane with that kind of a jury-rigged set-up. But I can really appreciate the advantage it gives you."

"I'll do some hard planning, but I know we could make Cabo San Lucas, in Baja, or Mazatlan, if we wanted to go over to the coast. What do you think would be better for the customs thing, Whitey?"

"Doc, as I recall, La Paz and Mazatlan are both international airports. I would think that Cabo San Lucas would be the least likely to give you much trouble. It's farther away from anything, and they do like green-backs."

"I'll work it out. Thanks for the advice, Whitey."

"For the good of the order." Whitey paused, then continued, "Okay, Gents, when I select the destination field, Roberts here will furnish you with some pretty accurate charts. I'll advise him various landing codes, which he will have for you also. Then you can earn your money. Be careful. Don't arouse a lot of attention and do carry an abundance of dollars. Not much need for credit cards in that part of the world, especially where you'll be going. Any other questions? Comments?" Whitey looked at each one in the room. "Okay, that wraps it up for me. Mr. Roberts, do you have anything to add?"

"No, I think you've covered everything satisfactorily, McFrank. Gentlemen, I'll be in touch when we hear back. I'll arrange to have travel money, charts and whatever else is dictated. Doc, you can add the fuel modifications to the expense voucher you turned in, or just do another one. In fact, do it that way, do another one. I don't want to hold up payment on the training expenses." Roberts rose and held out his hand to the two Marines. He gestured for Whitey to stay.

Doc and Smoke rose also, shook hands with Whitey, then Roberts, and left.

After they left, and the office door was closed, Roberts turned to Whitey, "Washington is questioning your limiting your orders to just three months. Is there some kind of problem, Whitey?"

"No, I felt this was going to be a relatively short caper. State did most of the overall planning and selection of people prior to the company getting involved. As I see it, I'll get the goods to Cordero and cover our interests while he sets up. From there, I would think that the local replacement company man would be able to handle matters. It doesn't appear that much interface will be required. We're supplying and funding the operation. Cordero will really be answering to Cellini. Beyond that, you'll have company people operating out of the embassy, as usual. Have you heard anything about when the replacement will be there?"

"I haven't heard and probably won't be advised. I'm normally out of that loop. But in this case, it would be good to know the timetable. I'll see to that one. In the meantime, I'll relay your thoughts on your guesstimate. However, I get the feeling the agency preference is for a standard six month contract. Is there some specific reason why you don't wish to sign for six months now?"

"Mr. Roberts, with all due respect, keep in mind, I just returned from six months in that part of the world. It isn't my normal sphere of operation. I don't really care for the climate, or the people, or the politics. However, I do what is required. I feel the contract I submitted is worth my requested fee for the period of time specified. If my estimate is wrong, and the company desires my continued involvement on-site, we can cut another contract, or extension. Also, I should mention that I'm thinking about retirement when this operation is put to bed. In short, I'm not anxious to make a career out of El Salvador."

"Well, that's honest enough. I'll pass your feelings up-line, and inquire about a company man replacement schedule."

"Appreciated. If that's it, I have things to take care of before I go. I'll contact you when I'm in-country."

Roberts indicated acknowledgment. And with that, Whitey left the office.

Doc called Ron Miller at Tacoma Industrial Airport and discussed the feasibility of the fuel system modification that he had in mind. Ron pointed out that it was done all the time, especially in Alaska and other remote parts of the world. He explained that the left tank feeds the left engine, the right tank, the right engine. But, as with most multi-engine aircraft, there is a cross-feed system linking the left and right tanks together. Doc knew this, of course, but Ron was leading up to something. He explained, "That cross-feed system is located in the forward part of the wing root. It is accessible just under the floor boards behind the cockpit. What I can do is to tap into the cross-feed line, put in a stand pipe, bringing it up into the cabin. At the cabin end of the stand pipe, I'll install a quick disconnect female fitting and matching male fittings on the hoses that are attached to the two hand pumps. . ."

Doc interrupted, "Ron, just how good are those two hand pumps, with the drums, that are on the airplane? I mean, how fast will they pump?"

"Those are 'rotary barrel pumps', an old design; they've been around forever. They were designed to be used in fifty-five gallon drums. My grandfather used to buy them from the Sears catalog. As best I remember, they are rated at somewhere between ten and fifteen gallons per minute. You had better figure on ten gallons per minute, or something like that. It will take you about eight to ten minutes to pump those drums empty. They won't be dry; the suction pipe is far enough off the bottom to leave a couple of gallons in the barrel. They work pretty good. Your arm will get tired, though."

"Okay, so you're going to put a quick disconnect on the end of the hose and the other half of the quick disconnect on the pipe that you'll bring up into the cabin. So, with this set-up one person can hook up the hose, then go back to the barrel and pump for ten minutes or so and fifty gallons of av-gas goes into the fuel system. That it?"

"Yeah, that's it," Ron replied. He pointed out rather strongly that this would sure make this airplane a non-smoker. It would be hard to get rid of fumes, especially during and after fuel transfer. It could be a spectacular way to end one's life.

"That's fine, Ron, but what are you talking about for the time to do this modification?"

"I'll need at least three days, Doc."

"Sounds good, do it. I'm also going to need another four barrels. Do you have a source for some good ones, clean and suitable for av-gas?"

"I can handle that, Doc. No problem. Like I said, this is done all the time, especially in Alaska."

Doc told him to go ahead.

*   *   *

HEADQUARTERS, CENTRAL INTELLIGENCE AGENCY
Langley, Virginia

Clyde Hayner read the TWX again. He couldn't believe it. Some jerk Marine Colonel from a detachment in Seattle wanted to know what two of "*his men*" were doing with the agency, and why hadn't he been informed, etc., etc. The TWX carried endorsements from HQ, 4th MAW, Glenview, Illinois, forwarding the TWX directly to him, by name. Clyde thought that he had better show this to his Section chief.

Clyde knocked briefly and walked into Peter Jorgensen's office. Peter looked up, "Yes Clyde, what can I do for you?"

"I just received this TWX. Some jarhead Colonel out in Seattle is upset about our two pilots involved in the El Salvador shipment. It came to me by name. How would you like me to handle it?"

Jorgensen read the TWX. "It looks like your two pilots kept their mouths shut. How did these people get your name?"

"It must have come from Colonel Striker, the officer I spoke with at Headquarters Marine Corps. He handled the orders through 4th MAW Glenview." Clyde pointed to the TWX in Jorgensen's hand, "You'll notice the 4th MAW endorsement on the TWX. I didn't have any direct contact with 4th MAW," Hayner said, somewhat defensively.

"Okay. Why not go back through this Striker person, who was obviously bypassed, enclose a copy of this TWX and indicate that our office does not feel that Colonel what's-his- name in Seattle has a 'need to know'. That should frost his cookies, plus Striker will probably add his two bits worth of rebuke, especially when he sees that this clown went around him." Jorgensen handed the TWX back to Hayner.

"I like it. Thanks Chief."

"By the way, how is that program working, Clyde?"

"I spoke with Roberts recently and he informed me that the shopping list had been completed and the goods in-storage in Vancouver, B.C... One of our C-47's from Patrick is up there and the two pilots had received some sort of refresher or something like that, to be able to fly the airplane. They're going to leave in a couple of days. Roberts will let me know."

"Sounds good. Keep me informed."

"Yes Sir." Clyde took his leave. Returning to his desk he took out a message form and addressed it to Colonel Striker, HQ, USMC requesting that he advise Colonel Weston, U.S. Marine Corps, Detachment Commanding Officer, NAS Seattle--via channels; Headquarters Marine Corps, 4th Marine Air Wing, NAS Glenview, that he is to comply with prior orders and that further information is on a "need to know" basis, etc., etc.

He got the TWX out right away.

CHAPTER SEVENTEEN
A MONTH TO GO

Whitey McFrank stood at the top of the American Airlines Boeing 727 rear airstair and breathed in the hot humid air of Central America. *God! He'd never get used to the humidity. He reflected on his recent conversation with Harold Roberts and hoped that, as much as he would like the extra money, this gig would be over in the three months he had estimated. He was in more than sixty days now, as he stood here. El Salvador is one miserable place to have to be. With less than thirty days to go, he could handle it. Okay, stop your bitching, McFrank,* he thought, *let's get off this plane and get the job done that you came down here to do.*

Taking a last breath of what little cool air remained in the 727's cabin he started down the stairs, one of the last passengers to deplane. Walking across the tarmac was like walking across a large griddle. The heat rose in waves. Whitey could almost see mirages in the thirty-yard walk across the ramp to the terminal building. He finally made it. As he reached out for the handle of the door into the terminal, a man stepped out almost in front of him. The man had been standing to one side, watching the passengers as they entered the terminal.

"Señor McFrank?" He asked, although it was obvious he had already identified him.

"Yes, I'm Señor McFrank."

"Come this way please, Señor, there is no need for you to be bothered by customs. We have a car to take you directly to your hotel, courtesy of Señor Cellini

"Do you have some identification?" Whitey asked.

"Of course, Señor." And with that, the man handed Whitey a card with his picture, signed, stamped and sealed in plastic. Whitey recognized Cellini's signature. He handed the card back and motioned for the man to lead the way.

The driver stopped, turned and asked, "Do you have additional luggage, Señor?"

"Yes, two pieces."

"May I have your claim checks, Señor McFrank?"

Whitey reached into his inner jacket pocket and produced his ticket with the baggage claim tags stapled inside the folder. He handed the entire ticket folder to the driver. The driver walked over to the American Airlines baggage carousel, handed the folder to an American Airlines employee and said something to him Whitey couldn't hear. The employee disappeared into a back room and in a minute or two returned with Whitey's two bags. The driver picked up the bags and walked over to where Whitey was still standing.

"These are the correct bags, Señor?"

"Yes."

The driver turned and said over his shoulder, "The car is outside, Señor, if you will kindly follow me."

They passed the passengers who were waiting in line for customs processing. As they walked by the driver nodded to a customs agent, who was standing where he could watch the line of deplaned passengers. The agent motioned them on. They walked the short distance to the main terminal entrance. Parked at the curb directly in front of the entrance was the same black limousine Whitey recognized as one of Alfredo's. Standing beside the car, waiting, was a man in a nondescript uniform. He was wearing a holstered side arm. As the driver and Whitey approached, the guard opened the passenger door and then went to the trunk and opened it. The driver handed him the two bags and went around and got behind the wheel. As the guard was getting into the front seat beside the driver, the driver retracted the partition window between the front and back seats and directed a question to Whitey,

"Your hotel, Señor McFrank?"

"The Camino Real on the Bulevar de Heroes, Driver."

"Gracias." With that, he put the car in gear and pulled away from the terminal.

Arriving at the hotel, the driver retrieved the bags from the trunk. The guard got out of the car, opened the passenger door and was standing looking over the people around the entrance while Whitey got out. The driver handed the bags to a bellman who had appeared quickly, and turned to Whitey.

"Señor Cellini wishes you to call when you are settled, Señor."

"I'll do it, Driver, and thank you for your services." Whitey turned to go and was surprised when the uniformed guard saluted. He returned the salute in an offhand manner and went into the hotel.

Checked in and settled, Whitey called Cellini. After some moments Alfredo came to the phone.

"Ah, Señor White, welcome back to El Salvador. I hope your flight was a pleasant one."

"Yes, a long flight but pleasant. Thank you for asking, Alfredo, and thank you for having the car waiting for me."

"My pleasure Whitey, but if you're feeling rested enough I would be honored if you would be able to dine with me tomorrow evening."

"It is I who would be honored, Alfredo. I'm looking forward to it."

"Fine. I'll send the car, of course. Will seven be a good time for you?"

"Seven will be fine."

"Good. We have much to discuss. Tomorrow evening then, Whitey." Cellini hung up.

Whitey then called the American Embassy and asked for the Cultural Attaché. The call was taken quickly.

"McFrank at the Camino Real, room 212." Whitey said. The information was acknowledged and he hung up.

The next evening the car was on time. As Whitey walked out the main door of the Hotel Camino Real, it was pulling up in front. The right front door of the black limousine opened and the same uniformed guard jumped out and opened the passenger door. Again, he saluted as Whitey got into the car. Whitey acknowledged with more of a wave than a returned salute. They drove away.

At seven o'clock in the evening it was starting to cool down. The city of San Salvador was beginning to come alive. Traffic was picking up and there appeared to be more people out and about. They arrived at the fenced estate and were quickly passed through onto the estate grounds. The car followed the same route Whitey had traversed before; S-curves winding through the manicured foliage, forcing a slower passage. As the car pulled up at the main entrance of the large house another uniformed guard, who had been waiting, opened the rear door and saluted as Whitey stepped out. Whitey acknowledged the salute and thought that on this trip he was being rendered military honors for the first time in all of his visits to the estate and duty time served in this country. Unusual. He might ask Cellini if the opportunity presented itself.

As before, Whitey was escorted into the mansion, and down a hall to Cellini's office. He was shown in immediately. Cellini was behind his desk, but stood and came around when Whitey came in.

"Señor McFrank, I'm so happy you could make it. Come, have a seat and I'll fix you a drink. Scotch whiskey?"

"That will do nicely, thank you." Whitey watched as Señor Cellini went over to a service bar along one wall, then continued, "But, if you don't mind my asking, how did you know that I would be on that specific flight?"

Cellini turned, while still fixing the drinks, "I don't mind you asking. I spoke with your Mr. Jorgensen in Washington. He checked with someone and then called me back. I rather thought you would be pleased if someone met you at the airport. Did I offend you?" He turned back and finished with the drinks. He walked over and handed one to Whitey.

"No, I was just surprised. Very few people knew I was on that flight. And yes, I was pleased to be met and to avoid the hassle of customs. It was a nice gesture. Thank you."

"My pleasure, Whitey. After all, you are an invited guest in my country again and I felt you should be treated like one."

"One small question, if I may?"

Señor Cellini gestured for him to continue.

"Your men have saluted me on more than one occasion. Perhaps you can throw a little light on the situation to satisfy my curiosity."

Cellini laughed and then said, "But Señor, it is because I told them you are a very high ranking officer in the forces of the United States, but preferred to travel in civilian clothes. It was intended to bestow honor."

Now it was Whitey's turn to laugh, and he did. Lifting his glass in a mock salute he replied, "The honor is taken and appreciated Alfredo. Thank you."

"And now, Whitey, I must report to you that Colonel Cordero is in El Salvador and has purchased a ranch, which he intends to use as a base of operations. Are you familiar with the area north of here, near San Julian?"

"I know where San Julian is, but I wouldn't say I was familiar with that part of the country." Whitey said.

Señor Cellini continued, "The property is at the fifteen hundred foot elevation, about a hundred acres and has a small landing strip. It was formerly owned by a family member. It is quite nice. I know the Colonel is anxious to meet you face to face, and is looking forward to working with you. I could have someone fly you out there whenever you would like to go. It is about twenty five miles North of San Salvador, but a fairly long drive and over secondary roads for the most part."

"That would be very kind of you. I'll let you know when I would like to go out to his ranch. Has he started work on his project?" Whitey set his near empty glass down.

"I believe he has. He has been here a little over two months. I hear that he has enlisted several men, besides the men he brought with him. May I freshen your drink?" Cellini said as he got up and started toward the service bar.

Whitey handed him his glass, "Make it a light one, please."

"The family is very pleased with the promptness your company has shown in getting the Colonel here. I understand there is a shipment of some sort on its way also. Do you know when it will be arriving?" Cellini said this with his back toward Whitey. With the last question he turned and looked directly at him.

Whitey was surprised at the depth of knowledge Cellini had of this operation. He managed to not show it. Peter Jorgensen must have told him. "That is one of the first things that I will be doing, arranging for a delivery spot. We didn't think it would be wise to bring arms into the international airport here, in San Salvador. Do you have any suggestions, Alfredo?"

"Of course. And I agree. It would cause undue concern even though all of this special force activity is for the good of the government. El Presidente has been very aggressive with reforms. Enforcing customs and the flow of unauthorized goods into the country falls under that action. I assume you will be flying the cargo in a company airplane, not a commercial airliner." Whitey nodded in the affirmative. Cellini continued. "You might consider looking

173

at the landing strip at the Colonel's ranch. Do you know what type of aircraft will be used?"

"Yes I do. It will be a C-47. Do you happen to know how long that small landing strip is?"

"As I recall, it is about twenty-five hundred feet long. It is more than enough for a C-47 if the pilots have any skill at all."

"I know both pilots first hand. Not a problem. This sounds like an answer to one of my primary concerns. I had best take a look at it. Perhaps the day after tomorrow I could take you up on your offer to fly me out."

There was a soft knock at the closed door to the study.

"Come in," Cellini said in Spanish.

A servant came part way into the room and announced that dinner was ready. Cellini rose and gestured for Whitey to follow the servant. In the foyer, they were met by Señora Cellini and their daughter, Isabell Antoinette. The daughter had grown into a beautiful young woman since Whitey had seen her last. He was quite taken aback and it didn't go unnoticed.

"Señor McFrank, it is a pleasure to see the gentleman who used to bounce me on his knee look so surprised. Have I changed that much?" She asked, rather coyly.

"Yes. I'm stunned by the beauty you have grown into. You were always that cute little girl to me, Isabella," Whitey managed to say, using the more intimate name.

"My friends call me Toni now Señor McFrank, and you may also."

"I'm honored." Whitey said with great dignity as he took her arm and they continued into the dining room.

Dinner was a pleasant affair. Señora Cellini was a gracious hostess and the meal a work of culinary art. After the relaxing but lengthy dinner Señor Cellini and Whitey excused themselves and took brandy and cigars in Cellini's study.

174

"Señor Cellini, you have been blessed with two very beautiful women in your life. Your wife and your daughter," Whitey said.

"And I must agree, Whitey. Isabell has indeed grown into the mirror beauty of her mother. I was amused by the startled look on your face. You are not easily surprised Señor."

No further business was discussed. Two old friends discussing life, beautiful women and good brandy. All in all, a very pleasant evening.

Whitey was later driven back to the El Camino Real Hotel.

The following afternoon Whitey called Señor Cellini. He was put through immediately.

"Alfredo, Whitey McFrank. Thank you again for a most delightful evening. I would like to take you up on your kind offer to fly me out to Colonel Cordero's ranch."

"Whitey, it would be my pleasure. When would you like to go?"

"Tomorrow morning, early, if it would be convenient."

"My car will be in front of your hotel at seven, if that is early enough, Señor."

"That will be just fine, Alfredo. I am in your debt."

"Señor White, I have been known to call my debts…"

"….and I pay my debts," Whitey interjected and uttered a rare chuckle.

Cellini laughed. "Yes, I'm sure that you do. Señor White, please call me upon your return."

"I will. Thank you again for your kind assistance." Whitey hung up.

CHAPTER EIGHTEEN
A PIECE OF CAKE

The Cessna 206 arrived over the ranch at thirty-five hundred feet. The pilot pointed out the boundaries. The land surrounding the ranch was arid and appeared to be rocky. Immediately to the south side of the landing strip the terrain started to rise, continuing up into a good sized mountain. The ranch and landing strip were on a small plateau. Northwest of the ranch, over some good sized hills, lay the small town of San Julian. To the north and east lay more hills and some mountains. It was fairly rugged country.

Cellini's driver had been out in front of the hotel promptly at seven o'clock that morning. He drove to the airport, turning in at the General Aviation side and up to a flight service facility. When asked, the driver told him that it was owned by Señor Cellini.

Thanking the driver, Whitey went into the office. He was met by a good-looking young man who introduced himself as Raul Arango. He was to be Señor McFrank's pilot this cloudless morning. The pilot's attitude was warm and friendly. Whitey took to him right away. As it turned out, he was also an excellent pilot.

The flight out to the ranch was uneventful. The pilot chatted about his work, the fact that he was fortunate to have the good job that he had. Whitey asked if he flew with Señor Cellini much. The answer was that it was more frequent now that Señor Cellini was busier and didn't have time to stay as sharp as he would like. Raul was quick to add that Señor

Cellini was a very good pilot, but also a careful one. It was evident that Raul liked and respected his employer.

When they arrived at the ranch, the pilot flew down the runway to the east and did a left hand orbit, then flew down the runway west and did a right hand orbit. Whitey asked him what he was doing.

"This is the prescribed procedure, Señor McFrank. Colonel Cordero has issued warnings that no one is to land without prior permission and prior to landing, will fly the pattern that I just did. You will note, Señor, there are X's on each end of the runway. That is the international symbol showing that the airport is closed to landing traffic," the pilot replied.

As they were completing the pre-landing maneuvers Whitey asked, "What are your orders? Will you be staying and waiting or coming back for me, Raul?"

"My instructions were to leave you and return at your call, Señor."

"Good. Do you own a camera?"

"Si, it is a 35mm from Japan. They make wonderful cameras."

"When I call for your return, I would like you to take a roll of pictures of the landing strip and the area around it, such as *you* would like to have as a pilot flying into this field for the first time. Also, the buildings adjacent to the strip. Can you do that? I will be happy to pay you for your trouble."

"Señor McFrank, it would be my pleasure to perform such a favor for you. I would not be able to accept any payment. I will shoot a roll of thirty-six exposures. Will one roll be enough?"

That would be fine. I appreciate your assistance," Whitey was pleased and not averse to showing it. "I would like to show my gratitude in some manner, however."

"Perhaps a word to Señor Cellini....if you insist on showing your gratitude, Señor." the pilot hesitated not wanting to appear presumptuous.

"I will mention your assistance and flying ability personally to the head of the Catorce Familias."

While they had been talking, the pilot had been working his way down into a normal landing pattern. He turned to the east on a final approach and touched down gently on the west end of the runway.

Whitey noticed that the pilot had to apply power in order to taxi down to the east end of the runway where the buildings were located. He then pulled off of the runway on a pad and swung the airplane around with the tail toward the buildings. As the pilot was shutting down the engine Whitey asked him the length of the runway and the field elevation.

"Almost twenty-five hundred feet long, Señor, and about fifteen hundred foot elevation," the pilot answered, pointing to the altimeter. It indicated fourteen hundred and eighty feet.

As they were getting out of the airplane five men appeared carrying automatic weapons and one rather casually well dressed, quasi-military garbed gentleman. Whitey thought him to be *"the Coronel Cordero"*. Whitey walked around the tail of the airplane. As he did the one that he suspected was Cordero came forward with his hand out.

"Welcome to Rancho San Julian de Cordero, Señor McFrank. I am Coronel Emilio Raphael Cordero. We finally meet."

Whitey McFrank took his hand and studied this man standing in front of him. *This man that had requested him by name to be his in-country contact and liaison. Whitey wasn't sure he liked what he saw. Outward appearances were about as expected; five foot eight in height, trim figure, black hair--like most Latinos--and very black eyes. A smile was there, but it lacked warmth. Enough for now. Time will tell what this one is all about,* Whitey thought.

"Yes, we finally do meet. I must admit, Colonel, I was a little surprised that you knew me by name. I do not believe our paths have crossed."

Colonel gestured toward the hacienda. Whitey fell into step beside his host.

As they walked toward the ranch house Cordero answered Whitey's question. "We know some of the same people in Europe, Señor. Yours is an unusual name and when I heard it in connection with this fine little country I remembered it from other conversations. I sincerely hope that you were not offended at my request." The Colonel led Whitey into the large adobe ranch house.

"Not offended, Colonel, merely curious," Whitey turned his head and listening, noticed that the airplane had started its engine and was apparently getting ready to return to San Salvador. "The airplane is going back. I hadn't really intended to spend the night, Colonel."

"Oh, but you're my guest, Señor. We have much to discuss and what better way than in the seclusion and security of my own ranchero." The Colonel said this as a statement of fact, rather than a question. "And given more time, perhaps you would join me in hunting some jabali. My men have spotted quite a few of the wild boars on the ranch. Have you ever hunted pig, Señor McFrank? It can be quite an adventure."

"Only the two-legged variety, Colonel. But, as you say, given more time, it could be interesting."

"Then we must do that sometime. But come, let me show you to your room. I think we can fit you into something more appropriate for a tour of the ranchero. I have some men training for our upcoming missions. Do you ride, Señor? Or would it be easier to take a jeep?"

"Yes, I do ride, but given a choice, I believe I would prefer the jeep," Whitey said as they stopped at a door.

` "Here we are, Señor McFrank. My men have laid out some clothes for you and some boots that might fit you.

When you have changed, rap on the door and one of my men will bring you to me."

Whitey opened the door, noticing the key to his room was on the outside. The room was large. It contained a very large bed with ornately carved head and foot boards, a writing desk, three chairs, a closet and small window. A closer look revealed that the window had very heavy, but somewhat ornate, bars on the outside. In one corner was a small fireplace. In the other corner was a door leading into a connected bathroom.

Whitey carefully examined the room. The door jamb into the room from the hall had poorly concealed contact strips, which would send a signal somewhere every time the door was opened or closed. He located two pin-hole cameras and two listening devices. Cordero was very careful about keeping track of his guests.

On the bed were three pairs of khaki pants, three khaki, and military-type short-sleeve shirts and beside the bed were three pairs of knee-high boots. Whitey picked up one of the boots. It was beautiful; the leather; soft and supple. The smell indicated that the tanning had been done with great care. Whitey quickly changed. The clothes were sized incrementally and, after trying various combinations, he found a good fit. The middle pair of boots fit as if they had been custom made for him. He was ready. He went over to the door and rapped twice, as he had been asked to do. It was quickly opened. Whitey went out and followed the guard down the hall to where he was to rejoin Cordero.

The guard turned into a room at the end of the long hall. It was a large room off of a kitchen. It appeared that it had at one time been a room for the servants; eating, lounging or the like. Now it was being used as a briefing room. When Whitey entered he saw Cordero speaking with eight troops. Standing behind them were three other troops in a slightly different garb. They made Whitey think of senior noncoms in a U.S. outfit. Cordero turned when he noticed Whitey enter.

"Señor McFrank, you appear to be ready. Do the clothes and boots fit all right?"

"Yes, they do. Thank you." Whitey said rather crisply.

"Good. We can go then." The Colonel turned and said something in Spanish to one of the men standing in the back and then gestured for Whitey to follow. They went out another door to the outside at the rear of the ranch house. There was a jeep there and a trooper with an automatic weapon, standing beside it. The Colonel said something in Spanish to him and he got in the back seat. Cordero gestured for Whitey to get in the front seat and Cordero went around and got behind the wheel. As he started the engine he said, "We can speak freely in English, my man doesn't understand a word."

"Colonel Cordero, I was a bit surprised that you asked me to rap on the door prior to coming out. Are there special reasons for this? The door wasn't locked. Will I be sleeping in that room with a locked door tonight?" Whitey spoke rather bluntly and was obviously annoyed.

A burst of laughter broke from Colonel Cordero as he wheeled the jeep around the side of the house and drove across the east end of the runway. He was headed for a road that started there and went up the high ground on the south side of the airstrip. "Señor McFrank, do not be upset. The ranchero is very secure at night. I have roving patrols and the locked room is for your own protection. Some of my people are new and still a bit nervous. You saw some of them back in the briefing room. Naturally, the new ones stand the guard duty at night. You do not want to be roving around, inside or outside the house. If it bothers you, feel free to take the key to your room inside. Then you can lock it or leave it, as you wish. However, I would caution you about leaving your room."

"I'll do that. And it was not my intention to do any roving, as you put it. I can appreciate your need for security." Whitey was not completely satisfied with the Colonel's answer.

"We observe a strict curfew after dark and in the house when I retire for the evening. But enough about that. When can I expect the shipment of my requested items? I have been informed that you are coordinating the delivery."

"The shipment will be arriving by C-47. Now that I have seen your airstrip, there's no reason why they cannot be brought directly in here. Your strip is about twenty-five hundred feet long and no obstructions at either end. I was going to have the shipment brought into a remote strip. We did not think it a good idea to come directly into San Salvador. The present regime appears to be somewhat particular about arms shipments into and out of the country. If you do not object, I'll advise my office to get the flight headed down. As soon as I know their itinerary I will advise you."

"The sooner the better." Colonel Cordero was delighted and it showed.

They spent the rest of the morning touring the ranch. One of the out buildings had a large room that had been converted to a martial arts arena. Cordero was proud to show it off. Whitey recognized it for what it was immediately and commented.

"What discipline do you follow, Colonel Cordero?" He asked.

"I have the good fortune to have earned a Black Belt in Karate. Before that I was a student of Ju-Jitsu. Are you a student of martial arts, Señor McFrank?"

"Yes, I have earned some recognition in Karate. It is a relaxing exercise discipline."

"I would be honored to have a match with you some time, Señor McFrank."

"Perhaps we can do that, Colonel.

They returned to the ranch house for a lunch break. The Colonel had been saving the best for the last. In the early afternoon they drove over to an area where some temporary huts had been erected. There were about a dozen on each side of a mocked up 'street-like' area. The Colonel parked the jeep on a point of higher ground where they could see most of the make-shift village. They were no sooner in place when a truck drove onto the street and stopped. Sixteen men in two strings of eight leaped out of the back of the covered truck and quickly went down each side of the street. Less than thirty seconds were spent at each hut. It went like clock-work. In a matter of minutes the village would have been secured.

Whitey was impressed and said so. He then asked how long the men had been training. The Colonel told him that it had been a little over three weeks. It was obvious he was very proud of the progress his men had made.

"Once secured, what is your next step, Colonel?"

"We gather all of the villagers into the center of town. All of them. Women, children and the men, including the village priest. Then we discuss with the villagers the folly of assisting these 'Castroites' by providing food and shelter to them," the Colonel replied smugly. He was looking at Whitey straight on. Neither of them said anything for a while.

Whitey turned back to the action that was still taking place in front of them. He nodded and said, "Yes, they must learn that they are much better off under the Catorce Familia than they ever would be under a Castroite communist regime. They must be told."

The Colonel started the jeep and they drove back across the runway and to the other end of the property. They finished the tour and got back to the ranch house in time to get cleaned up and ready for dinner. The meal was excellent, the brandy adequate and then it came time for bed.

Upon retiring, Whitey took the key inside and locked the door. He mentally reviewed the events of the day. Colonel Cordero's attitude about discussing the Castroites with the villagers didn't quite ring true. The look in his eyes did not appear to be educational in any way. Quite the contrary. There was a real mean streak in this one, Whitey thought.

He slept lightly.

Over breakfast the following morning Whitey discussed the weapons flight. Colonel Cordero said that due to the terrain it would be much safer to come in during the day. Several aircraft pass overhead or over the valley to the north of the ranch. He didn't feel that an airplane on the runway would draw any undue attention. Especially a DC-3 with Latin American markings.

McFrank advised Cordero that he would arrange to be here when the DC-3 was scheduled to arrive. They would stay in touch.

Whitey asked for a telephone and called the telephone number Cellini's pilot had given him when he was ready to be flown back to San Salvador. The pilot said he would be there within the hour.

Colonel Cordero suggested they finish their coffee on a patio off of the dining room. It was a pleasant place, a small walled, garden. Being early, and at this altitude of fifteen hundred feet, it was comfortable. They would be able to hear the airplane from a distance. Whitey had changed back into the clothes he wore upon arrival. The Colonel graciously suggested that Whitey should keep the boots, if the fit was to his liking. And the clothes. Whitey thanked his host, commenting on the quality of the boots.

The plane arrived within the hour and a short time later Whitey was on his way back to San Salvador. Once they were airborne the pilot handed Whitey his camera.

"I took thirty-six exposures, Señor, of the landmarks that I, as a pilot, would be interested in. I took some pictures

184

from the air of the buildings on the ranch and surrounding area, and then from the ground, as I was taxiing down to the east end.

"It is much appreciated. I will speak to Señor Cellini, as I said," Whitey replied. "This is a very good camera, Raul. I'm certain that the pictures will turn out just fine. Would you like me to remove the film?"

"It hasn't been re-wound. Feel free to do that, or I will after we land."

Arriving at the hotel, Whitey called for a cab and took it to the American Embassy. Upon arrival he took the film downstairs to the area reserved for the intelligence people. It was very plain, no decor, merely concrete and fluorescent lighting. All the embassies he had operated out of were the same. Not unlike the ancient catacombs under European churches. Whitey had always felt that it was like some archaic dungeon; concrete floors and walls, no windows, heavy steel doors. All of which was necessary for the security of coding machines, radio rooms and the other things required for modern intelligence operations.

He went into the photo lab and arranged for the film development and standard eight by ten enlargements. He then put together a dispatch for the Seattle office. It would go out that night. The message explained the landing strip at the ranch and that photos and negatives would be forthcoming in the daily diplomatic pouch. It would take three days for the pictures to get to the Seattle office.

This change in landing site would simplify things greatly; no worry about coordination with ground personnel, customs or any of the other potential threat factors. It would be simple. Land at the ranch, unload, take-off again and land at San Salvador International to clear customs, refuel and return to the States. How do the aviators say it? *'A piece of cake!'*

CHAPTER NINETEEN
TIME TO GO

Ron Miller was as good as his word. The fuel transfer modification to the C-47 was essentially ready in the three days he had said it would take. He told Doc there were a couple of minor items remaining, but it could be flight tested. It was another day before Doc could get down to Tacoma to check things out. He called Smoke and asked him to come along to look things over. They discussed Miller's suggestion and agreed that it might be a good idea to flight test before leaving.

Miller had put in the quick disconnects they had talked about. He found a type that was essentially leak-proof. This would go a long way to holding down the fumes. Miller had picked up the additional four fifty-five gallon drums Doc asked him to find and installed them neatly and securely. The two hand-pumps and hoses 'the company' people had provided screwed into the original two drums. Miller modified the four new drums to the same configuration. The hoses would reach the modified cross feed valve from any of the drums. Ron had removed the original nozzles from the hoses and changed the ends to the new leak-proof quick disconnects. He had then installed the appropriate end fitting to the nozzles in the unlikely event that the crew wanted to use the hoses as originally intended, out a window and over the wing to a filler cap. Doc was very pleased with the thoroughness and quality of work Miller had done.

Doc and Smoke took the airplane up for a test flight. While Doc flew, Smoke went in the back and hooked up one of the drums to the cross feed valve. He transferred fuel easily. The hand pump worked effortlessly, and it didn't take long to pump fifteen or twenty gallons of AvGas from the drum into the cross feed valve and hence into the wing fuel cells. All of the aircraft fuel cells had been full when they taxied out. There wasn't much room to transfer. Smoke insisted that Doc try it.

"Bullshit!" Doc said, "I'm the aircraft commander. That's co-pilot work!"

"Hey, Asshole! Don't start pulling rank on me now, 'Ol Buddy. What if something happens to me? You've got to know how to do this." Smoke replied rather indignantly.

"Okay, all right, climb back up here and take the airplane. I'll give it a try. How many drums are full?"

Smoke came up forward and climbed into the right seat, "I think all of them are full, Doc. I signed the gas chit that Ron handed me and it sure had a lot of fuel on it. He topped off everything in the bird. He does sell fuel, you know. You'll only be able to pump fifteen or twenty gallons. This operation has represented a lot of revenue to Miller over the past few months. Don't you remember how he had the gas boy sticking a hose into one of the wing tanks before the props stopped turning when we'd return from a training flight?"

"You're right. Well, what do I do? Just clamp the other hose into the cross feed valve and start to pump?"

"That's it, Boss. Just turn the hand pump until you feel it pumping; it has to build up a little suction." Smoke said as he slipped into the co-pilot's seat.

"Right. Okay, you've got it," Doc indicated the passing of flight control to Smoke.

Smoke acknowledged by patting the wheel.

Doc climbed out of the left seat and went aft, disconnected the hose Smoke had used, got the other hose and connected it to the cross feed valve and went over to the drum the hose was connected to and started pumping. He was pleasantly surprised at how easy it was. Doc yelled over the sounds of the engines, "Hey, this is a piece of cake!"

Smoke yelled back to him, "Right. And I don't smell any fumes up here and I didn't smell anything while I was pumping. Do you smell any fumes?"

"Just a trace. It isn't bad. I think if we're careful and get some fresh air blowing through the cabin for a while after transferring fuel we could probably smoke. What do you think?"

"That sounds like a plan. I don't want to think about spending over a dozen hours in this tin can piece of shit and not being able to smoke!"

Doc kept pumping. "I think you're right. I don't want to think about it either." As he finished yelling this last comment up to Smoke he felt some resistance. He was through transferring fuel. "Damn, this works good!" He disconnected the hose, put it away and made his way back up to the cockpit.

Smoke glanced over at him as he slid into the left seat, "See? Now aren't you glad you tried it? By the way, whose turn is it for the landing?"

"I don't remember, but you can have it. Just don't be too good and make me feel bad. Compre? Keemo-Sabi? Uh, do you want the left seat?"

"No, this will do just fine. I'm going to start downhill. How about the 'Descent' and then the 'Before Landing' check lists?"

"Righto Cap'n," Doc said as he got out the check lists.

Smoke's landing did piss off Doc. It was a greaser. They taxied in. Ron met them and then the fuel truck pulled up and Ron's gas boy started topping off the wing tanks. Smoke motioned out his side and then turned to Doc, "See? Ron sure likes to sell fuel."

They finished the securing procedures and check lists and climbed out. Ron was at the back door to meet them.

"Everything work for you, Doc? Any gripes?" Ron Miller asked.

"It all worked just fine. There was very little fume generation, Ron. Those quick disconnects work well. The rest of the bird is okay. Have your lad check and fill the drums in the cabin. I expect we'll probably be leaving either tomorrow or the day after. Please send the bill into my office as soon as you can."

"Right Doc, be happy to. I'm going to miss you fellows. Any idea when you'll be back?"

"Not at the moment. Probably in a couple of weeks. We've got to get a move on, Ron. Thanks again for a job well done. You do nice work."

"Thanks. Do you want a system schematic to take with you? I could make one up for you."

"No, that won't be necessary. We've tested the system and it works okay. Kinda simple and straightforward, wouldn't you say?"

"Yeah, it is that," Ron replied.

Doc and Smoke made their farewells and walked across the ramp over to their cars.

When Doc got home he checked with his answering service. Hunter had insisted that he get one since he was keeping such irregular office hours. When he and Smoke left, all of his calls would be retrieved by Hunter and handled as best she could. Doc wasn't worried. They didn't have much working that couldn't wait. Smoke had taken care of the Aer Lingus thing. Everything else was just essentially tire kicking.

His service told him that he had a call from his father. This was the agreed upon signal for him to call Roberts. Doc's father had been dead for years. (If he did get a call from him it would certainly be long distance.) Doc called Roberts and then Smoke.

"My dad called, Smoke. We're to meet downtown at nine in the morning and check out the situation. I believe the mail has arrived." *Doc loved this spook talk. It made him feel like Bogart.*

"Sounds like a plan, Doc. Shelly has an early flight in the morning anyway. Do you think we'll be leaving right away?"

"Yeah, I kind of think so. You had best have your going away party tonight, if you're up to it, 'Ol Buddy."

Smoke chuckled, "Well, if I don't show up, you'll know why." He hung up still laughing.

At nine the following morning both Doc and Smoke were sitting outside of Robert's office being served a cup of coffee by Chris Mavis. She kept looking at Smoke. Finally she said, "My God, Mr. Barnes, are you all right? You look just terrible."

Doc started laughing, Smoke turned bright red and about that time Roberts opened his door and motioned them both to come into his office. Doc was still laughing as they went in.

"Is it a private joke, gentlemen?" Roberts asked.

Doc answered for the two of them, "Well, sort of. Smoke had quite a night last night and your lovely secretary was concerned for his health. I think she wanted to call an ambulance."

Roberts cleared his throat and then said, "I see. Are you well enough to fly, Harry?"

"Yes Sir. I'm just a bit tired. I didn't get much sleep last night." This caused another outburst of laughter from Doc.

"Very good then, because it appears that our Mr. McFrank would like you two to get started as soon as you can. Doc, is the airplane ready to go?"

"Yes it is, Sir. We could leave today. I have made arrangements with a moving firm in Vancouver. They will

190

pick us up at the airport when I call, drive to the warehouse and load the crates on a truck and back to the airport. It shouldn't take more than a couple of hours. Our flight time to Vancouver is less than an hour. Once loaded, I want to take-off immediately. I don't want to take any chances of somebody getting nosy. All of the paperwork is in order. I'll file a flight plan to Caracas, via Cabo San Lucas and San Salvador. We won't have to touch down in the States. Somewhere between Cabo San Lucas and San Salvador, we'll drop out of radar contact and divert into whatever jungle strip Whitey has arranged for us. That's where the planning is to date."

"Well, it won't be a jungle strip. You two had better take a look at the mail that came in yesterday. The situation has improved immensely. Colonel Cordero, who will be receiving the goods, has recently purchased a very large ranch some twenty-five miles north of San Salvador. It has a landing strip about twenty-five hundred feet long. Take a look at this map." Chief of Station Roberts directed their attention over to the table in his office. He had spread out the map and pictures that Whitey had sent up in the company pouch.

After a few minutes of examining the material Doc directed a comment to Roberts, "This does simplify things, doesn't it?" Redirecting his attention to Smoke he said, "The runway runs east and west with good clearance at both ends. The only obstacles appear to be the high ground just south of the strip."

Barnes commented, "Whoever took these pictures sure knew what a pilot would want to see. He got everything that I would need anyway."

"You're right, Smoke." Doc agreed, handing each of the eight by ten enlargements to Smoke as he finished looking them over.

"I assume, Gentlemen, that this gives you all you need to know to get the job done," Roberts said, and then added, "McFrank would like a rather tight itinerary. He wants to be at the ranch when you arrive."

Doc took a paper out of his briefcase. "Here's the flight planning data. We're an hour from Vancouver. Three hours to load and refuel. Once airborne from Vancouver we're approximately ten hours to Cabo San Lucas. I figure two to three hours to clear customs and refuel, then another six and a half hours to the ranch. I had planned six plus forty-five minutes from Cabo San Lucas to San Salvador. I'll run a copy of this flight plan log for you." Doc showed the flight log to Roberts who nodded in understanding. "Why not this? We'll fly to Vancouver late today, refuel tonight, get a good night's sleep and load in the morning. I'll call the moving company this afternoon and arrange to have a crew meet us at seven in the morning. You can count on our being airborne by ten. We have sixteen or seventeen hours of flying but we can handle that in a one-day period. The only variable will be the time on the ground in Cabo San Lucas and whatever complications arise with the customs people. If we run into any problems I can call here, unless I'm in jail for moving arms around."

"I'll give you a number to call," Roberts said. He went over to his desk and took out a small notebook. "Here, write this down: 'five, five, five, eight four six zero'. That's a secure number. And, it would be a good idea to call when airborne out of Vancouver and then again when clear of Cabo San Lucas....on the HF radio." He glanced up at McGarrity in a questioning manner. Doc didn't respond. "The frequencies are listed on the documents I will give you. Someone will monitor the frequencies during the times listed. As you know, HF is subject to time-of-day shift"

Doc jotted down the number. "Yeah, we're all checked out on the radio. It won't be a problem. Can I use this phone number that you just gave me, on the flight plan for a contact number?"

"That'll be okay. We'll answer the phone number as Acme Freight Company. The same with the HF. We'll be Acme Base, you'll be Acme Flight. It will work just fine." Roberts was pleased. "I have funds, in cash, for you." He handed Doc a large envelope.

Doc took it. It was surprisingly heavy. "How much is in here, Sir?"

"Twenty-five thousand dollars in various sized bills. Please keep track of your expenses. I'll have to account for it. Which means that you two will have to account for it to me, or it will be deducted from your fee. That's the way it works. You won't need to ask for a receipt for any bribe money you give to the Mexican customs man." Roberts was attempting a bit of humor. Nobody laughed.

"I'll take good care of this, Sir. We'll get receipts for things. We both know what an expense account is. We're not on Per-Diem are we?" Doc asked as an after-thought.

Roberts chuckled. "No, you are on what we call 'actuals'. And I'm sure that you'll do just fine. I have the other charts and aerial approach plates for Mexico and Central America that you requested. They're in this packet here." Roberts said this as he handed Smoke the map packet. "I didn't ask for charts and approach plates for the United States. You said that you had them."

"Right. We have all of those. I really appreciate your getting these for us, Mr. Roberts. We could have probably gotten them through the NAS Seattle Operations Department, but it would have raised some questions," Doc said.

They wrapped up their meeting, Roberts wished them the best of luck and they were out the door. Standing at the elevator Doc asked Smoke when he wanted to leave.

"It's almost noon now. Why not go home and pack and get going?" Smoke asked.

Doc thought about it for a minute before answering. The elevator arrived and they went in and punched the button for the lobby. "Okay. I still have a couple of things to do. I want to stop by the office on the way. In fact, I'll do that now. Do you want to stop by with me?"

"No, I checked with Hunter yesterday and my stuff is clear. The Aer Lingus thing is handled. I'll just meet you at the field. You have any idea what time you can get there?"

The elevator stopped at the ground floor. They walked outside and stood on the steps to finish their conversation. Doc answered Smoke's question, "I can be there by three. Do you want to handle the pre-flight and flight plan?"

"Sure, I can do that. You go ahead and do your things. I'll file for a fifteen hundred hour departure for Vancouver.

"Okay, I'll call the moving company from the office and verify the arrangements that I have talked over with them. They have a flatbed truck and a fork lift on a trailer that they tow behind their truck....or something like that. He told me, but I don't remember all the details. If we refuel in Vancouver tonight and they meet us at seven in the morning, we could get airborne by ten with any luck at all."

"Let's do it. I'm parked up the hill, so I'll see you at the airplane," Smoke said.

Doc drove over to his apartment on Queen Anne Hill. It only took him about a half an hour to pack. He checked his refrigerator for potential culture sources and threw out a couple of things. There was a full half gallon of milk, a couple of steaks and an unopened package of hamburger. He took the milk and foodstuff across the hall and gave it to his neighbor. He told her that he'd be out of town for a while and asked her if she could keep an eye on things. His neighbors were a struggling young couple with a little girl. The wife was at home during the day since their little girl wasn't in school yet. Doc traveled a lot and it was his habit to give them any food that wouldn't keep. They appreciated the occasional treats.

Fifteen minutes later Doc pulled into his parking place at Aries Enterprises. When he went into the office Hunter looked up expectantly, gathered up her notepad and followed him into his office.

"Well, this is it, Hunter. Smoke and I are gone for a bit. I'll try to call but I'm not sure what the situation will be at the other end, so I don't know when I'll be able to get to a phone. However if anything comes up, call this number. They'll answer as Acme Freight and will be able to contact us by HF radio and will know how to find us." Doc could see the questioning look on Hunter's face. "You have some questions I take it."

"It doesn't sound like a government office to me, Doc. Just some strange deal you're involved in. I guess you know what you're doing, but it sounds fishy." Hunter wasn't buying it.

"The Acme Freight thing is just a front for communications, nothing more. Anybody can listen in on radio transmissions. It's just a....well, don't worry. I can't talk much about this charter or I would, Hunter. It pays good and is worth our while in that regard. It's legal and safe. That's about all I can say, other than Smoke is at the airplane now and I'm on my way there to meet him in Tacoma. I came by to see if you needed anything else--any more checks signed, or anything."

"No, we took care of all that the other day. You might go back and tell Ross that you'll be gone for a while and for him to coordinate with me. I think he's a bit owlly about your promoting me to General Manager. You could assure him of his importance to the project and to the company, Boss. His vines seem to have some pretty tender grapes."

"I get your point, Hunter. I'll do that."

Doc went into the back, spoke with Ross and then came back through the front office. He stopped in front of

Hunter's desk, started to say something else, then just looked at her for a moment and finally just said good-bye.

Hunter watched him go out the door, wondering what that was all about. *Strange, that man is truly strange,* she thought.

CHAPTER TWENTY
THE FLIGHT

*James Francis McGarrity was flat on his back. It was warm and oh so comfortable. He could feel the slight breeze moving the air in a quiet manner. A soft hand touched his forehead. He opened his eyes. Looking down on him with the biggest liquid blue eyes was this beautiful creature. She appeared to be naked, from the little part of her he could see. He couldn't really tell; her long blonde tresses covered her breasts. She looked a lot like Hunter. That was a dangerous thought. He reached up for her anyway....*then the phone rang. It was his wake-up call. Damn! It seems that what could be the good dreams never get finished. Doc rolled over, sat up and answered the phone.

It was the hotel operator. "Good morning, Mr. McGarrity, it is five-thirty."

"Mnpf! ....uh, thanks."

God! What time is it? Zero five thirty! Why is it always a dawn launch? Well, at least this time it's only a launch out of bed! Every time he heard the expression he thought of the many times dawn occurred halfway to a target. That's the stuff that's best forgotten.

After a quick shower and shave he called Smoke's room at the Hotel.

"Ready to go eat, Pal?" Doc asked.

"Sure thing, I'll meet you in the coffee shop," Smoke replied.

Doc and Smoke met the moving company at the airplane at seven. Smoke would stay with the airplane, pre-flight, file and be ready for take-off. Doc went with the movers. The move went a lot faster than Doc had imagined; they were back at the airplane within the hour. Loading the heavy crates aboard and tying them down securely took the better part of another hour. But finally it was done. The airplane was ready to go.

Doc took the left seat; Smoke had filed and would handle the clearances. Besides, as Doc laughingly pointed out, that was the co-pilot's job. Smoke grumbled something about seniority among whores as he was strapping in. They got the engines started and Doc nodded to Smoke to call for taxi clearance.

"VANCOUVER GROUND, DOUGLAS, YANKEE VICTOR, WHISKEY ALPHA WHISKEY SIERRA, TRANSIENT PARKING, TAXI, I-F-R, CABO SAN LUCAS, OVER."

"ROGER, WHISKEY ALPHA WHISKEY SIERRA, TAXI RUNWAY ONE SIX, ALTIMETER NINER THREE, CONTACT CLEARANCE DELIVERY FOR YOUR CLEARANCE WHEN READY ON ONE NINER DECIMAL ZERO, OVER."

"ROGER GROUND, RUNWAY ONE SIX, FOR WHISKEY ALPHA WHISKEY SIERRA, AND CLEARANCE DELIVERY ON ONE NINETEEN ZERO, WHEN READY." Smoke replied. He turned to Doc, "You know, I'll be damned if I can get used to all the letters of our aircraft call sign instead of numbers. What a pain in the ass."

Doc had started taxiing as soon as he heard the runway designation. He answered Smoke, "Yeah, I had trouble with it when we were doing the type rating in this bird. Tough to get used to. But a hellava lot better than flying into El Salvador with a load of arms in an airplane with United States markings!"

They reached the end of runway One Six and turned into the run-up area. After completing their run-up and Take-Off Check List, Smoke switched to the Clearance Delivery frequency for their instrument flight clearance.

"VANCOUVER CLEARANCE DELIVERY, THIS IS DOUGLAS, YANKEE VICTOR, WHISKEY ALPHA WHISKEY SIERRA, I-F-R, CABO SAN LUCAS, READY TO COPY, OVER."

"DOUGLAS YANKEE VICTOR WHISKEY ALPHA WHISKEY SIERRA IS CLEARED TO THE CABO SAN LUCAS AIRPORT, VIA FLIGHT PLAN ROUTE. MAINTAIN RUNWAY HEADING FOR VECTORS TO ON COURSE. CLIMB TO AND MAINTAIN ONE THOUSAND, SQUAWK THREE ONE ZERO. CONTACT DEPARTURE CONTROL, ONE THREE TWO DECIMAL SEVEN, AFTER TAKE-OFF. CONTACT THE TOWER WHEN READY FOR DEPARTURE, OVER."

Smoke read the clearance back correctly and switched to the tower frequency then turned to Doc, "Got all that?"

"Right. Let's do it. Standard crew brief. We'll agree on the power readings, then the power is all yours to set fine. If you see anything give a yell and I'll abort. We're heavy but we've got ten thousand feet of cement. My clearance is 'runway heading and one thousand'. You got the rest."

"Got it. I'll call the tower." Smoke switched to the tower frequency and called the tower, advising that they were ready for take-off.

"DOUGLAS YANKEE VICTOR WHISKEY ALPHA WHISKEY SIERRA, IS CLEARED INTO POSITION AND HOLD, OVER".

"POSITION AND HOLD, FOR WHISKEY SIERRA." Smoke looked over at Doc, who acknowledged with a nod of his head.

They taxied into position on the runway, set the brake and brought the power part way up to clear the spark plugs.

"DOUGLAS, YANKEE VICTOR, WHISKEY ALPHA WHISKEY SIERRA, IS CLEARED FOR TAKE-OFF. CONTACT DEPARTURE ON ONE THREE TWO DECIMAL SEVEN, WHEN AIRBORNE. HAVE A GOOD FLIGHT."

Smoke answered, "DOUGLAS, WHISKEY SIERRA ROLLING, ROGER, DEPARTURE ON ONE THREE TWO POINT SEVEN. GOOD DAY."

They were finally on their way. And an hour ahead of schedule. The weather was forecast to be pretty good. They'd be in the glue during climb and most of the State of Washington. They would then supposedly be on-top from Portland to Red Bluff, California and then in the clear.

The climb-out was easy, they entered the overcast at about two thousand feet and remained solid instruments to their initial assigned altitude of eleven thousand feet. Vancouver Departure Control handed them off to Seattle Center. They were in and out of the tops until just south of Kelso when they broke out on top of the cloud layer. Clear and sunny above, a great day to be flying. Smoke called Acme Base on the HF set and let them know their departure time out of Vancouver, B.C.

There wasn't much to do except watch the gauges and enter data into the flight log. They would have to do the fuel transfer at some point, but there was still plenty of time to think about it.

Smoke reached down and picked up the oxygen mask stowed beside his seat. He checked to make sure it was turned on and oxygen flowing. He took a deep breath. Doc noticed.

"Feeling a little hung over, Smoke?" Doc asked.

"Mftdptd nd hi phrtd," Smoke replied.

"I didn't get that, Smoke. Are you Okay? Take your mask away or I can't understand you," Doc said

Smoke took his hand down that was holding the oxygen mask to his face, "I said I farted and it is pretty awful over here."

About that time the cloud of gas had expanded to include the left seat of the small cockpit. "My God! I guess you farted! Something crawl up and die in you, 'Ol Buddy?"

"I'm just not used to big breakfasts," Smoke said as he put the oxygen mask back over his face.

They flew along for a while, both lost in their own thoughts. Finally Smoke took the mask down from his face, turned and hung it back up behind him. He looked over at Doc.

"You ever hear of what happened to Gene the Marine" Smoke asked.

Doc thought for a couple of moments.

"You know, I don't think that I saw him after that 'R&R' we had at Momma-Sans where you got introduced to the wonders of the Orient. In fact, the more I think about it, that was the last time I saw him. We'll have to ask around when we get back." It was quiet, except for the steady droning of the Pratt & Whitney 1830's.

Doc started laughing. It started as a few chuckles and then grew to out and out roaring laughter.

"What's so damn funny, Doc?" Smoke asked.

"I was just thinking about Momma-San's, Kimiko and that scream of yours," Doc said between breaks in his laughter.

Barnes thought for a couple of moments, obviously remembering too, then joined in with his own merriment.

"That was some R&R, that was," Smoke said, "Which scream? From the bath or the beads? Old Gene the Marine, some sense of humor he had."

"Both! The bath at Momma-sans had to be well over a hundred degrees. And when you made that running jump into it, I swear that you made it across that ten or twelve feet of hot water without getting wet above your knees!"

"And they say that man can't walk on water. I sure as hell tried to when I felt the temperature. Ah yes, but the beads. Now there was an experience to cherish and remember." Smoke looked away dreamy-eyed.

"I couldn't agree more. Right on!"

"But, you know, I sort of fell in love with Kimiko. I don't think I ever told you, but I went back several times after you returned to the States."

"No shit?"

"Yeah. Kimiko taught me a lot. She sure knew how to please a man." Smoke got quiet and lost in a lot of thought.

Doc thought about it also. The steady droning of the 1830's was almost hypnotic. He thought about Gene the Marine. *It was like yesterday.*

"Smoke, was that your first Japanese R&R?

"Yeah, it was also my first ride in a C-119 Flying Boxcar. Noisy damn thing. Couldn't hear yourself think. I don't know how 'ol Gene the Marine put up with it. And, just think, that's what our Reserve squadron is getting?"

"That's what Salty said, C-119's. You know, they used to be designated R4Q-2's. If you say that fast it gives you some idea of how folks felt about them. Then when the big change came about of having only one designation for an airplane regardless of which service it was in, came the big change over. R5D's became C-54's, the Navy-Marine designation of this thing we're in, the C-47, used to be R4D. And then...."

Smoke interrupted, "Goodness Doctor, you're just a world of information. I couldn't imagine how you could know all of that."

"Sorry 'bout that. But back to Gene the Marine. He invited me up in the cockpit for the flight to Japan on *my* first R&R. And then took me to Momma-sans. So I had the same experience. Bead jobs were a specialty of the house I think. But, you know Japan isn't anything like that now, Smoke. I

202

was talking to one of the Northwest Airline guys last Drill Weekend. He's on the Seattle to Tokyo run. He said that a Scotch and water on the Ginza is close to eighty bucks now! Can you believe it?"

"Yeah, and we paid what? Thirty six hundred yen for four days and four nights at Momma-sans. And that was about ten bucks American. Uh-huh, for all you could drink, bathe, eat and screw! Hell, it was almost worth getting shot at in Korea for those R&R's!" Smoke sighed in happy remembrance.

"That it was, that it was. But you say you kept going back after I rotated back to the States? Did you do the bead jobs with Kimiko each time?"

"Yea-ah, I sure did. Some fun!"

"Jee-zus, I don't see how. For me it was like I was going to turn inside out. I was with Jinsu and when we were screwing. I could feel her hands on my ass. But I thought it was just the way she was holding on. . ."

"Right," Smoke interrupted. "You had no idea she was shoving beads up your ass! No idea at all."

"Well, I knew she was doing something but, honestly Smoke, I really didn't know *what* she was doing. Gene had put her up to it just like he did with you."

"Okay. If that's your story, I'll buy it, 'cuz I didn't know what was happening either."

"But when I came and she pulled the beads out....it was like a trip hammer hitting my prostate gland. That's when I felt like I was turning inside out!" Doc thought for a moment, then added, "I think a man can only take one of those in his lifetime."

"Wrong!" Smoke said, a bit emphatically.

"You're a better man than I am, then. Once was enough for me."

Both pilots were lost in thought for a while, remembering. Their reverie was broken by a transmission from Seattle Center that Smoke had to respond to.

"ROGER, SEATTLE CENTER, DOUGLAS YANKEE VICTOR, WHISKEY ALPHA WHISKEY SIERRA, TO CONTACT OAKLAND CENTER ONE THREE TWO DECIMAL FIVE. GOOD DAY SIR."

Smoke changed frequencies. "OAKLAND CENTER, DOUGLAS YANKEE VICTOR, WHISKEY ALPHA WHISKEY SIERRA, ONE ONE THOUSAND, I-F-R CABO SAN LUCAS, OVER.

"ROGER DOUGLAS YANKEE VICTOR, WHISKY ALPHA WHISKEY SIERRA, SQUAWK IDENT, OVER" Smoke pressed the identification button on the transponder set. Oakland Center came right back, "RADAR CONTACT, DOUGLAS WHISKEY SIERRA."

Smoke's talking to Center on the radio shook Doc out of his reverie. Good memories, though, good people. He felt fortunate to have found the friend that he had in one Harry, The Smoke, Barnes.

"Where are we, Smoke? I haven't been paying attention." Doc asked.

"Coming up on Fort Jones, Doc."

Enough daydreaming Doc thought. *Back to work. They should start transferring fuel. There was room in the wing tanks now. They had been airborne over three hours.*

"Well, 'Ol Buddy, you can go start transferring fuel. Three and a half hours. We should be able to transfer all six drums. When you get tired of pumping, give a yell and we can trade places."

"Don't worry. I'll let you know. This co-pilot crap only goes so far, 'Ol Buddy, yourself," Smoke said as he climbed out of the right seat and headed back.

Doc took the clip board with the flight plan and logs and checked for their ground speed and fuel burn. He studied Barne's figures and notes. It wasn't to check up on him: Doc just wanted to see for himself.

Take-off and climb fuel consumption was as planned. Cruise burn appeared to be better than he had expected. It was less than a hundred gallons an hour. About ninety.

Smoke tapped Doc on the shoulder and stuck his head near Doc's ear. "There seems to be a problem. I can't transfer fuel. I've checked everything. The pump turns freely and then it feels like it hits a block. I tried the other pump and it did the same," he explained.

"Damn! You've tried everything, of course. Any ideas?" This could complicate things in a major way.

"Hey, you're welcome to give it a try, take a look, or whatever. I can't make it work. When we did the flight test everything worked easy. Now it isn't working at all. In fact, I insist you give it a look-see. You might catch something I overlooked." Smoke was not happy. He fully understood what it could mean if they had to land in the United States for fuel. He knew damn well they couldn't make Mexico without transferring fuel.

Doc motioned for him to come up and take over. Smoke climbed into the right seat and tapped the control column to indicate that he had assumed command of the aircraft. It was still on auto-pilot, so there wasn't much to do. Dodge birds, as the expression goes, and monitor the radio.

McGarrity went back. He uncoupled the hose from the stand pipe. Then coupled it back. He went over to the drum that was connected and checked the hose attachment to the pump. It was permanently affixed. He started pumping. The handle rotated freely. He could feel the suction pick up the fluid then it got harder to pump, then stopped altogether. He swapped the hose on the stand pipe with the other hose-pump assembly. Carefully checking everything, Doc then tried to pump from the second one. The same thing. He could feel suction picking up the fluid. Then stop. Smoke was right; it felt like the line was blocked.

Things had gone too easy. Now it looked like they might earn their money. If they land in the states, they'll sure as hell go to jail. There are big-time laws against moving around the type of merchandise that was in the crates. Let alone having that stuff in one's possession. Doc climbed into the left seat. He was lost in thought. Smoke left him alone.

"Okay, here's what we'll do," Doc said slowly, still thinking it through. "We'll use the HF set and talk to Acme Base. Let Roberts worry about this along with us. No sense in our being the only ones worrying. Maybe he'll have some ideas. One thing I know for sure, if we land anywhere in the states the customs people will take this airplane apart, let alone open a few crates. It'll be slammer-time, pal!"

"You're abso-fuckin'-lutely right, Doctor. And I have no desire to visit any concrete hotels," Smoke said as he reached for the trip file where the HF frequencies were stored. "Do you want to talk to them, or shall I?"

"You can just as well, but be careful how you phrase things. Anybody could be listening. Not that I give a shit, but Roberts would get excited."

"Right." Barnes dialed in the frequency listed for this time of day and tried a call, "ACME BASE, ACME FLIGHT, OVER." All that he heard was static and a small squeal. He adjusted the frequency back and forth a little and tried again. "ACME BASE ACME FLIGHT, OVER."
They could hear something faintly but couldn't make it out. Smoke transmitted again, "ACME BASE, ACME FLIGHT. . .GIVE ME A SHORT COUNT OVER,"

The same faint transmission came back while Smoke adjusted the frequency knob back and forth, "....foomph, ivtoph, foomph thREE, TWO, ONE, OVER."

"ROGER ACME BASE, READING YOU FIVE SQUARE, HOW ME? OVER."

".....-and CLEAR, GO AHEAD ACME FLIGHT, OVER."

"ACME BASE, ACME FLIGHT IS HAVING DIFFICULTIES WITH THE FUEL SYSTEM. UNABLE TO TRANSFER. PLEASE ADVISE BEST LANDING

SITE FOR COMPANY BUSINESS IN CALIFORNIA, OVER." Smoke turned to Doc. "That okay. Whataya think?"

"That'll tell 'em without violating security," Doc said. "Let's see what they come back with. Hit 'em again."

"ACME BASE, ACME FLIGHT, DID YOU COPY MY LAST, OVER."

"ROGER ACME FLIGHT, STAND BY ONE."

This got a chuckle out of Smoke. Doc gave him a hard look. "Don't you have any idea about the seriousness of our situation, Smoke?"

"Sure I do, Doc. But look *Pal,* we either have to laugh or cry. And who likes to see a grown man cry?"

"You're right. I'm sorry, Smoke...." The radio interrupted.

"ACME FLIGHT, ACME BASE, WHAT IS YOUR DECISION TIME FRAME? OVER."

Smoke looked over at Doc. Doc pointed to the clipboard, to the fuel 'How-goes-it' section. Smoke nodded understanding and picked up the microphone again. "ACME BASE, ACME FLIGHT, FOUR HOURS PLUS RESERVE, OVER."

"ROGER ACME FLIGHT, UNDERSTAND FOUR PLUS HOURS. REMAIN THIS FREQUENCY, OVER."

"WILCO, ACME FLIGHT STANDING BY. OUT."

"Let's see what the spooks come back with, Boss," Smoke said, "It should be interesting to see if they can do anything to discourage the customs folks from incarcerating us."

Roberts, the Chief of Station Seattle, had been called into the radio room when the aircraft had initially attempted contact. The news from the two pilots did not please him. Roberts went back to his office. He picked up the phone and called Peter Jorgensen. He was put through immediately.

Roberts explained the situation. Jorgensen was not pleased either.

"Dammit Roberts, I thought everything was tested and found to be okay. What in hell is the problem?"

"We don't know any more here than what I've already told you, Sir. Will it be possible to work anything out with the Customs Department?"

"I don't know. I'll get back to you." Jorgensen hung up and rang for Clyde Hayner. It took a few minutes for Clyde to get to his office.

The door to Jorgensen's office had no sooner opened when Jorgensen started in, "Who do we know over at Customs, Clyde?"

"We have worked with them from time to time." Clyde was a little taken aback. "Can you tell me what you need, Sir?"

"The arms shipment to our friend in El Salvador is about to be compromised. The airplane might have to land in the United States for fuel. Something has gone wrong with a fuel transfer system they installed out there."

"I see. How much time do we have?" Hayner asked.

"About four hours."

"Damn! I'll get right to work on it, Sir."

Jorgensen waved his hand in dismissal. Hayner hurried back to his office. He dug out his personal directory. There wasn't anybody in it that worked in Customs. *God Damn Marines!* He thought, *can't they do anything right! Here it is. A real good buddy over at State and best of all, he owed a favor!* Hayner dialed the number. John's secretary answered.

"Mr. Mays office, may I help you." Came a voice dripping with charm. *That lucky bastard,* Hayner thought.

"Yes, this is Clyde Hayner, at the agency, is John in?"

"What agency would that be, Mr. Hayner?" She asked sweetly.

"The Central Intelligence Agency," Hayner replied sarcastically, "Now may I speak to John, if he's in, that is."

"Thank you Mr. Hayner. Yes, he's in. I'll put you through."

In a moment John Mays came on the line. "Clyde, how are you? Sorry my girl didn't know who you were. She's new. What can I do for you?"

"Hopefully a lot, John. Do you have any connections over at Customs?"

"Of course, Clyde. What kind of trouble are you in? You sound hassled."

"Well, can we talk on this line?"

"I would think so, Clyde." John Mays chuckled to himself. *These spooks are all alike*, he thought.

Hayner outlined the problem without disclosing the final destination and cargo, other than it was somewhat sensitive and wouldn't stand up under much scrutiny. He did mention the aircraft markings and what that would cause the customs people to do.

"Let me see what I can do, Clyde. Are you at your number?"

"Yes. Oh, and John, this is pretty sensitive, the whole thing, I mean."

"I understand." They hung up.

John Mays couldn't contain himself. He laughed all the way into his Section Chief's office. He was still holding his side as he slipped into the chair beside the large desk. He had to wipe his eyes. His Section Chief, Bruce Mayo, waited patiently to find out what was so amusing. Finally, John was able to talk.

"I just heard the most *delicious* story. Those people over at Langley just can't do *anything* right. You just won't believe this. It seems....and mind you, this is ver-rry confidential....that an agency airplane is, as I speak, somewhere in California with a load of, only God and '*the company*' knows what. But whatever it is--won't pass customs. And in an airplane carrying some South American registration, or something. They can't transfer fuel and are going to have to land in Southern California, instead of their destination. We aren't allowed to know where *that* is, and do *we* know *anybody* at Customs that can help them out." John couldn't contain himself and broke up laughing again. By this time Bruce Mayo was also in hysterics.

"Oh God John, stop it! You're killing me. Is this really true? Your friend told you this?" Mayo asked. "I can't believe it."

"It's true. Every word. I may have some of the facts turned slightly here or there, but it's all true."

Calming down, Mayo said, "Well, what I understand is do *we* know anybody at customs who will tell their customs people at some place in California to look the other way when this airplane lands with a load of highly sensitive material destined for somewhere in Mexico, Central or South America. That it?"

"That's it, Chief. You do have a way of cutting through to the quick." Mays answered.

"If I had any sense I wouldn't touch this for anything. But you're right, it's delicious. I'll kick it upstairs and let's watch what happens.

It only took thirty minutes from the time Clyde Hayner called John Mays for word to go up the chain of command at State to the office of the Executive Assistant to the Under Secretary for International Security Affairs, Steve Hackett. He couldn't wait to call his old classmate at the agency, one Daniel Targo.

Dan Targo was head of the Mid East Affairs section. His secretary informed him the Assistant Under Secretary of State was on the line for him. Dan knew who it was. He picked up the phone.

"Steve, how the hell are you? To what do I owe this call from such an illustrious personage?"

Steve Hackett started laughing. He couldn't help it. After a moment of unintelligible mutterings he was finally able to talk, "I understand you folks have a major problem with some airplane full of contraband that is going to have to clear customs someplace in California."

"Steve, I haven't the foggiest idea what you're talking about. Could you be a bit clearer? We don't have anything going on in California."

"Well, it seems that one of your people called one of my people looking for a favor. Some airplane is flying down the West Coast with a load of something not nice and is going to have to land in Southern California because of a fuel problem. Your man wanted my man to exert some influence over at the Treasury Department....Customs Service, to be exact...to have them look the other way or something. I couldn't wait to call you, Dan, My Boy."

"Can you tell me who called? It might give me a clue as to what section is involved with this?"

"Hang on, Dan." There was the sound of Steve putting his hand over the telephone mouthpiece. Dan could hear sounds, but not what was being said. Steve came back. "Yeah, it was a Clyde Hayner. My guy says he's on the El Salvador desk. Will that help you?"

Let me check this out. I'll get back to you. And oh by the way, thanks for the call, Mr. Assistant Under Secretary. Uh, I owe you a big one, Steve."

"No problem, Dan. I thought this had gone far enough. I'll be curious to hear how it works out. Take it easy." They hung up.

Dan checked his directory. He found Hayner. The man worked for Pete Jorgensen. Dan knew who Peter Jorgensen was but didn't know him personally. He decided to call him just the same.

Jorgensen answered his own phone.

"Peter Jorgensen? This is Dan Targo in the Mid-East Section. Do you have a minute?"

211

"Of course. What do you need?" Jorgensen asked.

"I got a call from a friend over at State. He tells me Clyde Hayner called one of his people looking for a favor. Something about Customs and an airplane of ours in California. Do you know anything about this? They seemed to think it was pretty funny."

"Yes, I do know about it. Can I ask who called you?"

"It was Steve Hackett, Executive Assistant to the Under Secretary for International Security Affairs. He's an old classmate of mine and loves to needle me about things he hears about the agency. I have always encouraged him by acting really hurt," Dan explained. "It gives me a clue about what's getting out and about in the gossip circle."

"I understand, Dan. I appreciate your input. Let me get back to you." Peter hung up. He called Hayner and asked him to come to his office. It didn't take Clyde long to get there.

Jorgensen looked up as Hayner rushed into his office. "Clyde, who did you call about our little problem out in California? Was it someone in the Customs Service?"

Hayner cleared his throat. He sensed something was amiss. "Uh, no-o....I checked and didn't have any current contacts at customs, so I called a friend at State who owed me a favor. Is there some kind of a problem?"

"Well, you could say that. You left my office exactly twenty-two minutes ago," Peter said as he glanced at his watch, "And I have heard from Dan Targo, over in *our* Mid East Section, who had received a call from the Under Secretary for International Security Affairs, who seemed to know the whole thing. I won't be surprised if *we,* and I do mean *WE,* hear from our own Deputy Director of Operations! If not *THE* Director *himself.* Targo went on to say that the folks at State were having a good laugh about this. We look like a bunch of amateurs." Jorgensen paused and caught his breath, then pressed on, "What's done is done. Now here is what I want you to do. Go find someone who knows something about C-47's and explain the situation. If you need any details, call Harold Roberts. He's in contact with the airplane via HF radio. I'll deal with customs myself. Now get to it!"

Jorgensen's intercom came alive with his secretary's voice, "The Deputy Director of Operations is on three for you Sir."

Peter motioned for Hayner, who had started to get up, to stay put and reached for the phone. "Jorgensen here, Sir." Then he did a whole lot of listening. Hayner could occasionally hear some of the diatribe spewing forth when Jorgensen adjusted the telephone receiver against his ear.

Jorgensen was finally given a chance to respond. "Yes Sir, that's one way of describing the situation. It is really a very simple mission that has run into some unforeseen problems . . . well, yes Sir....we're dealing with the problem now, Sir. State was brought in by mistake, Sir." Jorgensen glanced over at Hayner meaningfully. "We haven't contacted anybody at Customs yet....uh huh, well we thought it would be in their ball park, Sir....no I hadn't considered the military....well....presently the airplane is in Northern California and we have about three and half hours more before they have to do something. That's right, Northern California. I'll do that, Sir." He hung up.

"Mr. Hayner, you heard my secretary say who that was. He is going to check with the military and see if we can't refuel the airplane at one of the bases out there. He will be getting back to me. You go find that expert on DC-3's. We'll talk more about this later."

Hayner nodded his assent and left as quickly as he could. When he got back to his office he called the Assistant Operations Chief, who he knew casually--their sons had played on the same soccer team--and explained that he needed a C-47 pilot as quickly as possible. No, not to fly, but to explain some systems problems. Next he called

Roberts in Seattle and asked for specific details about the transfer problem. Roberts would get back to him.

Ten minutes later Roberts called back. He had spoken with the crew and gotten explicit details, both the flight test and what was occurring now. Hayner had hung up and finished his notes about the technical things while they were still fresh in his mind.

It had been over an hour and a half since McGarrity and Barnes had heard anything from the company people. Smoke had just given their position report passing Sacramento when Oakland Center asked them if they had UHF communications on board. Barnes responded in the negative. Oakland told them to contact Air Force Tango Six on One Two Two Decimal Niner.

"What the hell is this all about, Doc? Any ideas?" Smoke was wondering aloud as he switched frequencies on one of their two VHF radios.

"Don't have a clue, Smoke. It must be some of the spook stuff helpin' us outta this fuel mess. Don't know."

"AIR FORCE TANGO SIX, THIS IS DOUGLAS YANKEE VICTOR WHISKEY ALPHA WHISKEY SIERRA, OVER."

The radio call was answered immediately. "DOUGLAS WHISKEY SIERRA BE ADVISED TANGO SIX IS A FLIGHT OF TWO EFF FOURS. WE WILL BE INTERCEPTING YOU IN APPROXIMATELY FIVE MINUTES. CONFIRM ALTITUDE AND ACKNOWLEDGE, OVER."

Doc and Smoke looked at each other in some wonderment. Doc spoke up first, "Ask them their intentions." Smoke nodded in acknowledgment

"ROGER TANGO SIX, WHISKEY SIERRA UNDERSTANDS FLIGHT OF TWO EFF FOURS. WE'RE AT ANGELS ELEVEN. ADVISE PURPOSE OF INTERCEPT, OVER."

"TANGO SIX FLIGHT WILL ESCORT DOUGLAS YANKEE VICTOR WHISKEY ALPHA WHISKEY SIERRA TO CASTLE AIR FORCE BASE. WE HAVE YOU IN SIGHT, TURN RIGHT TO ONE THREE ZERO FOR VECTOR TO CASTLE. START YOUR LET-DOWN AT THIS TIME. ACKNOWLEDGE, OVER."

Barnes looked over at Doc. McGarrity shrugged and said, "I don't know, but there's two of them and one of us. I think they'd win, Smoke. We better do as the man says." He reached up and pulled the power back a bit and started the airplane downhill.

"ROGER TANGO SIX, WHISKEY SIERRA IS OUT OF ONE ONE THOUSAND AND TURNING RIGHT TO ONE THREE ZERO FOR VECTORS TO CASTLE." Barnes picked up the chart and located Castle Air Force Base. He held up the chart and pointed. "Here it is, Doc. It's to the right of the airways near the town of Merced. Oh, hey! Look out your window!"

Doc glanced to his left to see a McDonnell F-4 Phantom on his wing. The F-4 had his gear down and dive brakes open trying to stay slow enough. Doc looked over and waved. There was no response from either of the two crew members of the Air Force fighter. "These guys look pretty serious, Smoke."

"Yeah. Mine do too."

Doc looked over to the right side and saw the other F-4 that Smoke was talking about. "Smoke, you stay on this frequency. I'm going back to Oakland on our other radio and advise canceling I-F-R, and so forth, just to cover our ass."

"Right"

Doc called Oakland Center. "OAKLAND CENTER YANKEE VICTOR WHISKEY ALPHA WHISKEY SIERRA IS CANCELING I-F-R, OUT OF ONE ONE THOUSAND. WE'RE IN ESCORT WITH AIR FORCE TANGO SIX FLIGHT, OVER."

"ROGER WHISKEY SIERRA, WE HAVE CANCELED YOUR I-F-R. YOU ARE CLEARED TO LEAVE THIS FREQUENCY. GOOD DAY SIR."

There was a light knock at his door. "Come in," Hayner called out.

"You the one needing a Gooney bird driver?" The man asked as he came in the office.

Clyde rose from behind his desk and held out his hand, "Yeah, I sure am. Thanks for coming over quickly. I'm Clyde Hayner, El Sal desk."

The pilot took his hand, "I'm Randy Mifflin. I know a bit about "Doug's", I hope I can help you." He looked around and sat down without being invited.

"*Doug's?*" Clyde asked.

"Douglas DC-3's, C-47's....Gooney Birds."

"Oh, sure. It took me a minute." Hayner referred to the notes he had taken from his conversation with Roberts. He explained slowly and in detail all he knew about the modification to the fuel system, tying into the cross-feed, the flight test working well and the problem they were experiencing now.

Randy didn't interrupt. He listened carefully. When Hayner was through Randy took a minute before commenting. Then he said, "I've heard of folks doing this. The bird has been around for a long time, you know. It should work good. Has anyone talked to the people that did the modification?"

Clyde was dumbfounded. Why hadn't he thought of that? "I don't think so, Randy. Let's go down to the conference room where there's a speaker phone and get Seattle back on the line."

"Good idea."

Hayner gathered up his notes and led the way. They went into the conference room and Clyde called Roberts. He came on the line immediately.

"Mr. Roberts, Clyde Hayner. Do you have the name and phone number where the modification work was done? I have a C-47 expert here who wants to talk with them."

Randy snorted in amusement at the term *C-47 expert*.

"No. But I can get it. Hang on." Hayner could hear Roberts talking to someone named Chris and talking about an expense file. In a moment he was back on the line. "Here it is. It's Miller Aviation at Tacoma Industrial Airport. Ron Miller is the owner. The number is area code two oh six, five, five, zero, three two three one. Let me know what you find out."

"Right. You're the one in radio contact. I'll get back to you." They hung up.

Hayner dialed the number in Tacoma. It rang several times, then was finally answered.

"Miller Aviation."

"Ron Miller, please."

"This is Ron."

"Ron, this is Clyde Hayner with the agency in Washington, D.C. We have a problem."

"Okay. How can I help you Mr. Horner?"

"It's *Hayner*." Clyde went on to explain what was happening, the crew's inability to transfer fuel from the fifty-five gallon drums.

Randy Mifflin spoke up on the speaker phone, "Randy Mifflin, Ron. Will you describe just how you made the modification?"

"We did it the usual way. This is done in Alaska all the time. Put a 'tee' in the cross-feed line, which is located just forward of the wing root, under the floor boards...."

Randy interrupted, "I know the airplane system, Ron. I'm a pilot and checked out in the 'Doug'."

"Okay, then from the tee we install a lever valve to prevent back flow up the stand pipe. Then the stand pipe comes up into the cabin area behind the cockpit, and I like to fit the end with a sealing quick disconnect. You put the mating disconnect on the pump hose from the drum...."

"Wait a minute. What's the lever valve? How does that work?" Randy interrupted again.

"I install an operating rod up into the cabin so the valve....oh shit! I'll bet that's the problem. Damnation! That's it! *The fuckin' valve's closed.* No wonder they can't transfer fuel!"

"I don't understand. We've been told that the crew flight tested the system...."

It was Ron Miller's turn to interrupt, "....the day they came down to flight test, I hadn't finished fabricating the operating rod and installing it. The valve was left open. I wasn't worried about them doing slow rolls. The sealing quick disconnect on the top of the stand pipe would hold the fumes. The lever valve is really a safety back up. The operating rod is so you don't have to lift the floor boards to open and close the valve. It was open when they flew the test. We closed it when the rod was installed and we refueled the airplane. Jee-zus, I thought I talked to Doc about the valve. But maybe I didn't. Damn, Guys. Hey, I'm really sorry. I hope this hasn't caused any problems."

Hayner had to turn away and keep a hand over his mouth to keep from screaming at Miller. Randy was still talking to Ron. Clyde got control of himself and jumped back in, "Look, Ron, I want you to call Harold Roberts and tell him about the valve and rod. He will get the crew on the HF radio and will relay instructions. Okay?" He gave Miller the Acme Freight telephone number.

"Right. You say they're still in the air, just unable to transfer and were going to have to land and refuel. I know that Doc didn't want to land until well into Mexico. I didn't know why and didn't ask. I'll call this Roberts and tell him to....well, I'll get it handled. Really sorry, Mr. Horner."

They said their good-bye's and hung up. Clyde didn't bother to correct Miller on his name. Hell, 'Horner' was as good as any. The important thing is that the flight could continue. It's a shame his buddy at State couldn't resist the opportunity to screw him over. Maybe he'd have a chance to get even down the road. He thanked Randy and offered to buy him a couple of drinks later. Randy declined since he had a flight, but asked for a rain check.

Clyde was more than happy to grant his request.

The C-47 was down to three thousand feet on a long straight-in approach to Castle Air Force Base when the HF set came alive. It was Acme Base calling to give them the information about the fuel system valve and how to operate it. Barnes told them to stand-by and went back into the cabin. In a moment he stuck his head back in the cockpit, "Works good, Doc. What do you want to do?"

"Shit! Let's ask these two fighter jocks if we can leave. In fact you pump gas and I'll talk to 'em."

"TANGO SIX FLIGHT, WHISKEY SIERRA. BE ADVISED OUR PROBLEM IS SOLVED. WE ARE ABLE TO CONTINUE OUR FLIGHT WITHOUT FURTHER ASSISTANCE, OVER."

"WHISKEY SIERRA CONTINUE YOUR APPROACH, AND REMAIN THIS FREQUENCY, OVER." The reply was terse and humorless.

"ROGER". Doc reached over to the HF set and picked up the microphone. He advised Acme Base that they hadn't been released yet and were still escorted by the Air Force. Acme Base told him to standby.

Smoke came back up and climbed into the co-pilot seat. "I transferred one drum for now. What's happening?"

"Everybody wants us to standby. You better get the Landing Check List out of the way, it looks like the Air Force wants our bodies on the ground."

They were one mile out on final approach when Tango Six got back to them. "WHISKEY SIERRA, YOU'RE CLEARED TO WAVE OFF FROM YOUR

PRESENT POSITION. CLIMB STRAIGHT AHEAD. CONTACT MERCED FLIGHT SERVICE ON ONE TWO TWO DECIMAL TWO WHEN CLEAR OF THE RUNWAY. OVER."

"ROGER, WHISKEY SIERRA IS WAVING OFF, THANK YOU AIR FORCE FOR YOUR ASSISTANCE. OUT." Doc hung up his mic and turned to Smoke. "Would you help me get this bird back to a climb configuration? With all this bullshit goin' on I'm afraid I'll miss something. You might want to let Seattle know that the crisis is over. They're still standing by."

What a cluster fuck!! He thought.

CHAPTER TWENTY-ONE
ONE BRIEFCASE

Whitey stopped at the front desk to check for any messages. The desk clerk handed him a note; he was to call the embassy. He went on up to his room. He knew from past experience that the telephones at the El Camino Real were fairly safe. Still one was always careful.

He called the embassy. "McFrank here," he said when the phone was answered.

"Just a moment, Mr. McFrank," the operator replied.

The ambassador's secretary came on the line. "Mr. McFrank, we received a call from the Policía Nacional. The head waiter at the restaurant where a member of our staff was killed has regained consciousness. The police thought someone from our embassy might want to talk to him. The ambassador asked me to relay the message to you."

"Which hospital and name or room number, please?"

"He is at the Hospital de Niños on the boulevard Los Héroes where it intersects Avenue Gustavo Guerrero. Room 219. The hospital is up by the Universidad de El Salvador...."

Whitey interrupted, "Yes, I know the hospital, it's not far from the hotel. Room 219. Thank you and thank the ambassador for me."

"Yes sir, I'll be happy to do that. Good day."

"Good-bye."

Interesting. Whitey didn't know that there had been any survivors from the floor staff of the restaurant. Most of the staff had been killed in the explosion, including some of the kitchen workers. This means that the head waiter saw who had placed the bomb. Whitey thought about the new information. He decided to go over to the hospital right away. He called the front desk and ordered a cab.

Arriving at the hospital, Whitey went directly to room 219. Nobody stopped him. There wasn't a guard outside of the room. He wondered about that. Whitey went into the room. There was a nurse bending over the patient, doing something with the dressings. She looked up when Whitey came into the room and said something in Spanish to him.

"Do you speak English?"

"Si. But you are to wait outside of the room until I'm finished. Do you have business with this patient?"

"Yes. But I can wait until you're through. No problem." Whitey stepped back outside of the room.

In a few minutes the nurse came out of the room. She went up to McFrank. "Now, perhaps you can tell me what business you might have with this patient.

"I'm with the American Embassy. Your Policía Nacional contacted the embassy and said that we might wish to speak with the headwaiter from the restaurant. I do not know his name."

"It's José Estado. He can speak to you but only for a few minutes. You can go in now. He speaks very good English."

"Thank you, Nurse, I won't be long," Whitey replied.

Whitey went into the room. José was awake and alert from having his dressings changed. Whitey went up to the side of the bed, held out his hand and said, "I'm with the American Embassy. The Policía Nacional felt that you might have some additional information. I'm investigating on behalf of the United States, the tragic bombing that took so many lives including our Agricultural Attaché."

"I have told the policía everything, Señor. However there was one thing that they took great interest in. The two briefcases."

"I'm not sure I understand. Two briefcases?"

"Si. Two men came in. They were in a great hurry. They asked to be seated in the back. The location was near where the young American always sat. They were both carrying identical briefcases. Yet when they left I distinctly remember seeing only one briefcase. I mean it was after I woke up here that I remembered the one briefcase. They left in a hurry, but only one of them had a briefcase. The other briefcase must have contained the bomb. That is what I told them....the policía."

"Would you recognize either of the two men if you saw them again, José?"

"Si. I....uh, oh...." José grimaced and took some deep breaths.

"Are you in pain? Shall I get the nurse?"

"No. It is all right. The pain comes and goes. I will be okay. Give me a minute."

José Estado closed his eyes for a few moments. His breathing became easier, then he opened his eyes and continued, "They were not from El Salvador, Señor. I recognized their accent. They were both from Venezuela."

"Are you sure, José?"

"Señor, as headwaiter I must know people. We Latinos have distinctive accents. They are as distinctive as your Norte Americanos' accents. The Venezuelan manner of speaking is fast and distinctive, unlike Mexican, Cuban, Colombian or Puerto Rican. I know accents, Señor. Both of those men were from Venezuela."

"I understand, José. I won't...."

The nurse came into the room. "Your time is up." She gave Whitey a hard look. "And I mean now."

"I was just leaving, Nurse. If there is anything we can do, his bill or anything special, please call the American Embassy. We will take care of it."

"That is very kind of you, Señor. I will tell the Administrator."

223

Whitey turned back to José Estado, shook his hand without saying anything and left the room.

From the lobby he called a cab and when it arrived, went directly to the American Embassy. None of the intelligence personnel were in the embassy. He left word for the Intel clerk to dig up anything and everything they had, including pictures, on known, or suspected, Venezuelan terrorists and to contact him at his hotel.

Whitey returned to his hotel. It was a lucky break, the two briefcases and the known accents. He remembered that he had met two Venezuelans recently. Colonel Cordero and his lieutenant. They were supposedly anti-terrorists. And how could they have profited by assassinating the Agricultural Attaché? It didn't make any sense.

But, finding the bombers is possible. Just barely possible. Maybe it would be a good idea to talk to Alfredo and check his resources. There was a very good chance that Alfredo's resources would exceed those of the agency's. He decided to call.

It took a while for Alfredo to get back to him. Whitey explained the situation and what he had learned, the two briefcases and the distinguishing accent, or dialect, identifying the two men as Venezuelan.

"This headwaiter, his name?" Alfredo asked.

"It's José Estado. He's in room 219 at the Hospital de Niños, out on the Boulevard Los Héroes. He said that he would be able to identify the two men if we had any pictures."

"Señor White, this is fortunate. I will have someone look into the matter. Not to change the subject, but how is the other matter proceeding? Have you heard anything?"

"Yes. That is one of the reasons I called you. The shipment is enroute. I want to be at the ranch when it arrives. Could I ask Raul to fly me out?"

"Of course. Feel free to call the flight service and schedule him as you require."

"Thank you, Señor Cellini.   I will keep you informed."

CHAPTER TWENTY-TWO
A DETONICS

The flight south had been essentially uneventful, other than the screw-up with the fuel transfer. As it turned out, all they had to do was pull the rod up to open the tee-valve in the cross-feed line and push it down to close the valve when they were through transferring fuel.

But the rod was barely visible. It only stuck up six or seven inches and was almost hidden by the stand-pipe. In fact, unless one knew what one was looking for, it would be easily, and *was,* overlooked. Once all had been resolved, the fuel transfer went easily. Doc and Smoke had taken turns transferring fuel from the fifty-five gallon drums to the wing tanks. Now facing them was the hurdle of clearing Mexican Customs in Cabo San Lucas.

They were about fifty miles out when Doc called for the Descent Check List and then asked Smoke to advise Cabo Approach Control that they would need Customs. Approach Control acknowledged their request.

They landed and were directed by Ground Control over to the transient fueling area. Ground Control advised them Customs would meet them there. As they taxied closer to the transient area, a line boy came out of a small shack and indicated a parking area. They pulled in and shut down.

The heat from the day was still rising off the concrete ramp. After a dozen hours of continuous engine noise, it seemed deathly quiet. With both pilot and co-pilot side windows open, one could hear the snap and crackle of the engines cooling down. Smoke finished the Shut-down Check

List, while Doc noted the chock-time in the Flight Log. It was 2233 local time; a little after ten thirty. Glancing up, Doc saw a car drive up and a uniformed individual got out and started walking out to the aircraft.

"*This must be customs*," Doc thought. "We've got company, Smoke," Doc said. "Here we go."

"Be cool, Doctor," Smoke replied.

McGarrity unfastened his seat belt, slid the seat back, raised the arm rest and climbed out and made his way aft, around the fastened down wooden crates, to open the cabin door. Walking aft, he turned on all of the main cabin lights. He grabbed the stair step which was stowed against the aft bulkhead, opened the door, jumped down, turned and placed the step in the door frame slots that were designed to hold the step in place. He turned back in time to greet the Mexican Customs official.

Holding out his hand, Doc said, "Buenos Dias, Senor".

"It would be more like 'Buenas Noches' at this hour of the evening, Señor. I would like to see your aircraft papers and cargo manifest. Do you have any passengers on board?" The customs official spoke in perfect English, ignoring Doc's outstretched hand.

The perfect English belied the Mexican's appearance. He was overweight, his khaki uniform was wrinkled and soiled. The visored hat had seen better days. It would make a crushed, fifty-mission hat look new by comparison He was obviously well educated, though.

Doc noticed that Smoke came out of the airplane behind them and was obviously going to put the pins in the landing gear. The gear pins mechanically lock and prevent the landing gear from collapsing or inadvertently retracting while the airplane is on the ground. He would be taking care of the refueling, too.

"No passengers. I'll get the documents for you, Sir. Would you like to come aboard?" Doc asked. It didn't look like this was going to go very well.

"Yes, I'll have a look while you're getting the papers." The official replied.

Doc climbed back into the aircraft, the official following close behind. Doc went straight up to the cockpit, grabbed his briefcase that held the cargo manifests, retrieved the packet that held the aircraft papers from the bulkhead behind the pilot's seat and went back into the main cabin. The official was looking over the fifty-five gallon drums rather curiously. He looked up as Doc returned and asked, "This is a rather unusual fuel system you have. What is its purpose?"

"We do a lot of contract work for the oil people. It takes us into the interior of Venezuela. There aren't many refueling facilities where we operate. We learned long ago to carry our own fuel with us." Doc waited for a reply. When none was forthcoming, it appeared his answer satisfied the official's curiosity. Opening his briefcase, Doc handed the official the cargo manifest and then placed the aircraft paperwork packet on one of the fuel drums where it would be handy.

Smoke came back aboard and made his way past them on his way up to the cockpit. Both Doc and the customs official ignored him.

The customs official examined the cargo manifest very carefully. He kept looking over at the crates, which were numbered, as if to verify the contents of each of them. When he finished the last page he laid the manifest down and reached over and picked up the packet that held the aircraft paperwork. He glanced at Doc, as if to ask permission to open the packet. Doc nodded his assent. The official took his time looking over the documents. Finally he looked up and asked, "Do you have any contraband on board?"

"No. Well, what do you mean by contraband?" Doc asked.

"Drugs, arms or cargo not listed on the manifest."

Doc started to answer in the negative, then decided on another approach. "Yes, as a matter of fact, I do," Doc said, following a hunch. "Just a moment, let me get it for you." He went up to the compartment behind the cockpit, where his luggage was stowed. Doc opened a small suitcase and retrieved a leather folder about the size of a woman's small purse. He went back to the customs official and handed it to him. The Mexican took it and unzipped the case. Inside was a small automatic. He looked up quizzically.

"Somebody left it on the airplane. I don't want it on board. It makes me nervous. Why don't you take it off my hands? If you look closely, you will see that it is called a 'Detonics'. It is forty-five caliber. It appears to be cut down in size from a standard forty-five ACP Colt. I have to clear customs in El Salvador also and I don't want to take a chance of having my airplane impounded."

"My department uses nine millimeter. I would have to buy the forty-five caliber ammunition. Isn't it expensive?"

Doc reached into his pocket and pulled out two one hundred dollar bills. He had placed them there for an opening like this. He handed the bills to the official. "Let me buy the ammunition for you in return for your doing me the favor of taking this 'contraband' off my hands. Speaking for myself, as well as for the company I fly for, we would appreciate this not being mentioned on any reports. We are going to be flying through here frequently on this current contract and wish to avoid any unnecessary problems."

The inspector looked at Doc for a moment, then, as if arriving at a decision, said. "As you wish, Señor. I will be happy to take this off your hands. It is a very unusual weapon. It's a shame you cannot legally carry it back to Venezuela." The Customs agent was admiring the weapon. Then hastily added, "But of course, you would not want to

229

have it on board going through El Salvador. That could be very costly to both you and your company." The customs official said this very seriously.

"I appreciate your helping me out, Sir."

"When are you planning to leave?" The official asked.

"We're going to refuel, have a bite to eat and then file. We'll probably leave shortly after midnight. Was there a special reason for your asking?"

"My replacement comes on duty at seven in the morning. It would be wise to follow your planned schedule. He can be very curious, which can sometimes cause delays. If you are planning frequent trips south, it is a good idea to arrive in the evening as you did tonight. I'm on duty every night with the exception of Sunday." The official paused for a moment for this to sink in and then continued in an official manner, "Capitan, you're papers are all in order, have a safe flight." He touched the visor of his hat in a token of a salute.

"Thank you. We'll take your advice and plan our trips through here on your duty schedule. Let me know how that cut-down gun works next trip." Doc said with a big smile, and returning the mock salute in a like manner. He was happy to have gotten through this ordeal. It could have gone badly.

The customs official held out his hand, saying "Inspector Sanchez."

Doc took it, saying, "Captain McGarrity." He walked the official back to the cabin door and out of the airplane. Once on the ramp, they shook hands again, exchanging pleasantries. The official left.

Smoke had come down out of the cockpit and was standing there when Doc turned around.

"That sure sounded easy enough, Doc. What gave you the idea to give him the gun?"

"Whitey told me these guys are nuts about guns. All Latinos, but especially those in official status of one kind or another. Police, army, and, in this case, customs. This guy is not your typical Mexican cop-type, though. Just looks the type. He is well educated and I was afraid if I tried to lay a bunch of money on him, he would have been offended. It was just a hunch," Doc said as he climbed back into the airplane. "Have you finished the flight plan?"

"Yeah, that's what I was doing while you played nursemaid to Pancho Villa. I think you may have calculated a tad short, 'Ol Buddy. I'm going to fill four of the drums."

"Hey, Pancho Villa was a bandit. This guy turned out to be all right. Two hundred bucks, a gun that Whitey gave us and one hellava lot of advice if we're ever going to be coming back through here. Okay?"

"S'alright."

"Well, he turned out to be a nice guy. That's all." Doc said rather petulantly.

"Okay, okay, I believe you."

Doc looked at Barnes for a moment to make sure he wasn't putting him on, then said, "I'll get the gas boy over here. You supervise the fueling. I'll go pay the landing fees and file the flight plan, grab a cab and come get you and maybe we can find some chow."

"Sounds like a plan, Doctor." Smoke started to turn away.

Doc grabbed his arm restraining him. "Hey, wait a minute. Where did I screw up the flight planning, Smoke?"

"You have us going direct, straight line from here to just off the coast of El Salvador.
I hate to be the bearer of bad news, but there are a bunch of rocks between here and there. I've redone the flight plan, keeping us over water, on down the coast of Mexico. It would ruin our whole trip making contact with some 'cumulo-granitus'; them rocks that will bring you to a sudden stop."

"Sorry about that. Glad you caught it. I'll get a move on."

McGarrity went over to the line shack and got the gas boy on his way. The boy didn't understand much English, but from what Doc could get out of him, it wouldn't be easy to find any place to eat at this late hour. He walked over to the tower and airport office. He entered the main terminal building and started down the hall. He passed a door marked "CUSTOMS", stopped and went in. Customs Inspector Sanchez was seated at a desk with the Detonics automatic all apart and the parts spread out on his desk. He was referring to a folded paper that had been inside of the gun purse along with a small cleaning rod. The official looked up, a bit surprised to see Doc.

Doc spoke first. "Excuse me Inspector. I hate to bother you, but do you know where my co-pilot and I could get a bite to eat?"

"At this late hour, everything is closed Capitan. But perhaps I could find something for you."

"I would certainly appreciate it. That's very kind of you."

"It won't be much, but perhaps enough to get you by until you land at San Salvador. Some sandwiches and coffee. Do you have a coffee jug?"

"I have a large thermos jug on the airplane. I'll go down and drop off my flight plan and pay the landing fees, then come back and bring the jug to you," Doc said.

"That's fine. Only stop back by here, Capitan McGarrity, and I'll take you to the airplane in my car."

"I don't want to put you to any bother. And, by the way, my name is *Doc* McGarrity."

The customs official stood up behind his desk and reached across with his hand stretched out, "My name is Juan Sanchez, Capitan McGarrity."

"Just Doc, Inspector Sanchez."

"Yes. Well then, just Juan, Doc."

They both chuckled. Then Doc told him he'd be right back. He went down the hall to the airport office to file. In a short time he was back and Inspector Sanchez drove him to the airplane. Doc jumped out and quickly got the coffee jug out of the airplane and handed it into the car.

"I'll be back in a short time, Doc," Sanchez said.

Smoke and the gas boy were still fueling the airplane. Doc went to see if he could give them a hand. Smoke waved him away. Doc went into the airplane, climbed up on a crate and took a nap.

He woke up when Barnes came in to open the over-wing hatch. Barnes went out through the hatch onto the wing and then back in dragging the fuel hose into the airplane. He started filling one of the fifty gallon drums.

"How much are you putting aboard, Smoke?" Doc asked.

"I've filled all of the on-board tanks. That makes eight hundred gallons and I'm going to fill two of these drums. That'll make a total of nine hundred and ten. Your flight planning paperwork showed six plus forty-five enroute hours. With reserve, all we would need would be close to the eight hundred gallons internal. I thought it wouldn't hurt to have a little insurance. We're going to be taking off before it gets warm. And we're a hellava lot lighter than we were out of Vancouver."

Doc yawned, "Sounds good to me."

"Well, I'm almost done. One more of these drums and that'll do it. What's the story on chow? I'm hungry."

"Everything's closed. Customs Inspector Sanchez is bringing us some sandwiches and coffee." Doc looked at his watch. "He should be back pretty soon."

"You're shittin' me, Doc. The Customs Inspector? You said that he's a nice guy, but this is unreal."

"Smoke, I don't kid about booze, pussy, in-flight emergencies or food. You should know that about me by now."

"You're right. You don't. But you threw me with the 'customs inspector' bit. I won't ask how it all came about."

"This inspector is the one that we should try to schedule our arrival and departures around. During his shift if at all possible. And like I told you before, all it cost was that Detonics McFrank gave me to use in cases like customs, police hassles and the like. I think I have made a friend for life. It's sure worth it."

"He was that impressed with the gun?" Smoke interrupted.

"Yeah."

Smoke finished filling the second fifty-five gallon drum and started back out through the over-wing hatch with the fueling hose. Doc started to help him when Smoke told him that he'd finish with the fuel hose, just to go pay the kid.

Doc climbed out of the airplane and walked over to the line shack to pay the fuel bill. Glancing up, he noticed car lights approaching the airplane. It was Sanchez.

"Buenos Narday, Seen-yor Inspector" Doc said as Inspector Sanchez got out of his car.

"Capitan McGarrity, don't try to speak Spanish. You're liable to offend someone with delicate ears. I have a wonderful meal for you and your co-pilot. Here, take the coffee jug and I'll get the food." He handed the coffee jug to Doc and leaned back into the car and brought out a cardboard box; it wasn't a small one.

"That looks like a lot of food, Juan. You must have bought out the restaurant. You shouldn't have gone to so much trouble."

"No trouble. My wife fixed this up for you. I told my wife you were a very important government official. She thought this would help further my career." Juan Sanchez said with a chuckle.

"You be sure to thank her for us, and you can add that we'll do what we can to further your career. You can say I said that. Come, I'd like you to meet my co-pilot." Doc gestured for Juan to go into the airplane. Doc called out for

Smoke to turn the interior lights back on and come down to the door. The lights came on.

As Doc and the inspector climbed into the C-47, Smoke came back from the cockpit. He saw Sanchez. "Hi there, you must be the Customs Inspector."

Doc stepped up, "Smoke, I'd like you to meet Inspector Juan Sanchez. He brought us some wonderful food, from the smell of things that his wife fixed for us." Doc turned to Sanchez. "Juan, this is my co-pilot, partner and best friend, Harry 'The Smoke' Barnes. His friends call him 'Smoke'."

"My pleasure, Señor Barnes. I would be pleased to call you 'Smoke'." Sanchez held out his hand.

Barnes took his hand and said, "I certainly appreciate meeting you. And thank your wife for the wonderful-smelling food. I'm famished."

"I'll leave you two to your meal." Turning to Doc, Sanchez said, "It's midnight now. How soon do you think you'll be leaving?"

"Probably crank it up and out of here before one. Is there something I should know?"

"Not anything that we haven't already discussed, Doc. Merely a question. I do wish you a safe flight and I'm looking forward to seeing you again," the inspector said as he climbed down out of the airplane.

"Thank you, Juan. We'll probably see you in a couple of days. We should be coming back through here, unless the company re-routes us," Doc called after him.

"I'll watch for a flight plan. Adios, Capitan Doc." Inspector Sanchez touched his cap visor, got into his car and drove back over to the terminal building.

Doc watched him drive away. He turned and noticed that Barnes was still standing there beside him. "Smoke, there goes one strange paradox. But what do you say we just load our ass into that big airplane behind you and hightail it out of here. This is getting too weird for me. Can you hold off your famine until we get airborne?"

"Yeah. I sure can. This is starting to spook me, too. I kept thinking he was trying to tell you something." Barnes paused then continued, "Yeah, let's do it."

"Right then. After you, my fine friend. You get the left seat, it's your leg. I'll pull the gear pins and kick the chocks. You can go ahead and get the engines started. Let's get out of here."

Smoke nodded and climbed aboard. Doc ducked under the wing and pulled the gear ground safety-lock pins, kicking each chock away from the wheel as he came back. He climbed aboard as Smoke was getting the left engine started. Doc knelt down and reached for the step, retrieved it, stood up and closed the main cabin door. As he came forward he stopped and checked the over wing window hatches on both sides of the cabin. Everything looked secure. He went on up to the cockpit, noticing that Smoke had put the chow within reach. Doc climbed into the co-pilot's seat.

"Where are you on the Check List, Smoke?"

"Uh, pick it up on the After Start Check List. I'm just finishing and will get the right engine started."

Twenty minutes later they were airborne. Much to their relief, there were no delays or problems. Doc reported to Acme Base on the HF radio that Acme Flight was airborne from Cabo. There was a quick acknowledgment, then silence. Base had clicked off.

"Well, I guess they don't want to talk to us, Smoke." Doc said as he hung up his microphone.

"Screw 'em then if they can't take a joke!"

CHAPTER TWENTY-THREE
CHICKENS, PIGS, GOATS OR COWS

Their route of flight would take them across the Gulf of California, down the west coast of Mexico, across the Gulf of Tehuantepec, staying well offshore of Guatemala, and into El Salvador. Following the coastline of Mexico was essential since the Sierra Madre mountain range contained some very high terrain. A lot of it stuck up into the air twelve and thirteen thousand feet. In one place it was above fourteen thousand feet. Radio navigation aids were scarce in this part of the world, and it was a very dark night.

Once past Tehuantepec, they would clear Mexican airspace. Their direct route would have them just offshore of Guatemala. Doc decided that by heading slightly further west, they could stay out of Guatemalan airspace. They would be able to maintain a good radio bearing off of the San Jose radio beacon on the west coast of Guatemala. It should be getting light about the time they would be at that position.

McFrank had mentioned that Guatemala was a nice place to avoid if at all possible. The government and especially the police or army were very corrupt. The United States did not have much influence in that country. It would not be a good idea to have to land there for any reason. Especially with a load of arms.

Once clear of Guatemalan airspace and entering El Salvadorian airspace they would drop down from their cruising altitude of eleven thousand feet to one thousand feet off the water. When they got closer to their turn-in point for

San Julian, they would go down on the deck, staying clear of everybody's radar.

That was the plan.

After taking-off from Cabo San Lucas they climbed to eleven thousand feet. Once level, and all the chores of setting up cruise had been accomplished, Doc and Smoke had a chance to eat. The meal was wonderful. Both Doc and Smoke felt they owed Sanchez a world of gratitude. It was so incongruous, Inspector Sanchez went to a lot of trouble for them. Yet, they had felt threatened for some reason. It was hard to put a finger on anything specific, but it sure felt good to get out of Cabo San Lucas. Maybe it had been the way he talked about his relief.

After they ate, Doc went back and sacked out on top of a crate.

Smoke was alone on the flight deck. There wasn't a lot to do. Monitor the engine instruments, make small adjustments on the auto-pilot to maintain their desired course and altitude and try to stay awake.

This was one of his favorite times. Alone in a cockpit, engines droning smoothly, things being as they should be, lots of fuel, nobody shooting at them. Life didn't get much better than this, he thought. In a couple of hours, looking to the east, from eleven thousand feet, he would be able to see the beginning glow of a new dawn.

Thinking, thinking, thinking. *Harrison Carvel Barnes the Second. Born with a silver spoon in his mouth, or his ass, he wasn't ever really sure which. He had been a good kid, not ever in too much real trouble or a bother to his parents. It was only later, in his teen years that he gave them grief but he made up for it by joining the United States Marine Corps. Boy! Wasn't THAT a smart thing to do! Guess he showed them, all right!*

Smoke chuckled out loud as he thought about it.

Dean Hedges, Dean of Men of Washington & Lee was a fair man. He was known to be rather tolerant of the student's pranks. But not this time! He didn't appear very tolerant at the moment, in fact, he was fuming! It was a Monday morning. It had been a very busy weekend. There had been some delay in getting Mr. Barnes into his office, since Mr. Barnes had neglected to attend his first class of the day. It was now ten o'clock in the morning. The Dean of Men was upset. His face was beet red and he was having problems getting words out of his mouth. Barnes just stood there waiting.

"Mr. Barnes! Just what in the hell do you have to say for yourself?" He finally managed to ask. It was unlike Dean Hedges to use profanity of any kind.

"I don't know what you are making reference to, Sir." Barnes answered, speaking reasonably and with an attempt at wonder as to why he was standing here in front of the man, tone in his voice.

"You know damn well what I'm talking about. It was one thing to steal the New Market Battle Flag from Virginia Military Institute, but to then drive around their town in a convertible, with the flag flapping until the police could find and stop you had to be the height of stupidity! But quite frankly, Mr. Barnes, it is one thing to deal with a historic item, and that battle flag is a historic item, but to then get the call from the Dean of Women over at Hollins College the following day about the little stunt that you pulled over there, was the final straw. You had yourself a very busy weekend." Sarcasm was dripping from every word.

"What was that, Sir?" Barnes asked feigning innocence.

"Mr. Barnes, you were seen and identified in the vicinity of the girl's dorm that had somehow ended up with a bunch of stray dogs turned loose inside....who had apparently been fed some form of laxative. THAT Sir, is what I'm talking about!"

"Oh." Barnes thought quickly. "Well, there is the matter of proof, Sir."

"Mr. Barnes. The nice thing about my position is that I don't have to prove anything! You Sir, are out of here. I'm sending notification to your parents with a full account of this year's so-called pranks; leading the panty raid at Hollins, the dogs turned loose in the girl's dorm there, the VMI flag incident and anything else that I can remember." The Dean paused to catch his breath, then went on in a more official tone, "You are hereby expelled. I want you off of this campus before nine tonight. Including all of your possessions. You will not be back. I can't imagine you ever being reinstated, Mr. Barnes, not as long as I'm the Dean of Men at this establishment! You're dismissed. Get out of my sight." Every word had been delivered with pointed clarity.

There wasn't anything left for Barnes to say. The Dean had made himself pretty clear. He turned and left the office.

Walking to his room in the dorm, Barnes formulated a plan. Dad would have his ass when he found out about this. Shit! He only had the rest of this year, a matter of a few months and he would have completed his third year. Oh well. The more he thought about it the more he thought the service would be a nice place to hang out for a couple of years. He had remembered hearing about a Reserve Program that would mean being on active duty for just two years, and he could even earn some G.I. Bill benefits.

Barnes was just finishing packing when his room-mate came in. Harry told him what had happened.

Paul Horn was a jock and from a wealthy family. He had been in on a lot of the pranks, but hadn't been caught or seen or identified. He was apparently home free, thankful that Harry hadn't involved him. This made him sympathetic to Harry's plight. Which came in handy. Harry needed some money. Paul Horn's weekly allowance far exceeded Barne's monthly stipend. Harry told Paul his intention to join the

240

Marines. Paul cautioned him on his choice, it could be tough. Harry had made up his mind, thinking about the dress blue uniform and how he remembered the way girls reacted to it, compared to the other service uniforms. Besides, John Wayne was a Marine. Right.

Paul's sympathy extended to purchasing a lot of things Barnes wouldn't be needing. He wanted Harry's portable typewriter, but Harry decided to keep that one item. Everything else, except his clothes, Harry sold. They promised to stay in touch.

Harry left the campus of Washington & Lee for the last time. It was barely two-thirty in the afternoon. His next stop was the U.S Marine Corps Recruiting Office in downtown Lexington, Virginia.

Staff Sergeant Grimm had been very understanding about Harry's need to get into the 'Corps' as quickly as possible. He had dealt with students from Washington & Lee and the VMI academy before. Especially those that felt going into the Marine Corps would be easier than going home in disgrace. Or so the applicant thought. The Sergeant's primary concern seemed to be the matter of any arrest warrants that may be outstanding. The processing time would take about three days. Did Harry Barnes have a place to stay?

Harry knew of a motel that he had used for other purposes. It even had telephones in the rooms. He had enough money, thanks to Paul Horn. Everything was set.

Sergeant Grimm pulled it off. In three days Barnes was on a train, on his way to the U.S. Marine Corps Recruit Depot, Parris Island, South Carolina. He had to leave his car in Lexington. Recruits were not allowed to have cars. The train ride from Virginia to Yemassee, the last stop before Savannah in the southeast corner of South Carolina, took close to twelve hours. Barnes hadn't changed clothes for a couple of days. He had packed all of his other clothes and locked them in the car. He was looking forward to a shower, *a good night's rest and some decent food. Stepping off the train in Yemassee, Barnes noticed a red sign with yellow lettering, directing him to an area for U.S. Marine Corps Recruits. He joined a group of other young men standing around in that area.*

They were quickly joined by the meanest Son of a Bitch in the world. There must be some mistake. He was here to volunteer to be a Marine. He probably shouldn't have mentioned that fact to the Drill Sergeant. He instantly became a matter of ridicule for this 'greeter of recruits'. He should have listened to Paul's advice and just gone home.

Barnes didn't want to remember boot camp. It was an extreme shock to his system. Selecting the Marine Corps had been one of the biggest mistakes he had ever made. On the other hand, becoming a U.S. Marine Corps fighter pilot was the smartest thing he had ever done. One thing was certain, going through Pre-Flight at the Naval Aviation Training Command was easy, compared to life as a Recruit in U.S. Marine Corps Boot Camp!

Dear old Sergeant Grimm, the recruiter, now there was a classic Son Of a Bitch! Barnes had thought he was signing up for a two year active-duty hitch as a Reservist. He should have read all of the papers carefully that he signed in the accelerated processing. He found out later he had signed standard enlistment papers and was IN for four fucking years! He found this out while being interviewed for various schools for which his two plus years of college education and General Classification Test scores qualified him.

The Naval Aviation Cadet Flight Training Program opportunity appeared as an oasis in the desert. It would be tough, but he'd sure as hell make it through. No way would he flunk out! It would mean going back to finish his four year hitch as an enlisted man. Not a chance. He had applied for flight training while still in boot camp. The tests were a snap, coming right from school, not to mention the incentive to change his present status, which had appeared to be a four year hitch as a U.S. Marine Corps infantry rifleman.

Pfc. Barnes somehow made it through Boot Camp. Nothing in his life had prepared him for that experience. He went to great pains to block it from his mind. It had given him an entirely new perspective on the small demands of his parents, the very liberal rules of a college campus and many other things in life that he taken totally for granted. Things like sleep, privacy in the bathroom, clean laundry, just normal everyday things that one didn't think a whole lot about unless they were suddenly taken away.

Nothing could ever be that bad again.

But finally he graduated and went home on leave. It was easy to make peace with his father. It was probably the Dress Blue uniform and spit shined shoes. His father was actually proud of him and even said so. His mother just cried. Enough of his old girl friends were impressed with the Dress Blues to make his leave a memorable one.

He returned from his boot leave to find orders to Pensacola! He had been accepted into the Naval Aviation Cadet Program. He was going to become a pilot, and then commissioned as an officer. Whew!

Flight training was a breeze. One hellava lot of fun and even as a cadet, he was treated like a human being. He made the scholastic honors list in every training phase. Barnes turned out to be a natural in the air, which was a pleasant surprise since he had not done well in sports while growing up. His father quickly got over the disappointment of his expulsion from school. He became prideful of his son's accomplishments. Dad flew to Corpus Christi and pinned on Harry's "Wings of Gold" when Harry graduated as a Second Lieutenant in the U.S Marine Corps. It was a proud day for father and son.

Smoke never forgot that day.

He also remembered the wonderful, wonderful leave. New York, his home town, was literally at his feet. The girls *just loved the Marine Corps uniform. This was even better than his boot leave. This time he wore his Officer's Dress Blues as much as possible. But then the girls seemed to like the greens almost as much. It was probably the wings. Those fabulous "Wings of Gold".*

At the advice of his instructor from his last phase of training, one Navy Lt. Stewart, Smoke had purchased several sets of miniature wings. "Coach Stewart", he insisted his three cadet students address him in that manner, after all they would be commissioned in a couple of weeks. They had to get used to the camaraderie existing between pilots of the lower commissioned ranks.

The miniature wings would come in handy on leave. You tell the girl of the moment that you brought these home for your mother, but you wanted her, the girl, to have them. Sort of like getting engaged. And being engaged, of course, usually carried certain intimate privileges. Coach Stewart referred to the miniature wings as leg-spreaders.

By the time the fourteen day leave was over Smoke remembered getting engaged to about four different girls. Ah yes, what a leave!

But all good things must come to an end. Second Lieutenant H.C. Barnes, USMCR was to report to VMT-3, a training squadron, based at El Toro, California. Sunny southern California. Maybe he would get a jet squadron, flying either the Grumman Panther or the McDonnell Banshee, take your pick. After all, he was a natural, or at least all of his instructors had told him so.

What did he get? Ten hops in a Corsair, and he was on his way to Korea as a replacement pilot. He was torn. It was like watching your mother-in-law drive over a cliff in your new car! Barnes had grown up during the Second World War. The Chance Vought Corsair was part of that history. He had only dreamed of what it would be like to fly one. He had flown the Grumman F6F Hellcat in his last phase of training down in Corpus Christi, had even carrier

244

qualified in it. He had thought the experience would be his last link to history. Not so. He was going to go to Korea and fly Corsairs, not jets.

But, it turned out that the Corsair was some kind of magic. You didn't get into it, you put it on. Jets could wait. He would get his chance to fly them later.

Memories, beautiful memories. *He had met Doc in his first squadron, along with Franklin, Wells, Randolph, and a host of others. All great people. And here he was. Eleven thousand feet, off the coast of Mexico, flying into God-knows-what. Life is good! God! Was he a lucky sumbitch or what? It sure beats the shit out of being a stock broker like his dad. And the great thing about it? His dad had agreed!*

They were approaching their San Jose, Guatemala check point when Smoke went back and woke up Doc. Smoke handed him a cup of coffee. McGarrity noticed it was a little past seven, Mountain Standard Time. He had reset his watch in Cabo San Lucas, but here, dawn had arrived.

"I need you to transfer some fuel, Doc. Then we can start downhill. We're coming abeam San Jose."

"Okay, I'll get right to it. How're you doin', Pardner?"

"I made it through the night. I'm pretty tired. It's better now that it's daylight. You can have the landing." Smoke went back up forward without waiting for more conversation.

Doc stretched the kinks out of his body. He sat on the edge of the long crate where he had slept and drank the coffee. They would be able to sleep in a real bed tonight. The thought sustained him. He got to work transferring fuel. He transferred both fifty-five gallon drums. He would have loved a cigarette, but his nose told him no way. He went forward.

Barnes had moved over to the right hand seat. Doc slid into the left, turned to Smoke and said, "I transferred all of it, both drums. Where are we?"

"I just finished the Descent Check List, so we can start down any time. We're well past the abeam point off San Jose. That's the Itzapa Radio Beacon on our number two ADF. The number one ADF is on, what I think is, Punta Remedios. The map of the San Julian area is there on the glare shield in front of you. I haven't got a good identifier on Remedios yet, but I think that's it. The bearing is as it should be anyway. Why don't you see if you can hear it? My hearing is all screwed up. You do that and I'll start this bird downhill."

"Okay. But my hearing isn't much better," Doc said as he slipped a headset on and adjusted the tuning of the number one ADF back and forth trying to get the identifying signal denoting the Punta Remedios homer. He pressed the headset tighter to his ears with both hands and closed his eyes. After a moment he looked up and turned to Barnes. "That's it. You had it, Smoke."

"I wasn't sure. How low do you want to go, Doc?"

"Why don't we just go in at a thousand feet? If we go much lower we'll lose radio reception. How far out are you?"

"It's only an intelligent guess, but from the bearings I have been taking I believe we're about thirty miles offshore and about eighteen to twenty miles north of our turn-in point. What we could do is to go on down on the deck for the twenty miles, turn in and when we hit the coast start climbing to a thousand or fifteen hundred feet. The strip, at the ranch, is about fifteen hundred feet field elevation. We won't get an altimeter setting, so it's going to be eyeball anyway. I've been using twenty-nine point ninety two barometric pressure for an altimeter setting all night, since we were over water and had planned on keeping it. Unless you have a better idea."

246

"No, that's okay, let's ease her on down. As we get closer the reception on the homer will get better and we can correct the track. I'll get the pictures of the area. I don't think we'll have any problems. When we get to the area, we have to fly a specific pattern. We're to fly down the runway to the east, do a left hand three-sixty, turn and fly back to the west, doing a right hand orbit at the west end. Then we can go in and land."

Doc got out of the left seat, retrieved his briefcase and was back with the pictures.

"This guy Cordero is kinda careful, isn't he?" Smoke asked as Doc climbed back into the left seat.

"Yeah, I guess so. We're lucky that we won't have much to do with him."

"If you're ready, it's your airplane, Compadre," Smoke said. He gestured command change of the airplane to Doc.

Doc patted the wheel, nodded and said, "I've got it." He adjusted the trim to his liking. Funny thing, that. It doesn't matter how well an airplane is trimmed up, when another pilot takes command, they invariably will re-trim to suit their taste.

It was quiet for a while, both of the pilots lost in their own thoughts. As if finally arriving at a decision, Smoke looked over at Doc and said, "You know, this flight pattern thing, there isn't any mention of altitude. What did you have in mind?"

"Hell, I don't know, I hadn't thought about it. And now that you've brought it up, I think I'm afraid to ask what *you* have in mind."

"I was just thinking we should make sure there aren't any chickens, pigs, goats or cows on the runway. One good way to insure that would be to blow some of the loose dirt away. It would discourage any critters from roaming around on our landing site. Plus, it would let the folks know we'd arrived. You haven't ever told me the itinerary that you gave

247

to Roberts to send to Whitey. What time did you tell him we'd be arriving?"

"I wasn't specific. I told him in the morning. Mainly because I wasn't sure of the time zone changes or what problems we would have getting out of Cabo San Lucas, so I didn't want to commit a hard number--just before noon on this date."

"It will be that, regardless of the time zone, from the way things look now. In fact, if the ADF needle is tracking, we're at our turn-in point now. I put us about twenty-five to thirty miles off shore. At this altitude we won't see the coast for probably another ten miles."

"Yeah, I've been watching the ADF. But, going back to our conversation about the flight pattern at the ranch, the more I think about it, the more I like your idea." Doc said, as he turned the C-47 onto the heading that would take them to the beach. He held the airplane at three hundred feet above the sea. Doc continued, "Since the first pass is supposed to be to the east, we'll be lined up, coming in from the coast. At low altitude, it might be difficult to spot the strip. I don't know. We could fly high and wide to check things out before committing."

"Doc, we know the ranch and airstrip are on the north side of that 4,700 foot high peak. The one just beyond is 6,500 feet and due west. On our left will be the tallest one at close to 8,000 feet. We've got the pictures of the area around the strip. Take another look, we've got lots of landmarks. All we have to do is thread our way between these little mountains. I say let's go for the low pass on our initial approach. I think we have enough data to do the job."

"Here, take the airplane, and hand me the pictures again," Doc said.

Smoke handed Doc the pictures, saying, "I've got it."

Doc looked at the pictures again, concentrating on what appeared to be the west side of the ranch. "It looks like the ranch sits in a sort of a half bowl. There is a rim to the west. When we clear it, it should be a simple enough matter to get a visual line-up on the runway. I agree, we can do it. Worst case would be off too far, one side or the other. You can watch for a couple of things in this one picture. I'll put it on top. Here, you take the pictures back and I'll take the airplane." Doc patted the wheel.

"You've got it," Smoke said as he reached for the pictures.

Doc took control of the airplane again while Barnes buried his head in the pictures. "Smoke, take a look, there's the mountains, and you can make out the beach line if you look close through the haze. We're here, 'Ol Buddy."

"Hand me the map. You just keep flying the airplane, Doc. Okay, you're tracking the ADF real good. As we get closer to the coast, you'll be approaching a tip of land jutting out into the ocean. The homer is on the left side, we want to be on the right side. You'll pass over an airstrip on the beach. That will be Banderas. We'll cross a coast road and pick up a secondary road leading from there right into San Julian. Elevation at San Julian is one thousand feet. So, we're going to want to start climbing as we cross the coast line."

"Got it." Doc was searching ahead through the haze, trying to pick out land details. He saw the point of land and started a swing to the right about ten degrees. "Okay, let's have some climb power. In fact, give me the Before Landing and the Landing Check List. Hold off on the flaps and gear. We'll carry the climb power setting for the low pass and approach. I see the secondary road. It sure isn't much to write home about."

Smoke had been busy in the cockpit setting up the check list items. He looked up, "There is a small town about ten miles in and then San Julian is another ten miles beyond. The first little town isn't named on this map."

"I see it. We're getting close, Pal."

"Right. Now look for San Julian. From the pictures and the map, I think the ranch should be to the right and just beyond the town and farther up the slope of the mountain. At least another five hundred feet. How high are you going to go?"

"High enough to avoid the rocks, Compadre. I was thinking about eighteen hundred feet or so. It looks like we'll miss all of the granite with that."

"Your call, Captain." Smoke pointed through the windshield, "There's San Julian."

"Got it. Watch for the ranch. Remember the strip has an 'X' on each end."

Both McGarrity and Barnes were looking intently out the window. Doc held the C-47 in a slight climb. They passed over San Julian about eight hundred feet above the ground. Doc noticed a couple of upturned faces as they passed to the south of the small El Salvadorian town.

"There's the strip! I've got it!" Smoke yelled out. "It's just a little farther to your right....at your one o'clock!"

"I see it!" Doc responded. He raised the nose to be well clear of a small ridged rise between the town and the ranch, then turned slightly right and headed for the west end of the runway, dropping down in altitude. He arrived over the end of the runway and held the transport about fifteen feet above the deck. They flew the entire length of the runway at the fifteen foot altitude, kicking up a trail of swirling dust in their wake, then pulled up sharply and executed a left hand climbing orbit, as specified in their instructions. Then right back down on the deck, flying the length, this time east to west, again at about fifteen feet above the ground.

Reaching the west end Doc pulled up sharply and executed a climbing right hand orbit, pulling back on the power and expelling energy in the climb. When the airspeed bled off, Doc called for the gear, then the flaps, as the airspeed allowed. Completing the orbit, Doc lined up and touched down right on top of the 'X' that had been painted on the west end of the runway.

He taxied up to the buildings on the east end, pivoted the C-47 smartly and shut down. Dust swirls, created by the two low passes, were still in the air.

There weren't any chickens, pigs, goats or cows to be seen anywhere.

Whitey had been flown in the night before by Cellini's pilot, Raul, in the Cessna 206. When the C-47 made its first pass across the field, he and Colonel Cordero were taking a late breakfast and just finishing their coffee out in the walled courtyard, when the thundering noise of the two Pratt & Whitney 1830's, driving the relatively large transport, and still carrying climb power, roared by, nearly over their heads.

"Madre de Dios!" Cordero exclaimed. Then remembering his guest, continued in English, "What in hell is going on?" He jumped to his feet, overturning his chair. Looking up, he saw the silver C-47 climbing and doing a left hand orbit. He kept watching until it came back down and disappeared behind the wall enclosing the courtyard, it was so low. It made the second pass the flight pattern called for.

"I believe your shipment has arrived, Colonel." Whitey said. But what was going through his mind was something else! *Goddamn Marines! Like he had said to Roberts, they were unpredictable! He had to chuckle to himself, though, it certainly was spectacular.* Whitey followed the Colonel back through the house and out to the strip. They emerged from the house in time to see the C-47 touching down at the other end of the runway. Their vision was obscured by the dust still in the air from the low passes.

Several of the Colonel's men had joined them, automatic weapons at the ready, looking to their leader in confusion for some sign. Colonel Cordero waved his hand to one side briefly and that was all it took for his men to visibly relax. Lieutenant Dominique Paredes came running up, slightly out of breath.

"Colonel, what is this? I couldn't see the aircraft registration. Is this the shipment?" he asked.

"Yes," Colonel Cordero answered without taking his eyes off of the transport in front of him. He shook his head briefly, as if to clear his mind, then directed his attention to his lieutenant. "Señor McFrank has already identified the airplane. And, you saw that the flight pattern flown was correct, of course."

"Of course." The lieutenant replied without hesitation.

The rear door of the airplane opened, Doc jumped down, turned and Smoke handed him the stair step which Doc fitted into the hatch sill. Doc turned and saluted the group as they approached. Colonel Cordero and Lieutenant Paredes returned the salute. Whitey reached out and shook hands with both Doc and Smoke, then turned and introduced them to the Colonel and his Lieutenant.

The Colonel was all smiles as he held out his hand and said, "Welcome to El Rancho San Julian de Cordero, Capitan McGarrity and Officer Barnes. I extend the hospitality of the hacienda and hope I can make your stay a pleasant one."

"Thank you, Colonel, but we have to get unloaded and into San Salvador as soon as possible," Doc said, then added, "We could use a bite to eat, if it would not be any trouble."

Nothing was said about the low passes.

Colonel Cordero told Lieutenant Paredes to have his men unload the airplane. Doc wanted to stay with the airplane while it was being unloaded. Lieutenant Paredes assured him he knew about tie-downs and no harm would come to the airplane. They would probably open and unload the crates aboard the airplane since there wasn't any freight handling equipment at the ranch.

The Colonel, Whitey and the two Marines went into the house, and on out to the walled courtyard. Cordero rang for the cook. When the cook arrived, Cordero asked McGarrity and Barnes to tell him what they would like to eat. The Colonel then told one of his men to show the two pilots where they could refresh themselves.

A short time later, Doc and Smoke joined Colonel Cordero and Whitey McFrank out in the courtyard. They were no sooner seated when the cook, followed by a helper, brought their breakfast and placed it in front of them. The two pilots dug in with enthusiastic gusto.

They had finished eating and were on their second cup of coffee, when Lieutenant Paredes came out to the courtyard and reported that the unloading had been completed.

Colonel Cordero acknowledged the report and then turning to McGarrity, asked, "How soon do you have to depart?"

"We should be leaving now, Sir. Our flight plan called for the first landing in this country to be San Salvador, for customs. We're counting on a lack of strictness."

"I understand and won't keep you. But next time, plan to stay and enjoy the ranch."

Whitey McFrank spoke up then, "Gentlemen, do you have room for a passenger?"

"Sure, Whitey, you can ride up front with us, on the jump seat," Doc said, then turned back to Colonel Cordero, "Please extend our appreciation to your cook for the breakfast. It was excellent. And thank you again for your kind offer."

They took their leave. The Colonel and Lieutenant Paredes walked them out to the airplane. Whitey had gone to collect his things and quickly rejoined them. They were airborne a short time later.

CHAPTER TWENTY-FOUR
FLAMING HOOKERS

When the C-47 was airborne and the Climb Check completed, Whitey tapped Doc on the shoulder and asked, "What the hell was that arrival air show all about?"

"Smoke here suggested it, Whitey. He was concerned that there would be a bunch of goats or chickens on the runway. I agreed wholeheartedly and thought it would be a good idea to insure a clear path. Besides, there wasn't a word about any specific altitude to fly on the pattern information sent to us. Did it cause some sort of a problem for you?"

This comment invoked some rare laughter from Whitey. "It was a bit of a surprise. No, it didn't cause any problems for me, but it sure got Cordero's attention. I'll admit, it was spectacular."

This was Smoke's leg to be in the left seat, so Doc could turn and give Whitey more attention. He pressed on. "What's the story with this Cordero fellow, Whitey?"

"He has been brought in to deal with some of the negative activity that Castro is causing in this part of the world. Cordero is supposedly pretty good at his job. I don't know much about him, myself. What did you think of him?"

"Well, he was gracious enough. However, I had the feeling that now I know what it would be like to face a cobra while in a corner. I don't think this Colonel is a very nice person."

Whitey smiled. "You're probably right, Doc. I'm inclined to agree with your analogy." He patted both pilots on their shoulders. "Well, you lads did a good job. Did you have any plans on when you would like to return and what you would be taking out of here?"

"Yeah, we're going to get a good night's sleep, refuel and head north." Doc looked puzzled for a moment, then asked, "What do you mean about taking something out of here?"

"Doc, you have an empty airplane. El Salvador is a major producer of coffee bean. The country is essentially run by the Catorce Familia, the fourteen families. And they are a major part of the growing and exporting of coffee, worldwide. I happen to know one of the more influential family members, and you could do yourself, himself and me a favor and probably make yourselves a couple of bucks in the process. That is, if you're interested."

Barnes turned to Doc and Whitey. "Gentlemen, if you'll excuse me. Doc, we're closer than I thought, you had better call the tower for landing clearance and get the check lists out of the way."

"Righto, Smoke, Me Lad." Doc reached for the microphone, "Whitey, I'm very interested, but let's talk about this over a meal, or something. I have some work to do now. We have to get this thing on the ground."

"No problem," Whitey replied as he sat back on the jump seat he was occupying.

Doc turned back to the task at hand. He contacted San Salvador Approach Control and got a clearance. In a short time, they were on the ground, cleared customs, and, with Whitey's help, arranged for servicing the airplane. While they were clearing customs, Whitey called Cellini's pilot and asked his advice for servicing. Alfredo Cellini had a major interest in the flight service where the Cessna 206 was based and they could handle all service problems that might be needed as well as the fueling. Security could be provided as well.

The flight service people provided transportation to the hotel. Whitey told the lads he had made reservations for them at the El Camino Real, the hotel where he was also staying.

"You'll like the rooms, the food is great and service to match. It is truly a world-class establishment, Gentlemen. What would you like to do first?" Whitey asked of them both.

Smoke spoke up, "Considering it's noon o'clock, or thereabouts, I would like to bathe, take a nap, and then make an evening of it. What do you say, Doc?"

"It certainly sounds like a plan to me. What happens with the night life here Whitey? Do you have to marry these girls to have a good time?"

"Why, Doctor, I'm ashamed of you. Are you considering fornication without benefit of blessings from the church? This is a Catholic country, Doc. That type of activity is frowned upon. The ladies of the night, down here, are referred to as 'putas'. And they are available in every size, shape, and talent. If you will let me know your requirements, I'll be happy to arrange something suitable. And you, Smoke?"

"I intend to be a very good little boy, Whitey. I have enough at home, when it's there. It wasn't always so, believe me, but that's the way it is now. Thanks, anyway."

"Whitey, I haven't paid for poon since my Japan 'R&R' days." Doc said, and then continued with some hesitation, "Why don't we just see how it goes. Right now I'd like to take a bath and get some sleep, also."

"I realize you two have had a pretty rough twenty-four hours. I want you both to know that you did a damn-good job. Get your rest and give me a call when you wake up. If I'm not in my room, call the desk and they'll tell you where I can be found. It will probably be in the bar. Hey, tell me if you don't want to do anything tonight. If you just want to sleep, I'll understand."

"Thanks, Whitey, but I've discovered that a person shouldn't try to catch up in one shot, you just get on a merry-go-round. If you haven't heard from us by eight-thirty or nine, give us a piss-call, if you don't mind." Doc said.

McFrank took this last comment in stride. Doc was right. And, he agreed. You get the sleep back in stages. Seeing as how he used to yo-yo back and forth between the Northwest and Europe, jet lag, time zone changes, being up for twenty-four hours or more was something he knew a lot about. "You're absolutely right, Doc. If I haven't heard from you two by eight-thirty or so, I'll give you a call. Well, gents, we're here. Give your bags to the boy hurrying out here. I'll take care of the driver. You're all checked in, you just have to pick up your keys."

Smoke spoke up, "Thanks Whitey, this is very thoughtful of you."

"Yeah Whitey, thanks," Doc joined in.

"No bother, you earned it. I'll see you lads later tonight."

Rosa Mendez was still angry as she got out of the taxi in front of the El Camino Real Hotel. She had slammed the door a lot harder than she had intended. The driver muttered a curse as she walked, or rather stormed, into the hotel.

Rosa Marie Mendez had been born in Peru, the daughter of a prominent rancher and coffee grower. She had enjoyed an excellent education and upon graduation spent a lot of time traveling with her father. On one of his coffee cartel trips to El Salvador she had met the dashing, then Lieutenant, Miguel Garcia Mendez, of the San Salvadorian state police, the Policía Nacional. She had fallen helplessly in love with the suave, handsome officer. His family background was acceptable and, after a suitable period of courtship, they were married. The ceremony was attended by many members of the Catorce Familia and other dignitaries. Rosa's family was well thought of in Peru as well as in many other Latin American countries. Rosa's father was a member of the coffee cartel and spent a great deal of time in El Salvador.

Now Capitan, Miguel Garcia Mendez, and Rosa Marie had been very happily married for two years--that is until about two o'clock that afternoon. Capitan Mendez was in the back country on a patrol chasing Castroite guerrillas. He wasn't due back for another week. While looking for something else, Rosa had found some letters from Capitan Mendez's mistress. Rosa was devastated.

So! She wasn't good enough in bed for her handsome prince charming. Was that it? He was the only man she "knew" and all that she knew had been taught by him. She had always been willing to try new things. She had never denied him anything! The discovery had sent her into waves of crying and despair.

As the time wore on, however, her misery changed to anger. Then angry revenge. By eight o'clock, she had bathed, dressed in the tightest, most daring, shortest black dress she owned and called a cab to be taken to the El Camino Real, which she knew to be frequented by visiting businessmen. It was the finest hotel in San Salvador.

It was her intention to have several drinks and then to get even with the conniving, cheating bastard she was unfortunately married to. That was her intention.

At nine o'clock sharp, Doc and Smoke walked into the bar. They made their way over to a table where Whitey was sitting.

"Evening, Gents. You look all rested and ready for bear. What would you like to drink?" Whitey asked.

"Scotch and water, Dewar's if they have it," Doc replied.

"I'll have the same." Smoke said, then continued, "What were you talking to Doc about taking a cargo north, Whitey?"

Whitey motioned to a waitress and gave her their order and another for himself. Turning back, he said, "I was telling Doc that you gents have an empty airplane, El Salvador is a major grower and exporter of coffee bean and that I knew some of the more influential folks who are involved. It would be a way of making a few honest dollars and would certainly account for a flight into the states with a foreign-registered airplane."

"It sure sounds like a good deal. I don't know anything about how we would go about getting rid of it, though," Smoke wasn't putting the idea down as much as declaring his ignorance.

Doc turned to him, "You know, I've been thinking about this. Smoke, remember, down at the southern end of Boeing Field there's a company called Associated Grocers. Big outfit. They're wholesalers. Hell, we've flown over them a thousand times, taking off or landing at Boeing. We could land, clear customs, go sell ten thousand pounds of coffee to 'em and unload. I like it. The engines would still be warm. What kind of money are we talking about, Whitey?"

"You will be able to buy the coffee bean at somewhere around forty or fifty cents a pound American, roasted whole bean in fifty-pound sacks. I'm sure you'll be able to get a couple of bucks a pound at the other end. But say it's only a buck and a half, that's still ten thousand dollars in your jeans. How much expense money do you have left?"

"Whitey, we didn't use any to speak of in Cabo San Lucas." Doc told Whitey about Inspector Sanchez, the Detonics and their 'box lunches'. That got another laugh out of him. Doc was beginning to think this spook had a sense of humor after all. It was about the third laugh since they met.

Even at fifty cents a pound, the ten thousand pounds of roasted, whole-bean coffee, would only take five thousand American dollars. They had plenty of cash left. Whitey suggested getting together with Alfredo Cellini in the morning. He would arrange the meeting. Business over, the three of them got down to some serious drinking.

Smoke got up to go to the head. "Excuse me, Gents, I have to drain a sump. Be right back."

On his way back to the table he ran into Señora Rosa Marie Mendez. That is, he literally ran into Rosa. She ended up on the floor. Her tight skirt had ridden up high on her thighs and, coupled with the few drinks she already had, made it difficult to get up. Smoke had been standing frozen, admiring this very beautiful woman, lying at his feet and hadn't moved.

Recognizing that Smoke was an American, Rosa said, in English, "Are you going to continue to just stand there or will you be kind enough to help me up?"

Harrison Carvel Barnes came to his senses. Taking his eyes off of her beautiful body he reached down and took both of her hands and slowly lifted the lovely creature to her feet. He kept holding both of her hands.

"I should introduce myself, Señorita. My name is Harrison C. Barnes, and yours would be....?"

"If you will kindly let my hands go, I will tell you," Rosa said. Barnes abruptly let go and she continued, "My name is Señora Rosa Marie Mendez. And if you'll kindly step aside, I would like to return to my table."

Barnes released her, stepped back and took a good look. She was about five foot, two inches tall, had a beautiful bust line, slender hips, lovely legs, dark hair not quite to her shoulder and cut in bangs, flashing black eyes and a terrific smile that Harrison C. Barnes was just now getting bestowed upon his countenance. His visual inventory had noted a small tear in a seam near the bottom of the very form-fitting, black dress.

"I'm afraid I have been the cause of damage to your dress. I would like to pay for either the repair or replacement, Señora Rosa Maria Mendez. Perhaps you would allow me to buy you and Señor Mendez a drink, while we discuss where I can send suitable funds."

Rosa turned slightly, bending to see the damage that Smoke had pointed out. It was just stitching in the seam that had come apart. She must have spread her legs in the fall and stretched the tight dress beyond the strength of the threads. She looked up at the handsome American standing in front of her and said, "It's nothing, just some threads came loose in the seam. You won't be able to buy Señor Mendez a drink since he is not with me." She hesitated, thought for a moment, and then continued, "We are separated. However, I will accept your offer. And it is Marie, not Maria." She had made a decision. This American would be the tool of her revenge against the cheating, conniving husband that had brought her to this appointment with infidelity.

"Fine then, let me escort you back to your table and you can get your things and join me and my friends."

"Your friends....?" Rosa hesitated. She wasn't sure if this would work out with what she had in mind.

"Yes, I'm with two friends, but I hadn't planned on spending the entire evening with them." Smoke had detected something, he wasn't sure what.

"Well all right then, but just one drink."

Rosa led the way back to her table where she picked up her jacket and then followed Smoke around a corner and over to his table. As they approached the table, Doc and Whitey saw them coming and stood up as they got closer.

Smoke stood to one side, presenting his find, "Gentlemen, allow me to introduce Señora Rosa Marie Mendez. And Rosa, this is Whitey McFrank and Doc McGarrity." He pulled out a chair for her to sit. The others sat, also.

Rosa turned to McGarrity, "Are you a medical doctor?"

"No, Señora, it is a nickname from our military days," Doc replied.

Rosa turned to Barnes, "Your two friends, they both have nicknames and do you have one as well, or do I call you Harrison?"

"You may call me anything you like, Rosa, but I do have a nickname. It is 'Smoke'."

"Smoke? That is very unusual. May I ask how you came by this nickname?"

"Only after you tell me what you would like to drink, Señora Mendez"

"You may call me Rosa, and I would like to have a whiskey and water."

Smoke motioned their waiter over to the table and placed drink orders all around. He then turned back to Rosa and explained that it was the name of a gambling card game played by Marine Fighter Pilots. He had a reputation of being very good at it, and one of the squadron members hung the nickname on him. It stuck.

Rosa was obviously impressed by the fact Barnes was a pilot. "And both of your friends, they are pilots as well?"

"Doc is also a former Marine Fighter Pilot." Turning to McFrank, "Whitey? Are you a pilot?"

Whitey spoke up, "I've done some flying in my time."

"For some reason, I rather thought you had, Whitey," Smoke said. "But did you know that Doc here is the VMA-216 'Flaming Hooker' Champion?"

"I just can't imagine what that would entail," Whitey said with a chuckle. "The thought is frightening. In fact, I'm indeed afraid to ask what a 'Flaming Hooker' is."

"It's a drink, Whitey. *Real* pilots drink 'Flaming Hookers'. And not many have the courage to stand up to a champion like Doc here."

Whitey cocked his head to one side, "Why do I wish I were somewhere else right now, I wonder and ask myself." He spoke as if he was thinking out loud. "Are you inferring, Mr. Barnes, that *I* do not have the courage to take your champion on?"

"I wouldn't dream of even thinking that, Mr. McFrank. However, if you're of a mind to attempt the impossible, I'm sure the Doctor will oblige you." Smoke said.

"Hey! Don't I have anything to say about this?" Doc asked.

Both Whitey and Smoke turned to him and said in unison, "No!"

Rosa was taking all of this in and finding it quite amusing.

"Okay, I'm in," Whitey announced, "Now tell me what in hell kind of a drink a 'Flaming Hooker' is."

Doc spoke up, "A 'Flaming Hooker' is a shot glass full of very good brandy. It is placed in front of the player and lit. The player must pick up the shot glass and down the drink in one motion. The trick, of course, is to not miss your mouth. You would set the front of your shirt on fire. Also, it is not very wise to let the drink burn very long. The glass can get too hot and burn the hell out of the corners of your mouth. Like most Marine Corps games, it isn't very adult, and can be harmful to your health. I should mention the fact that if the brandy used is not very good, a floater of high proof rum is sometimes used, just for the flame. I'm sure this establishment will have a good brandy, where the rum wouldn't be necessary."

"I'll go along with your premise, Doctor, that it doesn't sound very adult. However, I accept the challenge and the opportunity to wrest a championship crown from the head of a United States Marine Corps Officer."

"Done. And I accept the challenge. Smoke, call the waiter over and we'll start with ten each. Line 'em up!" Doc said pride fully.

They made small talk, essentially about coffee beans, while the drinks were being prepared. Rosa surprised and impressed them with her knowledge of the coffee commodity. The drinks came, and they were ready to go.

Doc and Whitey each had their ten full shot glasses lined up in front of them.

In an announcer's voice, Smoke said, "Gentlemen, light your brandies!"

"Uh, Whitey, don't use your lighter, use a match. It's much easier," Doc advised.

The two contestants each lit one of their drinks, picked up the glasses and downed the flaming drink in one smooth motion.

"Are you sure you haven't done this before, Whitey? You did it just like a pro."

"Doc, I merely followed your advice and suggestions. But now is not the time to chat, now is the time to get on with this charade. When you're ready, Sir."

"Right you are, Mr. McFrank. I'm ready."

They repeated the actions of the first pair of shot glasses and went on to the next, without a word, merely nods to insure staying together.

Smoke told Rosa this would probably go on for the rest of the night, or until one of them passed out. He suggested that they move into the dining room and get something to eat. Rosa realized she hadn't eaten anything, other than some tea and toast upon arising that morning. She was getting hungry. She agreed, without thinking anymore about her stated "just one drink".

They ordered dinner. Smoke selected an appropriate wine that would complement Rosa's selection. He suggested a pre-dinner martini, to 'clear the palate'. They chose to forego appetizers.

The good food and excellent wine loosened Rosa's tongue. She told Smoke about discovering the infidelities of her husband and her decision to separate. Rosa insinuated that she had been separated for some time. Smoke asked what the good Captain Mendez was doing these days. Rosa told him the Capitan spends most of his time in the back country chasing guerrillas. In fact, that was where he was as they spoke.

The dinner was over, the dishes cleared. Smoke had ordered Amaretto for their after dinner drinks. Rosa had only taken one sip of her drink when she decided she had enough and now was the time to act. She reached over and put her hand on Smoke's arm. She looked him straight in the eye.

"Smoke, I want you to take me to your room. Don't ask me any questions, just do this please."

It came as a surprise. This was obviously a woman of class, not some puta. There must be something behind this request that Smoke could only guess at. Whatever it was, here was a gorgeous creature who was asking him to make love to her. He was not going to be judgmental.

Smoke quickly called for the bill, signed it and included a generous tip. He helped Rosa to her feet and guided her out of the dining room to the elevators. In the elevator, he held her close. The elevator stopped at his floor and they got out.

Smoke unlocked the door, opened it and stepped back for Rosa to enter ahead of him. Once inside, he closed the door behind him. He turned as she came into his arms, looked up smiling and pressed her body close to his. She reached down and undid his belt.

He learned once again in his lifetime, how unaffected and *real*, foreign women, women who were not North American, could be.

Smoke reached down and picked Rosa up in his arms. He carried her into the room and gently placed her on the bed. He slipped his shirt off, kicked his shoes over in the corner and lay down beside her.

"Could you help me with this dress? I would like it to not get torn any more than it is."

"Of course, little Rosa," Smoke said as he sat up, then stood. He reached for her and helped her to her feet. Smoke pulled her close and again kissed her passionately.

Pushing him away, she said, "Smoke, please, the dress."

Smoke gently helped her out of her dress. She wasn't wearing a brassiere. Her panties were the skimpiest things, and quickly followed the dress. He started to get back onto the bed, but Rosa stooped down, picking up the dress and under pants and placed the dress over a chair to keep it from wrinkling. Smiling, she turned back to her selected lover and moved cat-like onto the bed. Smoke looked down at her for a minute, taking in her beautiful body. Her breasts were small, but firm. Her ass was a work of art. He quickly shed his pants, skivvies and socks and joined her on the bed.

Again, they kissed passionately. The touching of their bare bodies close together fueled the passion more. Their tongues thrusting into each other's throat. They kissed and kissed. Smoke pulled back for a moment and caught his breath. Rosa was breathing heavily and didn't open her eyes. He kissed the juncture of neck and shoulder and up behind her ear, then down onto her chest. Smoke took her breast into his mouth, kissing and softly sucking at the nipple. It was hard as a rock. Then he moved down onto her flat stomach, kissing and licking. Rosa was moaning and rolling slightly back and forth but not enough to disturb his aim. Smoke knew the direction he was heading and wouldn't have been put off. He quickly arrived at that juncture of pleasure. It was sparsely covered with soft, black hair and glistening with perspiration from the heat of their passion. His tongue explored the lips of her pussy, quickly finding her clitoris, then darted into the cleft. Rosa cried out with her pleasure. Smoke brought her quickly to a climax with his act of cunnilingus. He turned back up, rolled her on top of him and impaled her onto his now rigid member. Rosa's passion was raging, and being on top gave her the freedom to express it. Smoke raised his hips, thrusting to match her movements. She was climaxing again and again. Finally, Smoke couldn't stand it or wait any longer. He joined her passionate height and let himself go with her. Rosa collapsed, her face buried in the soft hair of his chest. He held her, caressing her body. They lay this way for some time. Finally, Smoke gently rolled her off of him. He reached over to the night stand for his cigarettes, then remembered that they were still in his shirt pocket.

Oh well, so much for couth, he thought. Barnes untangled himself from this lovely creature, got up, got the cigarettes, lit two and handed one to Rosa. Thinking some more, he went into the bathroom and brought back a towel. He gently toweled the perspiration off her body and the love juices that were staining the bed cover. Nothing had been said as yet.

Rosa looked up at Smoke and said, "I have never in my life experienced love-making like that before, my darling Smoke, never. I have only read about things like that." She giggled softly as she thought about it, then pronounced, "We must explore some of the other things that I have only read about, before this night is over."

Smoke smiled, thinking of a few of the things he would like to share with this beautiful Latin lover lady.

Doc looked over at Whitey with a new respect. They had just finished their number ten 'Flaming Hooker'. Whitey had only missed once, half the drink splashing down on his chest, setting his shirt on fire. He had quickly extinguished it. Not a word had been uttered. Doc had waited, then together they had lit the next shot glass in line.

"Whitey, you've got some kind of balls, my friend. What do they call that down here? *'Cohones grandes'*, or something like that, 'large eggs'. Your miss-sh on number seven could have gotten serious, but you kept going. I'm impressed." Doc paused for a moment to release a small burp, then went on, "My record was-h seventeen, or rather it took me seventeen uh, hooksh...or hookers, to become the squadron champion," Doc's voice was noticeably slurred.

Whitey nodded. "S'alright. It burned a little. I let the glass get too hot, it slipped just enough for me to lose my hold. Dumb game. How often does your friend Smoke put you in thish position? Having to defend your crown? Some friend," Whitey remarked.

"Hey! That guy carries his nuts in a wheelbarrow also, Whitey. Plus the fact he saved my life." Smoke went on to tell McFrank about the bridges at Sinanju and how Smoke stayed with him, even making a second run into the target that he didn't have to do.

"Do you have a friend like that, Whitey? One that lays his ass on the line, with, and for you?" Doc asked.

Whitey grew thoughtful. He hadn't worked with many partners, preferring to work alone. But one man came to mind. "Yeah, I do. His name is Colonel Bob Sexton. Like you say, he carries his balls in a wheelbarrow. He was 'special forces' back before there was such a unit. We saved each other's ass in Thailand once or twice, and a rather hairy situation in Laos. Later Bob did some work directly for the company in Europe and we ran into each other again. I forget who helped who out that time, but it'sh always been give'n take. Probably like you and Smoke. Doesn't matter who's ahead, you'd still lay your ass on the line for 'em."

"Right on!" Doc said. He motioned the waiter over and said to bring ten more brandy shots for each of them.

Whitey went on. He shared the real funny caper about the exploding light bulb with Doc. Finishing up, he said, "Doc, I haven't told anybody these stories. I guess I don't have to tell you that they shouldn't be repeated. And this isn't liquor talking. I trust you and I trust your friend Smoke. You're both my kind of people. I'll be honored to call you my friends. I don't say this to many."

This got through to Doc. He looked Whitey straight in the eye, held out his hand and said, "Ernest Herman McFrank, I'd put my ass on the line for you anytime, Pal!

You can fly my wing, or I'll fly yours, and I only say *that* to the deserving."

The drinks arrived. Doc and Whitey carefully, with somewhat exaggerated movements, lined up their ten shot-glasses each. Very slowly they nodded to each other, lit their drinks one at a time and downed them. Not a drop was spilled. They continued, in silence, until the seventeenth glass was downed. Whitey held up his hand halting the contest.

With great care pronouncing his words, he said, "I do not wish to take your crown, Doctor, but am honored to equal your record. And now I wish to find my bed and fall into it." Whitey motioned the waiter over and signed the bill. He pushed his chair back with some effort, stood and gestured for Doc to stand.

Doc got to his feet with some difficulty saying, "Oh Great Co-Champeen, I heartily agree. That'sh a wunnerful idee."

With that, the two semi-adults wandered off to find the elevator, their rooms and their respective beds.

CHAPTER TWENTY-FIVE
COMMODITIES

It was a rather quiet group that met for breakfast at nine-thirty the following morning. McGarrity and McFrank both looked like something left over from the "Wreck of the Hesperus". Barnes, on the other hand, just looked wasted, but with a somewhat dreamy look.

Doc spoke up first. "Smoke, I want you to meet the 'co-Flaming Hooker-Champion' of VMA-216. Or is it Flaming Hooker co-Champion. He matched me seventeen, one for one, and then helped me to my room."

Whitey interrupted him, "Doc, I thought you were helping me!"

They all had a good laugh over this proclamation. Doc looked over at Smoke and asked him how his evening went.

"Well Fellows, a gentleman doesn't talk about things of that nature. And if I did, you probably wouldn't believe me anyway."

This comment brought more laughter. When things subsided, Whitey said he was going to arrange a meeting with Alfredo Cellini for the coffee buy. He wanted to know what would be a good time and when did they want to leave.

Doc just shook his head, "I need another day of rest, and it damn well better be a day of rest, before strapping the airplane to my butt. Smoke here looks like he could use some non-energetic sack time. Later today I want to call the office. What is it? Two-hour time difference?"

"No, it's three hours. El Salvador is on New York time," Whitey remarked.

Doc glanced at his watch. "Okay, why don't I call after we finish breakfast, while you call Cellini? Is that his name?"

"Yeah, his real name is Alfredo Cellini. His friends, of which I am one, call him 'Alfredo'. He is a leading member of the Cartorce Familias and a grower of coffee bean."

Smoke spoke up, "Well, if we want to be in the commodity business, namely coffee, we should probably start with him. If we want to fly down to Peru, we could contact Rosa's father. He is a grower also. You two were too involved in your drinking game to hear what she had to say about the business. She knew quite a bit about coffee."

Both McGarrity and McFrank looked real hard at Barnes. Doc said it for both, "Smoke, you asshole! Your big mouth is what got Whitey and me doing the 'hooker' thing, and you have the balls to accuse us of playing games. Damn you! It's your fault that I feel like hell. Whitey, why not shoot this bastard?"

"Well, Okay Doc, if you say so. Right here and now?" Whitey asked as he started to reach behind his back for the small automatic he always carried there.

"NO! Oh *please* let me live. I won't put you two through any more misery....you need me, Doc. I can help you fly the coffee home." Smoke said in mock fright, then added, "Besides, *I've* got to get better myself to die as it is!"

This got them all to laughing again.

"Okay, okay. Whitey, let him live, but he has to get the breakfast tab." Doc said.

Whitey nodded assent. "Gentlemen, it's ten-thirty. I'll call Alfredo and set up our appointment. I'll try to get us in right after lunch. Doc, you can call your office in a bit. I'll call your rooms and let you know what I came up with," Whitey suggested.

271

Harrison C. Barnes took care of the check.

About an hour later there was a knock at Smoke's hotel room door. He had been resting. He got up to answer it. Doc was standing there with the strangest look on his face.

"My God! What's the matter, Doc.? You look like someone has died." Smoke was truly concerned.

"Someone has, Smoke....someone has." Doc shook his head as if trying to remove the thought.

"What the hell, who?"

"Ken Herring, you know, Hunter's husband. He's dead. A heart attack."

Barnes thought about this for a moment, "Who told you? Uh, when did it happen? I mean, you obviously called the office, but she's not there, is she? Tell me. Maybe you had better start at the beginning."

"Okay." Doc gathered his thoughts together. "I called and Ross Bigelow, our engineer, answered the phone. Ken died yesterday. Ross said that Hunter called him from the hospital yesterday. Ken had been awakened by chest pains early in the morning, Ross didn't say what time. Hunter and their son had started to drive Ken into Seattle. They live in Bellevue, remember. Anyway, they got as far as the toll plaza on the Evergreen Point Floating Bridge and he collapsed. The toll collectors called an ambulance. They took him to a hospital in Bellevue but Hunter told Ross he was 'D-O-A'. The doctor told her it was a massive heart attack, the type that nothing could have been done to prevent or help. I guess she's pretty shook up. What a dumb thing to say, of course she's shook up. I really like that woman. I hate to see her hurting like this." Doc was obviously upset.

"What can we do, Doc? God! He was awfully young, wasn't he?"

"Funny thing, I had always assumed he was close to Hunter's age. But then when I promoted her she said something that led me to believe he was quite a bit older. I only met him a couple of times, but didn't notice any apparent age difference. I don't really know, Smoke. What should I do?"

"Call her, for God's sake. Do you have her home number?"

"Not with me. I could call Ross back and get it, I guess. That would be the easiest, easier than trying to go through 'Information' from here. Can I use your phone? I'll call from here."

"Sure, by all means. Call her."

Doc placed the call to Seattle, spoke to Ross again and got the number. He placed the second call, this time to Hunter's home. It rang several times before it was answered.

"Hello?" a weak voice said.

"Hunter?" Doc asked.

"No, this is her daughter. There has been a death in the family, she can't take any calls right now."

"I know. That's why I'm calling. Will you tell her James McGarrity is calling from El Salvador? I'll hold."

"I don't know, Mr. McGarrity. I'll tell her, but I don't know....hang on."

It seemed to take forever, but finally Hunter came to the phone. "Hello." It was a quiet voice, in obvious hurt.

"Hunter, Doc McGarrity. I'm so sorry about your husband. Is there anything I can do?"

"No. I just won't be able to run your company, Mr. McGarrity. I don't know when, or even *if*, I'll be able to come back to work. There's so much to do here. I don't know where to begin or how long it will take....I just don't know what to tell you...."

"Look! Hunter! Don't do this to yourself. Just take it one step at a time. I'm coming home. It'll take two days, but I'm coming home. I'll help you. Don't worry about the company. Smoke can handle things. I'll be there for you. Hello? Are you still there?
Hello?"

"....I'm here. I'm sorry. This isn't your problem. You don't have to come back. Finish what you have to do....oh, I don't know what I'm saying. We'll be okay. I have the kids here to help me. We'll get by. I can't talk anymore now. Thank you for calling." She hung up.

Doc slowly hung up the phone. He kept his hand on it for a moment. He turned to Smoke. "This is terrible. Don't ever repeat what I'm going to say to you." Doc got up and started to pace. He turned to Smoke and shrugged. "I think I'm in love with that lady. I fell in love with her a long time ago. The moment she walked into my office looking for a job. I've always put it out of my mind before....well, because she was so happily married and all. But now things are different. I've got to get back and help her, Smoke. I've got to."

"Hey. I understand. She's quite a lady. I could fall for her myself. We'll go get this coffee thing and hit the road my friend. We can leave tonight if you want."

"Smoke, I'm upset, but I'm not stupid. We're in no condition to fly for some sixteen or seventeen hours. We'll do the original schedule that I proposed earlier. If I'm going to help her, I've got to *be* there, not spread over some Mexican hillside because I have my head up my ass! But thanks. I appreciate your support."

"Whatever it takes, Pal, whatever it takes." Smoke laid his hand on Doc's shoulder. "Come on, let's go find Whitey and bring him up to date."

"No. You'd better call his room. He doesn't like people knocking on his door."

"Right. I forgot." Smoke reached past Doc and picked up the phone. He dialed Whitey's room.

"Hello." It was a brusque answer.

"Whitey, this is Smoke. We just got some bad news from Seattle. We're going to have to get back as soon as we can."

"I got through to Alfredo. We can meet with him right after lunch. He is sending a car. Do you want me to cancel?"

Smoke turned to Doc and repeated what Whitey had said. Doc indicated for him to go ahead. Smoke answered Whitey, "No. We'll meet with him. Don't cancel. Uh, how about dress?"

Whitey said for Doc and him to be downstairs at one. What they were wearing at breakfast would be all right.

Barnes and McGarrity were in the lobby a few minutes before one. At precisely one o'clock Whitey came into the lobby, motioned for them to follow, and proceeded across the entry court toward a limousine waiting at the curb.

An hour and a half later they had completed the transaction. Ten thousand pounds of prime-roasted coffee beans in fifty pound sacks, two hundred sacks, at forty-three cents a pound American. Alfredo told them that they should not settle for less than a dollar eighty per pound in Seattle. He would have the cargo at the flight service station in the morning, along with a crew to load it. They could pay him then.

As they were enjoying a whiskey, Smoke asked Señor Cellini if he knew a Capitan Mendez of the State Police. The question startled Whitey, but he couldn't stop Smoke without being too obvious.

"Si. I know of this person. Why do you ask?"

Whitey spoke up. "We heard the name at the ranch. The Captain is not one of Colonel Cordero's men so we were wondering about the connection."

"That's right. He isn't one of Cordero's men, but he is acting as a liaison between the Policía Nacional and the organization Cordero is putting together. You have piqued my curiosity. What was it you heard?"

"Only the name and something about some information. It wasn't clear and I didn't want to ask too many questions. My curiosity was aroused also, which is why I asked you," Whitey answered with a straight face.

"That is all I know, Whitey. Do you want me to make inquiries?" Cellini asked.

"Not now. Maybe at a later time." Whitey wanted the matter to drop.

"Whitey, about that other matter. The data and pictures regarding Venezuelans? I've told my people to send what we had over to the *policía* with a suggestion that someone take them over to Señor Estado at the hospital."

"Oh, good. I appreciate that." Whitey said.

They were soon back at the hotel. Whitey hadn't said anything to Smoke in the car, but when they got back and were out of the car walking toward the hotel doors, Whitey said in a low voice, "Don't ever do that to me again, Barnes. It was not very smart. You forget, this is a Latin American country. These people are very macho. I don't know how Alfredo would take it, but Mendez would kill you without a moment's hesitation, and then probably kill Rosa. They consider it justifiable homicide in this part of the world."

"Sorry. Rosa had said some things I felt you should know about. That's the only reason I brought it up. Thanks for covering my ass, Whitey. I was trying to help."

"As it turned out, you may have helped more than you realize. I just don't like surprises." Whitey made a gesture of dismissal. "But enough, let's go have a drink."

They proceeded into the bar. Doc pointed out that since they would be flying tomorrow, maybe it would be a good idea if he and Smoke just had coffee. They had joined Alfredo for a drink so as not to offend. Whitey didn't object.

"I have some things to do this afternoon. I'll meet you tonight for dinner, if you like. And I'll plan on going out to the airport with you in the morning. What time did you want to do that? Cellini will have his people there early to load the airplane. He is not a typical Latin, where everything is late. My guess is they will be there at eight o'clock. You can give me the forty-three hundred dollars for the coffee. I'll put it in an envelope and personally give it to Alfredo. You said you have plenty of money?" Whitey asked.

Doc said, "Sure, we started with twenty-five thousand in cash from Roberts. I've only spent money for loading the cargo, fuel and fees in Vancouver, plus the fuel and fees in Cabo San Lucas and the two hundred dollars to Inspector Sanchez. I have receipts for everything except the bribe money. And I'll need money for fuel here and one other stop, but we have plenty."

"The company folks only think in big terms, Doc. Add the two hundred bucks to the forty-three hundred for the coffee and put down forty-five hundred for the bribe. Roberts doesn't really expect to see any of that money back, but you have to get a little creative in accounting for it. I'm sure you'll manage. Remember, you'll have the hotel bills as well." Whitey was trying to explain how things worked in the spook world.

Doc acknowledged the input. They wrapped things up and agreed to meet for dinner. Stopping at the front desk, checking for messages, Smoke was handed an envelope. Whitey and Doc both chuckled, then Doc said, "Well, I'll meet you for dinner, McFrank, but it looks like Smoke may have other plans."

The note was from Rosa, of course. Smoke tore the envelope open, read the short note and motioned for Doc to wait. He told Doc that it looked like he was going to be tied up this evening but he would meet in the lobby at whatever time Doc decided.

"Okay Smoke, I'll leave a message as to the meeting time tomorrow morning. It is going to be a very long day, if we're going to fly straight through. I know I'm wasting my breath, but do try to get some rest. Good luck, Pal!"

"Just hope that El Capitan doesn't return early, my friend. Have a good time," Whitey added with a chuckle.

CHAPTER TWENTY-SIX
THE FLIGHT HOME

The jarring ring of the early morning wake-up call brought Doc out of his comfortable dozing. It was zero-five-thirty, time to hit it. He decided to give Smoke's room a buzz. It rang about six times before a sleepy voice answered.

"Barnes." Came the groggy answer.

"Wake up and pee, the world's on fire and we need all the help we can get."

"Ugh....uh yeah. Right!"

"You're going to need a good breakfast, Smoke, Me Man. Come on, up and at 'em. I'll meet you downstairs in twenty minutes for chow." Doc told him.

"Mnmphf!" Smoke hung up.
Twenty-five minutes later Smoke walked up and joined Doc and Whitey. "Thanks for the piss call, Doc. I'm famished," He said as he pulled out a chair and sat down.

Doc glanced up, "You look a hellava lot better than you did yesterday. Must have gotten a little rest."

"I'm ready to go home. Another night like last night and I'd just want to stay here. In fact, I'm considering moving down here as it is." Smoke remarked.

Whitey broke in, "Moving is a good word. Keep it in mind. A moving target is harder to hit, and you would be a target, Smoke, trust me."

"What do you do?" Smoke asked.

Doc answered the question, "You just get in the airplane and head north. You don't look back. Don't leave a forwarding address. You just leave. That's what you do.

Now, let's eat, check out and get this show on the road. Our ride to the airport will be out in front at quarter to seven."

The drive to the airport took longer at this time of day. San Salvador was becoming quite a bustling city with all of the big city pains, traffic just being one. The air was still clear but the threat of smog and the other ills of a modern metropolis were just around the corner. San Salvador was in an area surrounded by mountains that was subject to the same type of weather inversions as Los Angeles. The weather today would be perfect for the flight home.

They eventually arrived at the flight service facility. Doc asked Smoke to take care of fueling and servicing of the airplane. He and Whitey would handle the cargo doin's.

Whitey had been right, the truck with the coffee and loading crew had been there since about six-thirty. They were patiently waiting out by the airplane. Everybody turned to with their assigned tasks. Whitey took care of the cargo paperwork. Doc had given him the forty-three hundred dollars in cash to give to Cellini. Doc supervised the loading. Two hundred sacks of coffee have to be carefully tied down. There were some cargo nets with the airplane, but Doc needed two or three more. Fortunately, he was able to buy them from the flight service.

The loading and fuel tasks were finished. Doc and Smoke checked over the Weight & Balance very carefully. They were about two thousand pounds over gross with the extra fuel on board. If they left this morning, they'd be okay, it wasn't hot yet. Otherwise they would have to wait until tonight. They decided to go now. It was a nine and a half hour flight to Cabo San Lucas. It was nine o'clock now. By the time they got airborne, it would get them into 'Cabo' about seven-thirty local time. There wouldn't be any worry about customs, since they didn't have anything sensitive on board. The airplane paperwork was in order and they had good paper on the cargo. Cellini's export company manager had arranged for a customs broker to prepare the proper documentation. They could even spend the night in Cabo, if they wanted.

It was time for farewells. The two of them walked over to where Whitey was talking to a pilot he knew, who worked for the flight service.

Whitey introduced them, "Gents, I'd like you to meet Raul Arango. He's the pilot I told you about, the one who took the pictures of the ranch, and who arranged for the servicing here. Raul, this is Doc McGarrity and Smoke Barnes, two fellow aviators."

Doc shook his hand first, "A pleasure, Señor Arango. Many thanks for the fine photo work. I should have known the pictures were taken by a pilot. You sure captured all the things we needed to see. And, your company did a good job servicing our bird."

Smoke broke in, "Special kudos to your gas crew. We have some tankage, drums, on board inside the airplane and they didn't spill a drop in the cabin."

"But Señors, the pleasure and honor is mine. Señor McFrank speaks very highly of your flying skills. Perhaps on your next visit you would allow me to show off my country to you. I could arrange some suitable entertainment."

This comment was met with a lot of laughter from the three Americans. Whitey had to apologize for them in order to not offend Raul. He offered to explain at some later time.

"We would be honored to accept your hospitality, Señor Arango. But now we must take our leave. We're going to depart before the density altitude becomes a problem." Turning to Whitey, Doc went on, "Any messages for anybody up north? Do you know when you'll be coming home yourself?"

"No, and yes, to your two questions. My contract doesn't have much longer to go. I'll give you a call when I return. We'll get together then and maybe go for a sail on my new boat." Whitey responded.

"I didn't know you had a sailboat, Whitey." Smoke said.

"I don't yet but I will, soon after I finish things up here."

Doc held out his hand to the two   "Well, that's it then. We're going to get a move on. Smoke, why don't you file and I'll do the pre-flight."

"Righto, maybe Raul can direct me." Speaking to Arango, "Can we file from here and get weather?"

"Of course. Come, I'll show you. Again, my pleasure, Doc." He shook hands, then went into the building with Smoke. Doc and Whitey were left alone.

"Seriously, Whitey, anything I can do for you, I'll be more than happy to."

"No. Thanks, and I do appreciate your offer. You and Smoke did a good job. Nice and smooth without any hassles. But this is it for me, Doc. I've told the company that this is my last contract. It has another forty days to run and then Sandy, my wife, and I are heading to the South Seas via a motor-sailor."

"That sounds just great, Whitey. Please give a call when you get back to Seattle. I'm looking forward to seeing that boat. You're going to be doing something I've always just dreamed about. I'm envious."

"I'll do that. The second or third thing I'll do after I get home. Have a safe flight back and don't spend all the money in one place, My Friend."

They shook and Doc went out to pre-flight the airplane.

Less than an hour later, he and Smoke were in the air headed north.

Smoke had filed a VFR flight plan, via the coastal route. It was a beautiful day and forecast to stay that way.

They would enjoy the view. The trip down had been in the dark. They were both a little surprised to see how rugged the coastal country really was. It is one thing to see elevations marked on a topographical map and quite another to see the real thing.

They had been lost in their own thoughts and were strangely quiet. Once an airplane is in cruise, there isn't a whole lot to do other than avoid birds and other things occupying their airspace.

"So, tell me, how did it go with Rosa last night?" Doc asked.

"Hey, I meant it when I said that gentlemen don't talk about their conquests. But you're my best friend, partner and fellow aviator." Smoke paused for a moment. "You know, that girl was a virgin when she married the good Captain. Apparently he isn't a great lover. I thought all Latinos were great lovers. Just goes to prove that you can't believe everything you hear. Well, she said she wanted to try things she had only read about. Doc, let me tell you something, that girl sure must have done some fancy reading. I'd sure as hell like to read the books she must have read!"

"What do you mean?"

"You're my best friend, or I wouldn't be talking about this." Smoke thought for a few moments, then continued, "The first night I went down on her and it must have been a first time experience for her. She didn't know whether to shit or go blind. Thank God she went blind or it could have ruined everything. She stated then, quite flatly, that she intended to try all she had heard or read about. And I mean *all.*

"Okay, I think I get your point. Are you up to being a bit more explicit?"

"Well 'sixty-nine' was just the beginning. She wanted me to screw her in the ass. She wanted to be spanked and to spank me. That was kind of fun. Last night, she got into heavier bondage. I made the mistake of letting her tie me up first. She had brought a riding crop with her, along with rope, and the way she laid the riding crop on, I think I was getting what she wanted to give the captain. It was a big mistake on my part. She was quite apologetic and treated me very good afterwards, but I may have some marks that could be a little hard to explain."

This brought a good deal of laughter out of Doc. Smoke went on.

"I swear Doc, I learned that there are only seven orifices on a woman and she wanted my dick in all of them. Ears and nostrils just aren't big enough, and they don't stretch. I mean this girl got kinky. But I learned a few things from her. She kept saying we should try everything until it hurts, and then maybe a little more, in case we weren't doing it right. Is this explicit enough?"

"Okay, Okay. That's fine. I must say, you have some kind of balls to try all that stuff. But no golden showers?"

"What the hell's that?"

"That's when they piss on you."

"No shit?"

"I think they do that too. But I don't know the name of that act."

"That's disgusting!"

This brought them both down with laughter. Finally when he could breathe, Doc said, "It reminds me of a saying. Do you know the difference between 'kinky' and 'perverted'?"

"I thought I did, but I'm not sure anymore."

"*Kinky* is when you tickle your lover with a chicken feather. *Perverted* is when you use the whole chicken."

More laughter.

"Doc, how did you learn about all this kinky shit?" Smoke asked.

"My ex-wife and I joined a dirty book club, back in '62. Funny, when we divorced and were dividing up the community property we fought more over those books, who was going to get which ones, than anything else. People are sure strange. I'll have to loan you a couple of them. The interesting thing is most of them are classical in the sense that they were written in the seventeen and eighteen hundreds. Pornography has been around forever. The Japanese have some real art work. I'll tell you a funny story. Do you remember Del Patterson, they used to call him 'Dilbert'?"

"Yeah, I remember him. But I could never figure out why they called him 'Dilbert', he was one hellava pilot. I flew with him a couple of times at El Toro, when he was still in fighters. He went over to VMR-352, the transport squadron where you were, didn't he?"

"Right, that's where the funny story comes from. We were on our first flight to Japan. Del didn't go get into any trouble. He was rather a straight shooter kind of guy. He went shopping. Well it turned out he found a unique shop that had a lot of porcelain and figurines. He bought a set of dolls that were called something like the 'Seven Steps to Heaven', or something like that. Anyway they were in seven different positions screwing. Beautiful detail, almost down to each hair. Then he bought two tea sets. You know, the kind of thin porcelain you can hold up to the light and see a scene. Well, one set of cups and saucers had the 'Seven Steps to Heaven' and the other set had things like Mount Fuji, a temple bell, head and shoulders of a Geisha Girl and so forth. He had the one tea set shipped home direct to his mother, and the other set he smuggled back on the airplane. He was worried about sending pornography through the international mail service. So, he gets back to the squadron and he's showing off the dolls and so forth, then he brings out the tea set and describing the scenes and handing a cup to one of the guys for a look. The guy starts laughing like crazy and hands the cup back to Del. You guessed it. It's a scene of a temple bell. He quickly looks at the others in the set and sure enough, they're all very straight scenes. The wrong set got sent home to mother. He was from a small town in a farm community in Minnesota. Now stop and think about it....she's serving tea to the girls at the local bridge club meeting, or the like, and bragging about the tea set that her son had sent to her from Japan. Kinda gets to ya, doesn't it? I never did hear how it ended, how Del explained it or anything. Actually, it's more fun to just imagine the scene."

When their laughter subsided, Smoke said, "You're right, it is more fun to imagine the scene. Your point is well taken. Pornography has probably been around since before cave art. Most of the rest of the world recognizes it as art. Look at the temples in India. National Geographic can't even show photos of them, and *they* can show bare titties on natives! Well screwing has been around for a long time or none of us would be here. Only in America do we try to hide it or pretend all births are accompanied by a star in the east. Yeah, and for that matter, Del's mother wasn't supposed to know anything about sex. Americans are really weird about what goes on in a bedroom between consenting adults. Well, hopefully adults, or at least, consenting."

"You're right, Smoke, absolutely right. Like I said, I'll loan you a couple of the books. Not to change the subject, but what do you think? Do you want to spend the night in 'Cabo' or go on?"

"I don't care, Doc. You're the one that's anxious to get home. I wouldn't mind going on to somewhere in the states. I would like to sleep in a Holiday Inn and eat at a Denny's. Sounds crazy, I know, but a whole lot of exotic food doesn't really do it for me. I would love to have steak and eggs, with hash browns and brown gravy over the hash browns and some ice cold milk, served by a nice waitress who speaks English. Dumb, huh?"

"God! That does sound good. I'm not crazy about flying straight through either. You end up losing it at the other end, getting caught up on sleep. Let's refuel at 'Cabo' and head up to San Diego or LA and spend the night. Of the two, I think I'd prefer San Diego."

"I think we can find a Denny's in San Diego. Remember, they're open twenty-four hours, so it won't matter when we get there. I'll do the flight plan." Smoke got the paperwork and charts out. After a while he looked over at Doc.

"It's five hundred and ninety-five nautical to San Diego which works out to be four plus ten. We're making a better ground speed than I figured. If this wind holds, we're going to get to 'Cabo' about seven forty-five or eight. But they're on Mountain Time Zone, so that'll be six forty-five or seven o'clock local. Figure an hour on the ground for customs and fuel....say an eight o'clock departure and that'll put us into San Diego a little after midnight, local time. We gain another hour of time zones. How's that sound? Is it too late for you?"

"No, it sounds great, Smoke. If Sanchez is on duty we can probably beat the one hour on the ground. Did you check the AIM manual for customs in San Diego?"

"Yeah, we have to land at Brown Field, not Lindbergh. And, it's twenty-four hour availability for customs at Brown, but we may have to pay an overtime charge, since it will be outside their normal hours."

The rest of the flight into Cabo San Lucas was uneventful. The winds held and they touched down at precisely seven forty-two, local time.

CABO SAN LUCAS, MEXICO

Shortly after engine shut-down Doc noticed a car driving up to them on the ramp. He recognized it as belonging to their friend, Inspector Juan Sanchez. Doc unstrapped and went on back to the rear door and opened it.

"Hi Juan, have you shot the gun yet?" He yelled out to him as he jumped down and walked over to the car.

"Hello Doc, yes and you won't believe it. It shoots like no other forty-five I've ever fired. It is very accurate despite its small size. The action is so fast that when your arm is coming up in recoil, the slide going to battery brings you right back down on your target. It is a wonderful weapon. You must get one for yourself. Your next trip, you might consider bringing some down. I could sell them quickly."

"I'll look into it, Juan. Give me your address and I'll drop you a line with the information on whatever I can find out. By the way, the meal was delicious. We have some dishes for you. Please thank your wife again for us."

"It will be my pleasure. Do you have anything to declare?"

"We got ten thousand pounds of roasted coffee bean and lots of paper work, Inspector. We're going on to San Diego tonight. Do you mind if Smoke gets the airplane fueled while we do the declaration?"

"Sure. That's okay. Let's take a look at your cargo. There will be fees, of course. You can bring the paperwork and we'll go over to my office, then I'll bring you back." Sanchez noticed Smoke coming out of the airplane. "Ah, here's Señor Barnes."

"Hi Juan. That sure was a good meal the other night. Thanks again." Smoke jumped down out of the airplane. He turned and put the step in.

"Smoke, Juan is going to take a quick look at our cargo and then we'll be going over to his office. He said that you can go ahead and fuel."

"Okay, I'll see you when you get back."

Inspector Sanchez examined the cargo. He was familiar with this type of bagging and was only looking for obvious signs of tampering. The Inspector was intent on doing his job even though he didn't think these two enterprising young men were smuggling contraband through Mexico. It was his job to check, and check he did. Doc retrieved the paperwork and while Inspector Sanchez was looking it over, got the Inspector's dishes. The two of them drove off to the Customs Office.

Less than an hour later Doc and Smoke were in the air again, on their way north.

San Diego was a bit of a surprise. The customs people turned out en mass to look over this Venezuelan-registered airplane. The United States Government had recently started to react to the heavy flow of drugs across its southern border. Arriving in the middle of the night, coupled with the registration, set off bells in the organization. After a very intense debriefing and examination of the aircraft registration paperwork and customs documentation for the cargo, it was decided to impound the airplane until morning. Customs planned to initiate a thorough physical inspection of airplane and cargo at that time. Smoke and Doc didn't get their steak and eggs until after five in the morning. Even with the delay and hassles the meal was everything they had thought about. One thing that can be said about Denny's, they're rather consistent throughout the United States.

Then it was back out to Brown Field. They were told to be there by eight. On the way out to the airport, in the cab, Doc had a brainstorm. He discussed it with Barnes, who readily agreed it was a good plan. It could work without disclosing any sensitive information. When the taxi reached the field, Doc directed the driver to drop them off at Customs.

They went in and asked to speak with the Senior Inspector, or Agent or whatever the head man was called. In a surprisingly short time they were shown into an office.

"What can I do for you, Gentlemen? You're the crew on the Venezuelan DC-3, aren't you?" Chief Inspector C.T. Shannon was all business. Mid-fifties in age, gray hair on the sides, still dark on top, khaki uniform, complete with a silver and blue bar on each collar point.

They were not invited to sit down. Doc answered for them both, "Yes sir, we are. And I think that I can set your mind at ease as to the validity of the cargo. From what we heard last night upon our arrival I understand that our government is getting pretty fussy about flights from south of our border with the drug thing and all. However, I would like to suggest that, with all due respect, Sir, you call our State Department and ask about our country's relationship with Señor Alfredo Cellini, head of the Catorce Familias, in El Salvador. Besides being very influential in the government of El Salvador, he is a major producer of coffee. We were going to come back empty and ended up doing one of our Embassy people there a favor by purchasing and bringing this load of coffee to Seattle...."

Inspector Shannon interrupted, "Why would I want to go through all of that bother with the State Department, young man?"

"Well sir, to properly inspect our airplane you would have to damn near take it apart and the same with the cargo. I'm certainly not trying to tell you how to do your job, Sir merely that this is a very legitimate cargo and there is a relatively easy way to verify that."

The inspector thought for a few moments. "Give me the name again."

"It is Alfredo Cellini. He is head of the fourteen families down there and also owns the coffee plantation where the cargo was grown, and the export company, among other things."

"All right, wait outside."

Barnes and McGarrity left the office. Inspector Shannon's secretary went in and when she returned, offered them some coffee. They would have to go down the hall to another area where the coffee urn was located. As they left, Doc noticed the secretary was looking up a number in the U.S. Government AUTOVON Directory. When they got out of earshot he said to Smoke, "It looks like Inspector Shannon is going to check with State." He told Smoke what he had noticed.

"Great, maybe they won't take our airplane apart." Smoke said sarcastically.

They found the coffee mess. Typical Government Issue. An urn large enough to serve the *ship's company*. It had probably just been made. It might last the day. Whatever the case, by noon you could use the contents for paint remover. In the morning like this it was merely awful. Barnes and McGarrity were used to it. The Styrofoam cups added a certain something. But, it was hot. And black. They took their time going back to the Inspector's office.

It took the better part of an hour, but worth the wait, before the inspector was satisfied that the cargo wouldn't have to be checked a bean at a time. The airplane was another matter. When Barnes and McGarrity were allowed back out to the airplane, it was apparent that every inspection plate had been removed, some not put back. All inside fuselage padding had been unsnapped to inspect areas next to the skin, but it could have been a lot worse! Doc paid the import fees and then helped Smoke put the airplane back into shape. He asked him if he wanted to get some sleep or go home. Barnes opted to go home.

"What the hell, if we get tired we can sack out on the coffee bags. It will be a lot more comfortable than sleeping on those crates going down." He told Doc.

"That's a fact," Doc replied. "Hey, I'm in better shape than you are. I'll go file and you can go over the bird again. Once we're in the air and at altitude, you can crap out. With any breaks at all with winds, we can be in Tacoma in about six hours."

"You got a deal, 'Ol Buddy.

It was a little after ten in the morning when they had both engines turning, the Before Taxi Check Lists completed and ready to head out. Doc was in the left seat, Smoke riding shotgun. He picked up the microphone, after getting a nod from Doc. "BROWN GROUND CONTROL, DOUGLAS YANKEE VICTOR, WHISKEY ALPHA WHISKEY SIERRA, CUSTOMS HOLDING AREA, READY TO TAXI, I-F-R TACOMA INDUSTRIAL, OVER."

"ROGER DOUGLAS YANKEE VICTOR, TAXI RUNWAY THREE ONE, ALTIMETER NINER, NINER SIX, ADVISE WHEN READY FOR CLEARANCE, OVER."

"RUNWAY THREE ONE FOR YANKEE VICTOR." Smoke glanced over at Doc, "You got all that, Captain?" He said as he set the altimeters on both the pilot and co-pilot instruments.

"Uh, roger that, First Officer Barnes. Runway tha-ree one."

They taxied down to the run-up area for runway Three One. Smoke got two of the check lists out of the way and was ready for run-up by the time they got there. Doc swung the bird around and set the brakes. They completed the engine run-up checks, performed the Take-Off Check List and were ready to go. Doc told Smoke to give 'em a call.

"BROWN GROUND CONTROL, DOUGLAS YANKEE VICTOR, WHISKEY ALPHA WHISKEY SIERRA, READY TO COPY, OVER."

"DOUGLAS YANKEE VICTOR, WHISKEY ALPHA WHISKEY SIERRA, A-T-C CLEARS DOUGLAS YANKEE VICTOR TO THE TACOMA INDUSTRIAL AIRPORT VIA VICTOR TWENTY-FIVE LOS ANGELES, VICTOR TWENTY-THREE, FLIGHT PLAN ROUTE. MAINTAIN ONE ZERO THOUSAND, CONTACT SAN DIEGO DEPARTURE ON ONE ONE NINER DECIMAL SIX LEAVING TWO THOUSAND FEET, SQUAWK ONE FOUR ZERO ZERO. CONTACT THE TOWER ON ONE TWO SIX DECIMAL FIVE, WHEN READY FOR TAKE-OFF. HAVE A GOOD FLIGHT, OVER.

"ROGER, A-T-C CLEARS DOUGLAS YAnkee...." Smoke rattled off the clearance he had copied in rapid fashion.

"ROGER YANKEE VICTOR, READ BACK CORRECT. CONTACT THE TOWER WHEN READY FOR TAKE-OFF."

Smoke dialed in the frequencies that they had been given in the clearance on the two VHF transmitters; Tower and Departure Control and then set the transponder, leaving it on Standby. He and Doc went over the crew briefing that they did before every take-off; who was going to do what and then what they would do in the event of an aborted take-off. Standard Operating Procedure for any multi-pilot, multi-engine airplane. They were ready to go. Smoke picked up the microphone, "BROWN TOWER, DOUGLAS YANKEE VICTOR, WHISKEY ALPHA WHISKEY SIERRA HOLDING SHORT OF RUNWAY THREE ONE, READY FOR TAKE-OFF, OVER."

"ROGER DOUGLAS YANKEE VICTOR, WHISKEY ALPHA WHISKEY SIERRA IS CLEARED FOR TAKE-OFF, WINDS ARE LIGHT AND VARIABLE, OVER."

"DOUGLAS YANKEE VICTOR IS CLEARED FOR TAKE-OFF." Doc taxied onto the runway, locked the tail wheel and advanced the throttles, "DOUGLAS YANKEE VICTOR IS ROLLING," Smoke replied as he backed up Doc on the throttles and switched the transponder from Standby to On.

They both did a quick scan of the engine instruments, Doc patted the throttles, indicating that they were Smoke's for him to set the 'take-off' power accurately. Doc noted the time. It was ten twenty-three. They should be on the ground in Tacoma by four thirty in the afternoon, God willing.

On the climb-out, passing two thousand feet, Smoke called San Diego Departure Control. "SAN DIEGO DEPARTURE, DOUGLAS YANKEE VICTOR WHISKEY

ALPHA WHISKEY SIERRA WITH YOU, OUT OF TWO FOR TEN, OVER."

"DOUGLAS YANKEE VICTOR WHISKEY ALPHA WHISKEY SIERRA, SQUAWK IDENT, OVER."

"DOUGLAS YANKEE VICTOR, IDENT, OVER." Smoke answered as he reached over and pressed the 'IDENT' button on the transponder which would activate a signal on the Departure Controller's radar screen, identifying their radar return.

"ROGER, YANKEE VICTOR, RADAR CONTACT. TURN LEFT TO TWO EIGHT ZERO, INTERCEPT VICTOR TWENTY-FIVE, FLIGHT PLAN ROUTE, OVER."

"YANKEE VICTOR, TURNING LEFT TO TWO EIGHT ZERO FOR THE INTERCEPT, OVER." Smoke hung the microphone on a hook to his right. He turned to Doc, "Well, do you think you can handle setting up cruise all by yourself, or do you want some help?"

"You gonna go crap out now?"

"The thought had occurred to me, yes. Couple of hours, then I thought that I'd relieve you."

"Sure, go ahead. I'll let you know if I get too tired." Doc took the clipboard with the flight plan on it and put it up on the glare shield. He unsnapped his microphone and hung it part way over the side window clasp. The coil-cord would allow him to stretch it to his mouth when needed. He was ready to handle the airplane by himself. Smoke unstrapped and headed on back to the cabin.

Two and a half hours later Doc left the cockpit and went back to shake Smoke. The airplane had been holding steady on the auto-pilot. "Hey, rise and shine, we're coming up on Sacramento. It's your leg."

"Yeah, okay, I'll be right up. You woke me just as I was, I mean it was Rosa and....oh never mind."

Doc chuckled and went back up to the cockpit. He needed a couple of hours of rest himself. The weather had been good and reports indicated that it would be essentially clear all the way home. Engines were working good, plenty of fuel, and they were going home. Doc's mind wandered. He was thinking about how best to handle Hunter.

There would be no good way. Death is a terrible thing for those left behind. As much as he was attracted to Hunter, he realized how little he knew about her. She had three kids, two boys and a girl. That much he knew. He had only met Ken a couple of times when Ken had come by the office. It was a tough break. But he was sure attracted to the widow. He just didn't want to scare her off. Just be there for her, he thought. Just be there.

Smoke tapped him on the shoulder, "Where did you say we were?"

Doc pointed to the instrument panel, "Sacramento is on the number one VOR and that's Linden, behind us on the number two. We're still level at ten and I'm talking to Oakland Center on the number one transmitter, when they want me to." Smoke slid into the seat, checked the clipboard and strapped in.

"Looks like you've picked up some ground speed, we're ahead of flight plan."

"Yep, and the weather is 'C-A-F-B' all the way."

"I like it, *'Clear as a Fucking Bell'*. Don't even have to earn our flight pay. What are the poor people doing these days?"

"Not as much as this, that's for damn sure." Doc yawned and stretched, "Well, you've got it, Pal. I'm going to get some Z's. Wake me about Portland, okay? Or if you need me earlier."

"Right, I've got it," Smoke said as he patted the control column, indicating transfer of command.

Doc climbed out of the seat and headed back into the cabin. Smoke unstrapped and climbed over to the left seat.

The C-47 touched down at Tacoma Industrial Airport at four twenty two. The landing was exceptionally smooth, belying the fact that Harry Barnes had been up for some thirty hours. They secured the airplane. Doc said he'd call the following day and do something about selling the coffee.

They drove off. Barnes to his lovely live-in and Doc to an empty apartment.

CHAPTER TWENTY-SEVEN
AN INTERNATIONAL INCIDENT

The drive north over secondary roads, if they could even be called roads, had been miserable. Bumpy, hot and dusty. A strong wind was whipping up billowing dirt-laden clouds of dust and flies. The trucks had to go so slow the flies could keep up. They weren't just buzzing about, they were biting.

Lieutenant Dominique Paredes was in a foul mood. Riding in the jeep, leading the two trucks, was just as bad as being at the tail end of a column. He was being battered by the strong cross wind that was stirring up the dirt clouds. The wind didn't seem to effect the flies. This was their third foray in two weeks. All of the patrols seem to be far from their home base and in areas without decent roads. Word had arrived about suspected Cuban Communists having crossed the border into El Salvador at a small town called El Jalpa. It had been reported the town had a population of less than three hundred people. There wouldn't be any problems. His force of forty-five troops was more than enough to cow these simple, backward people. These thoughts cheered him up a little.

"Commandante, we seem to be coming to a village," the driver said, rousing Lieutenant Paredes out of his thoughts.

"Stop here." Paredes held up his arm signaling to the following truck. As the jeep came to a stop, Paredes stepped out and over to the side of the road making a motion toward the two trucks that had also stopped. A man stepped down from each truck and came forward at a trot to their Commander.

Paredes stood waiting patiently, slapping his thigh with a swagger stick that Capitan Mendez had presented to him. Capitan Mendez was with the El Salvadorian Policía Nacional and had been assigned to Colonel Cordero's Special Force as a coordinator. Lieutenant Paredes didn't have much use for the man. He was a strutting peacock, always elegantly attired in tailored uniforms of the whitest white. He had only gone on a few patrols with Paredes, and his main concern had always seemed to be keeping his uniform from getting soiled and how much would be his share of booty or ransom. The Capitan had discovered the game his assignment exposed him to. Instead of reporting it he had cut himself in.

He preferred to stay at the ranch with the Colonel. This suited Paredes. It provided a lot more freedom without a watchdog standing over him.

The Capitan had made a big thing out of presenting him with the swagger stick. He said that all officers should carry one. It was a sign of authority. And besides, it kept one's hands out of one's pockets. It was unseemly for an officer to be seen with his hands in his pockets. The Capitan was always concerned about his "command presence", as he liked to put it. Paredes grudgingly liked the stick. It was handy for making a point with one of his troops or with someone that he was seeking information from. It left a nasty scar on the cheek of the recipient. Yes, it was handy and an excellent symbol of his authority.

The two men came up to him, saluting smartly. "Si! Commandante!" They said almost in unison.

Lieutenant Paredes returned the salute by touching the swagger stick to the visor of his hat. "I want you to take your men and surround this small village. Leave one man from each of your platoons, with me." He paused for a moment, thinking, then continued, "Your two men, my driver and I will go directly into the village plaza. We will await you there. Work your men inward, door to door, bring everybody. Women, children, old and young, to the plaza. Leave two men at the road entrance leading into the village to make sure that no one leaves. Move quickly. Understood?"

"Si! Commandante!" They said, saluting again.

Lieutenant Paredes looked both steadily in the eyes, then gestured toward his hat with the swagger stick. The two platoon leaders executed an about face and moved back to the two trucks shouting orders. Their men spilled out of the trucks, checking their weapons and moving out with their leaders. A man from each of the platoons trotted toward the jeep.

When they came up to him, Lieutenant Paredes motioned them into the back of the jeep and told his driver to go slowly. They had gone about a hundred yards when they heard the sound of gunfire.

"Stop!" He said to the driver. It was quiet. Then, in the distance they heard voices. It sounded like words of complaint, but not distinctive enough to be understood. There were louder voices of authority, then silence. Paredes told the driver to go ahead.

About half way into the village they saw two dogs, dead, obviously having been shot. Paredes relaxed. Now the sound of gunfire was accounted for. If it had been otherwise the men would have gotten word back to him. When they arrived in the plaza townspeople were being herded into the center square. The driver pulled the jeep up to the fountain, driving around the fountain until he was abeam the small church that faced the square.

Paredes was steeling himself for what he knew was to come. He thought about this village and the village of his youth in another country. *It seemed to him that every village and town in this part of the world had a central square, a plaza, and every one of them had a fountain. Paredes had*

298

*often wondered which came first, the square or the town.
And how or who decided where the fountain would go? It
was a puzzlement. But the answers to things of that nature
would have to wait, it was time to go to work now.*

When the jeep came to a stop the two troops in the
back jumped down and held their automatic weapons at the
ready, watching the people being driven together toward
them. The two platoons had started herding the townsfolk
into the center of the village, doing a quick search of each
house as they went. As they came into the square the
townsfolk seemed to know what was expected of them,
forming around the jeep. The driver and two troops kept
them well back from Lieutenant Paredes, who had
dismounted and was standing up on the edge of the fountain.
His hands, one holding the swagger stick, were on his hips
and he was looking almost bored by the proceedings, just
watching what was taking place and waiting.

He was about to start speaking when one of the last of
his soldiers came through the crowd, making his way up to
him. Paredes watched as the trooper drew closer and then
handed up a tin container. Paredes reached down and took it.
He recognized what it was instantly. In his hand was a tin of
7.62 x 39 ammunition. These rounds were for a Russian-
made AK-47 automatic weapon. Markings on the tin
appeared to be Russian. They certainly weren't Spanish,
English or German.

"Where did you find this?" Paredes quietly asked the
soldier.

"Commandante, it was one of the first houses we
searched. A young boy tried to break away and run from us
but we have him. His parents have been crying and pleading
with us. My Sergeant is bringing all of them forward now,
Sir!"

Paredes glanced up and saw three townspeople being
forced through the crowd by his soldiers. An older woman
was clinging to a young boy, crying and pleading

299

unintelligibly. The man who was obviously the father was following, trying to appear brave. Paredes stepped down from the edge of the fountain and indicated for room to be made for them. They were pushed up to him.

Addressing the young boy of about twelve years of age he said, "Where did you get this?" There was no immediate answer. "I will ask you again, where did you get this?"

The boy stood impassively, not uttering a sound. Almost faster than the eye could see Paredes whipped his arm up and slashed the boy across his face with the swagger stick. The boy let out a scream, his knees buckled and he sank to the ground.

"Pick him up," Paredes said softly, addressing a soldier.

Two soldiers quickly each grabbed an arm and jerked the young boy up.

I will ask you once more," Paredes said quietly, his posture very non-threatening.

"I, uh....I stole it from some other soldiers that, uh," Sobbing, he couldn't continue. His hand that he had been holding to his face was leaking blood between his fingers. His sobbing continued.

"Take your time, lad. Tell me everything. How many were there?"

"Please, oh please, don't hit him again, please." The mother had pushed herself closer almost standing between Paredes and her son.

Paredes addressed the father, "Control your woman or I will lose my patience."

The man grabbed his wife's arm and pulled her back. Paredes didn't bother to look, having directed his attention back to the young boy.

The boy started to speak, "I don't know....a few, many. They stayed two days and then left. I wanted to steal a gun, but they were always with the soldiers...." He started sobbing again, then, gaining more control of himself, continued. "They were not of this country."

"When did they leave?"

The boy was in better control of his pain now. "They left three or four days ago."

"And which way did they go? Paredes interrupted.

"They went that way." The boy said as he pointed to the north. "That way, up into the hills. They took food from us, from many in the town, and left. Some left four days ago and the rest, three days....uh. ." Talking obviously hurt, the boy was sobbing again.

Paredes had learned what he wanted to know. "That's fine, lad." Turning to the mother he said, "Woman, take care of your son." The father stepped forward and helped his wife with their son. They made their way quickly out of the crowd and the square. The men let them go without bothering them again.

Lieutenant Paredes stepped back to the fountain and up onto the edge where he could look out over the people. He raised his hands to indicate to the townspeople to be quiet. It was unnecessary. The moment he stepped up on the fountain it became deathly quiet. No one wanted to attract attention to themselves. There were over a hundred people in the square, but it was quiet enough to hear birds chirping beyond the gathering.

"Who is your Mayor? I want him to step forward." Paredes waited. "Your leader....who speaks for this town?"

There wasn't a sound, not even the rustling of clothes. The wind that had made the trip miserable up to this little village had stopped. The mid-day heat hung in the air heavily.

Paredes waited a bit longer then shrugged as if he understood. "All right, if you insist on seeing my impatience demonstrated I'll be happy...."

Lieutenant Paredes was interrupted by a young man calling out, "Who are you? Why should we help you?"

Paredes gestured to one of the soldiers close to the young man. The soldier moved quickly to his side and hit him in the face with the butt of his automatic weapon.

Paredes nodded as if that was a satisfactory answer and continued.

"A young boy from your village steals a box of ammunition from some soldiers not of this country he says. He tells me that the soldiers were here for two days and none of you want to tell me who the mayor or leader of this miserable little village is. Is he a leader without eggs?" Lieutenant Paredes looks slowly around the faces, few of which will look directly at him, then continues. "A little boy, brave enough to steal bullets and said that he wanted to steal a gun. What? To defend you? His family? His church? Is he the only brave person in this village? And you saw for yourself, he was brave enough to foolishly defy me."

Now the sound of feet shuffling could be heard. The people nervously moving, but no murmuring or even whispering. Still no one came forward.

"All right, you are bound and determined to seek my anger, I won't disappoint you." Lieutenant Paredes directed his attention to his men, standing below him. "Bring five young, healthy, male villagers up here."

The soldiers quickly did his bidding. They had five men, aged in their late teens or young twenties.

Paredes stepped down from the edge of the fountain and asked them, "Will you tell me who the mayor or leader of this town is?" He spoke slowly and distinctly.

The men would not look at him. No one answered. Paredes addressed his soldiers again. "See if you can encourage them to speak."

The soldiers started smashing the butts of their weapons into the five men's stomachs and knees, then as they went down the soldiers began kicking them. The abusive acts were gathering momentum when an old car, with one of Paredes soldiers hanging onto the running board, came into the square, honking for people to clear the way. It came to a stop in front of the five men on the ground. The doors opened and a priest and some nuns got out of the car. The priest came bustling up to Lieutenant Paredes.

He appeared to be surprised at the scene in front of him. "What is the meaning of this? What are you doing to these people? This is part of my parish. Our Savior and Mother Mary have bestowed their power of protection over this town, they are my responsibility! I won't have you abusing these poor people!" The priest was starting to warm up with his tirade toward Paredes. He failed, or chose not to notice, the redness coming into Lieutenant Paredes' face. Advancing even closer, the priest raised his hand in a closed fist. He was going to strike Paredes. It was a threatening motion and a tragic mistake on his part.

Almost faster than the eye could follow, Lieutenant Paredes stepped back against the fountain, drew his side arm and fired three quick shots in succession. The priest, arm still held high, had been pushed back by the bullets hitting his mid-section. A startled look was on his face as he sank slowly to the ground. He was dead before he hit the ground.

The nuns and townspeople started to rush forward toward the downed priest and Lieutenant Paredes. Threatening yells and screams rang out. The people were pushing in. Without being given an order, the soldier standing closest to the lieutenant opened fire with his automatic weapon. The first rounds found the nuns, all of them, since they were the closest. As they fell the townspeople behind them took the soldier's fire. Then the other soldier and the driver started shooting.

The soldiers on the outskirts of the crowd couldn't see what was happening, but hearing the fire and thinking their lieutenant was in trouble, opened fire on the crowd in front of them. The townspeople had no place to turn. They were taking fire from all sides. Women, children, old men, it didn't matter. The crowd was packed and every bullet found a mark.

Paredes had leaped back up on the fountain ledge and was finally able to order the shooting stopped but not before many of the crowd were down, some dead, others screaming in pain. The smell of gunpowder and smoke from the firing hung in the air.

Paredes stepped down from the fountain ledge shaking his head. What a damn waste. How had things gotten so out of control? It was that damned priest! May he rot in hell! It didn't occur to him that perhaps losing his temper had caused this devastation.

He gestured for the men to get into the jeep. Nobody tried to stop or threaten them in any way. The driver backed the jeep away from a body and slowly drove out, carefully avoiding driving over the dead or wounded. The other soldiers fell in behind the jeep from their perimeter positions. They were watchful for any threatening activity from the villagers. None was forthcoming. Shock from the carnage that had taken place in the square drained all hostility from any of the surviving villagers.

The column of soldiers dispersed, the men making their way to their respective trucks. Paredes told his driver to stop and wait for the trucks. Nobody was speaking. It was if they were all thinking and reflecting on what had taken place. Even though the villagers hadn't been armed and attacking, the adrenaline of battle is slow to settle in even the hardest of men. They would not soon forget this day.

Nor would the rest of the world.

CHAPTER TWENTY-EIGHT
HEADLINE NEWS

It was carried by the international wire services and made the front page of most major newspapers in the United States. It was shocking. Five Catholic nuns and a priest murdered in El Salvador! World religious leaders were up in arms. Rome sent scathing dispatches to President Fidel Sanchez, of El Salvador. A meeting was called by the United Nations Security Council.

In San Salvador, President Sanchez requested an immediate meeting with the United States Ambassador. The Ambassador asked Alfredo Cellini to accompany him to the meeting with the President. It was a short meeting.

It has been said that shit rolls downhill. The same might be said of those involved in politics. And especially during a witch hunt. Placing the blame for this outrageous and shocking event was gathering a great deal of momentum. The atrocity was linked directly to the new force that had been formed to deal with terrorism and Communism in El Salvador. The force that had been put together by the United States Department of State by requests from the head of the Cartorce Familias. Facts that President Sanchez was well aware of.

Coming away from the meeting with President Sanchez, a very angry Alfredo Cellini got word to Ernest Herman McFrank, demanding a meeting with him as soon as possible. The time and place was arranged quickly. The car was sent to pick up Whitey, and he was escorted into the presence of the head of the Cartorce Familias immediately.

It was very obvious to Whitey that Alfredo was agitated. The man was pacing back and forth and smoking heavily. Whitey chose not to speak. Finally the pacing stopped. Alfredo turned and pointed his cigar at Whitey, "This man, this animal, this Cordero, he's the one responsible for this outrage! How could your country allow a man of this character to be placed in such a position of trust? 'Highly recommended' your State Department said. I cannot believe he would do such a thing!" Cellini was starting to sputter and his anger did not appear to be abating. The pacing continued.

Whitey spoke up. "Señor Cellini, I understand your being upset. This atrocity is bringing world attention to El Salvador. As you know, my department did not recommend this Colonel Cordero. However, I will do whatever I can to help your position," Whitey tried to calm the man in front of him, but Cellini didn't appear to have heard a word. He turned abruptly to Whitey.

"That is just the latest atrocity! I'm finding out more each day about this creature and his band of cut-throats. He hasn't been hunting rebels and communists, he has been hunting for wealth! We have reports of assassinations of some of the wealthier planters, kidnapping, and then their death. The pig doesn't even have the decency to free them after being paid the requested ransom. And, the Capitan Mendez that you asked about when you were here arranging the coffee purchase this Mendez is supposed to be the coordinator between Cordero and our military. I have learned that he has deposited large amounts of cash into his bank account recently. We, that is the families, we still have banking connections my friend, even though the banks were nationalized and taken away from us some time ago. I'm afraid our Capitan Mendez has fallen under the influence of this beast, Cordero. It is a shame. I have been close to his family for years. A very respectable family at that." Each sentence was punctuated by the pointing of his cigar. Alfredo was really working up a head of steam.

Whitey was holding his tongue. Alfredo stopped in front of him. He was breathing heavily and just staring into Whitey's eyes. Finally, McFrank felt he had to say something. "Alfredo, I will make an official report through my agency. I'm assuming that these allegations can be supported or you wouldn't be mentioning them."

Cellini interrupted. "Of course they can be substantiated! And the investigation is not complete. There will be more. Of that you can be sure!"

"Good. I didn't doubt you for a minute. This will be an official report. It will go all the way, Señor, all the way to the top."

After a moment, Alfredo Cellini nodded his head in the affirmative. He turned away and resumed pacing. "And another thing. The pictures sent over to Estado? Someone included pictures of Cordero and Paredes also, since they were both from Venezuela. They were not told to do that, it was just a fortunate occurrence. Well, Estado picked out both of them from all of the other pictures claiming that they were the ones in the restaurant. Everyone, including me, felt that it had to be a mistake. That it couldn't be. Neither one of them were in El Salvador at the time, and were not on any Entry Visa lists. Now I'm not so sure it was a mistake. You know how easy it is to get into this country. And false identity papers are always easy to acquire."

He stopped, having made a decision. Turning back to McFrank, he said, "I want you to go out to his *'El Rancho San Julian de Cordero'*," Alfredo Cellini said the name of the ranch sarcastically, and then he continued, "And I want you to talk some sense into this animal's head. How do you say it? Make him an offer that he will understand. If I had the authority to issue a termination order for both of those animals, I would. You must make him stop any further illegal activities until we can bring formal charges against him."

Whitey understood well enough. He also recognized that the man in front of him was under a lot of pressure from his President's office, that he was a Latin, with the temperament of a Latin, and a lot had been invested by both his government and the U.S. Government. This was going to be a sensitive issue. "Señor Cellini, I will do as you suggest and go out to the ranch and speak with the Colonel. I will make my report to Washington and discuss this with my local control, of course."

"Of course. You will get back to me and let me know when you will be going out there? I think it would be a good idea to send the Policía Nacional Coordinator, Mendez, out with you. Have you met him yet?"

"That is a common enough name, and I have met many people here. What is his full name?"

"It is Miguel Garcia Mendez. I know his family, and I've done business with his father-in-law. Mendez married one of the daughters, a beautiful little thing. I've known both families for years, his and his wife's. I'm sick at heart to think he has turned into a thief and murderer."

"You say he is the coordinator between the military and Cordero? I haven't had the pleasure of meeting him."

"Yes. He has been assigned to coordinate between the Policía Nacional and the special group Colonel Cordero heads up. There are those in the government that chose to keep the two units separate, but under some degree of control." This last comment prompted a snort of disgust from Cellini.

"I understand. I will advise you of my schedule, both going out to the ranch and when I return. I will use Raul Arango, your pilot, to go out and back. He is a good man, Alfredo, and a very safe pilot. I'm quite comfortable with him." Whitey was trying to get the conversation out of the formal structure that had prevailed. Cellini seemed to be relaxing a little.

"Si. You're right. He is a very good pilot. I use him also, when I don't want to do all of the flying myself. And sometimes I use him as a co-pilot with the Lear or the King Air. I'm glad you feel that way too." Cellini had calmed down somewhat. "And yes, do let me know when you're back. When you call with a departure time, I will see that Capitan Mendez is alerted to accompany you."

It was time for him to go. Whitey had lots to do. He took his leave.

Upon arriving back at his hotel Whitey took a cab to the United States Embassy. He went downstairs into the basement where all of the intelligence equipment was located and placed a call, on a secure phone, to the CIA-Seattle Chief of Station, Harold Roberts. He explained his meeting with Cellini, in detail. Roberts was very familiar with the news event about the priest and nuns. He didn't sound too surprised to hear about the other matters. He could well understand Cellini's agitation. When time permitted, perhaps Whitey could check with José Estado on his identification of Cordero and Paredes. Roberts told Whitey that he would have to check with Jorgensen for any heavy guidance. It was out of his hands, and certainly above Clyde Hayner's area of responsibility. Clyde ran the El Salvador desk, but didn't make heavy decisions. Even Jorgensen would have to clear a termination order with the Chief of Operations. Whitey didn't know how far this was supposed to go, heavy or not. He discussed the sensitivity issue, somewhat obliquely, since it was an area of strong political involvement. Roberts suggested that Whitey call Jorgensen from the embassy while he was there and give him the same information that he had uncovered.

Jorgensen had left for the day. It would have to wait until the following day. He decided to send a dispatch, then follow it up with a call in the morning. He took a cab back to the hotel.

Whitey called Sandy. He told her about the nuns, she had seen the news on Seattle television and said that it was also in the Seattle newspapers. Whitey told her he was going out to the ranch in a day or so, to see Cordero. The situation was turning ugly and he might have to extend his contract. He assured her that he would let her know if he was going to extend. To calm her down, he told her to push the boat schedule ahead. Get it going with Perry. Incorporate her changes and recommendations. Any changes that he had could wait until his return.

Jorgensen had the dispatch in his hand when McFrank called. He was aware of the situation and advised Whitey that for now he would have to reason with Cordero. He was not authorized to go beyond that action at this time. McFrank was to report anything unusual resulting from his meeting. Jorgensen expressed his confidence that Whitey would be able to handle things, convincing Cordero to be reasonable. He mentioned that he would bring this latest information from the restaurant maître d' to Ops and to the attention of State. They might have another solution, but it would have to wait for now. Whitey had his marching orders. It was his job to carry them out.

Whitey called Raul at the flight service and made arrangements to be flown out to the ranch the following day. His next call was to Cellini to tell him he would be going out the following morning. If Cellini still wanted Captain Mendez to go along the Captain was to be at the airport at eight.

Captain Mendez was prompt. Whitey had a chance to look him over pretty well without the Captain's knowledge, since he was in the back of the flight service lobby talking to Raul, when the Captain arrived.

Capitan Miguel Garcia Mendez was almost a caricature of a Latin military officer. He was about five foot ten, maybe a hundred and eighty pounds, black hair, pencil thin mustache and dark glasses. His impeccable off-white uniform was obviously tailor made. Well shined boots, belt and holster completed the picture. Captain Mendez even carried a riding crop in his left hand. Whitey took his time looking him over before making his presence known. Once noticed, the Captain came over immediately and clicked his heels together, rendering a smart salute.

"I am Capitan Miguel Garcia Mendez of the El Salvadorian State Police, at your service Coronel McFrank."

Whitey waved his hand in a casual approximation of a return salute. "I'm not a Colonel, Captain Mendez. If anything, my rank would be about equal to a Major in your service. But I do not wish to be addressed by rank." Turning and gesturing to Raul, Whitey continued, "And this is our pilot, Raul Arango. He answers only to Señor Alfredo Cellini."

Captain Mendez raised one eyebrow slightly, at the mention of Cellini's name, and with a brief nod of his head, clicked his heels again. It was obvious that he was uncomfortable not knowing the actual rank of this pilot in the pecking order of this mission.

Raul returned the head-nod rendered with a nod of his own equally short. Addressing McFrank he said, "Perhaps we should find our way to the airplane. Please to follow me, gentlemen." He led the way through the office and out through the connecting hangar to a Cessna 206 parked outside. Raul went around and got in on the left side. Whitey held the door and gestured for the Captain to get in the back. Then Whitey got into the right front seat beside Raul.

Less than an hour later they taxied up to the buildings at the east end of the airstrip at El Rancho San Julian de Cordero. The airplane was met by Lieutenant Parades, Colonel Cordero's Executive Officer. Introductions were not necessary.

311

Lieutenant Paredes extended the Colonel's apologies for not meeting them. At the moment he was interrogating a prisoner. Would Captain Mendez and Señor McFrank like to join the Colonel? Raul Arango was not invited. The pilot got back into the Cessna and departed.

The Lieutenant led the way down a long hall and into a section of the hacienda that Whitey had not seen on his previous visits. They entered a windowless room that may have been a large storage room in other times. In the middle of the room was a wooden arm chair bolted to the floor. Over in one corner were two large Dobermans', sitting and watching the proceedings. An Indian was strapped into the chair, his left arm strapped to the arm rest. His right arm was free, but held by one of Cordero's troops. The Colonel was bent over talking softly to the prisoner. There were two other troops in the room, standing back, but ready to assist the Colonel if needed. They were obviously enjoying the proceedings.

Glancing up, Colonel Cordero noticed his guest's arrival. "Ah, Señor McFrank and Capitan Mendez, what a pleasure. I was just reasoning with this young man and trying to convince him to tell me where the guerrillas are based. He doesn't want to tell me. When I heard the airplane I decided to wait until you arrived before I continued. We have developed a very unique method that is proving to be quite successful. Allow me to demonstrate."

The Colonel walked over to a small barrel on the floor, picked a ladle out of it and held it up to the prisoner's mouth for him to drink. He replaced the ladle and returning to the prisoner said, "José, can you hear me? Just nod your head. That's right. Now I'm going to tell you something and I want you to pay close attention. Do you understand? Nod your head. Fine. You are not going to leave this room alive. Yes, that is what I said. You are not going to leave this room alive. But, and this is important, you do have a choice. You can have a very quick, painless death with a bullet in the back of your head. You will not know that it is coming. That will be your reward for telling me what it is I want to know. The other option is not very nice. It will be quite painful, lasting for a few days. I will be feeding you to my dogs, a hand, arms and your legs before you slowly die. Let me show you what I mean."

The Colonel nodded to one of his men who brought up a small table on wheels that had a meat grinder mounted on it. Rolling it up to the right side of the chair, the open end of the meat grinder was just below the arm of the chair. As the small table was rolled into place the dogs became very alert. The two troops that had been standing back, forced the prisoner's right hand into the meat grinder while the third turned the handle.

The screams of the prisoner reverberated around the room. The dogs dashed forward and immediately started eating the ground meat and bone coming out of the end of the meat grinder. Captain Mendez turned and threw-up against the back wall. Whitey was able to maintain a stoic appearance even though he was disgusted with the scene he was witnessing.

Colonel Cordero motioned for the men to stop. He took a small portable propane bottle with a nozzle attached, opened the valve and lit it with a pocket lighter. His men held up the prisoner's arm. His right hand was missing almost to the wrist. Colonel Cordero cauterized the wound to stop the bleeding. Soon the screams were reduced to weakened sobs. The Colonel offered the prisoner another drink.

"Now I think that you understand me, José. You will please tell me what it is I need to know." The Colonel said this very quietly and patiently.

The prisoner José nodded his head and tried to talk. Only retching sobs escaped. Colonel Cordero offered another sip of water and told the prisoner to take his time. The Colonel was acting compassionately toward this very

313

subdued person strapped in the chair before him. After a few minutes the prisoner was able to talk. It was obvious he was still in great pain. Colonel Cordero offered him some more water and told him he would give him something to ease the pain when José finished telling him what he wanted to know. José told him the last guerrilla camp he knew about was outside of the small northern town of Citala, in the mountains, just across the border from Honduras.

Colonel Cordero stood. "Thank you José, now I will get you something for the pain in your arm." He nodded to one of his men who had moved and was standing behind the prisoner. The man took out a small caliber automatic and holding it close to the prisoner's head, fired a shot into his brain. The Colonel was good to his word. Jose's pain went away quickly.

The Colonel walked over to Whitey and Captain Mendez. "You see. It is quite effective. A little pain, a little mercy, a little kindness and a quick shot to the head that the prisoner doesn't know is coming. Yes, simple and effective. Come, let's go have some refreshments." Colonel Cordero gestured to his men to clean things up and then without another word, turned and left the room. Whitey and Captain Mendez followed.

When they got to the study the Colonel went to a bar and poured himself a stiff drink. He motioned the other two to join him. Mendez was quick to acquiesce. Whitey thought it a bit early but decided to go along with this animal. It wasn't the time to start making any waves. He would wait until he had the Colonel alone. Then, and only then, he would accomplish what he came here to do.

Colonel Cordero and Captain Mendez discussed how best to handle a raid on the guerrilla camp that was supposed to be near the town of Citala. They would have to move fast before the communists moved on to somewhere else. Cordero had been surprised to hear that the guerrillas had encamped in-country. They usually based in either Honduras or Guatemala and made excursions across the border. This was something new. Maybe it was time to get a little tougher, Cordero had suggested.

Whitey quietly sipped his drink and stayed out of the conversation.

It was late in the afternoon of the following day before Whitey had a chance to get Cordero alone. Captain Mendez had left with a detachment of Colonel Cordero's troops under the command of Lieutenant Paredes. Whitey and the Colonel stood and watched the two trucks and jeep drive off, on their way to Citala and the guerrillas.

They were alone. Whitey turned to Cordero. "Colonel, we have to talk."

"Of course, my friend. What is it that you want to talk to me about?" The Colonel turned as he said this and started back into the hacienda.

"We need to talk about the nuns, Colonel. The six nuns that have the world up in arms and this country on the evening television news. The incident has attracted world-wide attention along with the United Nations. And there is the matter of some wealthy planters or ranchers who have met with some misfortune."

The Colonel stopped dead in his tracks. He looked at Whitey in a very unpleasant manner. "Señor McFrank, what right and with what authority do you have to speak to me in this manner?"

Ernest Herman McFrank did not respond well to this type of confrontation. He was a man of action, not conversation. And he was certainly far from being a diplomat. "Colonel Cordero, I will only say this once, so listen very carefully. I speak with the authority of the Catorce Familias. I speak as a representative of the Central Intelligence Agency of the United States of America, and I speak to you as one man to another. What I say to you is to stop senseless killing, stop any interaction with representatives of the Catholic Church, even if they are known to be harboring guerrillas. You can get the guerrillas out another way. And to start acting like the man you were hired to be. Do the job, quietly, with dignity befitting an arm of the government that is paying you. That is what I have to say."

Colonel Cordero stood as if he had been hit by a bolt. After a moment he whipped out his gun. "I will relieve you of your weapon, Señor. Do not do anything foolish." He said as he stepped back out of reach. The automatic in the Colonel's hand didn't waver.

This response took Whitey completely by surprise. He would have expected anything else, but not this. Turning slightly, in order to keep his hands in clear view, Whitey took his Detonics from the small holster behind his right hip. Holding it gingerly by thumb and forefinger he slowly extended it to Colonel Cordero.

"Just drop it, Señor," the Colonel said.

"I wouldn't want to do that, Colonel Cordero, it has a hair trigger and I don't want to take the chance of it discharging. With your permission I will place it gently on the ground," Whitey said in response. Moving very slowly he placed the automatic on the ground and stepped back with his hands held away from his body.

The Colonel motioned him to step further back, and then called over his shoulder for a couple of his men who he knew to be just inside the door. They came out immediately and seeing what was taking place, put their own automatic weapons at the ready and covered their leader.

Colonel Cordero reached down and picked up Whitey's automatic. He told his men, speaking in Spanish, "Take him to the holding room, strip him, do a skin search and then give him some other clothes. Take two more men with you. No chances, do you understand?" They nodded their understanding. The Colonel addressed Whitey in English, "Señor McFrank, please do not attempt anything foolish. I do not want to have to explain to your superiors that one of my men acted rashly."

Whitey didn't say anything. He preceded the two men into the hacienda. They said something to two others in the first room. The two new men led the way down the hall to a room next to the storeroom where Whitey had witnessed the interrogation. Once inside, he was ordered to strip bare naked. One of the men took his clothes but handed him back his undershorts. The four left the room. Whitey heard a bolt. He didn't bother to try the door.

Whitey looked over the room. There weren't any windows. One light bulb in a ceiling fixture, a small cot on one wall, a small table and chair, and a bucket in the corner for his personal needs. He walked over and lay down on the cot.

He lay there thinking. Funny how things work out. His job down here was actually finished. The goods had been delivered, Cordero was chasing guerrillas, albeit too rigorously, and as he calculated the days, it occurred to him that today marked the eighty-fifth day of his ninety-day contract. It appeared that he was going into overtime, assuming he survived this idiot's idiosyncrasies.

He heard the door bolt withdrawn. The door opened slowly and one man came in carrying some clothes and a blanket. There were his boots, fresh socks, new khaki pants and shirt. Whitey noticed two men with automatic weapons standing back from the door in the hall and watching his every move. The man walked over to the table and laid the clothes out, then left without saying anything. Whitey got up, ignoring the clothes, he picked up the blanket, went back to the cot, covered himself and promptly went to sleep.

The next morning the same guard came in. Whitey sat up on the edge of the cot. The guard motioned for him to dress. As Whitey was putting on the clothes, he glanced through the open door and noticed the same two guards were in the hall with their automatic weapons at the ready. When he finished dressing the guard motioned for him to follow. He led the way down to the dining room where Colonel Cordero was already at the table. He rose when Whitey came in and gestured to a chair for him to sit and eat breakfast. Two of the guards took their place well back against the wall behind McFrank.

"Ah, Señor McFrank, I apologize for the temporary quarters last night, but sincerely hope that you managed to sleep well. Your old room is being prepared and you will be in there tonight."

"Colonel Cordero, how long do you intend to keep me here?" Whitey asked.

"I won't be foolish and ask for your parole while you're my guest. Suffice it to say, you will be closely watched at all times. I implore you to act accordingly. I do not wish an incident. Why don't we have breakfast and then I will take you out to the training area. We are starting another group of recruits." The Colonel didn't answer Whitey's question and it was obvious that he had no intention of answering.

"I understand then that I'm a prisoner," Whitey said with a degree of disgust.

"Ah, here's our breakfast. I took the liberty of ordering for you, Señor McFrank. We probably won't make it back to the hacienda until later in the afternoon. You had best eat heartily."

Again, Colonel Cordero avoided any answer to Whitey's status.

CHAPTER TWENTY-NINE
COFFEE AND CRABAPPLES

It was difficult for Doc to wake up. Being in his own bed in his own apartment was far too comfortable. He was still tired. A short nap on a coffee sack just doesn't make up for long periods without sleep. Doc knew that he had a lot to do and most important was Hunter. He didn't know how soon he should call. *Would it be too early? What can he say? 'Gee, I'm sorry your husband died, how about dinner tonight?'* God! What disgusting thoughts. His feelings for Hunter ran pretty deep. He hadn't felt this way about a woman for a long time. And he hadn't dared think that way about her until this tragic thing happened to her life. It was pretty confusing.

By the time he shaved, showered and had some coffee, he felt that he could handle calling her. It was a little before nine. He looked up her home number and dialed. The phone was answered on the third ring.

"Hello?"

Doc recognized her voice, "Hunter, this is Doc McGarrity. I'm back. Barnes and I got in last night. How are you doing?"

"Oh, all right. The service was two days ago. Things have started to slow down. The kids went back to school. All of the well-wishers have come and gone. I'm trying to put my life back together again. Uh....I'm glad that you're back safe and sound. I feel that I've let you down, but this couldn't be helped...."

"Don't be silly," Doc interrupted, "You haven't let me down. A lot of the responsibility I gave to you was in case I didn't make it back safely. Things are okay. You are going to want to do something, even though you probably don't need the money. People have to stay occupied or they tend to wither on the vine, so to speak. Your job will be waiting for you whenever you feel up to coming in."

"Well, I just don't know, Doc. It's too soon to make a decision right now about that or anything else, for that matter. I just don't know."

"Hunter. Look, I'm more than your boss. I want to be your friend. Is there anything I can help you with? Legal matters, financial? Any problems around the house?" Doc was almost pleading to be allowed into her life.

"Doc, I really appreciate your feelings and your offer to help. I'll certainly keep that in mind. At the moment I can't think of anything. I'm sure there are matters I'm overlooking. Boeing has been very helpful. Among other things, they provided me with a check list of sorts, things that had to be taken care of. Fortunately, we had a will so there won't have to be a probate. I can't think of anything else, Doc."

"Maybe lunch? We can go over where you left things when you had to leave the office. A business lunch. I have to be in Bellevue tomorrow. How about then?"

"You have to be over here tomorrow anyway? I guess that would be all right. Please call first. Do you know how to get here?"

"I have the address. Is it complicated?"

"No. Except, well....it's a dead-end street, but well-marked."

"Okay. Is eleven thirty all right?" *--Am I pushing?* He thought.

"That's fine."

"Good. I'll see you then." Doc hung up carefully, relieved that she had accepted. His next call was to

Associated Grocers. When he explained the purpose of his call he was transferred to the coffee buyer.

Yes, they certainly did purchase roasted whole bean. When could the buyer see a sample? Doc told him where the cargo was located. Doc would have to bring in a sample which he agreed to do. They made an appointment for one o'clock that afternoon. This gave him plenty of time to drive to Tacoma and bring back a sample. He decided to bring a whole sack.

The afternoon meeting went well. The buyer was impressed with the quality of the bean. He would let McGarrity know the next day.

The following day Doc McGarrity pulled up in front of Hunter's home promptly at eleven-thirty. The drive across the Evergreen Point Floating Bridge had been quicker than he had anticipated. The traffic was light at this time of day. He had to kill some time driving around Bellevue since he would have been early. But, he was here now, sitting in the car outside her home. He was nervous as a high school kid on his first date. He couldn't believe it. Doc let go of the steering wheel, took a couple of deep breaths, got out of the car and walked up to the front door. The house was set well back from the street. It was a long walk. It seemed longer than it was, of course. But eventually he got to the front steps and rang the doorbell. In a moment it opened. Hunter was standing there.

She stepped back to allow him to enter. Doc stepped into the entry and came up to her closer than he had intended. She had only stepped back a short distance. Hunter looked up into his face, her eyes misted and she fell, sobbing, into his arms. Doc held her tight and patted her on the back. Neither of them had spoken. He was content to just stand and hold her. Eventually her crying stopped. She pushed gently back away from him and stepped into the kitchen, which was to the left of the entry and took a tissue out of a box on the counter.

"Oh Doc, I'm sorry to have put you through that. I thought I had myself under control. Seeing you, somehow brought it all back. I guess that I have been trying to keep it in for too long. I'm sorry...." He voice trailed off.

"Hunter, please don't apologize," Doc interrupted, "I'm here to try to help you get through this the best I know how. If holding you while you cry will help, I'll do it some more." He reached for her.

Hunter stepped back. "No, I appreciate it, but I'm okay now. Is it chilly out? Will I need a jacket?"

Doc looked her over as if seeing her for the first time. She was wearing her frosted hair shoulder length and in a page-boy. It had been cut since he left. Her attire was subtle; a beige wool skirt, with a pale green sweater, and light brown loafers. She looked wonderful.

"No, it's warm, and we'll be in the car. Do you have any place in particular you'd like to go?"

She had steered him into the living room. "Yes, the Crabapple. It's in downtown Bellevue, in the square. Why don't you sit down for a minute while I fix my face? Then we can go."

"Your face doesn't need fixing, but okay. I'll wait here."

Hunter was quick about it. They left for lunch.

The Crabapple was a nice enough restaurant. It earned its name from a large tree right in front of it. Or, at least that was what Doc assumed, that the tree was a crabapple tree.

The food was good. Or, Hunter had said that it would be, or was, or something like that.

Doc wouldn't have been able to tell anyone what he ate. It might as well have been pages out of the telephone directory, he was so fascinated with Hunter's company. He couldn't get over the feeling. He had worked with this person for several months, but she had been untouchable. Now it was different. He would have to be super careful though. It was a fragile thing. If he moved too quickly she would bolt. Doc wanted so much to just reach out and stroke her cheek. She was talking to him now and he hadn't heard a word, so lost in his thoughts of her.

"....the checks were one after another...."

Doc interrupted, "I'm sorry, what checks are you talking about?"

"The checks from the government. Aren't you paying any attention to me? There were two, about three days apart. The sums were substantial. I believe they were for the airplane expenses that you had detailed out for me prior to your leaving. Then another two checks came, still government, but a different color. One was for Harrison and the other for you. All of the deposit slips are in your in-basket, along with the final paperwork on the Viscount package from Aer Lingus. But you knew that was complete before you left. Didn't you?'

Doc had a hard time concentrating on what she was saying. He was watching her mouth move. It was the kind of mouth that should be kissed. Her lips were full. He hated skinny, thin lips. It made him think of nasty, cruel people. Dumb. People couldn't help how their lips were formed. It was a matter of genes. It just seemed that way. Hunter's lips weren't thin, they were just kissable. And Doc wanted to be the one kissing them. How was he going to do that? She had asked him a question and was waiting for an answer.

Doc took another drag on his cigarette while he tried to gather his thoughts about what she had been saying. *What was it? Something about the Aer Lingus thing?* He reached over and put the cigarette out. "Right. But I hadn't been paying much attention to the details, it was Smoke's deal. He was handling it. Have we received any funds on the package?"

"Nothing had come in before I left, Doc."

He loved the way she looked at him so directly when she spoke. In fact, he loved everything about this woman he was sitting with. Damn! He wouldn't be able to wait for the proper time to pass. He was going to screw it up, he knew.

"Uh, when do you think you might be coming back to work, Hunter? Ah, I'm not trying to rush you, it's just that you know about how things are supposed to work. I mean I really need you, Hunter....uh, for the business and all." *He realized he was rattling on and probably not making much sense. He couldn't believe he was acting like this, like some dumb kid on his first date. These kind of thoughts kept coming back to him. It was starting to piss him off!*

Hunter was beginning to sense that there was more to all of this than work. Her thinking had been turned inside to herself due to the shock and stress she had been experiencing. She almost thought it amusing if it hadn't looked so painful on this man sitting across the table from her. She thought that maybe she would see where this was all leading.

"It's flattering that you feel that strongly, Doc. I can't answer right now. But if you don't have any plans, why not come over Friday night for dinner and we can talk about it then.'

"Uh, thanks Hunter. I'd love to. What time?" Doc managed to reply.

"Seven? Would seven be all right for you? The bridge traffic should be manageable by then."

"Would you like me to bring anything? Wine, or something for dessert?"

"No Doc. Just yourself will be fine," Hunter said with a light chuckle.

Doc managed to get through the rest of the lunch and business discussion without making a fool of himself. He drove her back to her home and walked her to the door. They shook hands. Hunter thanked him for the lunch. He mumbled something in reply, turned and almost ran back to his car.

Doc drove to the office and called the coffee buyer at Associated Grocers. He was put through to him right away.

"This is McGarrity. Have you made a decision on the sample of coffee bean I left with you?"

"Yes. We're prepared to make you an offer."

Doc waited. The buyer didn't say anything more. "Well?" Doc finally said.

"Uh, usually the buyer and seller meet and then if the formal offer is accepted, the papers are signed and it is done."

"I'll be happy to meet with you. How much?"

"Well, if you insist on a price on the phone, we're prepared to offer you a dollar-forty a pound. Are you talking with others?" The buyer asked.

"No. but maybe I should be. I think you can do better. My sources in El Salvador said that this shipment is worth at least a dollar fifty."

It was quiet for a moment. The buyer was thinking. "I can do a dollar forty-seven and we will pick up. That is my final offer."

"Done. When would you like to have the shipment?"

"You said the shipment was in fifty pound sacks, like the sample and still on the airplane in Tacoma. Is that right?"

"Yes, it's at Tacoma Industrial Airport, right across the Narrows Bridge up on the bluff. There are signs just as you come off the bridge. Tell your driver to stay in the right lane. What time?"

"Well, it's after one now, say three o'clock. Will he have any trouble finding you?"

"No. Tell the driver that it is the only DC-3 on the airport. I'll be at the airplane at three. Have him bring a helper. Those sacks are heavy. Will he be bringing a check?"

"No, we'll mail the check to your office. Fourteen thousand seven hundred dollars less the brokerage fees."

"There won't be any brokerage fees. I'm the broker, the seller and the collector." Doc was getting a little annoyed.

"Oh, of course. Thank you Mr. McGarrity. Will there be more shipments?"

"There might be. I'll stay in touch." Doc hung up the phone.

His next call was to Barnes. It was answered on the fifth ring.

"Hello."

"Hey! Are you still in bed? We've got work to do. I sold the coffee and we have to meet the truck at the airplane at three. Can you do that?"

"Yeah. Shelly left this morning on a flight. I was resting. Three o'clock? I can do that. I'll meet you there. How much did you sell it for?"

"A dollar forty-seven and they're picking up. We have to help them load, though."

"Forty-three cents to a buck forty seven. We make ten thousand four hundred for a couple of hours work and it gave us a nice bed to sleep on. Shit! Hellava deal Boss! I'll meet you down there. Well, where are you now?"

"I'm at the office, why?"

"I'll come down there, then we can talk on the drive down to Tacoma. When do you want to leave the office?"

"No later than two fifteen. Be here by two. Can you handle that?"

"Sure, see ya soon." Smoke hung up.

Barnes walked into the outer office promptly at two o'clock. McGarrity had Ross Bigelow, the engineer, in his office. Ross was bringing him up to date on the cryogenic shipping container. Doc motioned Barnes to join them. Smoke shook his head *no* and went into his own office. Doc took the file on the Aer Lingus package and took it into Smoke.

"You don't want to join us?"

"No, I don't know anything about that stuff yet. I just wanted to look through my mail until you're ready to go."

"Okay. Here's the Aer Lingus file. Hunter had put it in my in-basket. You might want to check it over. I'll be ready to go in a couple of minutes."

They talked business for most of the drive to Tacoma, then Doc mentioned that he had lunch with Hunter that morning. Smoke wasn't too surprised. He needled Doc a bit about it. Doc asked how his homecoming had gone.

"It was Okay until Shelly saw the welts on my ass when we showered together. Then all hell broke loose."

"Oh really," Doc said with a chuckle.

"Yeah, I told her that I had backed into some electrical wiring, they were electrical burns." Smoke explained.

"And did she buy it?"

"I don't think so, but she pretended that she did. She might move out."

"Smoke, you ought to quit screwing around."

"Hey Doc! I wasn't looking for pussy when I ran into Rosa. I had no intentions of playing on Shelly. It was the farthest thing from my mind. Shelly is a neat girl and all that I've ever wanted in a woman, but we're not married. So I succumbed to the charms of a Latin lady. I'm only human!"

"Yeah, well you *succumbed* twice! That's a little more than just coincidence. Rather it comes under the heading of pre-meditated, I would think."

"Je-zuss Doc, am I on trial or something?"

"Hell no. I don't blame you for succumbing, even twice. But don't play the saint with me. What I meant was if Shelly ever finds out she's liable to cut your balls off. That's all, Pal. Those southern broads take that shit seriously. And the northern ones, eastern ones and the western ones, for that

327

matter. Shit, they all do. And it isn't really any of my business. When you get nutted maybe I can find a position for you as soprano in a boys' choir." Doc said with a laugh.

"Thanks. I'll hold you to that one," Smoke said, laughing in return.

Doc turned off the west end of the Tacoma Narrows Bridge and onto the access road leading up to the Tacoma Industrial Airport.

The Associated Grocers truck and crew were on time. The off-loading went quickly and Doc and Smoke were on their way back to Seattle by four-thirty. They owed Whitey a favor, big time. Thanks to him, they had made over ten thousand bucks. Not bad, not bad at all.

By Friday afternoon Doc was as nervous as a whore in church. Barnes couldn't stand it any longer.

"Doc, what the hell is wrong with you. You're acting crazy!" Barnes was exasperated. "Are things happening that I don't know about? Bigelow thinks that it's something he's done."

Doc kind of waved his hand as if to dismiss the question. Barnes wouldn't let up.

"Come on. I'm your partner, dammit! What's goin' on?"

Doc tried to avert his eyes, but Smoke kept getting in his face, eyeball to eyeball. Doc gave it up. "Okay, okay. It's nothing to do with the company, or at least, not directly. I told you when we were down in Tacoma, I'm invited to dinner tonight. At Hunters'. I told you." Doc kept waving his hand and trying to turn away. Smoke wouldn't let him go.

"You mean all this jumping around, slamming drawers shut and not talking to anybody, all this because you're invited to dinner at Hunters'?"

Doc nodded in the affirmative.

"Jee-zus Kee-rist McGarrity, pull yourself together, man. If it's this bad for just dinner, I can't imagine what it...."

Smoke shrugged and looked up for some heavenly advice. When none was forthcoming, he continued, "....well, never mind. I mean, it's not a date, for God's sake, it's just a dinner."

"Yeah, a dinner. In her house. With her kids there, wondering what I'm up to and me not being able to say anything straight, without making a complete ass of myself....and hardly able to walk across the room without walking into a wall. I'm telling you, Smoke, I've never felt this way about anybody before."

"Maybe you'd better tell her so she doesn't think you're a complete idiot."

"Have you lost your mind? The funeral was just last week. He's hardly cold yet. I can't do that. Not only would she think I'm an idiot, it would remove all doubt!" Doc stopped for a moment to compose himself. "No, I'm going to have to pace myself and take this thing one step at a time. I'm just a little nervous, that's all."

"Right! Just a little nervous. You might say that." Smoke shook his head and turned to go back into his office. He stopped and looked back, "Hey Buddy, 'Ol Pal, please let me know if there's anything I can do to relieve the strain."

"Thanks Harry. I'll do that. It's something I have to work through. Thanks for your concern. Say something to Ross, will ya? I don't want to talk to him right now. He still hasn't earned the bonus. I don't know what his problem is."

"Sure, I'll say something to him. Good luck tonight."

The afternoon wore on. Doc kept looking at the clocks on the wall of his office. There were five clocks. They were set and labeled. Local, Chicago, New York, London, and Paris. It seemed that every time he checked, it was just ten minutes later. *He was thinking it was like waiting for the priest and the warden to take him down the hall to the chair. Funny, to die sitting down. Better than the gallows, where your knees would be shaking. Damn! He was going to have to stop thinking like this!*

By four thirty, Doc had some degree of control of himself. He decided to leave and fight the traffic across the floating bridge. Maybe he'd pick up some flowers in Bellevue. *Would that be okay? Fuck it! He'd do it anyway. To hell with protocol!*

He told Barnes and Bigelow he was leaving. He'd see everybody Monday. Nobody said anything. Barnes gave him a thumbs up. Ross just nodded. Doc left.

Traffic was fairly heavy across the Mercer Island Floating Bridge. Concentrating on his driving gave Doc more time to settle down. He took the Bellevue turn off and wound his way into the small downtown area. He saw a florist shop and pulled in. He got back into his car with a dozen yellow roses. He drove out of the downtown area and direct to Hunter's home. It was a little before six. He was too early. What had she said, seven? Whatever. Seven it would be. He turned the car around and headed back into the downtown area. He spotted a nice looking establishment, The Hindquarter, and decided it would do. He went in for a couple of drinks. It would help settle his nerves.

Doc nursed two drinks, watching the clock. At ten minutes to seven, he got up, paid his tab and made his way out of the rapidly filling bar. The Friday night happy hour was in full swing. The Hindquarter appeared to be a popular watering hole. The drive to Hunters' took up the remainder of the ten minutes and then a little more. It was four minutes after seven when Doc rang the doorbell. It opened immediately and there she was. Just standing there with a pleasant expression on her face. Doc tried to say something and just some noise came out of his mouth. In desperation he thrust the bouquet of yellow roses at her. Startled, she stepped back a pace, then, chuckling softly, took the flowers.

"Doc, you didn't have to do this, but they're beautiful." She turned, taking them into the kitchen. Doc followed her.

"I....uh....just thought they could, you know, maybe brighten up the house a little. I hope they're okay."

"They're fine, just fine, Doc. May I fix you a drink? What would you like?"

"Oh, uh, scotch and water would be fine, if it's no bother. Or, uh, I could fix it while you're doing the flowers. Just tell me where things are." Hunter was going past him to get a vase out of a cabinet in the hall. Doc was half way following her and she was back with the vase.

"I could use one too, if you want to fix them. The scotch is in the cabinet up over the refrigerator, ice trays in the fridge and the water is here at the sink. I'll get you a couple of glasses. Here, hold these," she said, handing him the flowers. She opened another cabinet and took down two short, squat glasses. "Will these do?"

"Yes, they'll work fine." Doc handed her back the roses and took the glasses. He managed to get the ice trays and some ice and the drinks fixed without any problems. When finished, he handed her the drink and raised his glass in light salute. "To better days, Hunter."

"Thanks Doc, and yes, to better days." She took a sip out of her drink. "Now, you can go over to the kitchen table, sit down out of my way while I finish getting dinner."

The evening was a small success. McGarrity met the three children. The daughter, Shannon, was seventeen, a son, Kerry, sixteen and a young son Dean, aged nine. They were all well-mannered and seemed to enjoy his company. The older son gave him a couple of long looks but accepted him as his mother's boss and someone who cared about her. The daughter appeared to be happy that her mother was enjoying herself and coming out of the deep grief she had been experiencing. It was going to be okay. It would take time, but it was going to be okay.

He was even invited back.

CHAPTER THIRTY
CAUSE FOR CONCERN

Sandy McFrank had been marking the calendar since Whitey had left for El Salvador. Tomorrow was Saturday, the 7th of February, and "Day 90". Whitey should be coming home. She hadn't heard from him since when? Damn! She wished that she had written it down. She thought about it, relating to things that she had done. Then she remembered, it was the last week in January about mid-week. He had said something about some Catholic nuns being killed and that he had to fly out to the ranch the next day. He had told her that it was getting 'ugly' and that he might have to extend but if he did he would call and let her know. It wasn't like him to not call, especially if he said he would. Normally he wouldn't have committed to calling. But if he committed, he called. And he hadn't. She decided to call Harold Roberts.

She was put through right away. "Hello, Mr. Roberts? This is Sandy McFrank. Have you heard anything from Whitey?"

"No Sandy, I haven't." Roberts said.

"Well, tomorrow is the last day of his contract. I've been keeping track. Has Whitey extended?" She asked.

"I haven't heard from him, but maybe he did that through the embassy. If that's the case, I won't hear anything until next week. I can let you know."

"Would you please?"

"Of course. Is everything all right, Sandy? Do you need anything?" Roberts asked.

"No. I'm all right. It's just that if he was going to extend he said he would let me know. It's not that he calls frequently, he doesn't. Unless, that is, something is going to change from an original plan. Then he does."

"I see. Well, I'll check with the home office and let you know. If you need anything in the meantime, give me a ring. Okay?"

"All right. Thank you Mr. Roberts. Good-by." They hung up.

The weekend came and went. Then Monday and then Tuesday. Wednesday morning Sandy called Roberts again. This time she was put on hold for a couple of minutes. Finally he came on the line. "Roberts here."

"Mr. Roberts, Sandy McFrank. What is going on?" She was a bit testy. She hadn't appreciated being put on hold for so long and she hadn't appreciated not being called with news about her husband.

"Now Sandy, don't get upset. I haven't called you because we're still checking. I haven't heard anything as yet. You know communications in that part of the world are not the best."

"That's not true!" Sandy interrupted. "Every time he has called it was like he was calling from Tacoma. San Salvador has an excellent telephone system. You're stalling."

"Perhaps I was making excuses, Sandy. I should have said that communications in the field are not exactly AT&T. But never mind." Roberts was attempting to get Sandy calmed down. "I'll check with the El Sal desk and find out. I'll get back to you."

"Okay. I'll wait for your call. Don't be long."

Good to his word, Roberts called back in about ten minutes.

"Sandy, Roberts here. Whitey was called out into the field. He is on an extended tour of the back country. The home office automatically extended his orders. I'm sure he will call you as soon as he gets back to San Salvador."

"Thank you. I appreciate your letting me know." She suspected that either he didn't know or he was holding back information for some 'security' reasons.

Sandy waited another week. It was now the eighteenth of February. Eleven days into the new contract. Not a word from Whitey, Roberts or anybody. It was obvious to her she wasn't going to get any help from 'the company'. Whitey had always told her that if she was in any kind of serious trouble she should call Colonel Bob Sexton, U.S. Army (Retired). It took her some time to find his number. It was right where she should have looked in the first place, in their personal telephone directory under "Emergency" numbers. Bob was retired now. She couldn't remember where he was living, then noticed the area code two-oh-two, that was the Washington D.C. area. She dialed the number. It was answered on the second ring.

"Sexton," came his firm, gravelly voice. It had been a long time since Sandy had spoken with him, but she knew that voice. It wasn't one easily forgotten.

"Bob, is that you?" She asked from habit. "This is Sandy McFrank. Hello?"

"Hello Sandy. Yes, this is Bob Sexton. What's the matter, Love?"

Sandy told him what had happened. No word, Whitey telling her that things were getting ugly. And the ninety day contract running out and the company saying that he was out in the field and her suspicions from the way Roberts was handling her. The other end of the line was quiet. Then Sexton spoke.

"Sandy, I want you to stop and remember very carefully everything that Whitey told you about this operation. I want to know the names of the players, the game plan, everything. Take your time. All of the details. This may be very important."

"Well, it's funny that you should ask in that manner. As you know, we didn't usually talk much about his assignments. This was going to be his last contract. He is planning on retiring. We are going to buy a sailboat and do some serious cruising before he gets too old, so he said, anyway. I don't know how old he thinks he is, he's sure young enough for me. God!" She paused for a moment to reflect on what she had just said. "Anyway....so in this case I know quite a bit about what's going down because of it being his last contract. We talked more about this than we have ever talked about any of his jobs in the past."

Sandy told him, without caring about any telephone security, about the Communist guerrilla activity, Colonel Cordero, Alfredo Cellini and the Catorce Familias, the company C-47 with the Venezuelan markings, the two Marine pilots and the arms shipment to the ranch. While she was telling what she knew, Bob Sexton would stop her and ask more questions. He knew Alfredo Cellini very well, having done a job for him some time ago. Colonel Cordero he had only heard a little bit about. He was curious about the Marines. When she finished Bob told her he would call her back and to stay by the phone. He wanted to talk to some folks at the home office.

Sexton's first call was to Peter Jorgensen. Peter wanted to know what Bob's interest in all this was. Bob told him that he was acting as a friend of the family. What the hell was this about a contract extension? Peter didn't know anything about that, but if it was the case, naturally McFrank would be suitably compensated for whatever time he put in. Bob asked to speak with Clyde Hayner. He was transferred over. Hayner didn't know anything more than Jorgensen had.

Sexton called Alfredo Cellini. When Sexton identified himself to whoever it was who had answered the phone Alfredo came on the line immediately.

335

"Señor Sexton, how good of you to call. What can I do for you?" Alfredo Cellini remembered this Special Forces Colonel very well. He respected and almost feared this man. He remembered...

Colonel Bob Sexton had responded to a request by the Catorce Familias to handle an abduction of one of the relatives. A hired group of four mercenaries had taken the family member to Panama and was holding him for ransom. Sexton had found the four and also the person responsible and had moved quick enough to save the victim. The five people involved in the abduction were later found in a field, or rather their bodies were--in pieces. The rescued relative had witnessed the carving up. It was three months before he could talk about it. When asked, Sexton had said that those kind of people--abductors, only understood violence. The more outrageous the violence the better. It would serve as a deterrent. The incident was still talked about in some circles.

"Alfredo, I'm trying to find Whitey McFrank. When was the last time you saw him or talked to him?"

"It was the end of January. He flew out to Colonel Cordero's ranch near San Julian. As far as I know he is still out there. He was going to call upon his return and I haven't heard from him. Is there a problem?" Cellini was a little apprehensive.

"There might be. Tell me about this Colonel Cordero."

"He has been hired by the family to combat the Communist guerrillas in my country. He came to us recommended by your State Department. The agency placed him down here. We thought he was doing a pretty good job until the incident with the nuns...."

Sexton interrupted, "I heard about that. Not very bright on his part if he was responsible for that activity."

Cellini continued, "He was responsible and that was just the tip of the iceberg, as they say in the north. We are still investigating but it appears that he and his band of cutthroats are hunting for money, not communists. They are guilty of kidnapping, ransoming and then still not returning their victims. When we can prove this to be true, he will be dealt with. Whitey went out there to try to talk some sense into his head. We needed more time to look into the things that were beginning to come to our attention. I personally asked Whitey to buy me that time."

"I've heard a little bit about this Cordero, what can you tell me about him, what sort of a man is he?" Sexton asked.

"I've only spoken with him face to face a few times. I've told you all I know. From his actions I would be inclined to say that he is rather impulsive. He is very much the macho man, in control, but gives off the impression that he recognizes authority." Cellini was remembering how Cordero referred to him as El Patron.

"Okay. That will have to do for now. Take down my home number and also McFrank's home number...."

"I have both, unless yours has changed," Alfredo interrupted.

"I will be here in Washington or out in Seattle. Let me know if you hear anything from either Whitey or Cordero. This could be serious."

"I understand and agree wholeheartedly with your surmise. Yes, it could be very serious. McFrank has been a good friend over the years, I would hate to see anything happen to him at the hands of that idiot!" Cellini said with some disgust.

"I appreciate your help, Alfredo." Sexton hung up.

Bob Sexton sat back in the chair and gave thought to all he had heard. He knew Whitey would not have been out of contact for the period of time that had transpired. Something was wrong. He suspected that this Colonel Cordero had somehow felt threatened or discovered and done something foolish like imprisoning Whitey or even something really stupid like doing him in. Whichever,

337

Whitey was still at the ranch. Alfredo would probably find out and let him know. In the meantime, if Whitey *was* still alive he would have to move quickly. Once a person is restrained it can easily deteriorate into the next step. The easiest way to cover a mistake of that order is to do away with the witness. Sexton decided to assume the restrained scenario and to do something about it. He called his old Executive Officer, Hank Stevaro, who was also retired and probably bored to tears.

"Hello." It was Hank.

"Stevaro, you 'Ol Sumbitch, can you handle some excitement in your old age, or do you want to live forever?" Sexton asked.

"Hey, Bob, what you got goin'? And shit yes, I am going to live forever! That is, unless I start tramping around the world with you again. Tell me, you're on to something aren't you? Tell me."

"Seriously, do you remember Whitey McFrank?"

"Sure. Is he still alive? God! He must be getting pretty long in the tooth. Yeah, I remember him. You two did some things in Laos not too long ago, didn't you?"

"Right. Well he may need some company. I think that he is under some obligation to remain a guest, maybe preferring to be somewhere else. I would like to talk to you about it. I'm headed out to Seattle and can stop in there on the way that is if you're interested."

"Yeah, I'm interested. Can you give me some idea of what you may have in mind?" Hank asked.

"I'm thinking about maybe getting some of the lads, probably fifteen or twenty, and fetching Whitey for a retirement party or something like that. Do you still maintain beach party equipment connections?"

"That would depend on the complexity of the requirements. Small stuff is no problem. I have direct access to the local National Guard Armory in town."

"Good, we'll talk about it when I get out there. I'll probably be there sometime tomorrow. I'll call you when I have the flight number."

"Got it. Looking forward to seeing you, Boss."

Sexton called Andrews Air Force Base to see if they had anything heading west. There wasn't anything that would work for him. It would have to be commercial. Hank was in the Columbus Ohio area. He lived half way between Columbus and Dayton. Hank called it a ranch. Sexton was able to book a flight that would give him a three hour lay-over in Columbus, then on to Seattle via Chicago. He called Hank and Sandy, giving them his itinerary.

The flight out to Columbus gave Sexton time to think. A couple of things were obvious to him; the company wasn't going to do anything and Alfredo Cellini, well-meaning as he was, wouldn't act hastily. Cordero was unpredictable which made him a dangerous man. Somebody was probably going to have to go in and get Whitey out. This posed many problems. How many men did Cordero have at the ranch, how to get the extraction force into the area, how to get the necessary equipment into the country. He was thinking this was like many of the other operations Colonel Bob Sexton, USA (Retired) had run or been involved in. One minor difference; he didn't have the resources of the United States Government behind him this time. In fact, if he asked for help, the lid would be put on this thing faster than you could think about it.

Hank Stevaro was at the airline gate to meet him. They embraced and went to find a quiet corner, preferably where one could do something for a dry throat. They found what they wanted down the concourse. Sexton filled Hank in on what he knew and the calls he had made up to that point. Stevaro agreed that Whitey was probably a prisoner at this point and that he was probably not going to remain that way long. As for his interest, Hank wanted in. He would be able to provide anything in the hand-carry category of small arms

339

up to and including the LAWS hand rocket launchers. (Light Anti-Tank Weapon.)

"Hank, letting you in isn't a problem. I'm concerned about the ordnance. We might be able to get things from Cellini. But what the hell is your connection to the local National Guard? You've never talked about this." Colonel Sexton wasn't going to let this opportunity pass. It was almost too good to be true.

"It's a couple of things. One, I'm an advisor to the detachment and two, the Governor is a personal friend. As you may be aware the National Guard comes under State, not Federal jurisdiction. I got bored and this is a pretty good local unit. The Governor even gave me a commission. As for the equipment, I would only be borrowing it. If it makes sense, the caper you have in mind and something we can get backing for, even after the fact, there won't be a problem. On the other hand, if there's a problem, it'll probably become a big problem before it goes away."

"I see." Sexton thought about what Hank had said. "Okay. Look, here's what I'll do. When I get to Seattle I'll nail this thing down tight and then get hold of Cellini. Assuming the worst and we decide on an extraction, if we can get marching orders from him, our friends at the farm will fall into line. It would be the backing you mentioned. It's worth a shot."

"I think it'd work, Skipper. I'm not worried either way." Hank made his position very clear.

Sexton didn't respond to Hank's last remark. He would call him from Seattle, after speaking with Sandy and the two Marines who had been to the ranch, after he had sorted everything out.

It was getting pretty late when the Boeing 727 touched down at Sea-Tac International Airport. Bob decided to check into a motel out by the airport. He still carried an Air Crew identification card from Air America. It was a souvenir from the Thailand caper. He called the Hilton from the Courtesy Phone at the airport and found out they had a vacancy and air crew rates. Hellava deal, an eighty dollar room for thirty-two dollars. He decided to live it up. And the Hilton's jitney would pick him up at the baggage claim area.

His Air Crew Identification Card caused a raised eyebrow, but was accepted. He also noticed that a few looks came with the raised eyebrow. It was apparently becoming common knowledge that Air America was a Central Intelligence Agency fronted airline company. This amused Colonel Sexton no end.

When he got to his room he called Sandy.

"Hi, Love, I'm in town. I've checked into the Airport Hilton." Bob gave her his room number and then had a request. "Do you have the telephone numbers for those Marines?"

"Bob, you didn't have to do that. You are more than welcome to stay here. But hang on, I'll get the number for you." She put the phone down and was gone for a minute. "Here it is, the only number I have is for Doc McGarrity. The other one's name is Harry Barnes. His nickname is Smoke. Why is it all pilots seem to have those funny names?"

Sexton laughed. "I don't know, Sandy. Someone once told me that it was so they could yell at each other in a combat situation but I've never heard that kind of chatter. I don't know the answer. But, you're right, most pilots I've known have those funny monikers. I'll give McGarrity a call. I would like to take you out to dinner. Would tomorrow night be okay?"

"That would be fine, Bob. Call and let me know what time and what to wear."

"Will do. Thanks Sandy. I'll get back to you."

Sexton called Doc McGarrity. The phone was answered on the second ring.

"McGarrity." A voice said.

"McGarrity? This is Colonel Bob Sexton, U.S. Army Special Forces, Retired. I'm a friend of Whitey McFranks'. I would like to meet with you and discuss your recent doin's."

"Uh, I don't know about that. How did you get my number and what is your connection with the doin's, as you put it?"

Sexton interrupted, "Doc, I know this is unusual and I understand your need for security. I'm a *very* close friend of Whitey's and I would ask you to verify who and what I am with Sandy, Whitey's wife. Until you hear me out, I would just as soon you didn't speak with anybody downtown."

"Where are you? Give me a number. I'll call you back."

Sexton did as Doc requested. Doc called Sandy and heard enough about Bob Sexton to satisfy and enough from Sandy to realize what this was all about even though she was careful about what was said. Doc called Sexton back.

"What do you need from me, Sexton," Doc asked when Bob answered.

"I understand that you have been to the ranch. I would like to know the layout, location, personnel, attitude and anything else that you can think of. I need all the information that I can get my hands on."

"I have maps and a great set of pictures that were taken from the air and from the landing strip at the ranch." Doc told him.

"Jee-zus. That's better than I would have imagined. When can I see them?"

"How about tomorrow for breakfast. I can meet you out there. I'll call you from the lobby. Eight okay?"

"That's fine. I'll even buy. I've owed a couple of jarheads in the past and a couple of zoomie jarheads to boot. I'm looking forward to meeting you."

"Likewise, see you in the morning." Doc hung up. *Fuckin' dogface, zoomie jarheads, my ass!* He thought.

Doc had called Sexton's room and was waiting at the front desk when the meanest looking mutha in six counties walked up to him and identified himself as Bob Sexton. Doc decided that this guy could call him *anything he wanted!* He was quick to hold out his hand.

"Doc McGarrity, Captain U.S. Marine Corps Reserve, Colonel."

"You don't look anything like what I expected to see, Doc," the Colonel said.

"Oh? And what did you expect to see, Colonel?"

"Sort of a smaller person, eyes set real close together and blinking a lot, something like that."

"You must have been around Marine *helicopter* pilots. That's the way most of them look. And they shake a lot." Doc decided he was going to like this bad ass dog-face after all.

"You're right. And I was. Let's go eat and you can tell me how you met Whitey.

They made their way into the Coffee Shop, asked for a table in the back away from the suited businessmen who would soon be out on the street selling their wares. While they were getting on the other side of their first cup of coffee, Doc filled the Colonel in on their mission, Otto Schwartz, the flight and the ranch. Doc told him that he had brought the maps and pictures with him. They were out in his car. Their food arrived and they fell to. Between bites, Bob Sexton asked about the current location of the airplane, how they had managed customs and refueling. He was surprised when Doc told him about transferring fuel while still in-flight. Sexton chuckled at the part about the Mexican customs agent providing their dinner. A plan began to form. He suggested that he and Doc go back to his room where they could talk in comparative openness. Doc said he would get the maps and pictures and meet Bob at his room.

Doc made it to Sexton's room a few minutes later. When Sexton opened the door, Doc walked by him and over to a small table in front of the only window. There were two chairs, one on either side of the table. Obviously the arrangement was to take meals in the room. He pulled both of the chairs back out of the way, put his briefcase down on one of them and took out three large maps, in various scales, of El Salvador. He placed the largest scale map on top, then spread out the thirty or more pictures of El Rancho San Julian de Cordero.

Sexton had been watching. As Doc was spreading out the pictures, Sexton walked up behind him and looked over his shoulder. When Doc finished he stepped back and looked at Sexton and gestured toward the display.

Bob was impressed. He hadn't dreamed this much information would be available. He thought it time to share his suspicions.

"Doc, I think Whitey is being held captive by Cordero against his wishes. The situation could deteriorate quickly. One runs out of options rapidly after making that kind of move. From what I've learned about Cordero, which isn't all that much granted, tells me the man is unpredictable. I personally think that if Whitey isn't extracted out of there soon he won't be alive much longer. You've met this Cordero. What was your impression?"

Doc thought for a moment before answering. He thought back on the one time and that was when he and Smoke had arrived at the ranch with the shipment. "I met him only once. He goes by the title of 'Colonel Cordero'. He is small in stature, typical Latin features, black hair, eyes so dark they appear to be black. He was definitely in charge. His men seemed to fear, rather than respect him. He was very gracious to Smoke and me. He seemed to get along with Whitey. If anything, he held Whitey in awe. I don't know if this is helping you or not. Those were my impressions. I'm trying to remember and state them carefully. We arrived, his people unloaded the airplane while he fed Smoke and me. He invited us to stay, we declined due to the way I had filed our flight plan. We weren't supposed to be there. We had filed to land at San Salvador. He invited us back when we could stay longer. He wanted to show us how he trained his troops, our being Marines and all. Seemed like a prideful, macho sumbitch. That's about all I can tell you."

"You say that he invited you back?'

"Yeah. He wanted to show us his mock training village and how they ferret out the commies."

"Where did you say the airplane is now?"

"It's down at Tacoma Industrial Airport, as far as I know. The airplane is locked up and Miller has the keys. He wouldn't turn them over to anybody without calling me. Nobody has called so, I guess that the airplane is still there. A quick phone call will verify." Doc thought he knew what was coming next.

"Doc, what would you charge to take another little trip down to the ranch?" Sexton asked. "What the fuck do you mean 'charge'? First of all, I've already made a bunch of money, thanks to Whitey. Plus there wasn't any risk, it was a milk run, so to speak. And I feel a real kinship to Whitey. What kind of an operation will this be? CIA? Or Special Forces? I mean, are you here in any official capacity?"

"I'm here as a friend of Whiteys'. No official capacity. No support from our friends in Washington. In fact, you would have to steal the airplane. And this will not be a milk run, and it will involve risk. Now what do you have to say?"

This took Doc a bit by surprise. "Let me get this straight. You are going to go down to the ranch and *extract*

Whitey from the evil clutches of this little Latin dictator in a CIA airplane that you want me to steal and then fly for you. And you're thinking about taking a couple of other people with you to help. Is that it?"

Colonel Bob Sexton got cold. He looked Doc over slowly and then straight in the eyes. "I guess you could say that. It's putting it rather out of focus. But you could say that."

"Colonel, perhaps I didn't describe the operation at the ranch properly. Colonel Cordero has a small army of troops, that maybe don't like him all that much, but they are his to command. They are well armed, thanks to Whitey, Smoke and me. There is a flight pattern that must be flown prior to landing or they consider the airplane to be an enemy. I think I would like to know a little more about your plans before I venture into harm's way. I don't know what all you've heard about Marines, but one thing for goddamn sure, we're not suicidal!"

"I'm not judging you, Doc. Nor am I asking you to risk your life stupidly. I have a group of men I can call upon for this type of mission. They are extremely well trained and highly experienced in covert operations and operations of this type. I don't have to pay them, in fact most of them would probably pay me. Normally I would have to probably get there commercially, somehow arrange to have the right equipment and then make my way to the ranch, scope things out and go in at night. The force I'm talking about would number no more than twenty and that includes me. The troops I have in mind for this gig could take about anything up to and including the Hanoi Hilton. Your unique situation with the airplane throws an entirely different light on this operation. First of all, the airplane has been in there before. The markings are distinctive. You have been invited back by the man himself. Even though he has Whitey the way that he has, the fact that you know the pattern to fly, are an invited guest, all mean that you could get my team on the ground

346

with a high probability of not being fired upon. It would mean a frontal assault, with little chance for surprise, but that's my department to work out. Your knowledge of the objective and the pictures are invaluable to the operation. I can get pilots, that's not a problem, but not with your qualifications. Time is of the essence. And Whitey's time is running out. Those are the reasons why I don't think this is a suicide mission!"

It was quiet for a long time. The two men just stood and looked at each other. Doc remembered the night in San Salvador when Whitey had challenged him for the flaming hooker championship...*Yeah, Whitey, I'd put my ass on the line for you anytime. He had meant it. You don't say things like that without meaning it! You only say it to the deserving. And Whitey was one of the deserving.*

Finally, Doc sort of shrugged and then said, "Oh shit! Maybe I can get time off for good behavior. Maybe we can get the airplane back before anybody knows it's gone, maybe bears don't shit in the woods and maybe I think you're out of your fuckin' mind, Colonel, but I'm in. I'll need a co-pilot. Smoke is sort of involved. I shouldn't ask him to do this."

Colonel Bob Sexton smiled. He shook his head a little, then said, "You probably should let Smoke decide that for himself, Doc. He's probably as nutso as you are. Besides, if you don't ask him, he's liable to get violent. I'm saying this without having ever met the man. But if he's anything like you, and like most of the Marines I've known, he'll want to play."

"Okay, I'll mention it to him."

"Good. Let me know. I'll hold off finding you another pilot. I do have to make several calls." Sexton paused before continuing. "And it isn't quite as bad as you're thinking. One of the calls will be to Alfredo Cellini. Do you know who he is?"

"I've met him. Yes, he's some kind of head of a family down there, isn't he?

"That's one way to say it. More to the point, he's head of all of the families there. El Salvador is actually run by fourteen families. They're called the 'Catorce Familias'. Cellini is head of the Catorce Familias. It's my understanding that he was the originator of all this: Cordero, the arms shipment, the whole thing with our State Department and CIA. I'm going to try to get his backing for the mission. Then it will all be okay. I'll go on a verbal from him. It will bypass the committee thing we'd run into if we worked the problem from the U, S of A end."

"I understand. That sounds a whole lot better. I did know about the family thing. And, I'd just as soon miss the crow-bar hotel." Doc was quite relieved and it showed.

The Colonel chuckled. Yes, and I want to spend more time going over all the facts in detail from the time that you met Whitey. I want as much information as possible before I call Harold Roberts and Alfredo Cellini. We'll do this now, making notes, if you can give me the time."

"Let's do it." Doc said as he slipped out of his jacket.

CHAPTER THIRTY-ONE
A VISIT TO THE LIBRARY

Observing the training of the new group of troops would have been enjoyable for Whitey if it hadn't been for the four heavily armed men of Corderos' who were constantly on their guard watching him. They were careful to keep a proper distance and not allow any opportunity for moves that could change his status of guest. Cordero had been pleasant enough, maybe a little too much. Overacting was a term that came to mind. Whitey wondered how long this pretense was going to last. The good Colonel had gotten himself in pretty deep with this action.

As the day went on, Colonel Cordero was growing more and more apprehensive about his action. He admitted to himself that his action had been rash. But, what was done, was done. There was no turning back. Think, thinking, thinking. *Now that it was done, what could he accomplish with it? Ransom from the CIA? What did he want that he didn't have? Favors or concessions from the Catorce Familias? What did he need or want that he couldn't just take? This is a puzzlement, he thought. On the other hand, what to do about McFrank. The man had to be watched constantly. If let go, would he forgive? Would he seek revenge? How long before The Company would send somebody after him? The easiest thing to do would be to get rid of him and somehow blame it on the Communists. This would require more thought.*

They returned to the hacienda. Whitey was shown into the guest room he had occupied during his visits before.

He was curious as to how it had been prepared, as the Colonel put it. The first thing he noticed was the inside doorknob had been removed and a plate installed in its place. The door to the bathroom had been removed, allowing one of the pin hole cameras he had spotted his first time at the ranch to see a good part of the interior. The telephone that had been in the room was removed. Everything else appeared to be as before. Since he was still a prisoner, it was at least a comfortable prison cell. A major improvement over the prior night's accommodations.

He freshened up and then went to the door and knocked. The door opened slowly and one of the four guards, who had apparently drawn permanent duty, indicated for him to step back. As before, Whitey could see the other three guards out in the hall and very alert. They were the same four who had been with him since the night before, when this had all started.

The guard at the door managed, in broken English, to convey the fact that when it was time for Whitey to leave his room for a meal, or anything else, someone would come for him. They would knock and Whitey was to stay well back from the door.

Whitey indicated his understanding of these simple rules.

Approximately an hour later, Whitey had not been given his watch back, there was a knock at the door then it slowly opened. Whitey had been lying down and didn't bother to move. The guard motioned for him to get up and to follow. He was led into the dining room. Colonel Cordero was at his usual place at the head of the table. Whitey's place, to Cordero's right, the place of honored guest, had been moved a little farther down placing him out of reach. This fact amused Whitey. He sat down.

"Señor McFrank, I hope your old room will be more comfortable than the sparse accommodations you had to endure last night." Cordero held up his hand, indicating an answer was not solicited, then continued. "We are having jabali, wild pig, tonight. It is one that I took three days ago with a spear. In this part of the world it is considered proper to hunt pig with just a spear. Have you ever done this, Señor?"

"We spoke of this once before, Colonel. I have only hunted two legged pigs. And those I hunted with just about everything but a spear. However, I am looking forward to tasting the fruits of your hunt. Roast boar is tasty, if properly prepared." Whitey spoke without malice, in complete control. He would go along with this pig hunter as much as humanly possible.

The dinner was excellent. The pig had indeed been properly prepared. Over coffee and brandy Cordero told Whitey he would be gone for a few days. Whitey would be confined to his room. Would he like to select something from the library to read? The Colonel had some selections of American and English authors, both mystery and spy novels. Whitey took him up on his offer.

The following day Colonel Cordero drove into San Salvador. It took close to three hours to navigate the terrible roads until about eight kilometers west of Nueva San Salvador where he finally picked up paved highway for the remaining fifteen kilometers into the capital.

He had planned to call on Cellini to give him a report about the Communists operating out of Citala. He was informed that Cellini was with El Presidente and would not be available for two days. Cordero did not leave any messages. He had wanted an opportunity to mention that McFrank wanted to be in on the raid. Anything could happen during the raid, solving his present dilemma. It wouldn't be the same if he sent it in a message. He had some unfinished business in Costa Rica to attend to. It was his plan to contact Cellini upon return to El Salvador. He was only planning on being gone for two or three days.

The flight into San Jose was short but unpleasant. Cordero had to take an afternoon flight. The cloud build-ups that occur in the afternoon create a lot of turbulence. The Colonel did not like to fly to begin with. It was something that he avoided as much as possible. By the time the airplane touched down in San Jose he was in a foul mood.

Customs clearance in Costa Rica was normally pretty casual. When Cordero presented his passport the customs agent took an unusual amount of time examining it. He started checking some documents on a clip board. Glancing up, he asked Cordero to step to one side out of the line of arriving passengers and wait. The Customs agent picked up the phone and placed a call. Cordero couldn't hear the conversation but was beginning to get uneasy. In a few minutes a state policeman arrived and asked Colonel Cordero to follow. He was escorted down a hall to an office where a state police officer was seated behind a desk. The policeman who brought him handed Cordero's passport to the officer and then stepped back but stayed in the room.

The officer looked over the man standing in front of him. He wasn't sure he liked what he saw. He didn't bother to offer a chair, but cut right to the point. "You're Emilio Rafael Cordero, sometimes called 'Coronel Cordero'." This was not a question, but a statement. "We have been awaiting your return. Your reputation is well known in Costa Rica, Señor. We do have laws in this country regarding money, money coming into the country and money going out of the country. Your attempt to transfer funds from our national bank to the Canadian Imperial Bank in the Cayman Islands came to the attention of the authorities. There is no record of your bringing the funds into Costa Rica. There are some people in my government who want to discuss this matter with you Coronel Cordero." The officer continued to use the rank of Colonel sarcastically. Addressing the policeman standing behind Cordero he said, "Take this man downtown to headquarters. Here is his passport."

Cordero started to say something but the officer waved his hand in dismissal.

This couldn't be happening to him! That money was well earned and came from Nicaragua. He had asked for and received American dollars. He had wanted the monies sent to the Caymans, but the group for whom he had done the work insisted that it be transferred to where he was and that had been Costa Rica. It was a bank-to-bank transfer and he had thought nothing of it. He hadn't carried money into this country. This was absurd! He wondered if he had been set up.

CITALA, EL SALVADOR

The convoy of two trucks, led by a jeep, approached the town of Citala. Lieutenant Paredes told the jeep driver to slow down. The town appeared to be unusually quiet for this time of day. It was about an hour before noon. There were only a few people to be seen.

Citala was a small town situated in the northeast corner of El Salvador, high in the mountains and near the border crossing into Honduras. Approximately ten miles northwest was the border between El Salvador and Guatemala. The road into and out of Citala went into Honduras. Although the road wasn't heavily traveled, it was unusual to find a complete lack of activity. This fact bothered Lieutenant Paredes. He kept the pace slow coming into the town.

The jeep carrying Lieutenant Paredes and Captain Mendez came to a stop in the town square. The Lieutenant jumped out and motioned the two trucks that had been following, to pull up beside his jeep and unload. Quickly, the troops fanned out in groups of five from the town square. Lieutenant Paredes, Captain Mendez and the driver remained in the square. There were no sounds except for a barking dog somewhere off in the near distance.

353

Lieutenant Paredes walked over to a fountain that was in the center of the small town square. He sat on the edge and lit a cigarette. He would occasionally swat the flies away that were buzzing around his head. Captain Mendez stayed in the jeep. *He probably was afraid to get his pretty white uniform dirty*, thought Paredes. *God! He hoped that he wouldn't ever have to count on this strutting peacock if some shooting started.*

The first team returned with a citizen of the town. He appeared to be a worker, or peasant. He was very nervous. The men brought him up to their lieutenant. Paredes rose slowly, brushing himself off. He asked the peasant about the Cubans. The man appeared to be relieved when asked this question. He quickly explained he thought that the lieutenant and his men were more Cuban guerrillas. He told them about twenty or thirty men had been in the town. They had paid for all that they took. They didn't try to talk to anybody in particular or cause any trouble. They left on a road that goes south to San Ignacio. It parallels the Honduras border and winds up into the high country.

The man wasn't frightened and appeared to be fairly intelligent. He was a worker, which accounted for his lack of fear. Paredes had no reason to doubt the information. He would have to move quickly.

Paredes walked over to the jeep and honked the horn several times. People started to appear on the streets and the lieutenant's men could be seen returning. Paredes turned back to the peasant. He asked him how long since these men left the town. He was told they had left that morning. Lieutenant Paredes thanked the man, patting him on the shoulder and commended him on his citizenship. The man stood up straighter and said for the Lieutenant and his men to get "those invaders" out of his country.

Chuckling, barely to himself, Lieutenant Paredes signaled for his men to saddle up. They were going after the invaders.

It was eight kilometers to San Ignacio. Paredes didn't think the Cubans would be stopping there. *His map didn't show it but he thought the guerrillas would head east on some secondary road up into the mountains. That was their style, the mountains. They did it in Cuba, they did it in Nicaragua and they will do it here,* he thought.

The road to San Ignacio was National Highway Four. It was a connecting highway from Honduras into El Salvador and linking up with the Pan American Highway at The Capital; San Salvador. It was a terrible road; paved, but not maintained very well. It was the road that they had just driven into Citala. The Lieutenant hadn't seen any evidence of unusual traffic, military vehicles or anything like that. It was going to be time consuming to check each of the secondary roads branching off. They would start in San Ignacio. Three kilometers farther on was the town of La Palma; then an eighteen kilometer stretch to San Francisco Morazan. His map displayed several gravel and dirt roads up into the mountains out of San Francisco Morazan. His gut feeling was that he would find evidence of them at that juncture. He didn't dare to not check San Ignacio and La Palma, however. He knew Colonel Cordero wanted some results to offset suspicion about their activities. The recent flap over what they had done to the nuns was still fresh in Lieutenant Paredes' mind. They would search diligently.

EL RANCHO SAN JULIAN DE CORDERO

It had been six days and the routine hadn't changed. Whitey was wondering what was going on. All of his meals had been served in his room. The same four guards were still the only people who he had seen and they didn't speak English. Or rather one spoke only a smattering and understood less. On the fourth day he had been given a change of bed linen. The bath towels had been exchanged each day. Whitey had read the few books taken from the library the night before Cordero left.

He decided that if his imprisonment was going to be indefinite he might as well get some more books. He knocked on the door and stepped back. The door opened slowly. One guard came into the room once he saw that Whitey was back far enough from the door. Whitey could see another guard in the hall, weapon at the ready.

Whitey held up the four books that he had gotten from Cordero's library. He gestured out the door with the books, motioning that he wanted to get some more. The guard seemed to understand. He said something over his shoulder to the others. There was some conversation, but nothing was happening. Whitey decided that they had discussed it enough and started forward. The guards got pretty excited but Whitey kept walking. He didn't stop, but headed directly for the library. It was down the long hall and then another short hall and across from the Colonel's office. Whitey expected a shot to ring out any moment. He heard the guard's weapons being cycled but ignored the sounds and kept walking. Once at the library he went directly over to the section where the Colonel kept the English language copies and started to peruse the selection. All four of the guards took up station well behind him.

It took him a few minutes to select another four books. He could hear the guards getting restless behind him. He finally turned and gestured for them to lead the way back to his room. It was obvious they were not pleased with all that had taken place. They were muttering among themselves. The escort was as before, two guards in front leading and two behind him.

Whitey thought long and hard about this. They hadn't shot him, he had gotten away with it. He had taken charge, asserted a position and achieved more than just getting some reading matter. He hadn't seen any other men in the house while going to the library or returning. He thought he could hear kitchen noises down the one hall, but even that was a long way off and would only be the kitchen crew. A plan began to form. If the Colonel wasn't back soon he would need some more reading material and would have to do this again. However next time maybe things would be different. Four heavily armed men were difficult, but not impossible to get the better of, especially if they had no reason to suspect that he would try anything.

They hadn't even fired a warning shot. That was the important factor.

CHAPTER THIRTY-TWO
LEGAL AUTHORITY

Bob Sexton's first telephone call was to Harold Roberts, Chief of Station-Seattle. It was a waste of time. Roberts either didn't know anything or wasn't about to get involved in conversation with him. Sexton couldn't fault him too much since they really didn't know each other. Perhaps by reputation, but they'd never met.

Sexton's next call was to Alfredo Cellini. He wasn't in. Sexton left a message of *national importance* and his number at the Hilton. It took all of twenty minutes for the call to be returned. Bob caught it on the second ring.

"Sexton here."

"Señor Sexton, this is Alfredo Cellini. What have you learned?"

"Not a damn thing at this end, Alfredo. The agency isn't sharing any information with me, or Sandy, for that matter. I'm getting very concerned."

"You have every right to be, my friend. More and more is being found out about the activities of Coronel Cordero. He is not a nice person. His group has done more harm than the communists in turning the people against the administration. He should be terminated by our army. How do you say it? With prejudice? It would be an embarrassment to our government to bring him to trial. But the man has to be stopped."

"That's what I've been waiting to hear. Are you saying to me, Alfredo that you wish to have the special Cordero force neutralized and their contract canceled?"

"You have the authority to do this?" Alfredo asked after a pause to think about what Sexton had just said.

"No Señor, I don't. But *you* are in a position to give me the authority to do just that. And in the process I'll get Whitey out. If he's still alive."

"How would you do that?" Cellini asked, now fully understanding what Sexton was driving at.

Bob Sexton shared with him what he had learned from McGarrity, the airplane and even the invitation to return. He also mentioned that a group of Whitey's friends wanted to invite him to a beach party. Bob was careful with the words he used since they were not discussing these particulars on a secure line. He knew that Cellini was used to oblique communication, having worked with him before.

It took Cellini less than a minute to decide. "You have my permission to proceed, Señor Sexton. Force, as required, is hereby authorized. Is that formal enough? Do you need something in writing?"

"Hell no, Alfredo. Not for now. Your word is good enough for me. When the time comes you'll probably have to bail me out with my former bosses. But let's deal with that when we have to." Sexton paused for a moment, gathering his thoughts. "Well, time is of the essence. I'll get right on it. You will be advised of our departure date, mode of transportation and any particulars."

"Good. Call the same number and if I'm not immediately available, just leave a message. I'm looking forward to seeing you again and soon, Señor Sexton."

They hung up.

The list of names lay on the desk. Bob Sexton looked down at them, thinking what a great bunch of guys. Eighteen names. Hank Stevaro said that he wanted to get two more. One was Mark Dillman, an explosives expert and the other was Dan Hartmann. Dillman had served a hitch as a Navy Seabee, gotten out and then tired of civilian life. He decided on re-enlisting but wanted more action this next time around so joined the Special Forces. Hartmann was one fine crossbow archer. Serving together during Special Operations in Nam, Stevaro had known him to take out a victim at close to a hundred fifty yards using a special made Barnett crossbow with a scope. Hartmann also specialized in shoulder-fired weapons of the anti-tank variety. Very handy skills to have around.

At Stevaro's insistence Sexton had added them to the list in pencil. Both of these last two selectees were out of contact. Hank was trying hard to track them down. Stevaro had told Bob that he knew damn well they would want in and Bob had agreed.

Looking at all of the names, Colonel Bob Sexton knew that this bunch could take most any objective anywhere in the world. It was only a matter of insertion into the target area and how hard it would be to get back out. And there was the consideration of preserving life, the lives of his troops that is. Sexton had told Hank about Doc and the airplane. He outlined the whole routine that the two Marines had followed getting the arms out of Canada and down to the ranch in El Salvador. He even explained the flight, as Doc had related it to him. The customs in Cabo San Lucas and the friend they had developed there. If Hank could get the shopping list that Sexton wanted out to Tacoma? Did he foresee any problems? No? They would be non-stop to Cabo San Lucas and then non-stop again to their destination. It was time to call Hank back.

Sexton told Hank Stevaro to get the men headed this way now. If he couldn't get Dillman and Hartmann in one more day, to forget it. They were going to have to leave in three days, or whenever Hank could get the beach party goods out to Tacoma. They would have to ship via truck. Hank was planning on shipping directly to Miller Aviation at Tacoma Industrial Airport. Doc had provided the address and Sexton had passed it on. The shipment was out of storage, would be picked up the next day and headed to Tacoma. Hank would be following shortly. He wanted to try getting the last two men for a couple of days, but reluctantly agreed on just one more day.

The only remaining item on Sexton's to-do list was the co-pilot situation. He hadn't heard from Doc yet as to Barnes' decision. He called Doc at the office number he had been given.

"Good morning, Aries Enterprises, how may I direct your call?"

The totally charming voice stopped Sexton cold. He hadn't expected it. He somehow had assumed the company was quite small and Doc would be answering the phone.

"Uh, is Doc McGarrity in?" He asked.

"Yes, may I tell him who is on the line and the purpose of the call?" Hunter said this in a manner that was totally inoffensive.

"Sexton, uh, Bob Sexton. He'll know what it's about."

"Just a moment Mr. Sexton, I'll tell him you're on the line." Sexton was placed on hold.

A short moment later Doc picked up the phone, "McGarrity."

"Doc, Bob Sexton. What is the situation with Barnes? Does he want to go?"

"I don't know, I haven't talked to him about it yet. He isn't in the office but I expect him soon. I'll have to let you know."

"Okay. Please do, as soon as you know. The men are on their way. We'll have to leave as soon as the beach party goods arrive. They will be leaving Ohio tomorrow, by truck, and going direct to Miller Aviation."

"Like I said, I expect him in soon. We'll talk about it and I'll let you know. You'll be in your room? At the Hilton?"

"Yeah, I'll probably be on the phone, but keep trying." Sexton replied.

"You said that the men are on their way. How many are we talking about?"

"There are twenty now, counting myself and we're trying to get two more. That will be a total of twenty-two. Any problems?"

"We'll have to make it work. There aren't any regular airline seats aboard, just the bucket seats. You know, the canvas benches along each side of the airplane cabin. We might not have enough seat belts, or places for everybody. There is a jump seat in the cockpit and a radio operator seat behind the pilot's seat. We'll just have to make do for twenty in the back. Maybe I should rig a couple of straps like on a subway. What do you think?"

This brought a chuckle out of the very serious Special Forces Colonel. "I'm sure we'll be able to work something out. Let me know about Barnes. And by the way, Cellini has given me the official go ahead. It should keep us out of a concrete hotel."

"Right. That's good news. I'll get back to you about Barnes."

Hunter came into Doc's office. She was a little irked and it showed. "James Francis McGarrity, what is going on? This is my first day back on the job and I don't think I'm going to like what you're going to tell me. I couldn't help but overhear enough of your conversation with that Sexton person. Just where are you going to be taking twenty-two people and what decision does Harry Barnes have to make? This upsets me, Doc. What's going on? I'm waiting."

Doc didn't know what to say. He knew that she hadn't been eavesdropping she didn't have to. Conversations carried in the three front offices. Especially if it was quiet. Still, he wasn't used to having to answer to anybody. He had been single for some time now. As much as he dearly loved this creature in front of him, he just didn't know how to respond to her directness. She was waiting for an answer and it was becoming obvious that she wasn't going to leave without one.

"Hunter, please come in. Sit. I'm going to say some things to you that I've wanted to say for a long time. I know that it's too early, but the other things that I have to tell you about my conversation with Bob Sexton will upset you I know. So, if all of this is going to drive you away from me, you might as well hear all of it." Hunter started to say something, but Doc waved her quiet. He went on, "First, and probably foremost, I love you. I've loved you from the first day that you came into this office. I didn't know it then since I knew you were married. I learned early in life to avoid wanting things that were too far out of reach or that I had no business even considering. That was the situation with you. I had no business even considering loving you since you were so happily married. Then things changed. Listen kid, I wouldn't have wished your losing your husband on you for the world. But the facts are you did. And it changed things for me at that moment. I'm sure that you guessed from my actions when I was around you. I was tongue-tied, clumsy, a real klutz. On second thought, maybe you wanted to ignore it. I wouldn't blame you. I want our relationship to become more than the weekly dinners I've come to enjoy so much. I know, I know, it was all under the pretense of working you back into returning to the company. And that is something you're going to have to consider. This is a good job. It pays well. You have a world of responsibility and you do your job well. It isn't charitable. You're worth all that I'm paying you and more. But only you can be the judge if you don't like what I'm telling you. And now, getting to the other matter..."

"Doc, please. Enough. I don't know if I really want to know about..."

"Hunter, shut up. I'm going to tell you. Now you have more than a right to know. Barnes and I did a job for the CIA. It paid well. It was fun and really a piece of cake, as the saying goes. Things have turned bad. There is a real asshole down there. His name is Cordero. My guess is that he is the one responsible for the killing of those church people who have been in the news lately. Bob Sexton is a retired Army Special Forces Colonel who happens to be Whitey McFrank's best friend. Whitey is the agent we worked with in El Salvador and who, by the way, set up the coffee deal for us. Sexton believes that Cordero has taken Whitey prisoner and wants to go get him out of there. That is where Barnes and I come in. First of all, it has to happen fast. Sexton thinks, and I believe him, that this Cordero will kill Whitey if too much time elapses. It is his only way out. Cordero's, I mean. There are things about our earlier trip that you don't know about. I said that we did a job for the CIA. That job consisted of delivering a load of arms to this Cordero person. We ended up flying into a strip on his ranch. We had to fly a specific flight pattern or we would have been fired upon. The airplane has distinctive registration markings, Venezuelan, in fact. Cordero wanted Smoke and me to stay so he could show off his troops. We couldn't so he invited us back. That is why at least, I have to go back. I would be expected. That way we can get Sexton and his special people on the ground at the ranch. And quickly. I know all of this sounds crazy. We wouldn't be getting paid. I'll be using the airplane without the CIA's knowledge. Sexton says that if we wait for things to go through channels Whitey will be dead. He was able to get some legal authority from an El Salvadorian official, so we're covered to some degree. I don't particularly want to do this. I don't have a death wish. I'm not looking for any thrills. Once on the ground I intend to stay out of everybody's way. When it's time to leave, I'll fly the airplane back and hope that Whitey and the good Colonel Sexton can keep Smoke and me out of jail. That is, if Smoke decides that he wants to go. Now there you have it, Hunter. All of it. I can only say

I fully intend to come back. I intend to properly court you. I intend to make you my wife and I intend to love, honor, cherish and maybe even 'obey' you for as long as I live. And that, I intend to be for a very long time." He sighed. "Now you can speak."

Hunter's eyes had gotten big. For the last part of Doc's dissertation she had her hand up to her mouth. She kept shaking her head as if to clear the thoughts that were racing through her mind. It was a bit overwhelming and she was in shock. Yes, she had thought that there was more to Doc's attention than her coming back to work. She had known, but purposely not thought about it. Now his declaration of love was enough to shake her normal composure. But this wild flight back down to El Salvador to some animal who kills church people and wants to kill this CIA agent Whitey, or whatever his name was, all of this was proving to be an overload to her circuits. She didn't know what to say.

Doc didn't say anything. They just sat there looking at each other. It got so quiet you could hear the five clocks up on Doc's wall grinding away. And they were electric! Battery powered.

Hunter gathered up her thoughts and slowly regained her composure. She cleared her throat. Finally she spoke. "You certainly have a way with women, don't you? Is that it? I love you, I want you, now good-bye. Isn't there some song that goes something like that? I really don't know what to say, Doc. I'm impressed with your honesty and forthrightness. I don't have to tell you that if we were to have a relationship, it sure as hell would be getting off to a rocky start with you running off to get yourself killed." Doc nodded his understanding of her position but didn't contribute anything. Hunter continued. "I think it is best for both of us if I just forgot about your declaration of feelings toward me until you come back, if you come back. I think and hope you will, Doc. Truly I do. It is just easier this way. As for the company, you're right. This is a good job. There is a lot to it with just the aircraft deals. If Ross ever gets the temperature to stabilize, Freeze Flight will be off and running. You have saddled me with a lot of responsibility. I still have your 'power of attorney' and if, God forbid, something did happen to both you and Smoke, I would do something with the company and see to it that your next of kin, your child, in your case and Smoke's lady, in his case...plus Ross, got something out of all this. That hasn't changed from when you originally saddled me with this mess. I'm just in a better position to appreciate all of the ramifications since left with the same problems at home. I can and will handle those details. The other matter, I guess we'll just have to wait and see what hand fate deals us. That's all I want to talk about this for now. Besides, Smoke has driven up and you're going to have to do some selling to him." Hunter got up and walked toward the door.

"Wait, Hunter. I don't want to leave it like this."

She turned back quickly. "I do." She left his office just as Smoke came bustling in.

He watched her leave, somewhat in wonderment. He looked at Doc.

"Should I ask? --Nah. Forget it."

"Come in, Smoke, and close the door. I have something to talk to you about."

Sexton had been right. Barnes would never have forgiven Doc if he had kept him out of the thing. He was like a kid almost. His biggest concern was telling Shelly. But he would tell her.

Doc called Bob Sexton at the Hilton and told him they had a co-pilot.

366

THE SEA-TAC HILTON
Two days later.

The meeting had been scheduled for two o'clock in the afternoon. Bob Sexton had obtained a meeting room from the concierge. It was locked with a Do Not Disturb sign on it. Doc rapped on the door. It was opened quickly by a very large, very mean looking member of Sexton's troop. Doc introduced himself and Smoke. They were allowed to enter.

The room appeared small. It was thick with cigarette smoke. It felt small due to the size and type of people occupying it. It was one hellava group. Doc had niggling feelings of regret for Cordero. Just a thought. It passed quickly enough.

The maps and pictures that Doc had provided Colonel Sexton at their first meeting were spread out on the long, white tablecloth-covered, tables. The assortment of men were gathered around and everybody talking at once. Sexton looked up, saw them come in and then introduced them all around.

"There'll be three more coming, Doc. My Exec, Hank Stevaro, Dan Hartmann and Mark Dillman. They'll be here tomorrow and, we hope, so will the shipment. Are you two ready to saddle up?"

Barnes spoke up, "Yeah, but I'm going to need a good attorney, especially if I don't make it back." This evoked laughter all around. He went on, "But I wouldn't miss this for the world."

"I thought you were single."

"I am."

This last comment brought on more laughter. These men knew how their girlfriends and wives reacted to their specialized line of work. The Colonel waited for the hilarity to subside before continuing.

How about it, Doc. Is the airplane ready?" Sexton asked.

Yes. I spoke with Ron Miller this morning. He finished the twenty-five hour inspection I asked him to do a couple of days ago. He hasn't heard from anybody from the agency. The airplane is locked up. Ron has the keys, but if somebody came along to take the airplane back to Florida, they would have a hard time." Doc replied. "He also disconnected the batteries."

One of Sexton's troops spoke out, "You're the guys who are stealing the plane from the agency. What a trip! I got to hand it to you two. That takes some kind of balls!"

"Do you know something we don't?" Smoke asked.

Colonel straightened up from bending over the maps and pictures. "Hey! Enough! We have work to do. Doc, explain the flight arrival procedure that you told me about. The one you had to fly and the way you and Barnes executed it."

Doc reviewed the arrival procedures dictated by Cordero. The markings on the two ends of the runway indicating Runway Closed to Landing Traffic. There wouldn't be other aircraft on the field. Or Doc didn't think there would be.

"How hard would it be to drop a four man HALO team in the night before?" Sexton asked.

"What for?"

"Doc, I'm not used to being questioned, but if you must know it would be to put snipers on the ground prior to our landing. If someone decided that they didn't want us on the ground the team could discourage them from doing something about it." Colonel Sexton wasn't angry, merely lecturing.

"I understand Colonel and I'm not trying to tell you your business. But Sir, please remember, the airplane has been there before. It will fly the required pattern. We were invited back. All of those things." Doc paused to get his breath, then went on, "For those reasons I feel quite certain that I'll be able to get the airplane on the ground without taking fire. Nobody should get excited until your people come running out of the airplane. Then there's the matter of where do we land after dropping the HALO team? We won't have enough fuel to orbit until dawn and we can't land in San Salvador then take-off again."

"I see." Colonel Sexton was thinking about what Doc had said.

"And Colonel, I think I know but to make sure, what does HALO mean?" Doc asked.

"Uh, it means 'High Altitude Low Opening' parachute work. It gets folks on the ground without raising a lot of curiosity."

"You guys do that at night? Jee-zuss! If you misjudge, you can end up wearing a halo!"

"About it, Doc." The Colonel shrugged and returned to the issue at hand. "Okay, we won't do the drop. It would be for insurance purposes anyway. I guess I'll have to trust your judgment. Just remember, Doc, your judgment call is for all of these people here in this room and the three that are still enroute."

"I understand, Sir." Doc replied.

The rest of the afternoon was spent in heavy planning. Doc and Smoke didn't have much to do, other than answer questions from time to time about some part of the ranch or the hacienda. Both Doc and Smoke were asked to draw a map of as much of the house as they had seen. They did that separately, then compared notes and fine-tuned the drawing. They were able to make an intelligent guess as to where Whitey would be, if he was being kept in the main ranch house. It would only be a guess.

Since they hadn't gone into any of the other buildings on the ranch they didn't know any more than the pictures showed. Sexton didn't want them to leave the meeting, though, until he was sure that they wouldn't be able to contribute anything more.

As for their part in the extraction, Sexton made it clear their job was to get the airplane on the ground and to stay alive in order to fly out of there. They were to stay out of people's way. It sounded just fine to Doc. Smoke grumbled a bit, but Sexton shut him up.

As near as Doc could tell from the conversations going on around the table, there wasn't going to be any pow-wow upon arrival. Sexton considered these people the enemy. They were going to be treated as such. He told his people what Cellini had said.

The group was being divided up into two fire teams. Sexton would lead one, Hank Stevaro the other. The teams would be going in hot. Doc listened in wonderment as specific tasks were handed out. These people were *BAD!*

At a lull in the conversations going on around the table, Doc got Colonel Sexton's attention. "What is it, Doc? You have a question?"

"Yeah, I sure do. With all due respect, Colonel, what if Whitey is not being held prisoner, but is out in the field and out of contact. The main thing being, what if these folks are not the enemy?" Doc stopped for a moment to let what he said sink in. "I mean, just suppose that Whitey is healthy. Are you going to blow away a bunch of people based on what Cellini said? Was he that sure of their activity to issue a death sentence? Otherwise we've got a full international incident. A stolen airplane. Stolen arms and ordnance. I seriously doubt if any provision would be made for 'time off for good behavior'. The key would be thrown so fuckin' far away it would never be found!"

Colonel Sexton, U.S. Army Special Forces (Retired) thought about all that Doc had said for maybe a full minute. It was deathly quiet in the room. He and Doc kept looking at each other. Finally, Colonel Sexton spoke.

"I've known Ernest Herman Whitey McFrank since before his hair turned that color. He doesn't stay out of touch with his control or, in this case, with his wife for this kind of a period of time. If he isn't in touch, he's in trouble. It is that trouble we are going to solve one way or another. As for the international incident, as you put it, who is going to report it? We sure as hell aren't, and there will not be anybody around at the other end to talk despairingly about us. You can make book on that one, Doc." The Colonel paused, then went on, "The fact that Whitey went out to the ranch at the request of Alfredo Cellini, because of atrocities committed in the field by this bunch, is enough for me to consider them the enemy, leaving no question in my mind. I spoke with Cellini. He told me about Cordero, about his so-called force and their assignment. It has now been proven that many atrocities have been more than just linked to this force. They have done nasty things, Doc. Cellini didn't even want to stop them with the El Salvadorian army due to the political sensitivity. He doesn't want them to stand trial. He's not only issued a termination order, it was issued with prejudice! He will back us all the way. His backing will go a long way toward keeping our own government off our ass for the airplane and borrowed goods. Does that put your mind at ease? Have I answered your question?"

"Yes, Sir!"

"And, Doc, I'm not getting on your case. Your point is a valid one and well taken. The men in this room will and have, followed me anywhere. It is good that you brought up what you did. In answering you it gives me an opportunity to tell them some of the operational details." He stopped for a moment, allowing his gaze to sweep over each man.

"We're going in hot!" There were mutterings of agreement around the room. But Doc wasn't through yet, he had more to say.

"Okay Colonel, you're going in shooting. I understand. Now, one other thing. How about getting home.

371

How had you planned on doing that?" Doc was leading up to something, Sexton wasn't sure what.

"I'm not sure what you're talking about, Doc. Could you be more specific?"

"Well, we find Whitey and get out of there. Fly into San Salvador in order to refuel. We've got a bunch of well-armed men and the leftover ordnance. You and your troops are in battle dress. Shit, Colonel, the customs people will think you want to start a war. What's the plan for the other end?"

"Again, Doc, your point is well taken. My first priority, of course, is to get Whitey. Once that is accomplished we have several options. We can contact our embassy and get the spooks involved. There's our friend Alfredo Cellini. He should able to draw enough water with their Customs people, or we can bluff it. Just say that you've been operating in the back country when you call in for landing instructions. Not out of the country. You won't be on a flight plan. I'm not going to worry about that until we have to. Essentially, like I said, our best bet is Cellini and the spooks at our embassy. We'll call them immediately upon landing. One or the other should be able to keep us out of any problems. Our people should be pretty happy. After all, we would have done their damn job for them!"

"Okay. I just wanted to know. Thanks, you've answered all of my questions."

Smoke and Doc were to be at the airplane by noon, ready to depart when the shipment arrived. Sexton would have his people there no later than fourteen hundred, probably earlier depending on when the stragglers arrived. Stevaro had called, indicating they were on their way, all three of them. He had reassured Sexton that the shipment would be there by noon or before. He had contracted with a trucker who was going to be doing a back-haul out of Portland Oregon. The trucker picked up the shipment and would be delivering it personally before going into Portland. Unless something unforeseen occurred, the shipment would be there. In Tacoma.

Doc said they would be non-stop to Cabo San Lucas. He wanted to arrive sometime between one and three in the morning to avoid any problems with the Mexican officials. Doc was counting on dealing with a certain official that they had befriended.

"Another thing Colonel, chow. Noon to two in the morning is a long time. We won't be able to get anything to eat in Cabo, so there will be another period of six hours or so into the ranch. We're going to need some chow. Will field rations be a part of the shipment? You will be the last to arrive. Perhaps you can get box lunches from the Hilton. They are used to putting up meals for transient corporate aircraft."

"Good thinking, Doc. And yes, field rations will be included in the shipment. They can be the second meal. Your idea of box lunches is a good one for the first meal. If you can handle coffee and water jugs, I'll take care of the Hilton's cuisine for our repast out of here."

"Yes, Sir! Coffee and water for twenty-two souls. It's handled."

"Okay gents, that's it then. Enjoy your last night here. We leave tomorrow."

Doc grabbed Smoke, then said over his shoulder, "Are we dismissed, Colonel, Sir?"

This got a chuckle out of Sexton. "You're dismissed, Marines." He added a casual salute.

When Doc and Smoke got out to their cars, Doc asked about Shelly.

"Well, you know, I kinda thought maybe this could be the end of our relationship. You remember how she was the first time." Smoke looked at Doc, who nodded in the affirmative. "Well when I told her she was cooking grits and gravy, one of her favorite dishes. I made a point of staying out of her reach. Shit. She just said be careful, and if I didn't come back she'd hunt me down and kill me!"

Doc laughed. "That gal's something else.'

"Yeah, who'd guess that answer? I told her that we're not getting paid, we're stealing the airplane and there was going to be shooting. It was after I told her that when she said to be careful or she'd kill me. Sumpin else is right. I'll never be able to figure them out."

"Hey! Don't feel alone." Doc said. "Pick up a couple more gallon jugs, for the coffee, and I will also. Try to have them filled on your way down tomorrow. They'll get old and bad as it is. I'll get the water jugs. I like Seattle water. You know we've both drunk water all over the world and I've never tasted water coming out of the tap as good as we have right here."

"You're right! Okay, I'll buy several jugs, get the coffee and see you at the bird by noon or before. Are you going to try to see Hunter?'

"No way. She might change my mind. And then what would you guys do without me? Never mind, don't bother answering that one. See you at the bird. Have a good time tonight."

When Doc got home he sat down and wrote a long letter to his son Barry. Hunter's comments made him realize he hadn't paid his son much attention other than being on time with support payments. Of course, he saw him when he was anywhere near Southern California but he hadn't been much of a father.

It was a hard letter to write. He had originally intended it to be sent if he didn't make it back. And he wrote it that way. But then he decided to write another and mail that one tonight. It was equally difficult to write.

374

The first letter he put in a larger envelope with a note that it was only to be mailed if he didn't make it back. He addressed that one to the office, to Hunter's attention. He knew it would upset her, but it couldn't be helped. He vowed to himself that somehow he would let her know when they were clear of the target and on their way home, even if it meant calling the Seattle CIA office on the HF. That might not be a bad idea. They were going to have to let the agency in on the caper at some point anyway. Besides, Sandy would probably appreciate knowing Whitey was safe also. He would have to think about that one some more.

CHAPTER THIRTY-THREE
INTO HARM'S WAY

God! It was a beautiful morning! The sun was still below the horizon at oh six hundred. The sky was golden; and the sun, still behind the Cascade Range, etched the mountains so clear, they appeared to be a cut-out stage prop that you could almost reach out and touch. There was a crispness in the air. It felt good. This was going to be an okay trip. Doc got in his car and headed for the office. He was going to put the letters in his out basket. He had written a letter to Hunter as well. Not to be opened *unless*. It contained some explicit instructions on the company. He avoided talking about his personal feelings other than wishing her a good life and sorry that he wouldn't be sharing it. It seemed like enough had been said.

It didn't take long to drop off the letters and check his desk for anything that had recently come in. He opened the safe and took out the cash that he had withdrawn from the bank. They would need cash for fuel, landing fees and bribes. Their regular expenses, Doc figured they could charge on their American Express, hotels and meals; the normal tourist or business traveler things.

Everything else was okay. Hunter was very efficient. In the two days since she had been back things were cleaned up and organized.

Doc drove to Tacoma, planning to stop at a K-Mart or Payless Drug to get coffee and water jugs. Then he would find a Denny's and fill them with fresh, hot black coffee. He thought it would probably be a good idea to get some decent paper cups. What good would the coffee be without something to drink it out of? *Thinking, thinking, damn! He was good!*

It was close to ten o'clock when he pulled into the Tacoma Industrial Airport. He drove up to Miller Aviation and out onto the ramp, going directly to the airplane to unload the full jugs and his gear. The airplane was still locked up, so he piled everything up by the door. He got back in the car and drove it over behind the hangar, got out of the car and walked into the Miller Aviation office to get the keys to the airplane. Ron Miller was sitting in the outer office talking to two men who looked a little familiar. Shit! They were the two pilots who had flown the airplane up to Tacoma from Patrick Air Force Base, in Florida. They were obviously here to fly the airplane back. This was going to present a problem.

Doc decided to just take the bull by the horns. He walked up to the group. "Hi guys. Just get in?" Doc couldn't remember their names for the life of him.

The taller one spoke up. "We got in last night and stayed in Tacoma. It was a mistake. Not much fun."

The other one added, "Yeah, all the honeys around were working girls. They wanted money for a good time. What the hell kinda town is Tacoma anyway?"

Doc decided to keep them talking for as long as he could. "It's just your normal military town. There's McChord Air Force Base and Fort Lewis which is a large staging and training base for the U.S. Army. Both are on the south outskirts of Tacoma." He was thinking, *he had to keep them occupied until Colonel Sexton arrived. Looking at his watch. It was now a little after ten. He was going to have to keep them occupied until at least noon.*

"Well we stayed over at a motel south of the downtown area, right next to the freeway." It was the tall one talking again, "Heard a lot of airplane talk at the bar. Must have been fighter jocks from McChord."

The other one piped up, "How did the gooney bird work for you guys, get it all sorted out? Any problems?"

"We had some problems with the fuel system. We managed to make it work though. Miller here was going to fix everything and do the twenty-five hour inspection so it would be ready for you to take home." Doc looked over at Ron Miller and tried to mentally give him a message. "How's all that going, Ron?"

"Like I reported to you, Doc, she's all ready to go. The fuel system is okay." He replied.

Well, so much for that ploy, Doc thought. *"*Are you sure she can go today..."

"Doc, I told you it would be ready. And the shipment of stuff, that you were expecting, arrived this morning. The truck was here waiting when I came."

Doc groaned inwardly. Miller could have gone a long time without talking about that. It was too late. The comment had piqued the tall one's interest.

"What shipment? We weren't told about any shipment. We're just supposed to pick up the airplane and head back to Patrick. I want to get the show on the road." He turned to his partner, "Come on Walt, let's get a move on."

"Okay Steve, whatever you want. Shall I file?"

That's them, Walt and Steve. Now Doc remembered. The tall one was Steve and the other one Walt. "Hey guys, what's the rush? I thought that we were supposed to show you a good time when you came back. Smoke will be here any time now." Doc was trying to bait the hook.

"Nah Doc, we appreciate it, but we really got to get moving," Steve, who was apparently in charge, was starting to get agitated. "Besides, we're on limited per diem, and it's harder than hell to cover a good time. The Company is getting horseshit about heavy expenses."

"Well hey, what would you have done if the airplane was still in-check? Twenty five hour inspections can take time. If Ron here had the airplane scattered all apart and spread over the hangar floor, you would have to come back tomorrow and even then it might not be ready."

"You're right, Doc but the airplane isn't spread all over and we have to get going." Steve stood up. He glanced out the front windows of the office and noticed Smoke getting out of his car. Smoke had driven them both to Sea-Tac Airport when they had delivered the airplane. Steve turned back to Doc. "Here's your buddy. What was his name? Smoke?"

"Right. Smoke. You're sure going to disappoint him. He does like to party. And he knows the ones to party with. He's only been living with a gal a short time. He's going to tell you that you need an attitude adjustment. Your white count is way too high." Doc was still searching for a hook. "Have a cup of coffee and at least be sociable, Steve."

Steve waved to Walt to sit down. "Okay, but just one, then we've got to make tracks. I want to make Denver tonight."

Just then Smoke came bounding in, "Hey Boss, what's. . ." Then he saw the two CIA pilots and stopped short. He did some fast thinking on his feet. "Uh, hi fellows. We were wondering when you'd be back. I thought we were going to be partying. You were going to call, or did you just get in?" The latter was more of a statement than question.

Walt spoke up. "Hi Smoke. No, we got in last night. All the girls we tried to hustle were pros. They kept trying to take our money."

Steve added, "We're going to have to take a rain check Smoke. We're on a tight schedule and on limited per diem. We'll have to do party-time next time."

"That's a real shame Steve. You look like you could use an attitude adjustment. . ."

Doc broke in, "See what I mean, Steve? I told you that is what he would say. . ."

". . . and I know just the little number who will not only readjust your attitude, but she'll lower your white count and blow the wax out of your ears!" Smoke was starting to really get wound up.

Steve and Walt had made their way over to the coffee urn. Steve turned back, "You're sure tempting me Smoke, but I really think we had better start back today. But tell me about this little minx. Does she have a friend?"

That was all Smoke needed. He started telling about some of the Tacoma girls he knew and soon had everybody in stitches. Good 'Ol Smoke, he can sure spin a tale. A very funny guy. Close to an hour later three van-type station wagons pulled up. It was Colonel Sexton and party. They started piling out of the cars. There were boxes that probably contained box lunches. The men had small clothing-bag type luggage pieces as well. They were dressed in battle fatigues.

Both Steve and Walt got to their feet just as Colonel Sexton, accompanied by three of his men, and came through the door into the office. The Colonel appeared agitated and hurried.

"Doc, what the hell's goin' on? Why isn't the airplane open and ready to go? What's the problem?" The Colonel came right up to Doc, who had gotten to his feet, ignoring the two CIA pilots completely.

Doc gestured to the two pilots, "Colonel, I'd like you to meet Steve and Walt, they're the company pilots who are here to fly the airplane back to Florida." Turning back to the two CIA pilots Doc said, "I'm sorry guys, I don't remember your last names."

Steve spoke right up, "That's not important. What's this about the airplane being ready? Ready for what? I want to know just what the hell's going on here."

Colonel Sexton caught on quickly. Addressing Steve, he said, "Gentlemen, we are borrowing your airplane for a little excursion. . ."

380

"In a pig's ass you are," Steve interrupted. "You have no authority to use this airplane. It was brought up here for one job. That job is over. Now we're going to take it back to Florida. And that's the way it is!" Each sentence became more exact and louder.

Colonel Sexton moved quickly to stand in front of Steve. His face was about four to six inches away from Steve's face. The expression on Colonel Sexton's face was one of complete control, authority and defiance. This was a person not to be trifled with.

He spoke softly, but distinctly. Nobody had any problem hearing him, the room had become deathly quiet. "As I was saying Steve, we are taking this airplane on a little excursion. The job is not over. One of the company people involved is in serious trouble and we are going to get him out of that trouble. I don't have time for channels. The man in trouble doesn't have time for me to go through channels. You and your friend here, are not going to stop us, or hinder us in any way."

Steve started to say something. Colonel Sexton held up his hand stopping him, then continued, "You have exactly two choices. Pay close attention to what I'm saying. I don't have the time or the patience to repeat myself. Your first choice is as follows. We will tie you up and tell Mr. Miller here to untie you in eight hours, which is the time that we need to be out of any body's reach who might want to do something stupid. Or, and this is your other choice, you can go back into town, *since the airplane is not ready*," Colonel Sexton paused for the implication to sink in. "And come back tomorrow morning. The airplane will be gone. You can report it being gone to whomever you choose. You will be off the hook. Now, let me make myself very clear on one point, if you choose the latter and then do something equally stupid like not waiting until tomorrow morning to report the airplane gone, I personally, or one of my loyal compadres will find you and do serious hurtful things to your body.

That is not a threat. It is a solemn guaranteed promise. You will have been responsible for the death of a very brave man who is a loyal member of the same organization you work for and a very close friend of mine. *Do-you-understand-me?"* This last sentence was delivered louder and the Colonel had moved even closer. He stayed that way until Steve cleared his throat, preparing to answer. Sexton stepped back.

"Colonel, I do hear you. I do clearly understand your determination to do what you have set out to accomplish. And I would not, for the world, want to spend the rest of my life looking over my shoulder, nor would Walt here. But, since it is all in the family, would you let us in on some of the details of what your intentions are. Since we are in the same line of work I think that even if I don't have a real need to know, we do know how to keep our mouths shut. It would sure make me feel better about trying to put one over on my boss."

The Colonel thought for a moment. He made a decision. "Fair enough. Let's you and Walt and I go for a little walk. Mr. Miller shouldn't be involved in this anymore than he already is." The three of them left the office and started to walk toward the airplane. Colonel Sexton waved his people away who had started to follow.

Ron Miller spoke up for the first time. "Whew! Uh Doc, just how much trouble am I really in at the moment?"

"Ron, you're okay. Neither the Colonel, those two CIA pilots or Smoke and I would ever involve you. Don't worry about it." Doc turned to Smoke, "Do you have a couple of your harem cuties from Tacoma, or was that just bullshit you were flinging about?"

"Why Doc, would I lie about something as important as pussy? Of course I know some lovelies in Tacoma." Smoke sounded offended.

"Well, why don't you get on the horn and track down a pair. I have a hunch that our two friends are going to take the Colonel's offer. We might as well sweeten the pot."

"Good idea Doc. That's what I like about you; you're always thinking." This got a chuckle from Ron and the three men who had come in with the Colonel. Smoke went over to a desk with a phone and pulled out a small address book from his briefcase. He got to work.

The three men came back into the office. They walked up to Ron Miller. Steve asked Ron, "Is the airplane ready? And if not, when will it be ready?"

Ron understood now what his role was. Smiling, he said, "No sir, but if you come back in the morning I'll have it ready for you. I get here at eight."

"Right, we'll see you then, eight o'clock." Steve replied, smiling also. Turning back to Doc, "Well, it's a shame that you and Smoke have other plans. I was just getting warmed up about getting the wax buildup removed from my ears by that friend of Smoke's. You guys will owe us one."

Smoke called out from over at the desk where he had been busy on the phone. "Not so fast, hold on a minute," he called out to Steve and Walt. Turning back to the phone, he went on with his conversation with whoever was on the other end. "That's great, Candy, you won't be disappointed. I'll have Steve call you. Yes, right away. 'Bye hon." He hung up and looked up at the two waiting pilots.

"Owe, like hell. You guys are fixed up, as the saying goes. Here are the numbers. Steve, you get Candy and Walt gets Marci. Now don't screw this up, you two. These little beauties will be putting out on my say-so."

Doc broke in, "And, since you're on limited per diem, here's a little spare change to insure you're showing these gals a good time." He handed Steve two one hundred dollar bills.

Steve started to say something. Doc shut him off, "Hey, this is company expense money. We haven't been on limited per diem and our account is fairly liberal. I'm not buying you."

Steve laughed, "Okay. You guys have a good excursion. Hurry back. Frankly, we both would like to be going with you. The Colonel explained about the strip and all. It's best that it be you two, since you've been there before. Otherwise, I'd wrestle you for the seat, Doc."

"Appreciated. You guys are good troop." Turning to Ron, Doc went on, "Mr. Miller, why don't you have your gas boy drive these two gentlemen back to their hotel?"

"Right, Doc," Miller said, and went out into the hangar to get the gas boy.

"Hey, be sure to call the girls right away," Smoke said.

Everybody shook hands. Steve, Walt and the Colonel took a bit longer. Then the two pilots left.

Walking out to the airplane with the Colonel, Doc asked him, "You think they'll be okay?"

"I think so. I would be very surprised if it turned out differently. But how do you plan on flying south. Are you going to file a flight plan?"

"I've been thinking about that. We have a ton of fuel. I thought we'd take off and stay relatively low--thousand, fifteen hundred feet--and head over to the coast. Before we get to Astoria, head on out to sea, dropping down on the water. Head out twenty-five miles and then turn south. The ADIZ (Air Defense Identification Zone) is about twenty miles out. Then turning south we can stay out of U.S. air space. It will be light enough to be able to safely stay on the deck most of the way down. This time of year it will start to get dark in the LA area sometime around seven o'clock. That gives us seven hours to get there if we get our ass in gear now."

"That sounds like a good plan, Doc. I trust your judgment. I'll get the men and load the airplane. Miller says the freight we were expecting is in the hangar. You and

Smoke do what you have to do to ready the airplane for flight. We'll handle the rest."

"Got it." Turning to Smoke, Doc said, "You take the left side, I'll unlock the bird and do the cockpit; and then I'll do what's left of the right side."

They were in the air five minutes before noon. The take-off was to the south. Smoke, who was in the left seat, headed southwest toward Westport and the coast of Washington. They set up for cruise at fifteen hundred feet.

Doc looked over his left shoulder at Bob Sexton, who was sitting on the jump seat just behind them. "Colonel. Please go back and tell your troops they can move around but to do so with care. When we hit the coast and go down on the deck I don't want a lot of trim change. It will help if they stay put."

Sexton had to lean forward to hear Doc above the engine noise. "I understand. Right now, they're seeing to their weapons and the other items Hank Stevaro shipped to us. I'll pass the word though."

"Thanks." Doc turned to Smoke. "I figure we can get bearings off of Astoria, Newport, North Bend and Crescent City. They all have TACAN. Their DME will give us our miles 'from' so we can stay outside of the ADIZ. Will you have any trouble navigating?"

Smoke was a little surprised. "No, shouldn't have. Is that your plan? To stay outside of the ADIZ all the way to Mexico?"

"Yeah, we haven't talked about it. The Colonel and I did while you were doing the pre-flight. This is just for insurance if our two lads decide to blow the whistle. Why make it easy for somebody that might be looking for us. At the coast, we can drop down to four or five hundred feet, or lower and stay below radar. It might be too low to receive the TACAN or DME signals, but we'll still be able to receive the ADF. If we need to we can pop up occasionally for the

TACAN stuff. We'll have to hand fly it, but we've done that before. We'll trade off. Any better ideas?"

"No, I sure as hell don't have any. As for the CIA guys, I think Candy and Marci will hold their attention for some time. If they do decide to change their minds they'll probably be too tired to dial a phone."

This got Doc laughing. Colonel Sexton came back up to the flight deck.

"Did I miss something? What's so funny?"

"Smoke here says that if our two spook pilots hook up with Candy and Marci they won't have enough strength to dial a phone and tell on us." Doc explained.

Sexton chuckled, "You're probably right, Smoke. Doc, how's the plan going?"

"I'm working up the details now, Colonel. . ."

Smoke broke in, "How long do I have to wait, First Officer?"

"I already have it, Captain, Sir! We should be abeam San Diego, twenty-five miles out at seventeen thirty-five. That's five hours plus forty minutes after take-off, with a fuel burn of five hundred and sixty-five gallons. That's assuming, of course, our winds hold. Smoke, I called for a weather briefing before I left home this morning. That's what I'm basing this estimate on. We have lots of fuel and it looks like we'll have daylight for our wave-hopping. We might call Astoria Flight Service and get an up-date if you think we'll need one. We could use the old P-A-C airplane side number."

"If we're going to do that, let's wait until abeam Crescent City or even farther on down. But that's a good idea, Doc. What wind factor are you using?"

"It's northerly out of here and then swings around to a southerly about the Bay Area. I'm using essentially a no-wind factor. That was at ten thousand feet." Doc was looking at a piece of paper that had been in his pocket,

"Surface winds will be lighter and about the same, initially tail winds then they'll swing around on our nose."

"Here's the coastline, I'm going to take it down on the deck. Leave the power where it is, Doc; it's okay. You won't even have to re-lean."

"Wait a minute, Smoke. Look, there's a haze layer out there. Why not wait a bit, then go down on the deck. It won't attract any attention from shore that way. People just love to report an airplane going down." Doc said.

"You're right, Doc, you're right. Sure glad there's two seats up here. That's twice as much brain power." Smoke Turned to Sexton, "See Colonel? That's the way Marines do it. With brain power."

"Am I going to have to put up with this bullshit for the next eighteen hours?" Sexton replied.

"Abso-fuckin'-lutely, Sir! It's the Marine Corps' way to give the Army a hard-ass time." Doc said.

"Well Doc, you're right about that one. Marines have given me a hard time ever since I can remember. But, scrape away the bullshit and you'll find some real folks under it, I'm just as happy to admit." Colonel Sexton had one of his rare smiles on his face as he said this.

Both Doc and Smoke laughed.

Doc's estimate was right on the money. At seventeen thirty-five the San Diego TACAN needle swung through two seven zero degrees and the DME read 'twenty-five nautical miles'. They had made it without being intercepted. It appeared the two CIA pilots had kept their word. But the shit would hit the fan tomorrow!

Now that they were in Mexican air space, Smoke eased the airplane up to fifteen hundred feet and set the auto pilot. They could relax now. Doc asked Hank Stevaro, who was sitting in the radio operator's seat, to get their box lunches the Colonel had gotten from the Hilton. Colonel Sexton was in the back doing something with his troops.

Doc and Smoke swapped seats.

Opening the box lunches came as a pleasant surprise to both Marines. Doc couldn't believe it! "Hey! Would you look at this! Smoke, wouldn't it be a gas to have the Hilton fix box lunches for our drill weekend? I mean for everybody. This is something else."

Smoke just waved his hands, his mouth was full.

The next four hours passed quickly. As it got darker, Doc eased the airplane up to a safer cruise altitude. They were able to see well enough to stay just offshore. It came time to give Cabo San Lucas a call. Doc told Smoke to call, telling approach control they were canceling their I-F-R flight plan from Mexico City to Cabo and to request a straight in, visual approach.

"But Doc, won't that arouse their curiosity? We're not on any flight plan." Smoke couldn't understand where Doc was coming from.

"Smoke, there isn't supposed to be any V-F-R flying after dark in Mexico. Let them think someone forgot to forward our instrument flight plan. Since we're asking for a visual approach, they'll probably just forget it. Then we'll file out of Cabo for San Jose, Costa Rica, and cancel when we get out of Mexican air space.

"Got it. I'll give Approach Control a call." Smoke switched the number one communication radio to Cabo San Lucas Approach Control. "CABO APPROACH, THIS IS DOUGLAS YANKEE VICTOR, WHISKY ALPHA WHISKEY SIERRA CANCELING I-F-R MEXICO CITY TO CABO SAN LUCAS, WE HAVE THE FIELD IN SIGHT, REQUESTING STRAIGHT-IN APPROACH, RUNWAY ONE SIX, OVER."

"UH, DOUGLAS WHISKEY SIERRA SAY AGAIN YOUR FULL CALL SIGN AND I-F-R POINT OF ORIGIN, OVER." The person transmitting sounded hesitant.

Doc looked over at Smoke, grinned and gave him a thumbs up. Smoke grinned back and transmitted, "CABO APPROACH, THIS IS DOUGLAS YANKEE VICTOR,

WHISKEY ALPHA WHISKEY SIERRA. I SAY AGAIN, YANKEE VICTOR, WHISKEY ALPHA WHISKEY SIERRA, CANCELING I-F-R. REQUESTING STRAIGHT-IN APPROACH AND ALTIMETER IN INCHES. WE HAVE THE FIELD IN SIGHT, OVER."

"ROGER DOUGLAS YANKEE VICTOR, WHISKEY ALPHA WHISKEY SIERRA. YOU ARE CLEARED STRAIGHT-IN APPROACH TO RUNWAY ONE SIX. SHOW A LIGHT ONE MILE OUT, WINDS ARE LIGHT AND VARIABLE, ALTIMETER NINER NINER TWO, OVER."

"ROGER APPROACH WHISKEY SIERRA CLEARED STRAIGHT-IN APPROACH, WILL SHOW A LIGHT ONE MILE FINAL. OUT."

Smoke turned to Doc. "They didn't say anything about customs. What do you think?"

"I think that we shouldn't say anything either. But you know, Sanchez monitors the tower radio in his office. I'll bet you he recognizes our call sign and comes out to say hello at least." Doc thought for a moment, "We'll just have to deal with it. Let's you and me try to get refueled as quickly as possible in case he doesn't come by. If he does, I'll deal with him." Doc turned to Hank Stevaro. "Hank, will you ask the Colonel to come up?"

Hank went back to get his boss. Doc and Smoke took care of the Landing Check List. Smoke, like a good co-pilot, had already done the Approach Check List. They were about three miles out on a straight-in final approach when the Colonel made it forward. Doc told him about no required customs since the tower thought their point of origin was in-country. He explained about Juan Sanchez and that he expected Sanchez would meet them. Doc suggested Sexton take his cue from him. Sexton agreed.

"Okay, we're at one mile final. Smoke, turn on the landing lights. Colonel, please check the troops one more time, we're about to land." Doc started concentrating on his upcoming landing.

On the landing roll-out Smoke requested taxi clearance to transient fueling and advised the tower that they would be departing as soon as they had re-fueled. The tower cleared them as requested.

Doc swung the C-47 into the same fueling spot they had used last time. The gas boy was very good with his lighted wands. He seemed more awake this time. They shut down. The boy ran for the fuel truck and pulled up in front as Doc and Smoke were finishing the Engine Shut-down Check List. Smoke went back to open the fuselage side over-wing hatches. He told one of the troops to go out on the wing with him and he would show him what to do. Smoke went back inside and grabbed another troop and showed him the fifty-five gallon drum filling procedure. Doc had gone out to set the chocks and gear pins in place.

The gas boy had handed the fuel hose up to Smoke and the trooper up on the wing. Doc was talking to the gas boy when he saw a car approaching. As it got closer, pulling into the circle of lights from the ramp flood lights, Doc recognized the car as belonging to Juan Sanchez. Doc ducked under the wing, went over to the C-47's cabin door and called for Colonel Sexton to join him. He turned back as Juan pulled up and got out of his car.

"Buenos Noches, Señor Doc!" Juan called out and came up to Doc and the Colonel with a big smile and his hand outstretched.

"Good evening, Inspector Sanchez. Allow me to introduce one Colonel Robert Sexton, U.S. Army Special Forces." Turning to Sexton, "Colonel, this is my good friend Customs Inspector Juan Sanchez."

Colonel Sexton stepped a half pace back and snapped Juan a salute. Sanchez's face lit up like it had been hit with a klieg light. He straightened up, pulled in his stomach and returned the salute. He was obviously honored and delighted.

Doc guided Juan toward his car, gesturing behind him for Sexton to stay put. They walked far enough away to be out of earshot. Doc stopped and put his hand out on Juan's shoulder. "Inspector, your tower thinks our flight originated in Mexico City. A Customs Inspection is not necessary due to that belief. This is one flight you do not want to examine. Colonel Sexton, and his men are on a discrete mission in a country south of here. There are things in the airplane you do not want to see. We will be leaving as soon as we have refueled. I'll give you the landing fees. I trust you to understand what I am telling you, my friend." He looked at Sanchez directly.

Juan Sanchez understood his position. "Señor Doc, I came over to pay my respects. I heard your call to the tower and recognized the aircraft registration. You are right. A customs inspection is not required for in-country operations. Will you be coming back through here?"

"Yes Juan, we will. Perhaps then we can talk about this. In fact, I'm sure that my government will speak to your government alerting you to our itinerary."

"Good. I will look forward to your safe return, my friend." It was Sanchez's turn to salute Doc.

Doc slowly returned the salute. Juan started to get into his car, then turned and waved to Sexton, "Good hunting, Coronel." Juan drove off. Doc stood still and watched him disappear into the darkness.

Colonel Sexton walked up. "What did you tell him, Doc?"

"I told him that you were on a very discrete mission in a country south of here and that he wouldn't want to look inside of our airplane. I also told him we would be coming back through here and our government would probably tell his government to look the other way."

"I thought I saw you give him money. Was that a bribe?"

"No Colonel, I didn't give him bribe money. A bribe isn't necessary with this man. He has honor. And he is my friend. He knows that I wouldn't place him in a position that would discredit him. I gave him the landing fees. That is why we told the tower the flight originated in-country. He's off the hook."

"You do nice work, Doc. What do we have to do now?"

"Well Colonel, if you or your men can help Smoke in any way, do it. I'll use the fuel office phone to file our flight plan." Doc started back to the airplane. He told the men they could get out and stretch their legs. He went on up to the cockpit and got the paperwork for their flight plan. On the way back out of the airplane he ran into Smoke.

"I'm going to use the phone in the gas shack and file. You about done?" Doc asked.

"I will be by the time you're finished," Smoke replied.

"Are you filling everything? All of the drums?"

"Yeah, it can't hurt getting out of here. I don't know what plans you have after the ranch. I thought that this will give us a couple more options." Smoke added.

"Okay. I'll be back shortly. Do you have enough money to pay the gas boy?"

"No problem, Doc. Go file." Smoke turned back to monitor the refueling.

Thirty-five minutes later they were in the air. Runway one six again, with a slight right turn they were able to climb out on course.

Doc was thinking, it *was almost eleven o'clock local time. Their flight plan to San Julian called for a little over eight hours. That would put them into the ranch at about eight forty-five in the morning, local time. In time for breakfast. He would have to tell Sexton to leave the cooks alive.*

CHAPTER THIRTY-FOUR
THE BEACH PARTY

The little township of San Francisco Morazan was in the mountains, separating El Salvador from Honduras. The search had netted a fine catch; four members of the rebel band. Lieutenant Paredes wasn't sure if they were Cubans, Hondurans' or El Salvadorian rebels. He just knew that they were rebels. They weren't admitting to anything now but would soon spill all the details that Colonel Cordero would want to know, once Lieutenant Paredes got them back to San Julian and strapped into his Colonel's special chair. Paredes knew that this catch would please Colonel Cordero. He made the men drive all night in order to get back to the ranchero as quickly as possible. It was a little after eight o'clock in the morning when the trucks pulled into El Rancho San Julian de Cordero.

The Lieutenant immediately went into the hacienda looking for Colonel Cordero. The first men that he ran into were two of the four guards assigned to Whitey McFrank. Paredes was astounded when he was told that McFrank was being held under 'house arrest'. He couldn't understand why the Colonel would do a thing like this. McFrank was CIA! It must be serious. He would have to wait until Cordero's return.

Colonel Cordero had been gone for some time and nobody had heard from him. Nobody knew where he was or where he had gone. He had left. He hadn't said anything to anybody.

Lieutenant Paredes didn't understand any of this. The Colonel kept many things to himself. But this just didn't sit right.

First things first, however. He had the four prisoners brought in, stripped and put in the bare 'holding room' next to the interrogation room.

Paredes was in the kitchen getting the cooks busy. Two of them were to go down to the main bunk house that was being used as a barracks. They were to prepare breakfast for the main body of troops. Two were to remain at the hacienda to serve Captain Mendez, his two squad leaders and himself. He was directing this activity when he heard the airplane buzz the strip. He ran out into the courtyard in time to see, what appeared to be, the same C-47 that had delivered the arms and ammunition to the ranch. It was in a climbing turn then reversing direction for a return low pass at the strip. Paredes noticed that it was flying the prescribed flight pattern in the same manner as before, right on the deck!

This was a cause of uneasiness for Paredes. It didn't seem right. The Colonel hadn't said anything to him about more goods being delivered. What's worse the airplane could be here due to McFrank being detained. He didn't know what to do! However he hadn't become Colonel Cordero's second-in-command by inaction and stupidity. He quickly got some of his men. He told one of Whitey's guards to alert Captain Mendez and then get to the bunkhouse and bring the rest of the men to meet the airplane. He said to tell them to be alert and armed.

Lieutenant Paredes took the eight men that he had initially found out to meet the airplane. They would be ready. Paredes knew that it would take a little longer for the rest of his men to get up to the landing strip to back him up, if the need arose. He was hoping that it wouldn't be necessary to be backed up.

The large silver transport touched down at the far west end of the landing strip. Paredes could barely see it.

The air was still heavy with the blowing, boiling dust clouds that the low, buzzing fly-by's had kicked up. The airplane rolled out, slowing as it came to the east end of the runway. Then, as the speed permitted, the airplane swung sharply around so that the loading door was turned away from the hacienda. As soon as the airplane came to a stop, men dressed in battle fatigues and armed, came out of the airplane at a run and then threw themselves on the ground. Lieutenant Paredes' worst fears were realized. This was an attack group of some kind. These men were either here to get McFrank or to do great harm to Colonel Cordero's forces.

Lieutenant Paredes yelled for his men to open fire. He turned and started running back to the safety of the thick walls of the hacienda. He had reached the house on a dead run when he heard the sporadic fire of his men and the immediate return volleys from the attacking force. He hadn't dared to look over his shoulder to see the outcome of all of the firing.

He burst in the door of the hacienda to meet Captain Mendez accompanied by four or five men, "Where are the rest of the men? I told the man that I sent down to alert you to get all of the men! They're to come running, fully armed!" Paredes said desperately.

"What . . . what is happening? I hear firing. What is it?" Captain Mendez was trembling and clearly frightened.

"Get out there and stop those people. Get out there now! I'll get the other men. Hurry. Go quickly!" Paredes said to Mendez.

Mendez hadn't moved. He stood still, blocking Paredes passage down the hall. He was turning as white as his now-wrinkled, once-white uniform. Paredes still had his gun in his hand. He quickly brought it up and held it against Mendez's nose.

"Take these men and go out there and stop those people now or I'll blow your cowardly head off myself! MOVE!" Paredes screamed at the cowering officer. The

Lieutenant thought, *it was as I suspected. This strutting peacock is a coward. He's one that will run as soon as I turn my back!*

Paredes stepped back to allow the Captain to lead the men out. Mendez still hadn't moved. The Lieutenant glanced down and shook his head. A large dark spot was spreading on the front of the Captain's pants, and a puddle was forming on the tile floor of the entranceway. Mendez was wetting himself! This was the final straw. "GO!" Parades screamed.

Finally, oblivious to his having dishonored himself, Mendez lurched toward the door and the firing that was still going on. The men followed, looking down and being careful not to step in the puddle of fresh urine on the tile floor. They had seen the captain's fright.

Paredes ran through the house and out a back door toward the bunkhouse. He saw the men coming up the rise led by one of the men who had been guarding McFrank. Running to meet the men, Paredes told the guard to go around the south side of the house with half of the men and he would take the rest of the men and go around the other way. They started to split up when everybody stopped dead. They heard and saw the evidence of a large explosion that came from in front of the hacienda. Paredes knew that sound. It was a rocket or mortar! Louder than a grenade. The explosion was followed by heavy automatic weapons fire. He couldn't hear the lighter 'return fire' of his men.

Yelling at the guard to move out, Paredes took his troops to go around the north side of the hacienda in a flanking move.

Colonel Sexton had been the first man out of the airplane. He was followed quickly by his men. They ran a short distance from the airplane in order to attract fire away from the C-47. At twenty-five yards Sexton hit the dirt. His men did likewise. This was like a signal for the small group of Cordero's people to start firing. Sexton and his men immediately returned fire. They noticed one man turn and run back into the house. They made short work of the seven that had stayed to fight.

Sexton started to move his people up when four more of Cordero's troop came out of the house at a run. Another man that appeared to be an officer, stopped at a low wall forming a small courtyard at the entrance of the hacienda. All five started firing. Sexton motioned for Hartmann to move up with a LAWS rocket launcher. Stevaro and his squad quickly silenced the four men in front, while the officer ran from behind the wall back toward the door. He had just made it inside when Hartmann fired the rocket at a spot on the wall next to the door. In an explosive flash, the door and part of the surrounding wall erupted. Sexton, with his men firing heavy automatic weapons, rushed straight toward the opening that had just been created, some thirty or forty yards away.

Stevaro took his squad and started around the north side of the large ranch house. A short distance away they spotted about fifteen men coming toward them. Both groups saw each other at the same time. Everybody took cover. The ground was rough, covered with large rocks. A fire-fight broke out immediately. Stevaro noticed that these men were better organized and better trained than those that had fired at them in front of the house. The firing was slower, more deliberate and more effective.

Hartmann ran up and dove to the ground beside Hank Stevaro. "Henry, it looks like you could use a hand. Those folks have got some mighty big chunks of granite to hide behind! Let's see what I have here that might help."

Hartmann had taken another rocket launcher and was preparing it for firing. He then took two rifle grenades out of a knapsack tied around his waist, and placed them in front of him. Turning to Stevaro he asked, "What do you think, Hank, rockets or grenades?"

"Shit, Dan, let's do 'em all. You do the rocket, I'll fire the grenades!" Hank said as he reached for the two grenades in front of Hartmann. He noticed that they were 40mm Jump-Up Fragmentation rounds. They would work. He adjusted his M16 and loaded a grenade.

Dan laughed, "Right. Wait a minute." He looked over at Stevaro to make sure they were going to be on the same target. He aimed the rocket launcher at one clump of rock that Stevaro was pointing to, where several men had been seen to seek cover. "Ready? NOW!" He fired. The rocket ran straight and true, hitting a juncture between two of the larger rocks. Stevaro had fired at the same time. The grenade burst behind the rocks. The firing ceased from that group and lightened up from the others.

"Dan, try the pile of rocks over there!" Stevaro said as he pointed to another area to their right where pinning fire was originating. Hank loaded the second grenade.

Dan Hartmann eased around low to get a clearer picture of his target. He pulled another rocket launcher that he had readied up to the firing position.

This time Stevaro called out. "Ready?"

Dan took careful aim while shots were hitting all around him. He seemed to ignore the hazardous fire surrounding his position. He fired the rocket when Stevaro yelled out "Fire!"

Again, straight on the target. Both men hitting their selected targets. The firing stopped from that sector.

Three of his men took out a group to Stevaro's left. Hank signaled for his men to move up and secure the area. It didn't take long.

Thanks to the information that Doc and Smoke had provided, Stevaro knew there were a lot more men on the ranch. Playing a hunch, he directed his men to go back around the front of the hacienda to cover the south side. Hank guessed that he had met a divided force. The rest were somewhere. He thought the other side. That was the side closer to their airplane. It wouldn't do to have to walk home! He moved his people out quickly. He intended to keep his force between the airplane and anybody that could be headed that way.

Once inside the house, Sexton and his men stepped around the officer they had seen go into the main door. He was lying face down, partially covered with the rubble from the ruined door and wall. The hall that Doc and Smoke had sketched out in the house plan was dark either from rocket damage or someone had doused the lights. Sexton had taken the hall to the left with three men, Dillman to the right with four. They moved down the hall in opposite directions. The last two men in Colonel Sexton's squad were left to cover the entrance.

It was dark in the hall. The only light came from the entrance behind them and some sunlight filtering in the French doors at the other end of the hall. Bob Sexton was in front of his group. He saw movement ahead, a man was silhouetted against the light at the far end of the hall. Without waiting Sexton fired and then dropped to the floor. The return fire was fairly intense. One of his men fell heavily on him, knocking the wind out of him. Sexton got up and rushed, firing from his hip. It was effective. There had been three men in the hall. They were all down. Sexton returned to his fallen trooper. Two of his people picked up their fallen comrade and moved back to the entrance and the light. The man had taken hits in the thigh. He was unconscious either from blood loss or shock or both. As near as they could tell the bone was broken but the large artery in that part of the upper leg was still in one piece. Bleeding was fairly heavy, but not arterial. They set about patching him up with a pressure bandage. They would get splints and a stretcher from the airplane later.

Sexton heard a thumping down the hall where they had killed the three men. Carefully, they made their way back. Listening, the Colonel identified the thumping as code.

It was S-O-S. It was coming from a door. Carefully, Colonel Sexton reached for the door. He tried to open it. The door was locked. Feeling the handle, in the dark, he brushed a key that was in the door. Grasping the key, he turned it and opened the door.

"A man can't read a book with all the lights out. And the noise, my God! What noise? Can't sleep, can't read. Might as well check out of this place." Whitey was muttering and pacing the floor. Then turning and pretending to see Sexton for the first time, he said, "Oh, it's you. Why am I not surprised? And it's about time you got here. What kept you, Robert?"

"Whitey, you 'Ol Sumbitch. I'm sure glad to see your ugly face! We'll have to talk about all of this later. Right now we have some cleaning up to do. Are all these folk guilty of being bad guys? So far, we're only doin' them what's trying to do us. They fired first."

"Well, give me a piece and let's get to the rest of the doin'." Whitey said with a chuckle. "From what Alfredo tells me, they're all guilty as hell. They forgot their primary mission and have been involved with kidnapping, uncalled-for assassinations, uncalled-for brutality. I'd say offhand that they should all probably go, with the exception of the cooks. They're just cooks. I believe they're locals from San Julian. They're damn good cooks and I haven't had breakfast yet!"

"Okay, Cellini told me the same thing about the bad guys. So, there it is then. Let's hope the cooks have enough good sense to stay out of the way." Sexton replied.

When Dillman, who had taken four men and gone in the other direction, came to the kitchen he found two unarmed cooks hiding under a counter. He coaxed them out and brought them to the front entrance. He left them with the two men there and went through the rest of the house. It was secure. He met Sexton and Whitey. It was a joyful moment.

Dillman hadn't ever met Whitey, but meeting him meant their mission was successful.

There were still matters to attend to.

Sexton, Whitey, Dillman and the men started out the front. They left two of their men with the wounded one. Whitey noticed the body lying face down inside the entry to the hacienda. He walked over, looked down, and turned the body with his foot enough to recognize Captain Mendez. Whitey made a mental note to be sure to tell Smoke he was safe from being hunted down by a jealous Latin. *Ah yes, the world will be a better place without this one,* he thought.

Paredes had heard the heavy fire and explosions coming from the south side of the hacienda. He, and the group of about fifteen men that he was commanding, slowed their advance moving more cautiously. They had worked their way around to the front of the hacienda and could now see the airplane.

Lieutenant Paredes signaled to four of his men to circle out and secure the airplane. He and the remainder of his force moved toward the front of the hacienda. They were about fifty yards away when Paredes saw Whitey, in the company of others, coming out through the ruined entry. He held his hand up then brought it quickly down, signaling his men to drop and freeze.

Whitey caught the movement and dropped also. His actions alerted Sexton and the men coming out of the hacienda behind Whitey. Sexton crawled forward and came up alongside of McFrank. "Where are they?" He asked.

Whitey pointed off to his left. "Over there. I'm not exactly sure what I saw, but it was sudden movement . . . out about a hundred, maybe a hundred twenty clicks." Whitey was still looking in that direction. He hadn't taken his eyes off of the suspected target area. Then he saw some men making their way toward the airplane. "Look!" He said as he pointed in their direction.

Sexton noticed the four men also. "Right, I see 'em. It looks like they're heading toward the airplane. Let's hope Doc and Smoke see them."

"Why am I not surprised that those two Marines brought your people down here," Whitey said.

"They're good troop, Whitey."

Before Whitey could comment, Stevaro and his men came moving up from the north side of the building. Some shots rang out from the left. Paredes men now had some visible, moving targets, and were making good use of them. Stevaro's people returned fire and took cover. Sexton waved and got Hank Stevaro's attention. He motioned toward the airplane. Stevaro looked and then saw four men moving in that direction. He nodded back to Sexton, indicating that he'd take care of it. Whitey and Sexton heard Hank bark out some orders. Two men on the Stevaro's far flank started working their way toward the airplane.

Sexton returned his attention to the situation in front of them.

Whitey leaned his way and said, "They're damn good pilots but I don't know how good they are as infantry."

"Well, let's hope they're on their toes. It's a long walk home." Sexton took another look over the low wall they were behind toward the group firing at them. "What do you think, Whitey? They don't have a lot of cover out there. We should be able to flush them out."

"One would think so." Whitey said, looking over the wall also.

Sexton had briefed Doc and Smoke prior to landing that they should get out of the airplane and stay nearby but at a safe distance, in case it is hit by unfriendly fire. The airplane would be a natural target, especially if the extraction process becomes prolonged at all.

The two pilots had taken the Uzi's assigned to them, plenty of ammunition and the half dozen hand grenades left

402

for their use and moved away from the airplane. They had set up a post approximately twenty-five yards away on the south side of the airstrip, which was on higher ground. They had watched with interest and a high degree of trepidation, the assault on the main entrance of the hacienda.

Then they saw the rocket and resulting explosion take out the door and part of the wall.

"Jee-zus, Smoke. What the hell kind of rocket was that?" Doc exclaimed.

"Hey! You're asking me? My Marine Corps M.O.S. is the same as yours, remember? Airplane Driver. But I heard Hartmann talking about LAWS rockets and Three-Point-Five rockets. I happen to know that a LAWS is for tanks, its armor-piercing. What we just saw, I think, was a Three-Point-Five.

"How'd you learn about all that shit?" Doc asked.

"I used to be fascinated with armor. I thought that if I couldn't be a pilot I'd want to be a tank commander. But tanks ain't fun anymore. A grunt troop can take out a tank any number of ways. You remember the Bazooka from W-W-Two?"

"Yeah, what about it?"

"Well, that was just the beginning, Doc. Our people developed anti-tank missiles like 'DRAGON' and 'TOW', both of which are wire-guided. All the grunt has to do is hold optical crosshairs on the target and that's where the round will go. You can put it in the tank commander's shirt pocket! The other side has similar weapons. I guess that the latest hot deal is LAWS. Anyway, tank commanding can be hazardous to your health these days. So the only reason I know about this stuff is because of my interest in tanks."

"Okay, but whatever took out the door was spectacular!" Doc paused. "Listen. I hear firing coming from down around the north side. Can you see anything down there?"

"No, but I sure wish that I was down there with 'em!" Smoke said thoughtfully.

"You're out of your fuckin' mind, Smoke. You're one hellava aviator. Stick to what you do well and leave that stuff to those that do *that* stuff well." Doc thought about it, *what it would be like to shoot someone face to face. He had done his share of killing with an airplane, rockets, bombs, napalm, but somehow that was different. Face to face with another human being was something else again. The other person was just like you. With his own fears, hopes, probably a woman and maybe children. To just blow somebody away. He didn't know if he could do it.* "It's kinda cold, Smoke . . . kinda cold."

"Yeah, you're probably right, Doc. I just don't like sitting on my ass doing nothing."

"Hey! We're not doin' nothing! We're protecting the airplane like we were told to do."

"Well, it has gotten quiet. I wonder what's goin' on." Smoke tried to stand to get a better look. Doc pulled him back down.

"I was just trying to see, Doc. Hey. Listen. It sounds like firing coming from inside of the house . . . hear it?"

"I hear it. Just stay put. We don't want to give away our position." Doc suddenly grew intent. He was looking beyond Smoke at the south side of the hacienda. "Look over there Smoke." Doc pointed in the direction he had been looking.

Smoke turned and saw what had drawn Doc's attention. Some men were making their way toward their position and the airplane. Smoke said thoughtfully, "Well, it looks like we're going to see some action, Doctor. How do you want to handle this?"

They watched the progress of four men who were moving cautiously toward the airplane. Doc and Smoke were on the south side of the runway, on the high ground. The airplane had been brought to a stop on the north side of

404

the runway approximately a hundred yards from the east end. Cover was sparse where they were, but it didn't appear that the four men had spotted them from the way that they were moving. They had almost reached the east end of the runway when Hank Stevaro and his men came around the north side of the hacienda. Paredes men started firing. Stevaro's group hit the deck, took cover and were returning fire.

"Smoke, we're going to have to wait for those four to get closer. I don't think that we can hit them with these Uzi's from any distance." Doc said, while thinking *this looks like it's going to be my face-to-face that I've wondered about.* "How far do you think you could throw one of those things?" Doc pointed to the hand grenades.

"Hell, I don't know Doc, maybe twenty-five or thirty yards . . . something like that. Why?"

"I'm thinking. They're four of them and two of us. If we can wait until they're within throwing range, without being spotted, then throw and follow up with shooting, we should be able to take 'em out." Doc said without taking his eyes off of the four who were headed their way. "What do ya think?"

"It's as good a plan as any, Doc. Keep in mind, once we stand and throw, we're a target. If they're alert . . . and I have every reason to believe that they are . . . we might take some fire, as our Special Forces folks say."

"Would you rather wait and just use the Uzi's?"

"No, your plan is a good one, I was just pointing out that once we stand up we better make it all happen without any hesitation. Do you have any problems with that?"

"I guess not. I've always wondered about killing face to face, how I'd feel about it. You know, things like that. But I agree, when we commit it has to be all the way." Doc glanced at Smoke. "How do you feel about it?"

"Yeah, I've always wondered too. I guess that's the reason I wanted to go with Stevaro. I've always wondered."

Smoke paused for a moment. "Anyway, it seems that our questions are going to be answered. We just can't hesitate."

"Right." Doc said.

They watched as the four men drew closer. The men were being careful and appeared very alert. They were taking good advantage of what little cover was available. They would move toward the next selected rock or clump of taller grass one at a time or in pairs. The others covering. One good thing, they kept looking toward the airplane and not toward Barnes and McGarrity's position.

Barnes whispered to Doc, "We're going to have to go with your plan. See how only two are exposed at a time? We'll need the grenades for the ones that are covering, then we shoot the ones in the open. Okay?"

"You're right. About another ten or fifteen yards should do it. They'll be within throwing range. We'll have to wait until the back pair are within our throw." Doc whispered back. "The next set of movements should put them there."

The front pair took cover in some tall grass. One of them motioned for the back pair to move up. Doc reached for one of the grenades. Smoke picked one up also. They nodded to each other and carefully, holding the levers down, pulled the safety pins.

"Ready?" Doc whispered. Smoke nodded in acknowledgment. They both braced to jump up. "NOW!" Doc said in a half whisper, half shout.

Both Marines leaped to their feet, aimed and threw. As soon as the grenades left their hands, they started firing their automatic weapons. The pair of men that had been moving up and were in the open took hits. Then the grenades exploded over the covering pair. Doc and Smoke could hear screams from one for a moment, then it was quiet. Their grenades and firing had drawn attention from some of Paredes men who started firing in the Marines' direction.

They were too far away for their fire to be effective, but Doc and Smoke hurriedly took cover.

"Jee-zus! Damn! That was something!" Doc was panting heavily, the adrenaline taking his breath away. "You were good, Smoke . . . you were good!"

"Whew! You were good, too, Doc." Smoke was as out of breath as Doc. "I have had all my questions answered! You can have this infantry . . . Special Forces shit! I'll stick to airplanes, thank you very much!"

"Damn straight!" Doc was looking over toward where they had heard the screams. "Do you think we should check out those guys?"

"No!" Smoke answered emphatically. "Look!" Smoke pointed at the two men that Hank Stevaro had sent their way.

One of them was Dan Graves. Doc couldn't remember the other one's name. Graves walked over to where the screams had come from. A shot rang out. Graves went over and checked the other one, then rejoined his partner. They looked at the two that had been caught in the open, then came over to where Barnes and McGarrity were huddled behind some rocks. Doc and Smoke stood up to meet them.

"Looks like you two Marines did okay." Graves said to both of them.

"Dan, I heard a shot. Was one of 'em just wounded?" Doc asked. It had been the one that was his target.

"He was more than wounded, Doc. Half his face was gone and one arm. I just gave him relief."

"Oh." Doc had heard enough. He leaned over and threw-up into the grass. He retched again. Nothing came up the second time. Looking back at Dan Graves he said, "Good! Oh, uh sorry about that." He said as he motioned toward the vomit.

"Hey! Don't apologize. It happens all the time. Believe it or not, we don't like killing any more than you do,

Doc." Dan said this sincerely, not in a condescending manner at all.

Stevaro had observed the fire fight over by the airplane and noted that the situation was secure. He directed his attention to the group in front. He held up a rifle grenade as a signal to his men, the majority of which were armed with the M16 equipped with the M203 Grenade Launcher. Hank had provided his people with two types of rifle grenades; 'Jump-Up Fragmentation' and the high explosive HEDP Dual Purpose grenade. He had felt that those two types of rifle grenades, along with some standard hand grenades, would be enough for this operation. He had guessed correctly.

He loaded a HEDP, raised the leaf sight, aimed and fired the grenade for range. His selected target was approximately a hundred fifty to maybe a hundred seventy-five meters out. His round hit at a hundred fifty meters. It was effective. The men followed suit. It began raining grenades into the midst of the now twelve man force. Five or six of the enemies panicked and jumped up running, in an attempt to escape. They were quickly cut down by withering fire from Stevaro's men. The grenade barrage continued.

Finally it grew quiet. Hank gave the signal to move up. Carefully, covering each other and moving in pairs, the men made their way over the ground that separated the two forces. The grenades had done their work. There were no survivors.

Sexton called the men together. Whitey briefed them on the ranch lay-out. They would have to check the barracks building that was down behind the hacienda and the training village. That should do it. Sexton suggested that Hank take some men, use one of the jeeps, and check things out.

Whitey spoke up, "Hank, check the out buildings for a tractor or bulldozer. I know that there's one or the other around here somewhere. I want to bury the dead. Then, which one of these men is the demolition expert?"

"Mark Dillman. What do you need?" Hank replied. Dillman stepped forward at the mention of his name.

"I want to blow all of the buildings. The house especially. Do it, leaving the guest room as intact as possible. I'll show you." Whitey said. He called out to Stevaro, who was leaving, "Oh, and Hank . . . when you're checking out the property and come across some Dobermans, kill them."

"Any specific reasons, or should I ask?"

"I'll tell you about it later. Bring them back for burial with the dead men. Which reminds me, the officer in the pretty uniform that's just inside the door of the house, we'll take him back to San Salvador with us. I'll tell you about that later, as well."

"Got it!" Hank turned and motioned toward three men to accompany him. They left for the barracks behind the house.

Smoke, Doc and the two men who had supported them came up and joined the group. Doc came forward with his hand outstretched.

"Hi Whitey. You look pretty good. Are you okay?" Doc asked.

"Yeah, I'm all right. Oh Smoke, come over here, I'd like you to meet someone." Whitey motioned for Smoke to follow and went over to the entrance of the hacienda where Mendez's body still lay face down. Whitey turned the officer over with his foot. "Captain Barnes, I'd like you to meet Captain Mendez. Captain Mendez, Captain Barnes. It looks like you won't have to look over your shoulder, Smoke. This one won't be bothering you."

"It looks like he pissed his pants, Whitey." Smoke said as he looked down at the body in front of him.

"He did." Whitey replied, looking down at the body. "But that can happen after a guy gets hit. However having met this one, my guess is that it happened before he died." McFrank looked up at Barnes, "Your job is going to be to inform Señora Mendez of her husband's demise. We'll be taking the body to San Salvador with us. We've got to run this by Cellini but I'm sure, due to his family connections, he will probably be declared some kind of hero and buried with honors. I learned that he was involved in kidnapping and ransom activities and not a very nice person. It is good that he will have escaped the dishonor of a public trial or court martial. I'll fill you in on what to tell Rosa."

Smoke nodded and took his gaze away from the body at his feet. "I understand. I'll handle Rosa. It's the least that I can do. She is a wonderful person and doesn't deserve any disgrace rubbing off on her or her family."

Colonel Sexton started directing the men to bring the bodies to the rear of the hacienda. The open ground between the house and barracks appeared to be suitable for a common grave. They would have to wait for the bulldozer or tractor. Whitey took Mark Dillman into the house to show him what he wanted done.

While Dillman went about setting charges, Whitey sat down at the desk in the guest room where he had been imprisoned. Opening a drawer, he took out a piece of paper and wrote a note to his host.

My dear Colonel Cordero—

I do apologize for running off without saying good-bye or personally thanking you for your hospitality.

Duty called. Here is a five colon note for the cleaning lady. Sorry about the rest of the mess. It couldn't be helped.

I'll take you up on your offer for a pig hunt the next time we see each other.

Have a nice day,
E. H. McFrank

Dillman returned and assured Whitey that he had placed charges in such a manner as to leave the guest room relatively intact.

Hank Stevaro pulled up to the house in the jeep, with two more prisoners. Whitey identified them as cooks. He suggested to Sexton that they be released, along with the two from the main house. They were local San Julian folk, innocent of any wrong doing. Sexton let them take whatever food stuffs and other kitchen items with them. They took one of the smaller vehicles, loaded it and quickly departed.

A small bulldozer had been located and brought up to the area selected for burial. A wide trench was scraped out of the dirt, large enough to take the dead. The bodies were placed in the common grave. Whitey looked at each body carefully. When his examination was complete, he gave the order to cover them.

Captain Mendez was wrapped in a sheet and canvas tarp, then loaded aboard the airplane. Dillman returned with his demo team. All equipment and personnel were loaded aboard. It was time to leave.

Colonel Sexton asked Mark Dillman when things were going to happen.

Glancing at his watch, Mark responded, "About another twenty minutes, Boss. Time enough to taxi down to the other end of the runway, well out of the way."

Fifteen minutes later they were airborne on their way to San Salvador. Sexton suggested to Doc that they fly one wide circular pass as they climbed out. All hands were looking out the windows when the buildings erupted in explosive flashes and smoke. It was spectacular. Dillman had done a good job.

CHAPTER THIRTY-FIVE
HEROES OF COURSE

"Smoke, before we contact San Sal Approach, try the HF set for Acme Base. Okay?"

"What the hell am I going to say if they answer? 'Hi! This is the plane thief calling....' Give me a clue, will you, Doc?" Smoke sounded a trifle pissed.

"Tell you what. You fly the fuckin' airplane. I'll call Seattle." Doc replied. "You've got it."

"Fine! I've got it!" Smoke, obviously pissed, tapped the yoke, taking command of the aircraft.

Doc fumbled around the cockpit looking for something. "Smoke, where is the HF card with frequencies versus time of day stuff?"

"It's in the packet behind my seat. The back section. You'll find the specific frequencies for the Seattle office in there also. What the hell are you going to tell 'em?"

Doc reached over and picked up the flight data packet. "I'm going to tell them Agent McFrank is safely aboard. We are proceeding to San Salvador, and for them to advise Mrs. McFrank. Then I'll see what they have to say. And, uh, sorry I snapped at ya." He opened the packet and took out the HF frequency data. In a couple of minutes he had the radio set up. He glanced over at Smoke who acknowledged the apology with a nod of his head.

"ACME BASE, ACME FLIGHT, OVER."

There was just the normal sounds of the ether, some snaps, a few crackles. No pops, though. Doc tried again.

"ACME BASE, THIS IS ACME FLIGHT, OVER."
He waited and listened. Then decided to give it another try.

"ACME BASE, THIS IS ACME FLIGHT. SHORT COUNT FOLLOWS. ONE, TWO, THREE, FOUR, FIVE, FOUR, THREE, TWO, ONE....OVER."

This time there was a return signal. It was weak and garbled. Doc fiddled with the tuning knob.

"--rREE, TWO, ONE, OVER."

"ACME BASE, ACME FLIGHT, SAY AGAIN YOUR IDENT, OVER." Doc asked to make sure he was talking to the Seattle CIA office.

"ACME FLIGHT, THIS IS ACME BASE, STANDBY ONE, OVER"

"ROGER ACME BASE, ACME FLIGHT STANDING BY."

Glancing back over his shoulder, Doc saw that they were alone in the cockpit. Doc turned to Smoke. "I'll bet that was the Duty Officer and he's gone to get Roberts. I think the shit is about to hit the fan, my friend."

"You're probably right. Is this where we find out how many years we get for stealing a government airplane?" Smoke responded.

"No, they'll wait until they can physically slap us in irons. And then...."

"ACME FLIGHT, THIS IS ACME BASE. SAY YOUR POSITION, OVER."

"Here we go, Smoke....ACME BASE, ACME FLIGHT IS APPROACHING SAN SALVADOR. BE ADVISED, WE HAVE V-I-P ON BOARD. IF YOU WOULD BE SO KIND AS TO ADVISE MISSUS V-I-P, YOUR CITY, OF OUR PASSENGER IT WOULD BE APPRECIATED. OVER."

There was a full minute of radio silence. Some pretty heavy thinking must be going on at the other end. Doc and Smoke looked at each other and shrugged.

413

"ACME FLIGHT, ACME BASE. ROGER YOUR V-I-P. WILL PASS THE WORD. CONTACT ACME BASE FROM BRANCH OFFICE SAN SALVADOR AS SOON AS POSSIBLE AFTER LANDING. OVER."

"ROGER. WILCO. ACME FLIGHT OUT."

"Well, what do you think, Smoke?" Doc asked.

"I think we had better ask Whitey to come up on the flight deck. We have to call approach control and what are we going to tell them about customs and such."

"Right, I'll go get him." Doc said as he climbed out of the left seat and headed back into the cabin. In a minute he was back with Whitey in tow. Doc strapped back in and tapped the control column to indicate he was taking control of the airplane. Smoke acknowledged and turned to Whitey.

"Mr. McFrank. We've just spoken with Mr. Roberts and advised him that you were on board and asked him to contact your wife with the news."

"Good. I've been talking with Sexton and he told me about Sandy blowing the whistle. I'm sure glad she did. If she hadn't, I would still be there." Whitey shook his head as if in a state of wonderment. "She hasn't ever interfered with my work before. I'm sure glad she did this time...."

Smoke didn't give him a chance to finish. "I have to contact approach control now and request an approach. Either they will or the tower will ask us if we need customs. It could get a bit dicey going through customs with your friends and their equipment. Do you have any suggestions?"

"Yes, but did you file a flight plan into San Salvador like before?"

"No, we filed from Cabo to San Jose, Costa Rica. Then when clear of Mexican air space we canceled. So we're not on record with anybody but Mexico and Costa Rico."

"Good. Tell approach control, when asked about customs, that your flight originated in-country and you do not require customs. As soon as you land request taxi clearance to Cellini's flight service operation. I'll call

Alfredo and have him speak to the head of the C-A-A down here before they determine that you couldn't have originated in-country. Sexton told me that Cellini is backing us up."

"It sounds good, should work. And now another little matter. Roberts wants us to call from the branch office as soon as possible after landing. I assume he means from the embassy. Is that where the CIA operational folks quarter down here?" Smoke asked.

"Yes, I'll handle Mr. Roberts. You lads call the El Camino Real and get us a place to sleep tonight. We also have to get Steve Howard and a few of the other lads to the hospital. I think the best way to handle it would be to use one of the flight service vans. Steve's in pretty good shape, a lot of pain, but that's to be expected."

Doc glanced over at Whitey. "I didn't know we had any casualties, Whitey. How bad is he? How many others?"

"A couple of other men took minor hits and should also go to the hospital to be checked over. Sexton engineered a real good operation. Cellini is going to have to cover that little detail with the hospital also. Another thing, though, I checked everybody going into the hole. Lieutenant Paredes was not there. Do you remember him, Doc?"

"Yes I do. He sat at the table with us when Smoke and I had breakfast." Doc answered. Smoke nodded that he remembered also.

"Well, he wasn't there. Another thing. Paredes, Mendez, and the troops returned the same morning. This morning. They had some prisoners with them. I don't know how many, but from the conversations I overheard, and my limited Spanish, I know it was more than one or two. At any rate, they may have been blown with the house. Pity. Not our fault. Just thought you should know. We did let the four cooks go. Keep in mind eggs and omelets, fellows." Whitey said, somewhat philosophically.

"Huh? I don't think I understand. Eggs?" Doc asked.

"You have to break some eggs to make an omelet. It's an old saying." Whitey said.

"Okay. There it is." Doc turned to the business at hand, "Smoke, give approach control a call. Tell them we're five out for a visual."

"Right." Smoke reached for his microphone and changed frequencies on the VHF radio. He set in the proper frequency. "SAN SAL APPROACH, THIS IS DOUGLAS YANKEE VICTOR, WHISKEY ALPHA WHISKEY SIERRA, FIVE MILES OUT FOR A VISUAL APPROACH, OVER."

"ROGER DOUGLAS YANKEE VICTOR, WHISKEY ALPHA WHISKEY SIERRA, PLAN RUNWAY TWO SEVEN, CONTACT THE TOWER ON ONE TWO ZERO DECIMAL SIX, OVER."

"ROGER APPROACH, RUNWAY TWO SEVEN, THE TOWER ONE TWO ZERO DECIMAL SIX FOR DOUGLAS WHISKEY ALPHA WHISKEY SIERRA. SWITCHING." Smoke changed to the tower frequency and gave another call.

"SAN SALVADOR TOWER, DOUGLAS YANKEE VICTOR, WHISKEY ALPHA WHISKEY SIERRA, THREE MILES OUT FOR LANDING RUNWAY TWO SEVEN, OVER."

"ROGER WHISKEY ALPHA WHISKEY SIERRA, CLEARED TO LAND RUNWAY TWO SEVEN, WINDS LIGHT AND VARIABLE, ALTIMETER ONE ZERO ONE THREE DECIMAL TWO, OVER"

"ROGER WHISKEY SIERRA CLEARED TO LAND RUNWAY TWO SEVEN, CAN YOU GIVE ME THE ALTIMETER IN INCHES, OVER."

"ROGER WHISKEY SIERRA....TWO NINER DECIMAL NINER TWO. WILL YOU NEED CUSTOMS? OVER."

"NEGATIVE CUSTOMS, ORIGINATED IN-COUNTRY. THANKS FOR THE ALTIMETER."

"NO PROBLEM, CONTACT GROUND ONE TWO ONE DECIMAL EIGHT, CLEARING THE ACTIVE."

"WHISKEY SIERRA, WILCO."

"Got all that, Doc?"

"Roger, Smoke. Finish the check list, will ya, and gear down now. I'll get my own flaps."

"Roger, roger. Gear down, props coming up." Smoke watched the gear indicator transition from gear up to gear down. "Gear in the green. Check list complete."

Doc greased the C-47 onto the runway, held the tail up, and then eased it down as their speed decayed. They were on the ground. As they cleared the active, Doc called out, "Up, open, off and forward." (This translates to landing flaps UP, cowl flaps OPEN, fuel boost pumps OFF and props full increase; or FORWARD.) Smoke contacted ground control and they were cleared to Cellini's flight service operation.

The line boy was out in front holding wands ready to guide them into the parking place he had picked out for them. Doc mentioned that he must have been monitoring ground control and heard them ask for taxi clearance. Doc pointed and said, "Look, there's Raul Arango, Cellini's pilot. He's coming out to meet us, too."

Doc brought the plane to a stop in the parking area as directed. He reached over and pulled the mixtures to kill the engines, and called for the After Landing and Secure check lists. While Smoke finished the check lists and flight logs, Doc got out of the seat and went back to open the door and hand the line boy the landing gear pins. As he passed through the cabin he told Whitey that Raul Arango was out there to meet them. Whitey followed Doc to the door. Doc noticed and was surprised to see that Sexton and his men had changed into, what looked like, casual or construction clothes. The only one in battle dress was Steve Howard, the badly wounded man. He was on a stretcher and could be covered easily. The other wounded were not easily spotted.

There were no signs of any guns or ordnance either. The troops had been busy.

Doc opened the cabin door, handed the gear pins to the line boy and jumping down out of the airplane, turned and placed the steps in the door opening. Whitey climbed down and, with Doc, walked over to meet Raul. They shook hands all around.

Whitey spoke up after the usual pleasantries. "Raul, I need a couple of favors. We have a badly injured man and some walking wounded who must be taken to the hospital. I need to get to the American Embassy and we have about twenty folks to get to the El Camino Hotel."

"Not a problem, Señor. First, of course, the injured man. Is he able to walk or. . ."

Whitey interrupted him, "No, he's on a stretcher. The others can walk. We don't need an ambulance, but a van would do nicely. I don't wish to attract a lot of attention to this situation."

"I understand. I'll get a driver and van. How many will be going with him to the hospital?" Raul asked.

"I don't know offhand, probably three or four." Whitey paused to think for a moment. "To simplify things, I'll take a cab to the embassy. Doc, it would probably be a good idea if you and Sexton came with me. That will leave seventeen or so to transport to the hotel."

"We can fit that many in two vans. You won't have to use a cab, I'll be happy to get you to the embassy." Raul said, then continued, "Are you ready to go now? Any special service requirements on the airplane, Señor Doc?"

"Nope. Just fill the wing tanks, we'll do the inside drums before we leave. And engine oil, of course," Doc replied. "I want to keep folks out of the cabin, including line personnel. There's some fairly sensitive cargo on board." Raul nodded his understanding.

Whitey caught Raul's attention, "Oh, and by the way, will you have someone call a suitable undertaker for the

418

gentry? We have Captain Mendez on board. You remember the good captain, you flew us both out to the ranch." Raul nodded, indicating that he remembered. "Well, his luck ran out."

Raul said he would get someone on it. He didn't ask any questions.

Whitey turned to Doc, "I'll get everybody rounded up. You go ahead and make the hotel reservations."

"Right." Doc turned and trotted into the lobby.

Upon hearing all of the arrangements, Smoke said he would rent a car and follow the van over to the hospital. That way they would have transportation to the hotel after they got Steve bedded down. Plus, he was going to need a car to call on Señora Mendez and give her the bad news about her husband. Whitey told him that it was a good idea but to wait until he got back from the embassy before going to see her. He wanted to discuss the matter with Alfredo Cellini.

Raul dropped Whitey, Colonel Sexton and Doc at the embassy. They would be in touch. There was going to be some sort of a celebration that night at the hotel. Raul was invited. He would be filled in on all of the doin's at that time, security be damned!

The three checked in at the embassy reception desk. They were directed downstairs, and to the end of the hall, to Charles Hammond's office.

Charley had been sent down to replace the operator who had been lost in the bombing of the restaurant. He was expecting to see or hear from someone involved with the "Whitey McFrank" caper. Hammond had already received a call from Roberts in Seattle and had been briefed the moment that radio contact had been concluded with the C-47.

Hammond was young. He was fairly small in stature, maybe five foot six or seven in street shoes, slight of build, sandy colored hair that tended toward being naturally curly and he had an attitude. This was his first field operations assignment. He intended to make a mark for himself.

Whitey led the way down the hall, followed by Bob Sexton and Doc. When he got to Charley's office, the door was standing open. He tapped lightly to get Hammond's attention, then entered the office.

Charley glanced up and seeing the white-haired man standing in front of his desk said, with a slight touch of arrogance, "You must be the famous Whitey McFrank. You and your group are in a world of trouble, My Friend."

"Yes, I'm Ernest McFrank. I am not your friend. And I resent deeply your remark about any of my friends being in trouble." Whitey spoke slowly and distinctly.

Hammond rose quickly on his feet, still behind his desk. "You resent it, huh? Well, let me tell you, Sir, there is a matter of unauthorized use of a government airplane, and furthermore, if one of you is Henry Stevaro, you're in trouble for the unauthorized procurement and use of some weapons and accompanying ordnance. If that isn't enough trouble, Sir, I'm certain that there will be a lot more when the company finds out how all of that weaponry was put to use! And, you're absolutely right, I'm not your friend. But you're certainly going to need one! And, I for one uh......"

Hammond hadn't quite finished his little speech when, in a flash, Colonel Bob Sexton, U.S. Army Special Forces (Retired), stepped up to the desk, reached across and grabbed Hammond by his shirt front and pulled him off his feet and half way over the desk. Then bringing his face just inches away from Hammond's face, Colonel Sexton spoke quietly. "Listen to me, you little shit, if anybody is in trouble it is you and the people you work for. I put the team together to extract Mr. McFrank from the hands of a flaming asshole that you idiots didn't bother to really check out. And if I hadn't extracted him you would be writing a nice letter of condolence to his widow. Before you take it upon yourself to throw your weight around some real men you had better check with all of your bosses and also some representatives of the government of this country that you are currently serving in. Have I made myself clear to you, asshole?"

Charley Hammond tried to talk, but only gurgling noises came from his mouth. Sexton released his shirt front and throat.

".....Yes, Sir! I'm sorry....I mean, I didn't mean to..."

"Never mind all that. Direct Whitey to the scrambler phone so he can check in with his control. And then stand by. Don't go away or do anything to make matters worse. Got it?"

"Y-ye-yes, Sir! If you'll let me get off my desk . . . I'll uh, take him to the phone."

Sexton released him and a very subdued Charley Hammond led the three men down a hall to another room. He pointed to an enclosure with a desk and telephone. Whitey went over and sat down at the desk. Colonel Sexton and Doc remained standing back to give McFrank some degree of privacy. Hammond scurried away, heading back to his office.

Whitey picked up the phone and dialed the Seattle office. It was answered immediately.

"McFrank here for Roberts." There was a momentary wait. Whitey was starting to show evidence of some impatience, then Roberts came on the line.

"Harold? McFrank here....I'm fine. Thank you for asking....my contract? Well, the first one has expired. Go ahead and initiate the second ninety days and double the amount.....that's right, double.....Oh, and I'll need to add a couple of folks......no, besides Barnes and McGarrity.....I'll send a list of names in the pouch going out of here tonight.......what?.....Oh, about twenty.....that's right, twenty. Usual contract fees where there might be some loud noises and harm's way.....yes, there were some loud noises......no loss of personnel, some wounded, but all okay....uh-huh, one that will probably be in the hospital for a couple of days...I will send a full report, but not in tonight's pouch, maybe tomorrow or the day after. There is another matter that has become somewhat serious. It is about Colonel Cordero. You might want to speak directly with Alfredo Cellini. I'd strongly recommend your speaking directly with him......right. Directly.....Uh-huh, not through an intermediary from down here. Okay? And by the way, this second element of the mission will entitle McGarrity and Barnes to the bonus amount discussed.......uh-huh, I knew you'd agree to that one......right, they earned it."

Whitey chuckled, then went on, "And I appreciate your calling Sandy.....right after the radio transmission? I see, I'm a VIP now am I? I'll have to speak to the lads about that one......Harold, I figured you had a hand in it and I want you to know I appreciate it. Thank you, my friend......well, I'm going to throw a party tonight for twenty-two people at the El Camino, wish you could be here. Then I'll come home, go buy a sailboat and sail off to someplace where you can't call me......that's right......I'll do it. Thanks again Harold, I really appreciate all you've done. I'm going to call Alfredo now and bring him up to date. Give me twenty minutes or so, then call him.......Right. Talk to you later." Whitey hung up the phone, turned and looked at the two men standing there, expectantly.

"Well?" Sexton asked.

"You heard my side of the conversation. If Roberts has anything to say about it, you and your troops will get paid hazardous duty rates. And you and Barnes, Doc. There's still a lot a flak floating around about the airplane and the material Stevaro absconded with. Roberts understands the Cellini thing and, assuming he says what you said was his position, Roberts will be able to put the airplane and ordnance stuff to bed. The company pilots who came up to fly the airplane back to Florida, didn't raise any kind of fuss. Roberts was a bit taken aback about it." Whitey was interrupted by Doc and Bob Sexton breaking into laughter.

"Maybe there's something that you fellows might want to share with me?"

"Later, Whitey. Later when we can give you the whole story. Shouldn't you call Alfredo Cellini now, though?" Doc said to him.

"Right. I'll do it now." He picked up the phone again and dialed the embassy operator. "I'd like a local line, please. Right. This is McFrank." After a moment he dialed Alfredo's private number. It was answered immediately. "Señor Cellini, please....I'll hold."

Alfredo Cellini came on the line.

"Señor Alfredo, Whitey McFrank.....thanks, I'm okay......I owe it to Bob Sexton......of course, I felt that you would remember him.........right, he certainly is. You were right about Mendez. We brought him back with us.......no, that won't be necessary, he's already paid the highest price......yes, quite dead. However, he was married to a wonderful girl, from what you told me, and I thought maybe you might not want to cause her any undue pleasantness....good, I thought you would want it that way. One of my men, Smoke...if you remember, will go tell her. He will say that he died honorably, leading his men against the communists.......well, yes, he was out in front for a while, but then he ran........right. Well, I asked Raul Arango to have someone at your flight service call a suitable undertaker........Of course, if you want to do that, it would probably be appreciated by his widow. There is another small matter. The lads told Approach Control that their flight had originated in-country and they wouldn't need customs......well, you know, Sexton and his people wouldn't have looked too good to any customs folk, especially when the folk got to their luggage......yes, an amusing situation. Perhaps a call to somebody? Thank you. Colonel Sexton told me your position on all of this. Harold Roberts, Chief of Station Seattle will be calling you shortly.........right......there are some things he will need your help with....of course. To change the subject for just a moment, we are having a bit of a celebration at the Camino tonight and would be pleased if you would or could attend.......well, earlier would probably be better than later......right, you know how the boys get.......Sexton will be happy to fill you in on the operational details. We can talk about it this evening, say eight o'clock? ....good! I'm looking forward to seeing you also, Alfredo. Your wife and daughter are invited too......I understand. Probably better that way. At least we'll expect to see you then. Yes. Bye for now, Sir." Whitey hung up.

"He's going to call the flight service and find out what's been done about Mendez, and then he'll take care of the details. Smoke is still to go see the widow Mendez. That's it, Gents. We can head for the hotel, a shower--clean clothes which I'll probably have to buy--and then we can get the party organized. What say?" Whitey asked of the two.

"I say that you have reached a splendid decision. Why don't I go and encourage the asshole to arrange a car for us heroes? And won't it be fun when he finds out that we are? Sexton raised his hands, palms up, in a gesture of greatness.

"That we are what?"

"Why heroes, of course."

CHAPTER THIRTY-SIX
THE PARTY

The embassy driver dropped them at the front lobby entrance of the El Camino Real Hotel. As they walked into the lobby, the concierge hurriedly came forward to meet them.

"Ah, Señor McFrank, you and your party are all checked in. You have the Presidential Suite and the rest of the top floor. The others are already there. We moved your things from storage where we put them when you disappeared. I'm so happy to see you back with us. If you will come with me, I would like to personally take you up to your suite."

"The Presidential Suite? I don't understand." Whitey was somewhat taken aback.

Doc spoke up, "Uh, I arranged that, Whitey. There are nineteen rooms plus the Presidential Suite on the top floor. I wanted to keep all of the men together, so I just took the whole floor. The management had to move a couple of people, but I instructed the Manager to make it worth their while. The Presidential Suite has four bedrooms. I know that we'll have a couple of empty beds, but so what."

"You're absolutely right, Doc. So what! We'll keep the party confined to that floor. The management will be pleased to have it confined." Turning to the concierge, Whitey said, "We'll be expecting guests. If you will be kind enough to direct them up, it would be appreciated"

"Of course, Señor McFrank. This way please."

The Presidential Suite was sumptuous. Large double entrance doors opened into a small foyer, and then the suite. It consisted of a large sitting room, a smaller living room-type area beyond and four bedrooms, with their own baths, off to the sides. Two bedrooms on each side. The sitting room had a grand piano at one end, and a large bar that was currently being tended, by a hotel bartender. Several of the men were already gathered around the bar taking advantage of the refreshments available. The room contained three davenports, three overstuffed chairs, some tables and other smaller pieces of furniture. There were tapestries on the wall, denoting some historic event or other. Two beautiful chandeliers hung from the high ceiling. All in all, the room was exceptionally elegant. Two of the four bedrooms were off to the side of this room, one with a raised crest on the door. Sexton's men insisted that this room would be for Whitey. Sexton took the room next to it.

The living room area connected to the sitting room was smaller. It had two davenports facing each other with a large coffee table between them. Small chairs, paired with lamp tables were located in the four corners of the room, allowing for separate intimate conversation areas. More tapestries and one chandelier finished the elegant furnishings. The remaining two bedrooms were off to the side of this room. Doc saw that someone had put what looked like some of Smoke's things in one of the bedrooms. He took the other one.

The concierge had shown the suite with some pride. As well he should have. The suite and furnishings were beautiful. Doc asked that he send a piano player up about seven and arranged for a buffet. Whitey asked that a representative from the men's clothing shop come up and take his measurements. He would need some clothes. The concierge left to attend to his guest's wishes.

426

Whitey, Colonel Sexton and Doc had just started their first drink when Smoke arrived. He came right over to the three men.

"Gentlemen. I'm happy to report that Steve Howard is out of surgery and resting peacefully. He asked if maybe a couple of the guys would bring him a drink. Then he fell asleep." Smoke pointed to Doc's drink and addressed the bartender. "One of those please." Then he continued his report. "There was some fuss about his dress and the fact that he had gunshot wounds. I suggested that the head Doctor contact Señor Cellini. The Doctor knew who Cellini was. Then the problem went away. The other men returned with me. Their wounds were superficial. The Doctor just kept shaking his head."

"Good." Whitey said. "Smoke, you had better go light on the booze until you handle the Señora Mendez situation."

"Just one, then I'll get cleaned up and go visit the widow. I don't really have anything suitable to wear, though," Smoke said.

"The concierge is sending up someone from the clothing store just off the lobby. Why don't you get something from him? A blazer and some nice slacks, would do the job," Whitey said. "Don't worry about money. All of this will be expense account stuff; and, besides, you and Doc are both back on the payroll, including hazardous-duty pay scale."

"Hellava deal! They weren't upset about the airplane?" Smoke asked.

"There's something supposedly very funny about that situation. When Roberts told me that the company pilots didn't complain, Sexton and Doc here broke up. Why don't you folks let me in on the joke?" Whitey looked at each of them. "I'm waiting."

"Go ahead, Smoke, they were your friends," Doc feigned innocence.

427

"Well Whitey, it went something like this. They showed up to fly the airplane back to Florida on the same morning we were going to depart for El Salvador. They were not going to let us have the airplane. Colonel Bob here made them an offer that they couldn't really refuse, as the saying goes. He suggested that we were going to use the airplane, that they had a choice of either being tied up for eight hours or going back to their hotel and entertaining some friends of mine. Then they could come back out to the airport the following morning and report the plane gone." Smoke looked to Bob Sexton and Doc for affirmation.

"Smoke. What friends? Perhaps you could elucidate," Whitey asked, guessing what was coming.

"I know a few young ladies that I sort of ran with before hooking up with Shelly. They're good sports and enjoy a fun time so I fixed up the two pilots with two of the more aggressive types. Our guess was that they wouldn't make it out to the airport the following morning. Maybe the next, but even that would be 'iffy'. I mean those two ladies are something else, let me tell you. Aggressive probably isn't the right choice of words."

This got a chuckle out of Whitey, but then turning to Sexton he asked, "Weren't you taking a chance on them not reporting you immediately, Bob?"

"Sure, there's always a chance that one's judgment is wrong. You and I are both still alive, Whitey, because our judgment has been more right than wrong. I told them our intended mission. Hell, they both wanted to come along and they didn't even know you."

There was a knock at the door. It was opened by one of the men. A dapper man came in, followed by a helper with a rolling rack of men's clothes. The rack held jackets, suits, evening wear and shirts. He was directed over to Whitey.

McFrank outlined his needs, had measurements taken and then turned Smoke over to the clothier for his requirements. Complete wardrobes were arranged; shoes, socks, underwear and the selected outerwear for both men. McFrank asked if any of the others needed anything. He got no takers.

The clothier had been instructed to handle Barnes' requirements first. He assured Smoke that he would have the outfit ready within the hour. He hurriedly left to make the necessary alterations.

Smoke asked Whitey how he would find the home of Captain Mendez. Whitey went to the phone and called Alfredo Cellini. In a few minutes he came back to the bar with the address written out.

"Here." He handed it to Smoke. "When you go downstairs to leave, ask the concierge for directions. I've spoken with Cellini about this matter. You are to tell Rosa that her husband died bravely fighting the communists. He will be buried with full national honors. The government is handling all the financial arrangements. She will be contacted by the funeral director to arrange for a suitable time for the ceremony. Got that? Any questions?"

"No Sir. But what if she sees through the bravery and honor bit. Can I tell her the truth?"

"Smoke, I've given you the official position. Anything that you do beyond that is your call. I don't know the depth of the relationship between you and Rosa....and it's none of my business. However, she will have to attend the ceremony for appearances. She will know her responsibilities. You do whatever you want."

Smoke nodded acceptance and understanding. Turning to Doc, he asked, "Will you bring the clothes in when they arrive? I'm going to go get cleaned up."

Smoke picked up his small handbag, containing his shaving kit and a change of underwear, and went into the bedroom next to Doc's and closed the door. It appeared that he was upset.

The concierge had given Barnes a map of the city. The home of Capitan and Señora Mendez was across town, over near the Casa Presidencial. With the map and excellent directions he had been given, Smoke didn't have any problems. He pulled up in front of a wall with the address on the stucco. He parked, got out of the car and walked up to the gate. He noticed a doorbell set into the wall. He pushed it and thought that he could hear a ring somewhere. In a few minutes a maid came and opened the gate. She said something in Spanish that Smoke couldn't understand. He asked for Señora Mendez. The maid let him enter, then led the way through a heavily foliated courtyard into the house. It was cool and quite comfortable in the house. Smoke didn't know if it was from air conditioning or the design of the large, impressive home. The maid indicated that he was to wait in the foyer. She left to get Señora Mendez.

Rosa Mendez came down the hall, and then spotting Smoke, hurried up to him. Her eyes were big and she was clearly agitated. Approaching him, she held out her hand and speaking in English said, "I'm Señora Mendez, what can I do for you?" Her eyes were wildly searching his.

Smoke understood the inference and responded in a like manner. "Señora Mendez, I'm Harrison Barnes. I'm with a government agency working with the El Salvadorian militia. I'm afraid that I have some rather bad news. May we go somewhere to talk?"

Startled, Rosa said, "Of course, this way please." She led the way back down the hall in the direction that she had come and stopped at a door. Opening it, she stepped back, indicating that Barnes should enter first.

Brushing by her, Smoke entered the room. It was a small library and sitting room or den. Maybe fifteen by twenty feet in size. It was quite elegantly furnished. *Captain's pay in the El Salvadorian Army must be pretty good,* he thought. Rosa came into the room, closed the door and came up to Smoke.

Whispering, she said, "What are you doing here? My husband could come home at any time? --Are you insane?"

Taking his cue from her, Smoke spoke quietly. "My darling Rosa, do you have any love for that man or are you still angry and disgusted?"

"I truly hate him, Smoke. In your country I would divorce him in a minute. But this is a Catholic country. Divorce isn't done. My family would disinherit me. How would I live? It just isn't easy. I don't know what to do." Her voice trailed off.

Smoke took her into his arms and held her for a moment. Then he pulled back and placed his hands on her shoulders. "Señora Mendez, your problems are over. The bad news that I had for you is not that bad. Come, sit down." He led her over to a small sofa and sat her down. Kneeling in front of her, he continued. "Capitan Mendez will not be coming home tonight or anytime. He is dead. The official report is that he was killed in action fighting the communists. He will be buried with full honors, as befitting an officer of the El Salvadorian Militia, killed in action against the enemy. Instead of being the disinherited divorcee, you are the widow of a State hero." He paused, still holding both of her hands and looked deeply into her eyes.

Rosa had caught her breath when Smoke first said that her husband was dead. There was a fleeting moment of guilt, as she thought that she had wished him dead, but it quickly passed. There was a moment of remorse and sorrow for what had been before she found out what he was really like. Rosa Maria Mendez was no hypocrite. She accepted the facts as they were. There would be no tears. She looked down at her hands.

Glancing back into Smoke's eyes she said, "You said the official report. Is there more that I should know? You're holding something back, Señor Barnes, what is it?"

"I don't know all of the facts, Whitey does. You can speak with him if you desire. I can only tell you that Capitan

431

Mendez was not a very nice person. But you had already found out that fact. He was also not a very brave person. But whatever his faults, he has paid the highest price of redemption."

"I see. How much is known about his faults?"

"Apparently Alfredo Cellini knows some facts. He is the one that told Whitey McFrank. We are having a reception at the El Camino tonight, celebrating the freeing of Whitey from imprisonment by Colonel Cordero. I believe that Whitey invited Señor Cellini to the gathering. I would like to invite you also. You would naturally want to meet the men that your husband last served with and whom he led in battle. That would not violate your mourning requirements....if you get my meaning.

"Yes, I understand. I would like that. I must change into something suitable." Señora Mendez looked around the room, lost in thought. A thought occurred to her. "How did you get here? Do you have a car?"

"Yes. But there is something else. Señor Cellini is taking care of all of the funeral arrangements. The funeral director will call to inquire about your desired schedule. Whitey said that you would understand your responsibilities."

Rosa interrupted, "Yes, Harrison, I know what is expected of me. Do not be concerned. Will you drive me back home after I have paid my respects to his comrades?"

"Yes, certainly."

All right, now I must prepare myself and change. You may wait here. Would you like anything? A drink?"

"No thank you, Rosa. If you don't mind, I will look over your library."

"Please do. We're....er, I'm very proud of it. I won't be too long."

When Smoke and Rosa returned to the Presidential Suite the party was in full swing. An elaborate buffet had

432

been set up. The piano player was playing, surrounded by drinking troops trying to get him to play some Special Forces drinking songs. The attempts came close enough. The singing drowned out the piano anyway.

Whitey, Doc, Alfredo Cellini and Colonel Bob Sexton were at a table near the bar. Smoke guided Rosa over to the table. Whitey saw them approaching and stood, the others followed suit. Alfredo Cellini came from around the table and took Rosa into his arms. He held her close for some time. Finally he held his arms out straight, each hand on a shoulder and spoke to her in Spanish. It sounded as if he was offering his condolences over the loss of her husband. She accepted gracefully.

"But Señor Cellini, we must speak English out of respect to our hosts." Rosa said in English.

"Of course, Señora. Allow me to introduce them to you. On my right is Señor Ernest McFrank, his friends call him Whitey," turning to the man to his left, "This is Colonel Bob Sexton," then gesturing across the table, "And Doc McGarrity, who isn't really a medical doctor. Gentlemen, this is Señora Rosa Maria Mendez, the wife of the gallant Capitan Mendez, who led you in the battle against the enemies of this country."

Whitey stepped forward and taking her hand, brushed his lips against the back of it. "We are honored that you would meet with us, Señora Mendez."

Colonel Bob Sexton was next. Taking her hand, he executed a half bow, saying, "I regret that we must meet under these circumstances, Señora."

Then it was Doc's turn. He also kissed her hand, "Señora Mendez, thank you for coming. It must be difficult for you."

Rosa responded for the first time, "You are all so kind. I had to meet the men with whom my husband served. Thank you for inviting me."

Barnes made a place at the table and held a chair for her. He had been studying her interplay with Señor Cellini and the others. He was beginning to understand the noblesse and class of this lady. His initial meeting and the night they had spent together was not in keeping with the character of this incredible woman. Smoke had been exposed to one small facet of her character--the result of a woman betrayed and the vehicle of revenge that she had chosen. It wasn't the Rosa before him tonight.

Rosa asked to be excused for a few minutes. She got up and as she did the men at the table also stood. She was joined by Señor Cellini and they walked arm in arm into the foyer and out into the hall, away from the noisy festivity.

Doc took the opportunity to ask Smoke a question. He leaned over, and speaking quietly asked, "Was anything said about the dark side of her husband?"

"Sort of. She had come to truly hate him. She felt that she would be stuck forever. People of her station do not divorce in this country. It isn't done. I don't know if those were her exact words, but it was something like that. I had told her that Señor Cellini knew more about the problems surrounding her husband and that she should speak with him about it. Apparently she is doing just that at the moment. No memories are all bad. Rosa had feelings for this person, and she still does to some degree. However, I personally think she is relieved to find her problems solved."

"Well, she certainly seems to be taking it okay. I wonder if Cellini will tell her the truth." Doc said under his breath.

"I think she wants to know. And if Cellini sees, really sees that, I think he'll tell her."

Whitey turned from the conversation he was having with Bob Sexton. He leaned over to them. "I couldn't help but overhear part of your conversation. Alfredo will tell her if he feels it won't be too painful. You can bet on that one. These people deal with their problems fairly directly."

434

Whitey looked over toward the entrance to the suite, "They're coming back now. Rosa is certainly in control of herself."

Smoke and Doc watched the two approach. Smoke couldn't help but notice the composure and dignity that carried Rosa into the room. He was impressed. All thoughts of a repeat performance of their previous activities were the farthest things from his mind.

Rosa walked directly up to Smoke. "Señor Barnes, will you be kind enough to see me home now?"

"Of course, Señora Mendez." Smoke answered.

Rosa turned to Whitey, Doc and Colonel Sexton, who had stood as she came up to the table, "Gentlemen, it is my pleasure to have met you. My husband was honored to have worked with you. I'm grateful as well. I must leave now. Thank you again for all of your kindness and condolences." She turned and walked back toward the entrance to the suite, stopping briefly and shaking Señor Cellini's hand. Smoke followed her out.

Alfredo Cellini came up to Whitey, Doc and Sexton. "I will take my leave now also, gentlemen. Enjoy your well-earned celebration." Turning to Whitey, "Please give me a call tomorrow when it is convenient."

"Certainly, Señor Cellini, before noon."

Smoke and Rosa drove most of the way to the Hacienda de Mendez in silence. As they were approaching the gate, Rosa finally spoke up. "Señor Cellini told me enough of the facts about my husband for me to realize it is much better that he died than for him to face the charges that would have been brought against him had he lived. I am truly grateful to you and the men who insisted on this charade. I know that it is being done for my sake and the sake of my family. I just want to say the words of appreciation." Smoke stopped the car at the gate. Rosa continued, "You'll forgive me, Señor Barnes, if I don't ask you in. I would like to be alone now."

"I understand, Señora Mendez." Smoke replied. He got out of the car and came around to open her door. He helped Rosa out of the car and walked her to the gate. She pushed the bell.

Smoke stood looking down at this beautiful woman. Taking her hand he brushed his lips against the back of it, bowing slightly. As the servant approached, in response to the bell, Smoke waited for the gate to be opened, then turned and walked back around to the driver's side of the car, got in and drove away. No other words had passed between them.

The party was in full swing when Barnes returned. He tried to catch up with the festivities. It was no use. The troops were too far ahead of him. Finally he gave up and went to bed. Maybe they would think about leaving tomorrow. Or at least do the flight planning required for their flight home. There would be many stops required to drop off the troops, once they get to the States.

CHAPTER THIRTY-SEVEN
ALL BUT THE PAPERWORK

The loud ringing of the telephone rudely awakened Whitey. This was one time that it took a few moments to orient himself. God! Why do people drink like that? He knew better. The telephone kept ringing--and ringing. His hang-over was building a full head of steam.

"All right! All right! Damnation!" Whitey was saying out loud as he fumbled for the phone, finally getting it off the hook. "HELLO!" He screamed into the telephone.

"Good morning, Señor McFrank," came the voice of a young lady, "This is the hotel operator. It is ten o'clock. You asked to be called at this time."

"Hurumph! Yes....gracias." Whitey hung up the phone. Now he remembered. *He had to get hold of Cellini before noon. Better get a move on. Oh God! The pain. It hurts to move. Some party. Sexton and his lads do like to party on.*

Whitey lurched out of bed finding his way into the bathroom. He bent down to turn the shower handle and almost fell into the bathtub. He got the cold water turned on and stepped into the shower. Whitey tried to make the cold water wash the cobwebs out of his mind, swearing to himself to never, but never, drink like that again. He felt that he had to get better just to die!

The cold shower wasn't working for his hangover. His brain was still numb. Maybe some coffee would help. He went into the bedroom and called room service for a pot of coffee, a Bloody Mary and a pitcher of ice cold orange juice. He went back into the bathroom and shaved.

Whitey was dressing when he heard a noise out in the suite. He went over and opened the bedroom door into the main sitting room. The room service waiter was trying to push a cart with his order through the cluttered mess. There were six or seven bodies lying around. A trooper was sprawled out on one of the davenports and the rest of the troops were on the floor in various poses. Whitey noticed, he had to look twice--the hotel piano player was laid out under the grand piano. Someone had crossed his arms and placed a flower in his hands. The lads had obviously fed him several drinks. Whitey didn't remember much about that. He motioned for the waiter to wheel the cart into his bedroom.

The waiter brought the cart over to a table along the wall and set out his order. Whitey signed the receipt, adding a generous tip. The waiter hurried out, closing the door behind him. Whitey listened for and heard the outer door to the suite close. He gently sat down at the table and reached for the Bloody Mary.

There was a knock at the door.

"Come in." He managed to call out.

The door opened. It was Smoke. "I thought I heard you in here, Whitey. Have you seen the mess in the sitting room?"

"Yeah. Want some coffee?"

"Thanks, I could use some. I was going to go downstairs and get something to eat. Would you like to join me?"

"This is about all I can handle in the way of nourishment for now, Smoke. Grab a cup and there's a pitcher of orange juice. Help yourself."

"Those Special Forces troops come close to putting Marines to shame in the drinking department. Everybody was too far ahead of me by the time I returned from taking Rosa home. I gave up trying to join you folks. Nobody was making any sense. I just went to bed. Now that I see the shape you're all in I'm glad I did."

"How many bodies are out there?"

"I counted eight, and that includes the piano player. Did you see him? The flowers?"

"Yeah. I didn't have the strength to laugh." Whitey finished the Bloody Mary and poured himself some coffee and a glass of orange juice.

"I hate to say it, Whitey, but you look worse than when you and Doc did the hookers. I sure hope you feel better than you look."

"Thanks a lot, Smoke. I really needed that!"

"What's your schedule? Are you going back with us, or do you know yet?"

"Probably not. I have a meeting with Cellini today. It will no doubt mean that I'll be down here for a bit yet."

"I'm not trying to pry into your business, Whitey, but whatever you have to do, please be careful and not get yourself thrown into a hoosgow, or whatever. I've had enough excitement to last me awhile."

"Not to worry, my friend, not to worry. We know who the bad guys are. Now it's simply a matter of cleaning up the mess."

"That's an interesting analogy. Don't we have people to do that sort of thing?"

"Yeah. And I'm the people....or one of them anyway. In the parlance of the agency, I specialize in janitorial services."

"I won't ask!"

"Good. Don't." Whitey poured himself another cup of coffee. "I'm beginning to feel human. Smoke, do you have any idea when you'n Doc'll be leaving?"

"No. I have to go over to the embassy and do the report thing for Roberts and find out about U.S. Customs 'cuz of the stuff we have on the airplane....and that sort of thing. I have a car you know. Do you need a lift to Cellini's or do you need to go to the embassy?"

"Let me call Cellini and find out when he wants to get together. He'll probably send a car. If you're going to be at the embassy for the time that it will take to do the report thing, as you put it, I'll probably meet you there. It doesn't matter really. You're not going to get out of here today anyway. We can plan on having dinner together, unless you have made other plans."

"No. And if you mean Rosa, she is taking her role very seriously. Play time is over, Whitey. I'm glad that I had a chance to see this side of her though. I'm impressed. She's quite a lady."

"That she is, Barnes that she is. They grow 'em like that down here."

Cellini had told Whitey that he would send a car. Smoke went on over to the embassy.

The first person he saw was Charley Hammond who was just coming out the door of his office. Charley was extremely apologetic and wanted to make up for his indiscretion when they had arrived from the ranch. He went back inside of the office, taking Smoke by the arm. When he found out why Smoke was there, Charley couldn't do enough for him; set him up in a room to work and even helped him do the report, knowing how the format should be and also how the company liked things stated. Charley left him to work on the report and sent a Telex to Washington to get the Customs arrangements started. He returned to find Smoke finishing the report. He read it over and made a couple of suggestions. Barnes didn't have any argument and, in fact, appreciated Charley's input.

It took three days for the agency to make arrangements with the United States Customs Service to clear, without inspection, a C-47 carrying the Venezuelan registration YV-WAWS, upon landing in the United States.

The Customs Service requested that the flight crew clear customs in Corpus Christi, Texas, direct from San Salvador. Then the airplane could proceed to any destination in CONUS. (Continental United States.)

Two days following the party, Doc and Smoke got with the troops and figured out where everybody needed to be dropped. It was essential that they get Hank Stevaro and his beach party goods back to Columbus, Ohio. The sooner the better. Bob Sexton, and four others said that would be close enough and they could disembark there for points farther east, using commercial air.

They would haul Steve Howard out of the hospital and take him home to Lincoln, Nebraska. Lincoln was close enough for six others. The rest of the crew opted to be dropped in Denver, Colorado. Doc and Smoke would continue to Tacoma Industrial Airport and home.

They were set. The flight planning was done; money was transferred to designated accounts; Hank Stevaro was off the hook on the borrowed beach party goods as long as there weren't too many delays returning everything.

It appeared that everybody was happy.

The flight back to the states went okay, thanks to the agency paving the way with Customs. The registration on the airplane raised a few eyebrows when they landed around the country but no problems.

It was a little after five in the evening when they touched down in Tacoma. Miller was still there and said that he would take care of the airplane. Doc went over to his car. Smoke had his car at Millers' also, so he was taken care of. They agreed to be in touch late the following day. There would have to be a debriefing at Robert's office. They had been working on the airplane logs during the last leg of the flight so all that remained was entering the time for engine shut down and getting their gear out of the airplane. The guys had been a big help in keeping the bird clean and squared away, so there wasn't much to be done along those lines. They were able to get out of there by six thirty.

The drive to Seattle took close to an hour, due to evening commuter traffic.

Smoke drove up to his house. He noticed that Shelly's car was gone. He went in and checked the bulletin board. Sure enough, she was on a flight. She wouldn't be home for another day. *'Shit and damnation,'* he thought. *'What the hell; I need a drink!'* He turned around and headed for the Red Baron. It was only a couple of blocks away. *Maybe Heidi would be working tonight.*

Doc debated driving by his apartment for a quick shower and change of clothes, since he was still in his flight suit, then decided against it. He headed east to Bellevue.

It was eight o'clock when Doc got out of his car and walked up to Hunter's front door. He didn't know what he was going to say. He just knew that he had to see her and hold her. He rang the doorbell. He could hear a dog barking somewhere in the house, then heard someone coming to the door, trying to calm the dog. The door opened. It was Hunter.

Doc just stood there looking at her. His eyes misted. He couldn't speak. The lump in his throat had grown too large. Hunter inhaled sharply and put her hand to her mouth when she saw that it was him. She didn't say anything.

Hunter's daughter came up behind her mother. "Who is it, Mom? Someone for me?" She asked. Then seeing that it was Doc, went on to say, "Are you two going to just stand there looking at each other? Can't you ask him in, Mom?"

It broke the spell. Hunter stepped back and gestured for Doc to come into the house. He stepped in and muttered, "Sorry about the smelly flight suit....I just had to see you . . . didn't want to take time to change...."

Hunter reached up and put her finger on his lips. She stood there looking up into his eyes, still not speaking.

Hunter's daughter, Shannon couldn't stand it. "My God, you two, kiss, hug or something! You both look stupid just standing there, gawking at each other! I'll leave the room." She headed down the hall, laughing.

Hunter's youngest son, Dean came out of his room trying to see what was going on. Shannon grabbed him on her way down the hall. "You can come with me Dean-o, I got something to show you." Young Dean followed her on down to her room.

Hunter and Doc came into each other's arms. Doc kissed her again and again. He kept telling her that he loved her, wouldn't leave her again, missed her, and other sweet nothings. Hunter still hadn't said anything. Of course, Doc hadn't given her much of a chance. She pushed him away to get her breath.

"James Francis McGarrity, give me a break! Why didn't you call? Why didn't you let me know that everything was all right? I've been worried sick about you....and Smoke. Well, to be honest, it was mainly you," She dropped her eyes and blushed a little, then kind of shaking her head she looked back up into his eyes and went on, "Don't ever do that to me again, Mister. Do you hear me? Now come in here and tell me what happened." She took his hand and led him into the living room and over to a sofa, sat and pulled him down beside her.

He started at the beginning and told her everything up to the battle at the ranch. That he missed her like crazy, the stolen airplane . . . the company pilots arriving to take the airplane back to Florida, Smoke's girlfriends. He thought about her all the time. The flight and then the battle. (Doc left out the party and Mendez.) Had he mentioned that he loved her? He went on to say that the company had forgiven everybody and what's more, was going to be paying hazardous-duty pay and bonuses. It had turned out rather well. That he didn't ever want to be apart or away from her again.　He and Smoke had only missed one drill weekend....and that he loved her. Or, had he told her that?

Hunter blushed again. "What am I going to do with you, Doc? You have told me that you love me. I believe you. I just need a little time, okay? You're not the easiest person to get used to, you know. I do have deep feelings for you....and they'll grow. But they need time. Can you handle that, my Marine?"

Doc glanced at his watch. "No. How much time do you need? I only have a couple of minutes....and the rest of my life to spare! Dammit woman, tell me now!"

This startled Hunter. Then she chuckled, "Okay Doc, you got it....my undying love and affection. And yes, I do love you or I wouldn't have worried about you as much as I did. Now come here and give your lady a kiss!"

Doc complied with her request.

They were married three months later. It would have been a week sooner but Doc had to make up a Reserve Drill Weekend that he had missed.

CHAPTER THIRTY-EIGHT
MAIL

There was still no trace of Colonel Emilio Raphael Cordero or his deputy, Lieutenant Dominique Paredes. Alfredo Cellini had told Whitey McFrank that it was his intention to have the U.S. State Department put out a termination contract on both of them. Whitey wished him well, but went on to tell Alfredo that he was going sailing. They were at Cellini's town house, in the study, having a drink even though it was early in the day.

"Come now, Whitey, you and I have been friends for a long time. I'm telling you as one friend to another that I'm going to request that you be assigned the termination contract. I'm not doing this for any obscure reason. I'm doing this because I know that you will get the job done and in quick time! I would strongly advise you to stay in San Salvador for at least three more days. I should be able to get the orders cut in that period of time. It wouldn't make any sense for you to get on an airplane and then have to turn right around and come back. There will be time enough for sailing. Besides, just think about it, the world will be a much better place without those two." Cellini got up, intending to freshen their drinks.

"No more for me, Alfredo."

"What? Are you going religious on me or the like?" Cellini raised his eyes in supplication. "Whitey, you are a much nicer and more patient person when you've had a couple of drinks. Now don't let me drink alone at this time of day."

"Well, only to keep you company, Alfredo." Whitey paused for a moment then continued. "Have you started the request through channels? On the termination order?"

"It was discussed during my meeting with El Presidente. I believe that his office was putting something through. I haven't started any formal requests as yet, but as I said, I intend to. Is there a special reason for your asking?"

"Yes, it will probably go down then. Since I'm the logical asset, I was trying to get a feel for the timing. The trail can cool down quickly. But you said the President was going to do something. That being the case, I think you're right. Three days will probably be enough." Whitey took a pull on his drink, thinking about the problem. "Alfredo, I'm going to need a lot of help picking up the pieces of the trail. Will you grease the skids . . . or oil the gears with the Policía Nacional, I'm going to need several men working on this case? At least initially."

"Certainly. And I think it would be a good idea to check for all of his known cars that have been registered in El Salvador, with descriptions and licenses of the cars along with the pictures we have of the two of them. The pictures should also be sent to the border check points. Pictures--the ones that were inadvertently sent to that headwaiter who survived the restaurant explosion. Wasn't that a break? Nobody was told to send the pictures of those two; it was done only because they were Venezuelan."

"Sometimes the gods do smile, Alfredo."

Two days later Whitey received word at his hotel to contact the Embassy. Charlie Hammond took his call and advised him that he had some priority mail. Whitey told him that he would be right over.

The envelope hadn't been opened. It was marked "ADDRESSEE'S EYES ONLY; TOP SECRET, (Destroy If Not Delivered within 48 Hours)".

446

All of the markings were enough to raise the curiosity of the most callous. Whitey decided to not open it until he returned to his hotel. Charlie was obviously disappointed, but thought better about asking any questions. Whitey signed for the envelope and left without any further discussions.

Upon opening the envelope and giving the single page order a quick scan, Whitey determined that it was as he suspected. The words leaped out, "....*TERMINATE CONTRACT WITH PREJUDICE...*" The time allotted was "--as required."

He burned the envelope and put the single page order in a special place in his briefcase. It was placed with expense account forms and other business correspondence that wouldn't attract any attention or interest to customs people. He had learned early in his game that the best place to hide something sensitive was to leave it in the open. It had worked for many years.

Whitey had been in constant daily contact with Sandy since being brought out from the ranch. He was not looking forward to placing the call this time, but it had to be done. She answered on the second ring.

"Hello," came the voice from the most wonderful lady on the face of the earth.

"It's me, Babes, I'm going to be delayed for a few days."

"What does a few days mean, Whitey?"

"Just that. A few days. I have some cleaning up to do; then I'm free to come home to you, and we can get our boat. How's that coming?"

"Ernest Herman McFrank, don't you dare try to change the subject. You hear me? I want to know what's going on!"

Whitey took a moment to gather his thoughts. His lady sounded a bit pissed. How to talk about this without too much violation of security. "Look Babes, it is just a matter of taking care of a couple of items. Two, to be specific. It won't take long and I don't have a lot of choice in the matter. I don't see any personal problems, if you follow."

"Bullshit!"

"Wait a minute. Don't interrupt. The control factors are mine, my darling. Not to worry. Schedules, time and place, all of these factors are my call. No surprises. And I promise to be in contact with you each and every day. I can't be specific as to time since I'll be moving around; just each day."

"You're not just saying these things to make me feel good, Whitey." The tone of voice had changed from anger to one of concern.

"No. I'm trying to discuss what I can as straightforward as an open line will allow. And with that, I've said too much, Babes."

"Okay. I understand." It was quiet for a moment then she added, "Please be careful, my sweet man. Just be careful. I love you."

"I love you too, Sandy. I promise to come home to you soon. I'll call you tomorrow."

Whitey worked on the follow-up plan for the Policiá Nacional. He was a bit surprised at the cooperation and major assistance that he was being given. Good to his word, Cellini had set him up with the Commissioner of Policiá directly. The Commissioner had immediately started the men searching for cars registered to Cordero. They had been given pictures of both Cordero and Paredes. The pictures sent to the border check points were accompanied by orders not to detain them, only to advise immediately of their crossing and vehicle description. So far nothing had developed. The two men had disappeared.

448

CHAPTER THIRTY NINE
PAROLE

Colonel Emilio Rafael Cordero had been pacing back and forth in his cell, as was his habit. The pacing generated the only air movement in the already hot and musty cell. It was still early in the day and he knew that it would soon become almost unbearable, even for one like himself. He had been born into this hot and humid climate that was so prevalent in the countries bordering the Caribbean Sea. The fact that San Jose was in the mountains of Costa Rica, and the climate cooler and drier than sea level, made it possible for him to retain his sanity. But now, even that was becoming harder to do. The small area of a cell, without a window, no air circulation--it was horrible.

Born into a middle class family and raised in Caracas Venezuela, Colonel Cordero had always prided himself on his adaptability to his surroundings. Climate or hard work, it mattered not. The inactivity of confinement was proving to be the hardest thing that he had ever had to endure.

He heard footsteps approaching. He couldn't see anything since his cell door was solid except for an eye-level grill and cover that could only be opened from the outside. This was obviously for purposes of observing the cell's occupant. It was opening now and a voice ordered him to stand away from the cell door. In a moment the cell door was opened.

"Come with me and bring all of your things. Move!" The harsh voice of the guard was no stranger to the Colonel. He had been hearing it, along with others, for better than three months. Cordero had tried to befriend some of the guards to no avail. They were all non-communicative and of similar nasty attitudes. They had taken his money for food, until the money ran out, then he had been forced to eat prison fare. He calculated that he had lost more than ten pounds. He had always been proud of his build, keeping trim and in good shape. Now he felt that he was too thin.

Trying to get something from the guards without money was useless. He had given up long ago. With money, anything was possible; a better cell, food, a woman, whiskey, drugs, anything.

He remembered the day that had landed him in this prison. Never formerly charged, never told why or how long he would remain imprisoned--only that he had been accused of money trafficking into the country of Costa Rica. It was senseless! The money had been well earned and came from a contract with the United States Government for some work that he had done in Nicaragua. Colonel Cordero had asked that the money be sent to the Caymans, but the group for whom he had done the work insisted that it be transferred to a bank in Costa Rica. It had been a bank-to-bank transfer. He hadn't carried any money into the country. He had thought nothing of it. This had to have been a set-up for some ulterior reason. He had often thought about various ways to get even with those responsible. It was one of his ways of passing the time.

He had thought about that and other matters over the past months, wondering what Paredes had done about the contract. Lieutenant Paredes had left the ranch with a detail of men the morning of his confrontation with McFrank. Cordero had not intended to be away from the ranch for any length of time. He had driven into San Salvador with the intention of conferring with the head of the Catorce Familias, Alfredo Cellini, in an attempt to smooth things over since McFrank confronted him, claiming to be speaking for the family. He had been informed that Cellini was with El Presidente and would not be available for a few days.

Cordero had decided to transfer banking funds from Costa Rico to El Salvador. This was something that he had put off doing, but it would be smart to do now that he was settled in. It was his intention to remain in El Salvador for some time. The small country offered many opportunities for a smart man.

He had taken a flight to San Jose. When clearing Costa Rican Customs, he had been detained, then taken before an officer of the State Police and hence into these cells. No charges, no formal arrest, no nothing. His offers of bribes had been ignored. In fact it was as if he had been ignored completely. Ignored for three months.

The prison guards moved him at least once a week. One cell was the same as the other, with the exception of which side of the prison building. On the west side, the late afternoon sun had a tendency to heat up the cells even more. When his money ran out it became the only side available to him. San Jose was high in the mountains of Costa Rica, and the climate was almost comfortable. Generally speaking, of course, and not referring to the inside of a prison cell block.

It was the filth that Colonel Cordero couldn't stand. He was very particular about his surroundings. Here was a man who enjoyed his creature comforts--his dress, neatness and diet. All of those things were in short supply currently. Bathing was sorely missed. He was only able to get a quick shower once a week. More frequently, if he had money, of course. His hair was unkempt, mustache scraggly, and he had grown a short beard since it was easier to trim than to shave with the few toilet articles that he had been able to purchase.

And now they were moving him again. Carrying the few possessions he had managed to accumulate over the past three months, Cordero fell into step behind the surly guard. To his surprise, they left the cell block and continued toward the front offices. This was an area that Cordero hadn't seen. They stopped outside of a door marked "Superintendente". The guard knocked on the door.

"Come," resounded tersely from within the office.

The guard opened the door and motioned Cordero inside, following closely. Once inside the large office, the guard stepped around Cordero and up to the desk. The guard saluted smartly. "Here is the prisoner Cordero, El Commandante," the guard said.

The Superintendent returned the salute nonchalantly and said, "You're dismissed."

The guard turned and left the room. As he did so, Cordero noticed that there was someone else in the office. It was Parades, his lieutenant!

"Sainted Mother of Jesus!" He thought. *"Maybe my ordeal is over!"* He turned back to the Superintendent, trying to pay attention to what was being said.

"....arranged for your release. Here are some papers for you to sign, and then you'll be free to go." The Superintendent was motioning toward some papers on his desk.

Cordero stepped forward and leaned over the desk to get a better look at the papers. He noticed that they were bank papers. He looked up at the Superintendent questioningly.

Meeting his gaze head on, the Superintendent said, "Just sign the papers and you'll be free to go. I suggest that you leave Costa Rica without hesitation. Senor Paredes has an airline ticket for you. You are to be out of the country within twenty-four hours."

Cordero picked up the papers and read them carefully. His shoulders slumped with the realization of the enormity of what he was being forced to do. He knew that it would be futile to argue.

"Most of my funds will be released to your government, El Commandante, when I sign these papers." He waited.

"Yes. The fines against your crime are substantial. If it wasn't for your sponsor, Senor Paredes here, we wouldn't have bothered doing this. You are fortunate to have such a person working on your behalf." The Superintendent paused for a moment; then said very slowly, "Now...sign...the...papers!"

The tone of his voice left no doubt that the conversation was finished. Cordero reached for the pen that had been placed near the papers, and quickly signed. He left the papers and pen on the desk and stepped back. The Superintendent looked the papers over, seemed satisfied and handed one set back to Cordero. He motioned to a bulky package on the floor beside the desk. It was obviously his civilian dress and personal items taken from him upon his internment.

"Pick up that bundle. It is your clothes and personal items, including your passport. You may keep your prison clothes as a reminder of your illegal actions."

The Superintendent activated his intercom and told someone to come into his office. He continued to look the papers over, now ignoring Cordero, still standing in front of his desk holding the bulky package. In a moment, another guard came into the office.

The Superintendent looked up and said, "The prisoner is released. Escort him and this gentleman to the main gate."

Paredes got up quickly and took some of the things Cordero had brought into the office. Cordero carried the bundle. They turned and followed the guard out of the office. In a short time they were out of the prison. The guard hadn't said a word to them, speaking only to other guards at each set of doors.

Once outside, Paredes motioned toward a car that was parked close by. They quickly got in and Paredes started the car. Only then did they dare to speak.

"My Coronel. I apologize for the time that it took to find you. Nobody knew where you were. I traced you through your car left at the airport, the airlines, passport control and finally to the bank here. When I discovered that the account was frozen by the government, it led me to you." Paredes was humbly seeking pardon for things not of his doing.

He had driven a short distance away from the prison. He now pulled the car over and parked in order to be able to devote his full attention to his leader. He turned in the seat, looking directly at Cordero.

Sensing that it would be wise to keep this valuable loyalty, Cordero graciously accepted his lieutenant's attitude. "My friend, I made the mistake of not telling someone my plans. I acted rashly. You had left on patrol. I only intended to go into San Salvador and meet with Cellini. He wasn't available. The trip to San Jose came about on a whim. As it has turned out, an expensive whim, not to mention the three months of hell that I have been through. But tell me, what is the situation at the ranch? The search for the Castro Communists?"

"Patrón....the news I bring you is not good. We have been blamed for atrocities against the church. Someone informed the Catorce Familias that it was our doing, the killing of the priests and nuns. Then there was a raid at the ranch. The Americanos came in by the airplane that delivered the arms to us. They were there to obtain the release of the CIA Agent McFrank. They killed most of the men and blew up the main ranch house."

Paredes paused to allow this dreadful information to sink in. There was no reaction from Cordero. The lieutenant continued.

"Because of the church accusations and the Americanos and their CIA, we are not welcome in that country. I wouldn't be surprised if there was a price on our heads. I learned from the cooks the Americanos spared and released, that there has been an intensive search for both you and me."

"What of our money? Were you able....no, of course not."

"Wait, my Coronel. I went back to the ruined house and retrieved the gold. Your wise action of hiding gold for emergencies was well founded. That is what I have been using for funds in my search for you. There are several bars left. I haven't tried access to any of the banking. Not in El Salvador or here in Costa Rica. Like I said, only the information about the frozen account which led me to you. You can see from the papers you signed, about a third remaining is ready to be picked up, or you can transfer it later. That much I do know."

Colonel Cordero thought about all that his lieutenant had told him.

"The superintendent mentioned that you had airline tickets. For where?"

"Part of the arrangements for obtaining your release included taking you out of Costa Rica. I booked our tickets to Caracas."

"Good. We still have a few connections and can go anywhere from there." Then, making a decision, went on to say, "But right now, I want to bathe, get into some clean clothes and have a decent meal. Tomorrow, we'll drive out to the hacienda where we were staying here in San Jose. There is some more gold, not much, but we're going to need all of the funds we can lay our hands on. Be careful that we're not followed."

"Si, my Coronel!" Paredes said briskly, turned and put the car in gear.

CHAPTER FORTY
JANITORIAL SERVICES

With the help of Cellini's assets, Cordero's car was found at the San Salvador airport. Whitey was able to pick up Cordero's airline trail leading him to San Jose. Whitey chose to travel under a diplomatic passport that would also allow him to carry an attaché case with a diplomatic seal on it. In this way he was able to carry a weapon and other items necessary to carry out his termination assignment. There would not be any problems passing through Costa Rican Customs.

Once clear of customs in San Jose, Whitey went to the airport police office. They were very helpful and it didn't take long to find out that Cordero had been detained some months ago. The officer in charge gave him directions to the prison where Cordero had been sent.

Whitey rented a car and drove out to the prison. Upon showing his credentials at the prison gate he was led into the Superintendent's office.

The Superintendent had been alerted from the gate and was expecting the visitor. When Whitey was brought into his office he rose, came around his desk and extended his hand in greeting. "And to what do I owe this visit from a representative of the United States government?"

McFrank was carrying credentials identifying him as an Assistant Attaché to the El Salvadoran diplomatic contingent. He took the outreached hand. "My name is McFrank. I'm looking for a prisoner that you have here by the name of Cordero. Emilio Rafael Cordero. He is a Venezuelan."

The Superintendent motioned for Whitey to sit as he returned to his desk and sat down. "I'm afraid that you are a day late, Señor McFrank. The prisoner Cordero was released yesterday. I believe that he is on his way to Caracas. A Señor Parades arranged his parole. He had airline tickets for them both. Cordero has been asked to leave Costa Rica within twenty four hours of his release from prison as one of the conditions of his parole."

"When was he released yesterday?"

"He was released at four o'clock. It is now nearly noon. You may be able to catch him at the airport. Check with Passport Control. They keep records of passengers arriving and departing Costa Rica."

Whitey rose, gesturing for the man in front of him to remain seated. "Thank you. I must be gone then. Please don't get up."

"But Señor McFrank, wouldn't it be better to call from here to see if they're still in-country? You Americans are always in such a hurry." He reached into his desk for a personal telephone directory and dialed a number. He was put through to Passport Control and in a matter of minutes was able to determine that neither a "Cordero" nor a "Paredes" had cleared Departure Passport Control. The Superintendent then called another number and from what Whitey could overhear, was able to determine that the Superintendent was inquiring about afternoon flights to Caracas, direct or connecting. There were two direct; the first at one thirty-five and the other at three fifteen. There were a few other flights out of the country before the four o'clock deadline that would possibly connect with a flight to Caracas from other immediate destinations. He jotted down the information and when finished, handed the piece of paper to McFrank.

"There you are, Señor McFrank. I hope you accomplish your mission, whatever it is." The Superintendent rose and held out his hand.

Whitey rose also. "Thank you for your help." He shook hands and left.

McFrank drove directly to the airport. He parked in front of the entrance to the terminal. He showed his diplomatic identification card to a policeman standing near the entrance. He wouldn't have to worry about being ticketed, or worse.

The first thing he did was to check Passport Control again. The same people were still on duty and were very cooperative even though Whitey didn't have the airport police officer with him this time. Neither Cordero nor Paredes had cleared. Next he checked the car rental counters. At the Hertz counter he found what he was looking for; a black Ford Fairlane four door sedan had been rented out to a Dominique Paredes the day before yesterday. It had not been returned.

Black was a very unpopular color for a car in this part of the world, with the exception of limousines. Black absorbs the heat. The girl at the Hertz counter said that it was the only one in their fleet and always the last full-size car to be rented. Nobody wants it. Señor Paredes was so insistent on a full size sedan that he didn't mind the color.

Whitey thanked her and left. He hurried back to his car, thinking that the black car would stand out even in heavy traffic. The gods again, showering favors in his direction.

Near the entrance of the airport was a slight rise where Highway One curves away from the entrance to the Aeropuerto Internacional Juan Santamaria. It would make an excellent vantage point. The car that he was looking for would have to enter the airport complex at this entrance, regardless of which direction they would be coming from. The shoulder of the road was wide enough for him to park and wait. Whitey glanced at his watch, it was getting close to two o'clock. They would have to show up soon to make a direct flight. For some reason, Whitey didn't think that Cordero would want to do any connecting. He would want to get out of the country and back to his own turf as soon as possible.

At two fifteen Whitey spotted a black sedan coming toward him from the direction of Alajuela, the next town northwest of the airport. It was turning off of Highway One onto the access road to the airport.

Whitey started his car. He reached over to the briefcase on the passenger's seat, opened it and took out his Detonics with the fitted silencer attached. In one smooth motion he chambered a round without taking his eyes off of the black sedan. He started to close on it in order to check the license plate. The Hertz counter girl had been kind enough to furnish him with it.

Yes! That's it! And they're both in the car. It looks like Paredes is driving, Whitey thought. He fell back away from the rear of the Ford Fairlane in front of him. *Now, how to do this. I can't blow them away in front of the terminal; there are too many people around. Paredes will probably drop the Colonel off at the main entrance of the terminal and then go turn the car in. Maybe I can scare 'em into doing something stupid.*

Whitey gunned the car and drove up and hit the Ford's rear bumper. He was close enough to see Paredes look into the rear view mirror with a startled expression on his face. Paredes made him all right. Cordero turned in the seat and stared at him in astonishment. Whitey was in luck. Paredes reacted. He swerved around the car in front of him and took off. Whitey was barely able to stay within two car lengths behind him. They passed the terminal entrance and down toward Highway One.

Paredes barely missed a car that was just turning into the airport entrance. He cut across, bouncing over a low divider in the road and was forced to take the connecting

459

road onto Highway One, heading into San Jose, ten short kilometers away.

Whitey started closing the distance. He had fallen back when it appeared that Paredes was going to hit the car turning in. He would have thought that Paredes would have wanted to go in the other direction. Maybe the near miss had forced this choice of roads.

Traffic was light and Whitey wanted to get them off the road. They were approaching a cemetery entrance. Whitey pulled up alongside and fired twice at Paredes, then hit his brakes to fall behind in case they returned fire. The Fairlane began to swerve from side to side. Whitey could see Cordero trying to steer from the passenger side. Paredes was slumped forward, and from the way the car was acting, must still have his foot on the gas. The Ford got closer to the right side of the road and finally lost control completely, leaving the road, rolling over and over, down a small embankment, taking out some of the fence surrounding the cemetery. It hit a couple of headstones, breaking them off, and then came to rest upside down against the side of a good sized tomb.

Whitey was stopped and running over to the Ford as Cordero was climbing out. He waited for the Colonel to get to his feet then moved a little closer. He raised the automatic and started to take careful aim.

"Wait! Señor McFrank, don't shoot! I am not armed. You can see, I am not armed. You are here to kill me. That I know." Cordero raised his arms out to his side to indicate that he wasn't armed. "I spared your life at the ranch, you owe me something for that at least. We are both students of the martial arts, why not give me a fighting chance to die '*Mano-Mano*'? He put his arms back down, standing a little taller and waited for Whitey's response.

"I don't owe you a damn thing Cordero. And yes, I'm here to kill you and your henchman, Paredes."

Cordero interrupted him, "He is dead. Both of your shots rang true. He died instantly."

"That's as it should be. And sure, I don't mind killing you with my bare hands. In fact it will be my pleasure." Whitey stepped well back, removed his jacket, and placed the silenced automatic on it. Cordero removed his jacket as well. They moved toward one another, slowly circling. Whitey was careful to circle back in order to stay between Cordero and the weapon he had placed on his jacket.

As they closed Cordero reached down to his belt and hit a release button hidden in the buckle's design. A stiletto appeared in his hand. The prison people hadn't discovered the secret of the beautiful belt and buckle that Cellini had given him upon their first meeting.

The flash of the blade got Whitey's attention. "You bastard, Cordero! I should have known you would do something like this. Honor means nothing to you. I'm going to hurt you for this before I kill you."

As Whitey moved in Cordero spoke in a tense, husky voice. "Now I will do to you that which I should have done when I had you locked in my home. You....you are the one responsible for destroying it! This beautiful knife-belt was given to me by Alfredo Cellini. It is only fitting that I use it to finish you."

"The way I see it, Cordero, you didn't have the 'huevos', or as we Americans would say, the 'balls' then, and you don't have them now or you wouldn't need a weapon to do the job."

They were both moving in and out, feinting one way then the other. Whitey spoke up again, taunting, trying to get Cordero angry. "And by the way, it sure is a poor excuse for a knife. You're lying. Some woman must have given it to you or did you take it away from her? She must have been either eighty years old or too small or sick to resist you."

Cordero was starting to get red in the face. Whitey kept it up. "Come to me you sweet thing, show me what you can do with that toy. I forgot to tell you that in my country, that the larger the belt buckle the smaller the penis! From the

461

size of the belt buckle you're wearing you must have the penis of a little boy!"

It worked. Cordero's Latino machoness boiled over. He momentarily lost control and charged. He thrust the knife towards McFrank's chest. Whitey stepped back, absorbing the rushing onslaught, blocked the attack with his right forearm across to his left. Cordero would have anticipated a block to the outside. This took him by surprise. McFrank grabbed Cordero's knife hand wrist with his left hand and placed his right forearm under Cordero's upper arm, locking him in an upright position. This put tremendous pain on Cordero's elbow.

Whitey calmly addressed his opponent, "Cordero, just so you know what is about to happen to you, this technique is called *Huai Zhong Bao Yue.* It means 'Embrace The Moon In The Chest'." Cordero was screaming in pain from the pressure on his elbow. Whitey went on as if lecturing to a slow student. "If you think this hurts, there's more!"

McFrank applied more pressure, bringing Cordero's heels up off the ground. "Now I want you to listen to this very carefully."

Whitey applied final pressure and the tendons in Cordero's arm broke loose and the elbow snapped with the sound of a dry sapling, causing Cordero to almost pass out from the excruciating pain. His screams became deafening.

"Now you see....you're not listening. I don't think you heard a single tendon snap. Well, as long as I have you in this position I will try to duplicate with your help, the screams of all the people you have tortured and murdered."

Whitey stepped to his left and swung under the broken arm, twisting it a full turn at the broken elbow. "This is called *Song Mot Shang Tian.* It means 'Send The Devil To Heaven'. Now asshole, get used to the pain because I'm not through with you yet." McFrank spun on his left foot and with his right foot kicked Cordero's knee backward and stepped down, forcing the kneecap down the front of the leg and breaking the knee. Cordero screamed and passed out from the pain. Whitey picked up the knife and waited for his opponent to recover.

As Cordero regained consciousness, dazed with pain, McFrank showed him the knife. "I suppose I should have done this while you were out but I didn't think it would be fair for you to miss anything. Now it is time for you to go home, you bastard, go home to hell." Whitey leaned forward and quickly shoved the stiletto up under Cordero's chin, into his brain. Death was quick.

Whitey took the belt off of the corpse and returned the knife to its place. He admired the workmanship. He went over to the car and verified that his two shots had indeed sent Paredes home to hell also. Cordero had told the truth for a change. Paredes was very dead. Both shots had found their mark in his head. They were two inches apart. Whitey was mildly disturbed with the spread.

It was time to leave. The entire incident had only taken minutes and no one had stopped to look at the scene. People in this part of the world don't like to give cemeteries much of their attention and Paredes car was practically out of sight from the road.

Whitey got into his car and turned around heading back to the airport. He was starting to shake. He held out his hand, noticing the tremors. It was rare for him to have been so cruel to an opponent....but Cordero had deserved all the cruelty and more. A quick death would have been too good for this one. Whitey needed time to mentally settle back into the world and rid himself of the loathing and resentment he felt toward Cordero.

After turning the car back in and waiting for his flight to San Salvador, he called Sandy. He told her his present location, reported that his mission was complete and he would be heading home in a couple of days. He would call again from San Salvador when he knew his firm departure date and flight schedules.

After hanging up Whitey realized that he had been too terse. He almost called her back then decided to wait until he was on the ground in San Salvador. Maybe by then he could get the poison out of his mind and sound like a human being to this lady that he loved so dearly.

CHAPTER FORTY-ONE
HOMEWARD BOUND

At ten o'clock the following morning Whitey was ushered into Alfredo Cellini's office. Whitey motioned for Alfredo to remain seated and tossed a sack on his desk.

"What's this, my friend?"

"Open it, Alfredo."

Cellini did as he was bid. He opened the bag and removed the belt with the trick buckle housing the razor sharp stiletto. He looked up questioningly.

"If you give out many of those and have a reputation or identity in so doing, I thought you would like to have this one back and not found on the late Colonel Cordero's body. The blood stains on the belt are his, by the way." McFrank paused for a moment to let that sink in, then continued. "My work here is complete, Alfredo. I wanted to drop this off and say good-bye. I'm leaving here, returning to my wife and we're going sailing. Don't ask for me anymore. We'll always be friends, but I'm retiring from government service and all such related activity."

"Ah Señor White, what can I say? I would like to hear about the end of your contract." Alfredo took note of the expression on McFrank's face and switched what he was going to say. "But, I guess the blood stains say it all. And the other one?"

"Two shots, both to the head. Very quick, very clean. It's over, Alfredo. I must be going."

Alfredo Cellini got to his feet and came around his desk. "As you wish, my friend. You will not be forgotten. And if your voyaging brings you to this part of the world, I would be most offended if you didn't spend some time with me and my family. You'll always be welcome, my friend, always welcome." With this last Cellini embraced Whitey, stepped back and shook his hand. The look of pride and affection that he bestowed on Whitey McFrank expressed his feelings as no words could.

Whitey saw it and understood. "Thank you, Alfredo. I'll keep that in mind. I know that Sandy would enjoy you and your family. I've spoken of you to her many times. But, now I really must take my leave."

"Of course. And you have your own car. So, if there isn't anything more that I can do for you I will reluctantly let you go. However I think that you should have the belt, as a souvenir." With that, Alfredo picked up the belt and handed it to Whitey.

McFrank looked down at it, admiring the quality workmanship. He nodded his acceptance, glancing back up at Alfredo.

"Good. I'm glad that you accept it, Señor Whitey. It is rightfully yours." He paused for a moment, then continued, "Bon Voyage. The thanks of my families and the people of El Salvador go with you."

Whitey left and drove to the American Embassy. He went directly down to the lower levels and into Charlie Hammond's office.

"Come on, Charlie, let's make this quick." He motioned for Charlie to follow him down to the cryptographic room. When they got there Whitey motioned for Charlie to sit down at the special crypto typewriter. "Just type what I tell you."

Charlie nodded without saying anything.

"To Chief of Operations, Headquarters....copies to...Peter Jorgensen, Arlington and Harold Roberts, Seattle. Mission complete. Subjects Cordero and Paredes terminated with prejudice, outskirts of San Jose, Costa Rica. Evidence left in place. No problems or witnesses. Departing San Salvador this afternoon. Contract complete. Forward agreed upon funds as usual. Consider this my resignation.....sign it Ernest Herman McFrank."

At the name, Charlie Hammond looked up then quickly returned to his typing without uttering a word. In a few minutes he was finished. Turning to McFrank he said, "I'll get this out right away. Uh, it has been a pleasure meeting you, Mister McFrank. I'm sorry that we got off to...."

Whitey interrupted him, "It's all right, Hammond. We all make mistakes. However in your chosen line of work, it pays to not make many. Try to remember, and with that, I'll be going. Please extend my best regards to the Ambassador."

"Yes Sir. Have a pleasant flight home, Sir."

"Thank you, Charlie. And you'll come to appreciate that the flights home are always the best ones. Especially if you have something worthwhile to go home to." He paused, then added, "I happen to."

Twenty-four hours later Whitey McFrank was attacked as he stepped out of the passenger jet-way from the American Airlines 727 at Sea-Tac International Airport. It was in the form of a young blond lady.

He hadn't quite reached the passenger waiting area when he was suddenly engulfed by this flying female that was all over him. He barely managed to stay on his feet.

"Hey, hey, it's me....I'm home. Sandy, stop for a minute. Wait!" Whitey had dropped his bags and was attempting to control this ferocious animal that was trying to devour him. Sandy stopped suddenly. She looked him straight in the eye.

"Mr. Ernest McFrank, you have retired from contractual services. It is over for you. That's it. Done. Or should I spell it out? We're going sailing. The only excitement will be our dealing with Mother Nature. And that should be enough to keep even you from getting bored. But now, you may come with me to our home; and when I'm through having my way with you, then you can tell me all about this last little clean-up escapade, about our friend Colonel Bob Sexton, and all of those other little details. But it can wait."

Collecting luggage and the drive home took the better part of an hour. Whitey had many questions about the boat but Sandy wouldn't say anything. They arrived at the apartment and went in.

"What the hell is this?" Whitey uttered in amazement. The apartment was bare. He went from room to room. Only the bedroom held anything, their box spring and mattress. And they were on the floor! There were candlesticks on each side. The kitchen did have a small table and two chairs. They were the ice cream parlor table and chairs that had been out on the small balcony of the apartment. "What's going on, Sandy? Where the hell is everything? Have we been robbed?"

"No my love, I've sold a lot of things and...." She noticed a look of alarm coming over her man. "No my sweet one, I didn't sell any of your things. Let me finish. Most of our stuff and your precious things are in storage. We're leaving in two days for Taiwan. Our boat is almost finished." This last bit of news was said in an excited, squeal. As Whitey started to say something, Sandy put her finger on his lips. "Mister Bob Perry has been very helpful with suggestions for me to get us ready for extended cruising. I'll go over the details and plans of our boat with you in the morning. Right now we have other things to attend to."

She took his hand and led him back into the bedroom.

The End

Made in the USA
San Bernardino, CA
03 October 2014